How We Are and How We Got Here
A Practical History of Western Philosophy

Douglas Giles
Elmhurst University

Real Clear Philosophy

ISBN: 978-1-7358808-8-4

Contents

PREFACE FOR INSTRUCTORS

This book helps students of any age or background learn about the story of philosophy in the Western world. I wrote it to fill the prodigious gap between books that oversimplify philosophy and complex works that are inaccessible to nonprofessionals (and many professionals!). I also want to give instructors of philosophy a textbook option that is affordable and accessible for students and includes important philosophers who are left out of the standard textbooks.

How We Are and How We Got Here is a distillation of what my decades of teaching has taught me about how students best learn about philosophy and why it matters. I kept several premises in mind throughout the book, the most important being that everyone can understand philosophy and be a philosopher if given the resources to do so.

How This Book Differs from Standard Textbooks

In writing this book for use in university courses, I wanted to avoid two pitfalls of standard textbooks on philosophy. One is the ridiculous high cost of textbooks that publishing corporations expect students to pay. Second is that standard textbooks don't adequately give students the resources they need to connect meaningfully with philosophy. These two pitfalls are partially connected.

The overuse of primary texts is confusing to students. Some instructors feel that philosophy is best taught through source material. I respect their choice, but I have seen too many students enter my courses who dropped out of a previous Introduction to Philosophy section in which the instructor threw complex source texts at them and expected them to sink or swim. These students sank and learned little to nothing. These students aren't stupid, and they aren't lazy; they weren't given the tools to succeed.

Therefore, this book is not a "reader." It is a book that explains the philosophers' ideas. That is its role—as a guide. I think that the role of a philosophy textbook is to be a secondary resource that helps instructors explain the philosophers' ideas, so this book references the primary texts without reproducing them. This saves page space for explanation and discussion, while keeping costs down for the students paying for the book. It also gives instructors more freedom to add whatever primary texts they deem fitting. Primary source texts are widely available in the public domain, and I encourage instructors to share them with students as I do in my courses.

Another key difference in this book is its emphasis on recent philosophy. Quite a few standard textbooks focus predominantly on ancient and early modern philosophy, giving students the impression that philosophy was a pursuit of the past. Some "readers" textbooks have recently added to their disjoint approach a few essays more recently written, but not in a coherent way that shows the current directions in philosophy. It is important to show that philosophy is an ongoing conversation that is continuing to engage with current social issues and break new ground.

This book includes philosophy's current engagement with social changes and real-life concerns and that includes covering current movements in social philosophy, feminist philosophy, and philosophy of race, among other current issues in philosophy. *How We Are and How We Got Here* includes more philosophers who are female, people of color, and nonheteronormative than probably any other textbook, and not as mere box-checking but acknowledging these philosophers' important roles in philosophy's effects on society.

What This Book Covers and Why

An important lesson I have learned from teaching philosophy is the importance of learning philosophy chronologically. Students benefit from learning how philosophy has developed by seeing how philosophers interacted with historical changes, and students gain understanding by appreciating how philosophers build on the ideas of their predecessors.

A historical, contextual approach to philosophy avoids the disconnected and fragmented view offered by topically arranged textbooks. This book shows how throughout history, philosophy connects with real life and our everyday experiences. It looks at philosophy not as an arcane collection of disconnected questions but as an ongoing dialogue in response to real-world problems.

Any book on the history of philosophy invites debate over who and what are left undiscussed. What I have tried to do is include the philosophers and ideas most influential to us today. I agonized over many dozens of decisions whether to go into more detail about particular philosophers and ideas. Obviously, I am making a set of value judgments in deciding what ideas are, and are not, significant, and every judgment that I have made is open for discussion. Nevertheless, I think it important to present philosophy to students as something pertinent to their lives and not merely as academic pedantry, so that principle guided my decisions.

This book is targeted to beginning to intermediate students in philosophy. Therefore, it does not delve into many deep details that are worthy of discussion because an analysis of them would not directly benefit the target audience of this book. The book's content is designed to help readers understand the basic content of the philosophers' ideas without confusing or intimidating them with opaque complexities. I have kept in mind the many, many questions that my students have asked over the years about philosophy because those conversations help reveal the issues most relevant to discuss in this book. A very important aim is that this book never talks down to students but includes them in philosophy's long conversation.

Of course, this book is designed to fulfill most schools' general distribution requirements. That is why its subject matter is Western philosophy. Philosophy departments need to satisfy the requirements handed down to them by their states and institutions, and, regrettably, non-Western philosophy is not part of those distribution requirements. There is a widespread ethnocentrism in U.S. education that leaves very little room for non-Western knowledge. A recent trend in some standard textbooks is to include a few paragraphs about ancient Chinese and Indian philosophers, but these inclusions serve more as sidebar curiosities. These textbooks give students the false impression that philosophy in China and India stopped more than 2,000 years ago, and I think this does more harm than good. Those two cultures, among others, deserve adequate attention and background in a book much larger than this one.

Also in the service of schools' general distribution requirements, this book does not cover logic or critical thinking. Most schools cover that material in specific critical thinking or reasoning courses. This book also does not include ethics because most schools teach stand-alone courses on ethics. Leaving out logic and ethical theory allows this book, and courses that adopt it, to spend more of the limited course time on the rest of philosophy.

I very much welcome feedback from instructors on ideas to improve this book. Like philosophy itself, this book is an ongoing process always seeking to be better in addressing the problems of the real world.

Best Regards,
Douglas Giles, PhD
Elmhurst University

ABOUT PHILOSOPHY

Welcome to this discussion of the history of Western philosophy. Make yourself at home. Whether you know a little or a lot, this history will hopefully introduce you to new ideas and spark your curiosity to investigate further for yourself. Because this is a chronological history that puts things into context, we'll start at the beginning.

The Beginning of Philosophy

The beginning of philosophy was. . . . To be honest, nobody knows. Its beginning is forever lost in the mists of prehistory. Sometime, somewhere, the first philosophical human being started to wonder about truths and meanings beyond the surface reality in which he or she lived. That would have been many thousands of years ago.

I've often wondered if the greatest philosopher ever was a sheepherder, someone who, having many quiet hours while tending sheep, was able to contemplate deeply about the nature of reality and humanity's place in it. Alas, we will never learn the insights of this greatest of all philosophers because the sheepherder never wrote them down.

My imaginary sheepherder leads to two other ideas. The first is that everyone is a philosopher who can have philosophical insights, or at least can be with a little effort. The second is that not everyone who has written about philosophy is a great philosopher.

These two ideas also apply to you. You can be a great philosopher if you put your mind to it. Plus, you don't have to agree with what famous philosophers say, even though they published their ideas and are notable for doing so.

In this book, I want to teach you about philosophy to encourage you to think for yourself. Philosophy is doing your own independent thinking, following the implications of your thoughts, and coming to your own reasonable conclusions.

What Is Philosophy? Philosophy Is a Quest

Let's first deal with some misconceptions. Many people, because they've been allowed so little experience with philosophy or have had philosophy taught badly to them, have a negative view of it. They see philosophy as the obscure arcane thoughts of odd reclusive men from bygone times. They see the study of philosophy as dusting off moldy ideas that have little relevance to their daily lives. **Not true!**

Literally, the word "philosophy" comes from the Greek words *philo* ("love") and *sophia* ("wisdom"). Thus, the label "philosophy" means "the love of wisdom." Clearly, though, the act of philosophy is much more than simply loving wisdom. It is deeper, broader, and more involved.

Many people have attempted to explain what philosophy is. Some have said philosophy is thinking about thinking, reflecting on experience, or a pursuit of truth. Philosophy is all of those things, but it is also something much more.

Here is my definition:

Philosophy is the active intellectual search for fundamental principles on which we can build a better life.

What does that mean? Let's look at the definition one idea at a time.

Philosophy is *active*.

Philosophy is not passive. If you submissively believe what you are told, you're not being a philosopher. Philosophy is about actively thinking for yourself (I can't emphasize that too much). An active mind is important for philosophy, and philosophers are never satisfied with comfortable feel-good answers. Philosophers question assumptions—especially their own—and the act of philosophy is a live and ongoing pursuit for better explanations, ideas, and understandings. The most important part in being a good philosopher is actively and open-mindedly listening to other people's ideas.

Philosophy is *intellectual*.

Yes, philosophy is engaging in active thinking. Philosophers do not accept ideas because they feel nice but because they make intellectual sense. You need to use your rational powers a lot when engaging with philosophy. That's intimidating, especially because what philosophy explores are some of the most difficult concepts possible. We need to think diligently and critically to explore these concepts, discuss them, and arrive at solutions.

Philosophy is an active intellectual *search*.

When we engage in philosophy, we are looking for something. Philosophy is not an aimless pursuit. Philosophers are not navel gazing, and we aren't thinking for its own sake. We have a purpose. Philosophy is a quest. We are searching for answers to our most pressing and vexing questions by actively using our minds. Instead of passively accepting superficial answers, philosophy searches deeper into topics, seeking to understand the essence of issues that affect us in our lives.

Philosophy is searching for *fundamental principles*.

Fundamental principles are the concepts that underlie our thinking and how we view the world. A main difference between philosophy and other intellectual pursuits is that philosophy searches for the meaning behind concepts and phenomena. Science is excellent at measuring phenomena and gathering data. Philosophy is exceptional for forming a worldview that strengthens our ability to perceive phenomena and make decisions about them. All of the data in the world can't give us wisdom. Philosophy searches for the foundations for our perceptions, understandings, and what we do in the world. Identifying the fundamental principles that underlie our world and how we perceive and think about it is necessary to understand ourselves and our world.

Philosophy has a purpose for its search for fundamental principles.

With few exceptions, philosophy's purpose is to improve our lives. This is one of philosophy's greatest strengths. Philosophers engage in philosophical inquiry with the hope of more fully understanding the world in which they live. Whether that understanding leads to practical benefits or the satisfaction that having answers brings, the goal of philosophy is improving the quality of human life. Different philosophers have had different views on how life could or should be improved, but one way or another, they all share the same desire to better the human condition through better understanding fundamental principles and how to apply them. When we understand the fundamental principles of what the world is and how we perceive it, we can build a better life for ourselves and future generations. Philosophy is the active intellectual search for that deeper understanding.

Thinking actively, diligently, and critically about the problems we face helps us to arrive at solutions and improve our lives. That is the answer to what philosophy is and why people engage in philosophy.

Philosophy in Context—Philosophy Is a Conversation

As you read this book, an important idea to keep in mind is that philosophy is *not* detached from the "real" world. You may have heard that philosophy is, as it is too often wrongly portrayed, obscure and weird thinking. The reality is that philosophy is a response by real people to the world in which they live.

Philosophers do not create ideas in a vacuum. All philosophers are, as we all are, embedded in a particular culture, time, and place. All philosophers are a product of their culture and are affected by their environment and the events of their time. Likewise, the philosophies they create are affected by their time and place.

It also works in the other direction. Philosophers affect culture and society. The ideas of the philosophers have shaped human society throughout history, a fact that is too often underappreciated. Philosophers have identified fundamental principles on which we can build a better life, and subsequent generations have used those principles to change their societies. The wisdom of philosophers has shaped many governments, businesses, and individuals. How we are today and how we think is a direct product of the thinking and writing of major philosophers. That reality is one of the primary things you will learn in this book.

The history of philosophy is the unfolding of a very long conversation. No philosopher starts from nothing. As you read this book, you will see again and again how philosophers are responding to the ideas of previous philosophers. They sometimes agree and they sometimes disagree, but they are always inspired by earlier ideas and take those ideas into account in building their philosophies. Through the process of people reading, conversing, and responding to ideas, philosophy developed over time, taking in social changes, always in conversation with society and the variety of philosophical ideas available. This book is a chronicle of significant parts of that conversation.

Keep in mind when reading each philosopher in this book that we have the benefit of many years of history that they did not have. You always have to try to put aside what you think you know today and how we think today and put yourself in that philosopher's position.

You cannot understand history without understanding philosophy, and you cannot understand philosophy without understanding history. That's why this book discusses philosophy chronologically. It begins at the written beginning of Western philosophy's history and shows how many major philosophers built on the ideas of their predecessors. Philosophy is enlightening because it is a quest to understand how we are, where we have been, and where we are going.

Philosophy in Your Life

You can now be a part of philosophy's conversation. We are all philosophers to one degree or another because we all wonder about the questions of reality, life, and society. The more you join in the conversation, the more insights you will get into society and the more you become a philosopher in your own right.

In this book, you will discover philosophers with whom you connect and ideas you've thought of yourself, as well as others who are totally different and new to you. Philosophy is a voyage of discovery, and you can have a lot of fun, if you are willing. Like with all good things in life, the more you put into reading and thinking about the material in this book, the more you'll get out of it. Enjoy!

Chapter 1

PLATO

To study and understand Western philosophy, we must begin with **Plato**. Plato wasn't the first philosopher, but we begin with Plato because he was the first systematic philosopher, meaning thinking of and writing about philosophy as a thorough approach to life. Western philosophy developed from Plato's approach to the problems facing ancient Greek society.

There is no overestimating the influence of Plato on philosophy and Western civilization. The questions he raised and the ideas he discussed echoed down through history. Plato's ideas didn't have much influence during or shortly after his lifetime, but in later centuries, his particular systematic approach to philosophy became one of the two main pillars of Western philosophy, the other pillar being Aristotle, who we will discuss in Chapter 2.

Present-day students initially find Plato's thought difficult to grasp. That is because the ancient Greek culture of Plato's time is foreign to our culture, which is no surprise. There are many centuries of history between us and the ancient Greeks. Our culture today is the product of a very long history, and a significant part of the foundations of Western culture are in the ancient Greek world. We sit at the end of a long story, and like any story, it is most easily understood by starting at the beginning. So, while Plato and the ancient Greeks may seem strange in their thinking, grasping the essence of Plato's philosophy is the beginning of understanding all of Western philosophy.

Plato was active as a writer and teacher from approximately 399 to 347 BCE. He lived in Athens, Greece, during a time when that city-state's power and prestige was in decline. Like so many other philosophers we will meet in this book, the social and political situation of his homeland affected his thinking. Athens had suffered an embarrassing defeat to Sparta in the Peloponnesian War, and that defeat called into question the belief among the Athenian aristocracy that Athens had a successful social system.

Plato's philosophy addressed the political and social uncertainty of his time with an eye to building a better society. The primary theme of Plato's philosophical system was how to live as good a life as possible. For Plato, a principal means to that end was identifying the fundamental principles that could provide stability for society amid the chaos of capricious leaders and deities. Plato looked first to geometry and mathematics because in them he saw order and certainty and the promise of a philosophical method and language to explain the world.

Plato's Writings

Plato wrote all of his works in the form of dialogues among two or more characters. We know that the characters in Plato's written works were real people, but we do not know how much of what Plato wrote were those people's actual words and ideas. Plato's lead character in his dialogues was usually his teacher, Socrates. Why Plato wrote in the form of dialogues is a mystery, especially given that Socrates apparently taught that writing philosophy was antithetical to actually living philosophically. Perhaps Plato's intention was to grant Socrates's ideas a form of permanency, even if Socrates didn't think that was important. This intention would be consistent with Plato's beliefs about the nature of Truth. It may also reflect Plato's desire to have a lasting effect on his society and to share with future generations the vision he had for society.

A common plot runs throughout the dialogues. Among the discussants, a concept such as Justice or Piety is mentioned. Socrates says he does not know the exact meaning of the concept, could someone please explain. Someone provides an answer, often a well-known someone who claims to be an authority. Plato frequently used the rhetorical device of inserting well-known Athenian people in the dialogues and having them express their views to Socrates. Socrates points out that the answer given by the alleged authority is merely an example of the concept, and he presses for a *definition* of the essence of the concept that covers all particular instances of it. Numerous commonsense definitions are examined and discarded as being insufficient to describe the essence of the thing being defined until eventually we are left with no definitive answer.

The lack of satisfactory conclusions in Plato's dialogues frustrates some readers, but Plato forces us to read between the lines, perhaps reflecting Plato's purpose in the dialogues. Plato possibly doesn't want to give the reader the answer but to ignite in the reader a desire to *find* the answer. In philosophy, answers cannot always be captured by mere words. Plato consistently expressed the view that truth cannot be expressed in static sentences, nor can the truth be described in elaborate rhetoric. Knowing truth takes time, and the person wishing to know truth must nurture and develop the intellect. The process of gaining knowledge requires many conversations. Knowing the truth is a life's work. Knowledge and other virtues must be cultivated by a student over many years.

To that end, Plato in 387 BCE founded an educational association that came to be known as the "Academy" after the name of the grove in which Plato held it. The Academy was not a formal school as we understand it today but an environment in which students could live and learn from their elders about philosophy.

Defining Justice

Plato's longest and most detailed dialogue was *The Republic*. Plato's central topic in it concerns the question of what justice is. For Plato, justice is both an ethical issue and a political issue. Justice defines how individuals should interact with each other and how society should be structured and ruled. In exploring justice, Plato uses his usual literary device of Socrates discussing the question with alleged authorities. They give Socrates examples and definitions of justice, and Socrates shows how each definition is inadequate to define justice.

In *The Republic*, Plato has characters in the dialogue give examples of actions and situations that they consider to be just, but examples are not definitions. The discussants in *The Republic* never come to an agreement on what justice *is*. Rather than go into the particular details of the complex arguments between Socrates and his interlocutors, let's step back to appreciate the complexity of the timeless and universal question of what justice is. How do you approach defining a virtue like justice? Justice is not something you can point to or hold in your hands. You cannot see justice. You cannot handle it. There is no instrument by which you can measure it. Justice has no color or texture or any material quality we can discern with our senses. And yet, do you not have a sense of justice and injustice?

Consider this example. For a class, you work long and diligently on a paper. You put in a great deal of effort and hand in the paper to your professor. Without even looking at your paper, the professor tosses it into the trash and says you failed. Would you consider that unjust? Why? Because you weren't treated fairly? What do you mean by fairness? Why should you be treated fairly, whatever that means? What does fairness have to do with justice? Perhaps you say that the professor was not doing the job a professor should do, like read a student's paper. OK, but why should a professor do that, and how is doing one's job justice? Take any other set of circumstances and you run into the same set of problems. You will find that you are giving other words for justice, like "fairness," "righteousness," "equality," and so on, but not actually giving a definition of what justice fundamentally *is*.

The point is that we find it much easier to feel that something is just or unjust than it is to define intellectually what justice is. Frustrating our attempts to define justice is that we have never experienced an example of perfect justice that we can use as a standard to judge particular circumstances. Nevertheless, we feel that we can judge whether we are seeing or not seeing justice. Although we cannot measure justice, we still feel that we can discern differences in levels of justice and injustice. From where does this knowledge come? What is the standard of justice by which we can compare actions and situations and know which are instances of justice?

Plato argued that there must be a singular, unchanging standard of justice. If the standard of justice was changeable or relative, then we would have no real standard by which we could make judgments. It would be as if the standard of measure that is a meter was changeable and was a different length in different times and places. If a meter was changeable, how could we know how long anything was? Only when we have a universal standard that says *this* is a perfect, exact meter could we then say with confidence that any particular object is a meter long. Using the same reasoning, Plato insisted that justice must be something universal and unchanging; otherwise, justice is a mere word expressing our whims and has no value.

If justice is universal and real, what sort of thing is it? Justice is not a physical thing like a tree or a person. So, justice must be a nonphysical, yet still real, thing. What kind of thing is that? How would we have knowledge about that kind of thing? First, we need to ask, what is knowledge?

What Is Knowledge?

Plato firmly believed that for knowledge to be genuine, it must be universal and unchanging because truth is universal and unchanging. Physical objects change, so knowledge and truth must be nonphysical. Therefore, genuine knowledge is not perceivable by the physical senses. True knowledge must be perceived by reason. Knowledge must also be connected to an objective truth. What is true must be true independent of individual perceptions or particular circumstances. For something to be objectively true, it must be true for everyone.

Plato makes a strong distinction between knowledge and opinion. Opinions are subjective perceptions had by individuals. We can have the knowledge that the temperature is 20 degrees Celsius because we can objectively measure that. But one person may feel that temperature is too cold, while another person feels that temperature is comfortable or even warm. How hot or cold it feels is a subjective opinion. Plato felt that opinions are not worth much because they are relative to the individual person; they cannot be considered knowledge.

Plato's problem with opinions ran far deeper than disagreements about how the temperature feels. Plato connected opinions with subjective sense perceptions, and he contrasted that with the connection of knowledge with objective reason. Plato agreed with the earlier Greek philosopher, Heraclitus, that our physical senses cannot be relied upon because they can be easily deceived by constantly changing appearances.

However, Plato did not go as far as Heraclitus did in saying that the physical world was unknowable because it was in such continual flux.

Plato observed that objects in the world fit into discernable patterns. We can identify qualities that particular objects share that allow us to identify them. For example, Plato and Socrates are particular entities, but we can call them both "human." The term "human" stands for a universal concept that refers to all particular entities that share the similar qualities that compose the definition of "human." When we look at particular trees that differ in their particularness, we can also recognize that they are all trees because they share similar qualities.

The crucial question that Plato asks is this: how is it that we recognize objects like humans and trees or concepts like justice and piety? Let's look at the example of this object.

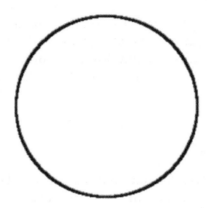

What is this object? If you replied that it is a circle, your answer is understandable but not exactly accurate. What is the definition of a circle? A circle is a closed curved shape made of points equidistant from a fixed point within the curve. Is the circle on this sheet of paper or electronic screen an object that fits the definition? Not exactly. If we measure the points with great precision, we will find that the "circle" on this page is not a perfect circle. If we look closely enough we see that the curve is not solid but made up of tiny points, and not every point is exactly equidistant from a center point. The object on the page is not a circle but an attempt to *portray* a circle.

Almost all objects in the visible world are like this, Plato is saying. All objects are imperfect copies of something perfect. But we can identify this circle (or any other object in the world) because we have some sort of knowledge of the perfect circle and use that knowledge as the measure of what a circle is. However, we have never experienced a perfect Circle, just as we have never experienced perfect Justice. And the capitalization is meaningful, as we shall soon see. The "circle" on the page is not actually a circle; it is merely an object that is "circular." It is an object that has qualities that cause it to resemble a Circle.

Plato's Forms

How do we come to the judgment that something is a circle if we have never seen a perfect Circle? Plato's theory is that we can recognize a particular object as a circle because the object partakes of the *Form* of Circularity and that we have knowledge of the Form of Circularity. When we have a sense experience of a particular object, we intellectually compare our sense impressions to our knowledge of the Form of Circularity and understand that the object is circular.

When we look at an object and think, "That is a tree," how do we come to this conclusion? Part of the answer is because of the information provided by our physical senses. We think it is a tree because it looks like what we believe a tree looks like, and perhaps feels, smells, and sounds like we believe a tree should. But to think it is a tree because it looks like a tree doesn't answer the question of *why* we think it looks like a tree. What *is* a tree anyway? How can we know that something is a tree?

Let's imagine that we are looking at three oak trees. Despite their differences, they share certain qualities in common, and this common set of characteristics we call "oak tree." This concept "oak tree" is a universal: it applies not just to one or even several objects but to a class of objects of a certain type. In Plato's philosophy, all oak trees are oak trees because they partake in the Form of Oak Tree.

Plato's theory of reality is that the particular objects of our sense experience are related to universal objective truths. Any particular tree is a tree in that it participates in the Form Treeness—in other words, the particular object is a copy of the perfect Tree. Remember our earlier example of the circular object. That particular circle is a copy of the perfect Circle. The object resembles a Circle because it partakes of the Form of Circularity. It is a particular instance of a universal Form.

We live in the world of visible objects, and in that world we find that particular objects have a set of constant, universal qualities. This is why we can identify and talk about objects in our world. For example, David, Juan, Svetlana, and Anushka are all distinct individuals, yet we can refer to each of them with the universal term "human." Despite their individual differences, these people share certain qualities. We use names for these sets of shared qualities like "human," "tree," and "justice."

Corresponding to the names are Universals that consist of the essential qualities common to all objects within that kind of object denoted by the name. When a botanist seeks to understand trees in general, he or she is seeking not knowledge about a particular tree but what is universally true about all trees. Plato would say that the botanist is seeking to understand the Form of Treeness.

According to Plato's theory, this relation between particular objects and universal Forms enables us to recognize qualities within objects. For Plato, we can think of every quality that we can think of—circularity, tallness, greenness, humanness—because we know the perfect, objective, universal Form of that quality. All circular objects have the Form of Circularity in common. We recognize an object as a "circle" because it participates in the Universal of Circularity and we know the Form of Circle. Back to our earlier discussion about justice, any occurrence of justice is an act that partakes of the Form of Justice. Likewise, in the realm of our thinking, we make judgments that something is just or unjust because we have knowledge of the Form of Justice and can thus recognize instances of justice when we experience them.

In Plato's view, reality is composed of particular objects and universal Forms. Particular objects get their qualities from the Forms. All objects that are beautiful have the universal Form of Beauty in common. However, and this is very important to Plato, particular objects are temporal—they come into existence and go out of existence. A rose grows from a bud and flowers into beauty but then withers and dies. The rose has lost its beauty, but does Beauty itself cease to exist? Of course not. The Form of Beauty never changes. It is unaffected by the world of particular objects that come into and go out of existence. A Form exists in and of itself, separate from any objects that partake of it.

Plato refers to "beauty itself" and "justice itself." We have knowledge of Justice itself, and by this Plato does not mean a someone's opinion of what justice is, but the Form of Justice. The Forms are not dependent on particular minds. They are realities that are independent of all minds. Circularity exists even if no human mind is thinking of Circularity; it exists even if there are no objects in the visible world that are circular. The same is true about Justice, Beauty, and all the other Forms.

If you find the reality of the Forms confusing, an example should clarify. Consider the multiplication table. Does it exist? Obviously it must, for it would be silly to say that $5 \times 5 = 25$ and $6 \times 7 = 42$ are not true or are not real mathematics. Where does the multiplication table exist? Yes, you can write the table down, but what you write are just symbols that represent the reality of the multiplication table. You have not created the truth that $5 \times 5 = 25$ by writing it down. Erasing or destroying the symbols that you wrote does not destroy the truth and reality of the multiplication table. The reality of the mathematics is not changed by what you or anyone else says or does in regard to them. Even if everyone forgot the multiplication table it would still exist and its content would still be true. Is it not also true that no human being invented the multiplication table but rather we each at some point learned about its existence?

How Do We Learn the Forms?

What, then, are Forms according to Plato? They are the true objects of knowledge. Like Truth, they are universal, unchanging, and nonphysical and thus are not perceivable by the senses, are objective, and are grounded in reason. The universal Forms are unchanging and perfect—a perfect Circle. But remember that we do not ever experience perfect Circles and perfect Justice in the visible world. The Forms must be real, not imaginary, so then where do they exist? The Forms do not exist in physical space; they are perfect entities existing beyond this visible realm, separate from all of the objects that partake of the Forms.

How do we learn the Forms? Plato means something different by "learning" than we mean today. For Plato, learning is a process of recollection. We learn by remembering the knowledge we already have of the Forms. What a good teacher does is awaken the dormant knowledge within the student. Although Plato never explains how, the knowledge of the Forms is in our psyche prior to our physical birth in this world. The ancient Greek concept of psyche is similar to what we think of as the human soul, but Plato associates psyche with our mental capacities. Plato believed that human psyches were uncreated and immortal. Having always existed, our psyches' knowledge of the Forms comes to us from a previous existence. Thus, we are born into this world with innate knowledge of what is true. Unfortunately for us, we have forgotten this knowledge from our psyche's previous existence. We just need to uncover this knowledge buried within our mental capabilities.

When we perceive a particular object, like a circle or a tree, our reason uncovers in our perception the object's resemblance to a universal Form. Through the insight of reason, we recollect our knowledge of the Forms, and this is how we identify what the particular object is.

For Plato, though, identifying particular objects was a secondary pursuit if not a waste of effort. Knowledge of the Forms is our one true goal. Plato said that rather than try to learn about justice from the limited and deficient particular examples of justice that we experience in the visible world, we learn what justice is by contemplating Justice itself—the perfect Form of Justice. We do not bother much at all with the study of objects on the visible world like trees and animals because they are not what is ultimately important. The particular objects merely point us to the Universal Forms, which are the proper target of our thinking.

We can access true knowledge of the Forms by using reason, which is independent of sense experience. This must be the case, Plato holds, because we can identify a circle despite having never experienced through our senses a perfect Circle. We know about perfect Circles and perfect Justice not from experience but through the innate knowledge in our psyches of the Forms. Our experiences of particulars in the world reminds us of knowledge we dimly remember, and, in recollecting our knowledge, we realize that the object partakes of the Forms, which should inspire in us the desire to study the Forms.

The problem with Plato's theory of Forms is how it works in the world. How exactly does an object partake of a Form? Saying a particular tree resembles the Form of Treeness is one thing, but Plato is also claiming that the particular tree gets its qualities from the Form of Treeness. How that works, he does not explain.

It gets more complicated when we think about the diversity of species of objects. Aren't an oak, a maple, and an elm all particular species of trees? Do they all partake of the universal Form of Treeness? Then why are they different species? Do particular oak trees partake of Oak Treeness rather than Treeness? A tree is a plant, and don't all plants partake of Plantness? Going in the other direction, the leaves of an oak tree are green, so the leaves must partake of Greenness, but the trunk is brown so the trunk must partake of Brownness. What about the oak tree's size, shape, texture, and other characteristics?

It would seem that every single quality of every object—its size, shape, color, texture, and so on—would have to come from a corresponding Form. How many Forms are there? How many Forms are in any particular object? And what about relative qualities like tall and short, thin and wide? Would a tree's height come from Tallness or Shortness? When a tree grows and its trunk widens, is it partaking of less Thinness and more Thickness? Plato's theory of Forms becomes complicated.

The Allegory of the Cave

Plato does provide some good explanations for his theory of Forms. His most famous is known as the Allegory of the Cave. In *The Republic*, Plato has Socrates tell a long, poetic story that explains the nature of reality and how we can have knowledge of it. Here's a paraphrase.

A group of people have been imprisoned in a cave since birth. All their lives they have been seated on the ground, their backs against a low wall that runs across the cave. They are chained such that they are unable to turn their heads and can only see straight ahead at the cave wall opposite them. (Yes, this is a strange story.) The only light in the cave comes from a fire that is well behind the prisoners that shines light over the low wall and onto the cave wall opposite the prisoners. Between the low wall behind the prisoners and the fire, other people regularly pass by holding up puppets of people, animals, and other objects. (Yes, this is a very strange story.) The prisoners are unable to see the people, the objects they carry, or the fire itself; they can see only the shadows of the objects cast on the wall in front of them. Consequently, having seen nothing else all of their lives, the prisoners believe that these shadows are all that exist. The prisoners can talk with one another, and the words they use refer to the shadows that pass before them.

Plato, through the voice of Socrates, now asks us to imagine that one of the prisoners is unchained and allowed to roam free. First, the prisoner turns around and can now see over the wall and see the puppets. The sight of these puppets thoroughly confuses the prisoner, who naturally had thought that the shadows were the true reality. Having had no experience other than the shadows, the prisoner assumes the puppets are illusions. Looking at the light of the fire blinds the prisoner. Its appearance is so foreign to all prior experience that the prisoner turns away and flees back to the familiar shadows.

We are then asked to imagine further that the prisoner is forcibly dragged up the cave entrance's rough and steep ascent and out into the sunlight outside of the cave. The prisoner first feels pain and anger at this rough treatment but once outside is immediately overwhelmed by the dazzling brightness of the sun. It takes a long time for the prisoner's eyes to adjust to the glare of the sunlight. At first, the prisoner is able to discern only vague shapes in the reflections of objects in a pool of water. Eventually, adjusting to the new level of light, the prisoner's eyes can now see the vividly real people, animals, and other objects of which the puppets in the cave are mere copies.

Thus enlightened, the liberated prisoner now knows the pathetic level of knowledge held by those who are still in the cave. Returning to the cave to share these new revelations and with the desire to set the other prisoners free from their ignorance, the prisoner now has difficulty readjusting to the darkness and is now unable to see the shadows on the cave wall. The enlightened former prisoner shares the knowledge of the greater reality outside the cave with those still imprisoned within it. Those still chained against the low wall refuse to believe the descriptions of the outside world and the real objects in it. They angrily ridicule the former prisoner as being crazy and no longer being able to function in their world of shadows. Ominously, Plato has Socrates say, "If they could lay hands on this person who was trying to set them free and lead them up, they would kill him."

Everything in the Allegory of the Cave is symbolic. The cave symbolizes the physical world in which we live. The chains symbolize our ignorance within the darkness of the cave of the visible, physical world. Within the cave are the particular objects in the physical world. The people carrying them to cast shadows on the wall symbolize human artistic activity, the shadows symbolizing artistic creations like sculptures created by humans as copies of the objects in the world. This interpretation matches Plato's rejection of representational art as empty foolishness.

The world outside the cave symbolizes the realm of the Forms. The Allegory of the Cave is teaching us that the objects in the physical world are mere copies of a higher reality—the Forms. The Forms are illuminated by a light above and beyond, symbolized by the Sun, a light that gives life and intelligibility to everything. The fire in the cave is inferior to the greater light that is beyond the world, and everything in our world is at best a pale copy of the realm of the Forms. The liberated prisoner symbolizes the philosopher, who now has knowledge of the Forms and understands that they are what is truly real, not the objects in the cave—

the objects in the world. Finally, the former prisoner who returned to the cave to try to teach the other prisoners symbolizes Socrates. Plato's teacher had discovered wisdom, but when he tried to share that wisdom with others, he was ridiculed. Eventually, Socrates was executed by his fellow citizens of Athens because his teachings were deemed to be corrupting other people. Plato uses the Allegory of the Cave to teach lessons in knowledge, reality, and politics.

Plato's Divided Line

The Allegory of the Cave presents Plato's view of reality as being divided into two realms. As we shall see later in this book, Plato's dualistic cosmology is the most influential and enduring aspect of his thought. Plato saw knowledge and reality as inextricably connected. The levels of knowledge correspond to levels of reality, and he drew a symbolic line separating the two realms of existence—the visible realm and the intelligible realm—corresponding to how we can perceive each realm. Everything in reality is either above the line or below the line. We can picture Plato's divided line and the two realms in the following way:

Plato's Divided Line

THE GOOD

Intelligible Realm:	Forms	Mind	Knowledge	Virtues	Unchanging
Visible Realm:	World	Bodies	Opinion	Shadows	Change and decay

Plato categorizes the different ways that we perceive and think and arranges them in the structure of reality. At the top is the fundamental principle of reality that Plato calls "the Good." It is the highest realm of existence, perfect in every way. Plato gives us little explanation about what the Good is, although from the Allegory of the Cave, we get the idea that it is the light of reason that gives the Forms existence and makes them intelligible to us. Plato writes: "The good may be said to be not only the author of knowledge to all things known, but of their being and essence" (*Republic* VI.509). The Good is the source of all things, providing existence and knowledge of existence, but is greater than everything else.

Above the divided line is the intelligible realm. In this realm are the Forms and the Virtues. They are perfect and unchanging and therefore fully real. This is a nonphysical reality we cannot perceive through our physical senses. Plato refers to it as the "intelligible world" because this realm is intelligible to reason. This highest level of knowledge is the realm of true knowledge through rational contemplation of the Forms and the Virtues, like Justice.

Below Plato's divided line are the changeable particular objects of the world. We exist in the visible realm of physical objects that we perceive through our physical senses. The visible physical world is a world of constant change, somewhat like Heraclitus's view that we can never step into the same river twice because the river is different every second. Plato says that the world of change is a realm of real objects that we can encounter by means of our senses and that we can take in sense information about them. However, Plato contends that because objects in the visible realm change, they are not fully real and we cannot understand them rationally. Our physical senses are so easily deceived that we cannot hope to learn much from observing the visible world. We can, at best, get only partial, temporary ideas about particular objects.

Clearly, Plato thinks there is a relationship between a particular object and the universal Form, but what that exact relationship is, Plato never quite answers. An incomplete answer may be found in the Allegory of the Cave. The particulars in the world are copies of the universal Forms. That means that each particular object somehow "participates" in the Form. A photograph "participates" in the reality of the object of which it is an image. An artwork participates in the same way; a human created it to symbolize an object. The more realistic the image in a photograph, painting, or drawing is, the more fully it participates in the object. However, this analogy falls short because it is still comparing one physical object with another.

Perhaps we can find a better analogy in the Allegory of the Cave—a shadow cast by an object. A shadow "participates" in the reality of the object that casts it. The particular objects are still real, just as a shadow is real. They are not phantasms or illusions. Still, a shadow is less real than the object that casts it. Like a shadow, the objects in the visible realm are real projections of something more real. Objects in the visible realm are projections of the Forms, but unlike the unchangeable and eternal Forms, the particulars change, and they eventually degenerate into nonexistence.

Somehow the Forms cause the existence of particular physical objects, although how Plato never explains. What is clear is that the Forms are the standards which we use to judge whether particulars are excellent or deficient. We can understand anything in the world in terms of the Form that gives it its existence and "what it is." The "what it is" is not just its physical characteristics but its function. To understand any object, we must understand the Form.

Philosophy of the Polis

Plato was the first philosopher to offer what we now call political philosophy. The word "political" comes from the ancient Greek word "polis," which means "the city." So, polis relates to political, and all things political are related to all things about the city or society because the ancient Greeks thought in terms of the city-state.

Like most later political philosophers, Plato was interested in how best to bring about a just society. In Plato's philosophy, true Justice is never arbitrary or subjective; it is always objective and universal. The goal, then, is to put in place social institutions that are objective and unchanging. Only such a structure will keep society well ordered. In *The Republic*, Plato sets out the social structure and institutions he thinks will best ensure a just society. He admits that his plan will probably never be implemented—utopian visions seldom are. Nevertheless, he offers his plan as a model to which we should aspire, even if we never achieve it.

Plato holds the commonsense notion that the functional political state relies on a division of labor. Rather than each of us doing everything—each one of us having to grow our own food, make our own clothes, and so on—we each should specialize in particular tasks that will allow us all to be more efficient and harmonious. For this reason, Plato thinks society should identify each human's special skills and train all members of the polis to be skilled workers in fields that best take advantage of those skills. In this strategy, every profession would be filled by those whose skill sets enable them to excel in their professions. This includes the leaders of government. Only those who show exceptional skill in making rational political decisions should be in government, just as only those who are exceptionally skilled at making clothes should be tailors. All levels and areas of society would be filled with the best candidates on the basis of skill in their assigned labors.

Not surprisingly, Plato thought that the skill most essential to leading a state was the ability to make informed, rational decisions. Therefore, political leaders must have knowledge of the Forms and the Good and be able to apply universal knowledge to particular situations. The humans with such skills are the philosophers, and, yes, Plato wants philosophers and political leaders to be one and the same.

Now, don't assume that this was self-serving on Plato's part. He's being prudent and consistent with how he saw reality functioning. Think about it. Just as we would want the physician who would heal the body to possess the skill and experience to make informed, rational medical decisions, we would want the political leaders who would heal society to possess the skill and experience to make informed, rational political decisions. If people who have trained to be critically thinking philosophers are the best at making informed, rational decisions, then isn't it only reasonable that political leaders should be philosophers? We've certainly seen how disastrous it is when political leaders aren't good at critical thinking.

In Plato's ideal society, the best trained and most rational people should be the leaders who guide the state. Unlike what we have seen happen far too often in history, Plato's leaders would not be richer or more privileged than others in society. These leaders would not benefit themselves; instead, they would dedicate their lives to serving the interests of society as a whole, completely forsaking all personal interest. Plato believed that it was impossible for anyone to be a good leader without proper training that began in early youth and continued until one was age 30. These leaders would have known nothing in their lives except training for leadership, having been picked as young as seven years old for their potential in reasoning. Plato didn't even call these people "leaders"; he called them "guardians." They are humans who dedicate their lives to guarding society from harm by using their highly trained skills in reason to keep society well ordered.

The next group in society are those who display willful, dynamic energy with strength of courage. Humans with those skills would be trained to be society's police and military. Plato called them "auxiliaries," in the original sense of the word as helpers and supporters. The auxiliaries use their skills to protect society from external threats—invading armies being a harsh reality in Plato's time—and from internal criminal and subversive threats.

The last group, the majority of society, are the producers, those who, as the name attests, have the skills to produce the various material things that everyone needs to survive. These are the farmers, miners, tailors, potters, carpenters, and other craftspeople; merchants; physicians; and other specialists. This group of humans is not at all less valuable to society than are the guardians and auxiliaries. Obviously, no society could survive without workers performing this work, and Plato values them accordingly.

Plato's ideal society is a meritocracy—a society based solely on merit or ability. He proposes that children, regardless of their parentage, be rigorously assessed at a young age as to their talents. Whatever superior abilities and aptitudes children possess will determine what occupation they will enter, and they will be trained accordingly. That means that the child of a cobbler could become a baker, soldier, or guardian. The child of a guardian could become a ditch digger. What mattered is which skills most benefit society. Plato's ideal society, in this one sense, is without strict class distinctions. The downside to this system is that once one's occupation is identified, one has no social mobility to be or do anything else. Once a cook, always a cook; you can never change professions. Personal ambition, we might imagine, would upset the system and disrupt social order.

Achieving a harmonious well-ordered society is probably Plato's top priority. Given this, he has a strong bias against individualism and the macro-expression of individualism: democracy. Plato did not want tyranny, but he also thought that democracy was harmful to society. Today, we place a high value on democracy—at least what we take to be democracy—so Plato's opposition to it sounds mistaken in our worldview. Right or wrong, Plato had a solid reason for opposing government by democracy. (You will find that philosophers can have good arguments but still reach incorrect conclusions.) He argued that a democracy ignores the fundamental principle that everyone should act for the good of society as a whole rather than for themselves. Instead of accepting their social roles, Plato reasoned, humans in a democracy seek personal advantage over others. Opposing factions emerge and struggle for power, and democracy can "promote [to leadership] anyone who merely call[s] himself the people's friend" (*Republic* VIII.558). Plato feared that someone with enough charisma and guile would grab power by securing the loyalty of enough voters. Once in power, the politician could become a tyrant and suppress those who might challenge the tyrant's power, and that would result in a state that is far from being just and well ordered.

That is Plato's warning against democracy, and history has proven his argument is not without some legitimacy. However, Plato also expresses disdain for the idea that humans should have liberty, free speech, and equal rights, so perhaps his opposition to democracy is not entirely for noble reasons. He dismissed such ideas of freedom as giving free reign to the lower appetites and ignoring the higher dictates of reason. By equating democracy with unruly passions, he dismissed it as beneath being human.

Plato's Influence

We end the chapter on Plato, but we never entirely leave Plato and his ideas behind. You will see throughout the history of philosophy how Plato's themes and ideas keep returning again and again. Plato's concern with the questions of how we know anything, what the nature of reality is, and how we can build a better society are still the most common fields of inquiry in philosophy. Philosophers have found Plato's answers to these questions to be either inspirational or regrettable.

Plato's idea of intellectual debate in which the truth must be demonstrated by reason became the model for philosophy. Propositions need to be demonstrated before they can be accepted as truths. Even more, propositions need to be defended from questioning in order to be true. The philosophical tradition of Plato has been one of using the tools of reason to demonstrate the truth and then applying those truths to life and society. Attached to that tradition, though, has been Plato's assumption that philosophical demonstration does not use worldly examples but higher principles. The Platonic approach does not deny the world, but it does downplay its relevance.

Plato's greatest influence has been his theory of the divide between two realms of existence and, specifically, the Forms. Many philosophers accepted his conception that there are universals and particulars. Even when philosophers strongly disagreed with the theory, their arguments remained influenced by Plato's conception of reality. As we go through the history of philosophy, watch for how varieties of Platonism arise.

Chapter 2

ARISTOTLE

Aristotle was the second pillar of ancient Greek philosophy. Like Plato, his influence on the rest of Western philosophy cannot be overestimated. Aristotle studied under Plato for years, but when Plato died in 347 BCE, Aristotle took a different path. Some students are surprised that someone would disagree with his or her teacher, but they shouldn't be. Philosophy is a conversation among thinking people, and thinking people frequently disagree because they think for themselves. It's not a sign of insolence to disagree, respectfully, with one's teacher. Aristotle, for example, held Plato in very high regard and wrote in opposition to Plato's ideas only after his teacher's death. Aristotle eventually wrote and taught in his own school, known as the "Lyceum" (Greek for gymnasium) because he took over a former gymnasium. He produced a large body of work, only a fraction of which survived intact. He was an active writer from 347 to 322 BCE.

Aristotle dealt with many of the same questions that Plato did about how we have knowledge, but Aristotle took an almost diametrically opposed view. Plato believed that the objects in the world were only copies of a higher reality—the Forms. Accordingly, Plato believed that studying the objects of the world was not fruitful because they were often not as they appeared to the senses and were less real than the universal Forms. Plato contended that what was needed was not the study of particulars but the study of the universal Forms—this would achieve real knowledge about what was ultimately real.

To the contrary, Aristotle believed that what exists is the world we perceive with our senses. The objects in the world did not depend on a higher realm of Forms. Therefore, the way to understand the world was to learn about objects by observing their qualities. Aristotle contended that observational study of the world would achieve real knowledge because the physical objects in the world are fully real and that, indeed, they were the only things that fully existed.

That, in a nutshell, is the big difference between Plato and Aristotle. It is why the famous painting by Raphael, *The School of Athens*, shows Plato (left) pointing upward and Aristotle (right) gesturing to stay grounded.

Plato reasoned from the universal Forms to the particulars, whereas Aristotle reasoned from the particulars to universal concepts. Aristotle's emphasis on examining the world and cataloging our observations foreshadowed modern scientific methods. Medieval protoscience took its inspiration from Aristotle's Categories, and his ideas on potentiality, actuality, and the four causes, all of which we'll get to a bit later. For centuries, philosophers chose whether they agreed more with Plato's or Aristotle's approach to philosophy.

Aristotle's philosophy of knowledge can be divided into three areas: how objects exist, how we know objects, and how objects change. These three areas overlap and are interconnected, but we'll discuss Aristotle's philosophy in that order.

How Objects Exist

Plato had argued that particular objects were the way they were because they partook of a universal Form. Aristotle countered that Plato's theory of Forms cannot explain how particular objects exist. Aristotle didn't object to the idea that reality consists of particulars and universals, but he had a problem with Plato's idea that the universals existed separately from the particulars. This ignited a debate that continued for centuries that came to be known as "the problem of universals."

What do philosophers mean by "the problem of universals?" Take the example of a sheet of white paper. It is a particular object. This particular object has a quality that we call "whiteness." This whiteness is real; it is a real quality in a real object. The question is whether whiteness itself exists as a universal apart from the object. Another example is baldness. The question is whether baldness can exist on its own, aside from there being a bald something. Socrates is bald, and it would be true that Socrates's baldness is real and a real characteristic of Socrates. However, does "baldness" exist outside of Socrates or anyone else?

Plato's theory of Forms says that "whiteness" and "baldness" do exist as universal Forms independently from all objects that are white or bald.

In other words, even if there were no white or bald objects, "whiteness" and "baldness" would still exist.

Aristotle disagrees. He maintains that universals exist *in* objects, not separate from objects. The particular objects that we see in the visible realm are what exists. This means that the objects in the world exist as they appear to exist without connection to a hidden, higher realm. These real objects Aristotle calls "substances" (more on substances later)— objects that we can describe by qualities such as "whiteness." These qualities are in the particulars, not in the observer or in a universal; they are objectively present only in objects.

Aristotle isn't, strictly speaking, denying universals. He is asserting that the universals are not themselves substances (independently existing entities) and that only particular objects are substances. Plato had confused universals with substances in thinking that because we can think about a universal like whiteness it must therefore exist as a real thing. It was from this reasoning that Plato concluded there is a realm of Forms.

To understand substances (objects) and the qualities that appear in objects, Aristotle says, we need to study those objects. He therefore developed a system of intellectual inquiry to study and explain objects.

How We Know Objects

Our beliefs about how objects exist leads us to how we believe we can gain knowledge of objects. This connection is true for Plato, Aristotle, and many other philosophers we will meet later. Aristotle's differences with Plato about the nature of reality meant that his views also differed about what knowledge is and how we can gain it.

What Knowledge Is

Aristotle's epistemology (the philosophy of knowledge) is very different from Plato's. Plato had concluded that we cannot gain knowledge of the physical objects we perceive through our senses because the senses are imperfect and easily mistaken about the changing material realm. Those physical objects are also less real, so Plato instead urged his students to study the realm of Forms. In contradistinction, Aristotle claims that knowledge comes from a study of particular objects. This is the case for both physical objects and nonphysical virtues like justice. Having a theory but lacking direct experience of the relevant particulars is deficient knowledge. Thus, Aristotle thinks it is a mistake to contemplate an abstract quality in isolation from its concrete manifestations. For example, he says that "musicalness" cannot exist unless there is someone who is musical. Therefore, if we want to understand "musicalness" we need to study musicians and what they do. Similarly, the knowledge we have is directed at the particular things we deal with in our everyday lives. Aristotle gives the example that a doctor, when healing a patient, does not try to cure the Form of Man but tries to cure individual men. (Aristotle has very little to say about women, who he saw as inferior to men.)

Aristotle stressed that knowledge requires going beyond appearances or first impressions. Our study of objects must be detailed and comprehensive. Having *knowledge* is more than sense experiences and more than familiarity with a collection of individual facts. A dog experiences smells, textures, and tastes, but the dog does not have true knowledge. Our inquiries need to go beyond knowing particular facts to understanding how these particular facts result from more fundamental truths. We need to reach beyond appearances to study the true causes of things; therefore, our study of objects is about uncovering the fundamental principles of how objects are. For Aristotle, we attain knowledge when we understand the first principles and causes of why things are the way they are.

Aristotle developed a detailed method of acquiring knowledge that is a kind of protoscience. Science is one particular way to approach to the world. We can contrast an artist's, a gardener's, and a scientist's interest in a tree.

The artist takes in the particularity of how the tree appears. In representing the tree in an artwork, the artist is interested in the particular play of colors in its leaves, the twists and turns of its branches, and the unique textures of its bark. The artist's aesthetic knowledge of the tree consists in how the tree looks and feels.

The gardener has a different type of knowledge because she knows what she needs to do to make trees flourish and increase their fruit. This knowledge has the form of "if you do this action, then this result will happen." The gardener has a practical knowledge of what works but doesn't necessarily understand why it works.

In contrast, when the scientist tries to understand a tree, she seeks to gain a general understanding of the universal characteristics of trees. To understand what is essential to being a tree, the scientist sifts out information that is irrelevant and what is unique to this or that particular case. To put it into Aristotle's terms, the scientist is abstracting the essence (essential qualities) of the tree from its accidental (nonessential) features. The scientist is not content to know only what helps make trees grow. She wants to account for how each individual fact fits into a system of facts and to understand the causes for each fact. Aristotle believed that full knowledge will show us that a particular fact could not be other than it is. That thought of Aristotle's was long influential in European society, as we shall see.

True knowledge is, therefore, far more than a list of facts. True knowledge results from a comprehensive inquiry into the universal nature of things and seeks the necessary connections among them. This true knowledge requires knowledge of the ultimate first principles from which particular facts about particular things can be derived. This approach establishes a high goal for how natural philosophy should be conducted. Too often today scientists are content with simply collecting observations and the "if you do this action, then this result will happen" level of knowledge, without an understanding of the larger picture and greater connections among all things. To be fair, most people are content with a low level of knowledge, and, after all, scientists are just people.

How We Gather Knowledge

Aristotle's approach to gathering knowledge stems from his fundamental conviction that the basic structures of human thought are congruent with the structures of reality. He believed that we can come to understand the things in the world by observing the world and properly reasoning about it. When we correctly reason from one proposition about the world to another in our mind, we are at the same time moving from one true fact about the world to another true fact about the world.

To guide our thoughts toward knowledge, we need to ensure that we use language that has the same structure as reality. As Aristotle puts it, "To say of what is that it is not, or of what is not that it is, is false, while to say of what is that it is, and of what is not that it is not, is true" (*Metaphysics* 1011b25). This is the first appearance in philosophy of a kind of correspondence theory of truth—that what we believe is true depends on whether it corresponds to the way things are in the world— and we will see many philosophers agree with this basic idea.

According to Aristotle, the basic structures of language, thought, and reality are revealed by the kinds of assertions we can make about things. Getting the structures of language correct will reveal not only the categories of our thought but also the categories of reality. Aristotle gives us a list of ten categories or ten kinds of questions we can ask about any object or concept. Aristotle proposed them as the ten irreducible classifications of objects. When we gather the answers for these ten categories, we have a good and thorough understanding of the object. Here is a table of Aristotle's ten Categories.

Table of the Categories

Category	Question	Example
(1) Substance	What is it?	A tree; a dog
(2) Quantity	What size is it?	10 meters tall; 9 kilograms heavy
(3) Quality	What is it like; what are its capabilities?	Flower-producing; loyal
(4) Relations	How is it related?	Larger than the others
(5) Place	Where is it?	On a hill; in the corner
(6) Time	When is (was) it?	Now; yesterday
(7) Position	What position is it in?	Standing; lying
(8) Condition	What state is it in?	Flowering; covered in fur
(9) Action	What is it doing?	Growing; sleeping
(10) Affection	What is acting on it?	Being blown by the wind; being warmed by the fire

Let's work through the Categories beginning with substance. The English word "substance" is the translation of the ancient Greek word *ousia*. Aristotle defines *ousia* as a permanent state of being. An object's *ousia* (substance) is the vital core of what it is and is its ultimate irreducible level of being. Aristotle says that substances "are the entities which underlie everything else, and everything else is either predicated of them or present in them" (*Categories* 5.6). This means that every particular object has a core something that is what it is, and for Aristotle, that is its substance. Substance has a privileged position in the Categories because it is independent of the qualities. All of the other qualities of an object are distinct from but borne by the object's substance.

When we consider the question, What kind of object is it? we are considering the *what* that it is—what is essential to it. Another word for Aristotle's concept of substance is "essence." As he states, "the essence of each thing is what it is said to be intrinsically" (*Metaphysics* 1029 14). When we answer, "It is a tree," we are saying that the qualities of the object are the definition of what a tree is. The essential qualities of a tree compose the definition of tree and are true for every tree. Every object has an essence, the distinct set of qualities that defines the kind of object it is. Aristotle further categorized substance into species and genus. Species indicated the first order of substances, and genus was the second order, a more general classification. Centuries later, scientists adopted Aristotle's species and genus in the taxonomy of all life.

We identify an object by its qualities. For example, every tree has leaves, so we identify an object with leaves as a tree, and we understand that possessing leaves is part of the essence of what a tree is. Important to Aristotle's theory of reality is that this substance that defines a tree is not a Platonic Form. According to Aristotle's theory, it is a mistake to reason that because all trees are similar, there exists "Treeness." This, according to Aristotle, was the mistake that Plato made, thinking that similarities of kind meant the existence of a universal of that kind. Certainly, all trees share similar qualities that we can understand by the concept "tree," but to say that there is a substance that is "tree" does not mean that there also exists a Form of Treeness.

The rest of the Categories build on the first category of substance, and we can use them to help us understand an object beyond the kind of object it is. Categories two through ten can be converted into questions we can ask about any object. The category of quantity is as straightforward as the name indicates. Considering a tree, we can ask quantitative questions like, How tall is it? What shape is it? and so on. Numerical measurements of an object fall under quantity.

The category of quality is less obvious. Here, we are asking what an object is like, what its distinct qualities are. That a particular tree can bear flowers distinguishes it from other types of trees. Cherry trees flower, but oak trees do not; thus, "flower-bearing" is a quality of cherry trees but not of oak trees. Relations compare a particular object to others—the object is bigger or smaller, narrower or wider, than other objects, and so on.

Place and time are as uncomplicated as they seem. They are informative categories because the time when we observe a tree is important because some trees can be different in summer and in winter. Place is where something is—the tree is on a hill—but position is different—it is the object's disposition within its place—the tree is still standing or it has fallen down.

Condition describes an object's current state and is usually related to the category of quality. A particular tree may have the quality of being capable of producing flowers, but it may or may not be in the condition of flowering right now. If a particular tree has lost its leaves, that tells us something about this tree; perhaps it is diseased. Similarly, a cat may or may not have fur, and a person may or may not be clothed.

Action is also straightforward: what is the object currently doing? Finally, "affection" in this context doesn't mean loving gestures; affection identifies the outside forces that are currently *affecting* the object. Right now, a tree is being blown by the wind or being cut down by a person. Yes, a cat can be petted and loved by a person, so that is the cat's current affection.

The Categories and their related questions can be applied to any object. We can ask, Where is Phillip? What is he like? What is he doing?

and so on. The answers we can gather to these questions help us to know about Phillip or any other object. Any physical object or social entity has myriad qualities and activities. That means that particular things have general qualities—many objects can walk or be green, for example. However, the reverse—that general qualities have things—is not possible. Within Aristotle's theory of objects, it makes sense to say "Phillip is walking," but it makes no sense to say "walking is Phillip." Phillip would exist whether or not he was walking or bald, but walking and baldness cannot have any separate existence from objects in which they are qualities. Therefore, substances can be the subjects of statements to which predicates (i.e., the other categories) can be applied—for example, "the tree is flowering" (flowering being a predicate of the tree) and "Phillip is walking" (walking being a predicate of Phillip).

Immanuel Kant (we will meet him in Chapter 8) called Aristotle's ten Categories a brilliant work of philosophical thinking. When the medieval philosophers (we'll meet them in Chapter 3) discovered Aristotle, they largely adopted his idea that the Categories can explain the irreducible kinds of qualities present in objects.

The Categories express Aristotle's belief that all of our knowledge is rooted in our sense experience of objects—that we learn about the world by observing it and gathering information. Using reason, we can abstract, generalize, and draw conclusions from what we learn through sense experience and thus achieve knowledge. Sense experience Aristotle called only potentially intelligible, whereas properly applied analysis makes things actually intelligible. Aristotle presented a method to discipline our reason in his book *Analytics*, which formed the foundations of logic and greatly influenced medieval thinkers.

Thinking of objects in terms of their substance also helps us see that universals exist in objects and are understood by the human mind. Using our reason, we can abstract from our sensory experience of particular objects the concept of universal substances, which Aristotle also calls the form of an object, like trees and humans. These thoughts are crucial to understanding how objects change, which is our next topic.

How Objects Change

One of the problems facing ancient Greek philosophers was the problem of change. Why and how do objects change? Plato had agreed with several philosophers before him that change was an uncomfortable dilemma. Their reasoning behind their discomfort was that perfection has to be unchanging. If something is perfect, it does not change. It was a common belief that anything that changed was not perfect. Plato's theory of the Forms addresses this—the Forms are perfect and unchanging. They are fully real, and the objects that change in the visible realm are less real.

Another problem vexing these philosophers was that change seemed to them to be a movement from nonbeing to being, something being created out of nothing. For example, it appears to our senses that an acorn stops being an acorn and an oak tree starts to exist. Some questioned how this can be, that an object of one kind can disappear and another of another kind appear in its place. The philosopher Parmenides went so far as to suggest that all appearances of change were illusions because the idea of something being created from nothing was nonsensical. Therefore, he declared, nothing ever changes. This type of thinking is what happens when reason is allowed to run free without being grounded in experience.

Aristotle accepted the reality that objects change. His view is consistent with his assumption that physical objects are the only entities that exist (rejecting Plato's Forms) and that physical objects appear to us as they actually are, meaning we can confidently gather information about them. Real objects undergo changes; therefore, change is real.

However, we still need an explanation of how objects change. How do acorns seem to disappear and oak trees appear? How does an oak tree have leaves in the summer but not in the winter? Plato's theory of Forms is powerless to explain the *changes* that we observe in objects. Aristotle needed to come up with an explanation for change. His theory is ingenious. He combines several concepts into an explanation of change that greatly influenced medieval and early modern thinkers. The concepts Aristotle used are form and matter, potential and actuality, and the four causes.

Form and Matter

First, let's look at Aristotle's concepts of form and matter. These concepts are absent from Aristotle's discussion of the Categories, but they are not at odds with them. To simplify Aristotle's complex description, we can say that a substance (see the earlier description of the Categories) is a combination of form and matter in a particular object. A tree is a substance that is also matter in the form of a tree.

What Aristotle means by "form" is not what Plato means by "Form." We'll capitalize Plato's Form but not Aristotle's form because Aristotle does not see the form as being a higher archetype as Plato had thought about the Forms. Aristotle's form is something present in objects in the world equivalent to the category of essence. Aristotle's form is the answer to an object's substance or "whatness." It's perhaps easier to see when we talk about a human-made object like a drinking glass. Its form is cylindrical, about seven centimeters in diameter and twelve centimeters tall; with a solid, closed bottom; and an open top, and it is used to drink beverages. That is what it is.

Every object has its form, its "whatness," and every object is also made of matter, its "thisness." The drinking glass is made of matter, in this case glass, and more specifically, this particular piece of glass. I can hold up the drinking glass and say, "This is made of glass," indicating its "thisness." Another object may have some of these qualities, the same size and shape, but if that object's matter is something flimsy or soluble, it can't be used as a drinking glass. It still has a "thisness," but its "whatness" is not the form and essence of a drinking glass.

Interestingly, for Aristotle, matter is nothing in and of itself. Matter is amorphous and characterless in itself and only is part of an object when form takes hold of it to create a substance. This is true even though we never find any matter that has not been formed—and how could we? What could matter without form be?

Matter in an object can be formed into a new object. In the case of a block of marble, a sculptor takes the marble matter and changes its form, its "whatness," from a hunk of marble into a finished statue. For an oak tree, the matter changed from the form of an acorn into the form of an oak tree. Aristotle's concepts solve one of the objections of earlier philosophers about change. The oak tree doesn't come from nonbeing into being; instead, existing matter in an acorn has been changed in form into an oak tree.

Form and matter are the two components of objects, and an object changes when the form changes, but we still need to know how objects change. Aristotle's next concept in his theory of change is the spectrum of potentiality and actuality.

Potentiality and Actuality

Change, for Aristotle, is a matter of potentiality and actuality. All objects that we perceive in the world have potentiality and actuality. Objects all have actuality because we can perceive them; if they didn't have actuality, then they wouldn't exist for us to perceive them. But every object also has potentiality—the potential to become something more or something else—the potential to change. We only find objects that have been actualized into what they are now. They are actualized but also contain the potential to actualize into something else. Only a perfect supreme being with perfect actuality could have no further potential. All the objects we experience are a combination of actuality and potentiality.

Let's consider an example to illustrate how potentiality and actuality help explain change. Imagine that I show you an acorn and ask you what it is. You would no doubt reply, "It's an acorn." Having previous experience with the qualities of acorns, you can identify the "whatness" of what I am showing you as being an acorn. (Don't you wish all tests were that easy?) If I then ask you what an acorn changes into, you would no doubt reply that acorns change into oak trees. That makes sense; we know from experience that an acorn is the seed of an oak tree.

Next, I ask you what it is in the acorn itself that informs you that it will change into an oak tree. You can't tell that by looking at the acorn. If we use all of the questions from Aristotle's Categories to ask about the acorn, there is nothing in the acorn's qualities that indicate it can become an oak tree. If you slice the acorn open, you will not find a tiny oak tree lying inside it waiting to emerge. True, today we have the technology to extract the acorn's DNA and match it to the DNA of grown oak trees, so, yes, today we can conclude that an acorn can grow into an oak tree because of its genetic makeup. Obviously, though, Aristotle did not have access to DNA information.

So how did Aristotle explain how acorns changed into oak trees? Furthermore, why is it that acorns don't turn into anything else but oak trees? They don't turn into maple trees. They don't become cabbages. They don't turn into beavers. Acorns only ever change into oak trees. How does Aristotle explain that?

Aristotle's explanation is that every object has a specific potentiality that determines what that object is capable of becoming. An acorn possesses only the potential to become an oak tree. It does not have the potential to change into a maple tree, cabbage, beaver, or any other object. Every kind of object—every substance—possesses a limited potentiality, and that is part of a substance that makes it a unique kind of object. Aristotle's explanation leads to the same conclusion as our modern DNA explanation, and Aristotle deserves credit for devising a rather accurate explanation based on the information with which he had to work.

Our acorn has the potential to become an oak tree, but that potential will be actualized only under certain circumstances. To demonstrate this, for years I carried an acorn in my backpack to teach about Aristotle's theory of change. (You could say that I used the acorn's potential to be a prop for a philosophy lesson. Clever, huh?) Anyway, the point is that for all the years that the acorn was in my backpack it never changed into an oak tree. That acorn has had the potential to become an oak tree, but it has never been able to actualize that potential because some jerk has been carrying it around for years in his backpack. If that selfish philosophy professor had instead planted the acorn in the soil and watered it, it could have actualized its potential to grow into an oak tree.

Interestingly, Aristotle seems to suggest that an object has the *desire* to actualize its potential. Medieval philosophers adopted that idea and saw every object in the world as striving to fulfil its goal as a substance—for example, the acorn desires and actively strives to become an oak tree. Whether or not Aristotle actually believed that an acorn *wants* to change into an oak tree, we can use his theory to understand acorns and every other object as existing along a spectrum of potentiality and actuality. An object has the potential to change in specific ways given the type of object it is. However much potential an object has, that potential must be actualized. Something has to happen to it. That is where the four causes come in.

The Four Causes

Aristotle developed the concept of the four causes to explain how any object's potentials are actualized. By the term "cause," Aristotle meant something broader than how we usually use the word. Today we use "cause" strictly in the mechanical sense of a prior event bringing about a result—for example, flipping the switch causes the light to turn on. Aristotle's thinking is wider. Aristotle uses the term "cause" to describe multiple factors that affect why objects change. A cause in the Aristotelian sense is one of several reasons why an object is the way that it is.

Aristotle identifies four causes—four different reasons that explain objects and change. Those four reasons are the material cause, formal cause, efficient cause, and final cause.

The first cause is the material cause, which is exactly as the name indicates. What is the matter of which an object is composed? Our acorn is composed of organic plant matter. A marble statue is marble. A human is made of organic animal matter. A wooden table contains wood. Simple.

The second cause is the formal cause. This also is as the name indicates—the form of an object, as we discussed earlier. The object's form and matter describe the object as it currently is. Our acorn is an object that is a mass of organic plant matter that is in the form of an acorn. An oak tree is a larger hunk of organic plant matter in the form of an oak tree. A marble statue of Zeus is composed of marble matter in the form of a representation of Zeus. Form plus matter equals a marble statue of Zeus. Simple.

The third cause is the efficient cause. This use of "cause" by Aristotle is the mechanical usage that we are most familiar with today. With the efficient cause, Aristotle is describing the external effects that have affected an object. The world is filled with many ongoing processes that affect various objects in various ways. These processes are causes that affect effects in objects. Effect is the root of the word "efficient," which means an immediate agent that produces an effect (whether or not it does that "efficiently," with little or no waste).

By understanding the efficient causes that have affected an object, we can understand why that object has its current form. We can most easily see this by considering objects made by humans. A marble statue of Zeus has the efficient cause of the human sculptor's act of sculpting marble into the form of a representation of Zeus. In terms of efficient causes, it's easy to see how the sculptor acts to create a statue, but how does efficient cause explain how an acorn changes into an oak tree? For the acorn, the efficient causes are the soil, air, sun, and water. These causes actualize the acorn's potential to change into an oak tree. Every acorn has the potential to change into an oak tree, but only when the efficient causes operate on it will that potential be actualized. The same is true with a block of marble. It has the potential to be sculpted into a wide variety of objects, but only when a human sculptor acts on the marble will that potential be actualized. Every object in the world can be affected by efficient causes and change that object.

Efficient causes are related to objects' actuality in that every object has its current form because prior efficient causes have changed it into its current form. The acorn's efficient cause is the oak tree that created it—an acorn is the seed of an oak tree. There's the circle of life illustrated in efficient causes: oak trees create acorns and acorns create oak trees and oak trees create acorns and … Oh, and which came first the chicken or the egg? Alas, Aristotle doesn't help us answer that question. Where Aristotle can help us is that we can observe any object in its current state and understand through efficient causes why it is in that state.

An efficient cause will only affect objects that have the potential to be actualized by that cause. For example, fire only acts as an efficient cause on objects that have the potential to be changed by fire. Fire melts the wax in a candle, but it will not cause a metal fork to change. Fire can cause an object that has the potential to burn to catch fire. In that case, there is a transfer of actuality to an object that has a specific potential to be so actualized. The various ongoing processes present in the world effect changes, with certain efficient causes interacting with certain objects and actualizing certain potentials in them.

Aristotle's fourth cause is the final cause. The efficient causes that affect objects go hand in hand with an object's final cause. The fourth cause is final in the sense that it has a destination (although not necessarily a termination). What is the end or purpose for any object? What is the function that it is meant to fill? That is the object's final cause—the end for the sake of which a thing has been constructed or has come to be. In Aristotle's writings, there is a strong sense that everything has a purpose, that everything is working toward its own end or goal. The final cause is an object's goal and purpose.

Remember what I said earlier: Aristotle suggests that an acorn *wants* to become an oak tree? That's because, in Aristotle's system, there is only one reason why an acorn exists—to become an oak tree. The acorn does not want to be squirrel food or a philosopher's prop, it wants only to become an oak tree. The final cause is inherent in the object's essence or form. Essential to being an acorn is the purpose of becoming an oak tree, whether an acorn actively desires it or not. Acorns either fail in that purpose, or they succeed in that purpose. The acorn in my backpack is a failed acorn, though it's my fault that it has not fulfilled its only purpose in existing.

In Aristotle's view of the natural world, every seed and every baby animal has the final cause of growing up to become the organism it is meant to be. When we look at human-made objects, the same principle applies. What is the purpose of a statue of Zeus? To be present in a temple dedicated to him. That purpose is why the sculptor sculpted the statue and why every other human decision was made about the statue. Why did the sculptor choose Zeus? Why choose marble? Why hire a sculptor in the first place? All of these questions are answered by the final cause of the statue.

In Aristotle's view of the world, everything is working toward its final goal and purpose. Acorns become oak trees, baby beavers become full-grown beavers, blocks of marble become statues, wood becomes tables, and so on. Everything is moving toward a purpose. If the efficient cause operates, then the potential that is related to the final cause is actualized and the object's purpose is fulfilled. Using Aristotle's four causes, we explain an object by answering four questions about it: what it is made of, what made it the form it is, what or who produced it, and what its purpose is.

A Table of The Causes

Cause	Tree	Statue
Material	Organic plant matter	Marble
Formal	Oak tree	Image of Zeus
Efficient	Soil, air, sun, and water	Sculptor's acts of sculpting
Final	To make acorns	To venerate the god

Community and Government

Not surprisingly, as on other topics, Aristotle's approach to the political state differed from Plato's. Plato had envisioned how the ideal state should be and reasoned from the perfect community to how we can structure ours. Aristotle's approach was to look at existing city-states' forms of government, comparing their similarities and differences and attempting to identify what worked and what didn't. Unfortunately, the data that Aristotle and his students had collected about the city-states of their time have been lost, but we do have Aristotle's book that was derived from that research. That book is called *Politics*, from the Greek word *polis* meaning "city."

Strangely and disturbingly, though, Aristotle begins his book, *Politics*, with a discussion of the necessity for hierarchies among humans. In short, he states that the Greeks should rule over the barbarians, men should rule over women, and masters should rule over slaves. He claimed that this hierarchical order was evident from the natural order of things.

I've previously mentioned that he saw women as inferiors (women's function was to supply men's everyday needs, he wrote), but he also believed that a large number of humans were inferior beings, fit only to serve as slaves (whose function is to supply superior men's everyday needs). He declares in *Politics* that there are natural slaves—humans whose essence includes being slaves, who from the hour of their birth are predisposed to be slaves. This seems evident and obvious to Aristotle. He basically argues thus: Are there natural slaves? Yes, because we see in the world that some humans are born enslaved. It is therefore morally acceptable to enslave those people who display, he says, a predilection to servitude. This quite absurd line of thinking shows how even the most intelligent of people can hold prejudiced views and how rational thought can be used to defend ideas that are not true.

Aristotle's grave flaws about women and "slaves" aside, he did make several interesting observations about political systems. He said that the two primary questions regarding political systems are, "Who rules?" and "On whose behalf?" He identified three structures of "who rules"—a single man (monarchy), a select few (aristocracy), and a large number (polity). To each one, he added the two possibilities of "on whose behalf"—ruling for themselves or ruling for the common good. When any of the three political structures ruled for the common good, they were good, although Aristotle gave preference to polity because it included a larger number of humans in decision-making (not women or slaves, of course).

But Aristotle warns that each structure could be perverted into benefiting only those in government. Monarchy can descend into tyranny, aristocracy into oligarchy, and polity into democracy. Aristotle had similar criticisms about democracy as had Plato, seeing it as leading to self-interested tyranny.

Aristotle proposed that the state should be governed by a constitution, a written rule of law to which all are subject, including those who rule. All citizens would have a voice in decision-making, guided by the state's constitution to act always to do what the common good requires. The weakness in Aristotle's conception is who the citizens of a state are.

The Twin Pillars of Plato and Aristotle

Are we done with Plato and Aristotle? Not in the slightest. Plato and Aristotle are the twin pillars of philosophical thought that form the foundation of Western philosophy. Every philosopher you will meet for the next seven chapters of this course is in one way or another responding to Plato, Aristotle, or both. The philosophers in chapters after that, with a few exceptions, are still strongly influenced by Plato and Aristotle, so always keep in mind what you have learned about them.

There is a temptation to disregard Plato's and Aristotle's ideas because of the ancientness of their ideas. This would be a mistake because, as I cannot stress enough, philosophy is a long conversation that builds on the ideas of previous philosophers. Even today, philosophers still discuss Plato's and Aristotle's philosophies and build on their ideas.

What about their ancientness? Should we reject Aristotle because of his views on women and slaves? Should we reject Plato because of his views on democracy and individualism? A big part of being a good philosopher is recognizing the strengths and weaknesses of arguments and theories. With all the philosophers we meet, we must take a critical look at their ideas and make discerning judgments about what we agree and disagree with—as long as we have solid reasons for why we make those judgments. We can, and indeed we must, make such discerning judgments about Plato's and Aristotle's ideas, taking the good and leaving the bad.

Chapter 3

THE NOT-SO-DARK AGES

It is a popular myth that philosophy, if not critical thinking in general, ended sometime in the 400s CE, and Christianity is usually blamed. The evidence belies the myth. The reality is that the method of medieval Christian philosophers was a normal continuation of a philosophical method that emerged in Greek philosophy long before the Christian era. Plato's philosophy was a dualism that saw the higher realm of the Forms as the truer reality. Plotinus followed with the teaching about the One. The centuries that followed the fall of the Roman Empire and the rise of Christianity saw Christian thought mature as a continuation of long patterns of previous philosophers. Christianity did not end philosophy but intertwined with it, largely continuing the concerns and issues present in Greek philosophy.

Plotinus

A huge influence on Christian philosophy was the non-Christian, **Plotinus** (ca. 204–ca. 270 CE). Plotinus is perhaps the single most influential philosopher in European history. Yes, even over Plato and Aristotle. That's because for more than a thousand years Plotinus was the primary source by which scholars understood Plato's philosophy. Most of Plato's writing had been lost by the 400s CE (more on that later in this chapter). For centuries, scholars knew that Plotinus was a Platonist, and scholars having access only to Plotinus assumed that Plotinus's philosophy was a continuation of Plato's. Obviously, he was inspired by Plato, but he took Plato in a new direction.

Plotinus was inspired by Plato to craft a cosmology that included a divine entity above and beyond the world. It was compatible with Plato and other philosophies of the Roman era, such as Stoicism, which taught about the divine *Logos* as the source of all wisdom and reality but from which we are largely separated. The idea of *Logos* inspired the writer(s) of the Gospel of John, and Plotinus's compatible philosophy further inspired Christian philosophers to synthesize Greek philosophy with their faith. Because the writings of Plato and the Stoics were lost, Plotinus's cosmology, expressed most fully in his book, *Enneads*, took hold, making him so influential for centuries.

Plotinus went beyond Plato in dividing reality into three, not two, levels. Similar to Plato, Plotinus thought of the levels of reality as a hierarchy of Being. The top level of Being was the One—the immaterial first principle that is self-caused and the cause of all other beings. At times, Plotinus equated the One with Plato's Good, and at other times, he suggests that the One preceded the Good in terms of Being. The latter is consistent with Plotinus's view that the One is so fundamental to everything that it is beyond all attributes, and, therefore, calling it "good" would be applying an attribute to it. The One is pure Being. We cannot describe it with words because the One is beyond words and descriptions. We can deduce about the One only what it is not—such as it is not limited. Calling it "the One" is the least inappropriate description.

The One is the source of everything that exists. Plotinus wrote that the One needs nothing, it desires nothing, and it thinks nothing, but it is so full of pure Being that its Being overflows and all of existence is an emanation from the One. An emanation is different from a creation, and this distinguishes Plotinus's cosmology from a religious creation story. A creation is an act of will. An artist creates, a builder creates; any creation is a product of a willful, deliberate action. An emanation comes out from a source, but the source does will or act to bring it into being. An imperfect analogy is how a natural spring is so full or water it overflows with water, but not out of an act of will. Also, a creation must occur in a particular time and space, but the emanations from the One are beyond time and space. They simply are. We can't even say they "happened." They eternally are.

If all of that is difficult to understand, it is because these ideas are beyond human understanding except for the effects. We can only acknowledge the reality that all that exists emanates from the One—the source of all Being. Plotinus borrows Plato's analogy of the sun to describe the One. It is the eternal light that illuminates everything without being diminished by doing so.

The first emanation (in terms of Beingness, not in terms of time—remember, these are emanations, not creations) from the One is what Plotinus called the *Nous*, meaning Intellect, or Divine Mind. (Warning: This is truly mind-bending stuff here.) Intellect is eternal and immaterial like the One, but it is not the One. It is a perfect overflowing emanation of the One. As Divine Mind, it intuitively—meaning immediately and without effort—knows the One and knows itself. The One cannot know itself because the act of knowing creates a separation of knower and known. Intellect can know the One, and Intellect can know itself. In knowing itself, Intellect intuits Plato's Forms. Yes, Plotinus adopts Plato's theory of Forms. The Forms have their being from the One, but the identity of each Form comes from the Divine Mind of Intellect. In other words, the One gives everything being, and Intellect gives the Forms their distinct essences. Plotinus adds that Intellect knows not only universal Forms but particular Forms of particular objects. For example, there is a Form of humanity of which all humans partake, but there are also a Form of Socrates, a Form of Plato, and a Form of every individual human. Everything is known by the Divine Intellect.

The second emanation from the One is Soul. Don't confuse this with the soul of a person; this is the concept of a world or universal Soul. Like the One and Intellect, Soul is eternal and immaterial, but interestingly, Plotinus wrote that Soul exists as a connection between the immaterial and material realms of existence. Soul has two aspects—a higher aspect that reflects Intellect and contemplates the Forms in the intelligible realm, and the lower aspect that descends to the visible realm to replicate the universal Forms in particular objects. Plotinus explains it as follows:

> [Intellect] possesses intelligible Forms; the Soul has received them, and ceaselessly receives them from [Intellect]; that is what her life consists of; the clearness which shines in her is the consciousness she has of her thought. The reflection which the Soul herself projects on matter is nature, which terminates the series of essences, and occupies the last rank in the intelligible world; after her, there is nothing but imitations [of beings]. Nature, while acting on matter is passive in respect [to the Soul]. The Soul, superior to Nature, acts without suffering [loss]. Finally, the [Intellect] does not act on the bodies or on matter. (*Ennead* IV, 13)

Emanating from Soul are the individual souls and bodies of all things in the visible realm, and Soul unites the cosmos as one living organism. This lower aspect Plotinus equates with Nature and all of life and movement in it. Soul does not consciously order Nature, but what order there is in Nature flows from the rational order of Intellect—the principle order to which the world is subject. In this division of the Soul, Plotinus is emulating Plato's divided line.

We individual humans are aspects of Soul, similarly divided into higher and lower aspects. We each have a soul—lowercase in distinction form the universal Soul (uppercase). Plotinus says that within a person's soul "there [are] two cities, the one superior, and the other inferior, which latter derives its order from the former" (*Ennead* IV, 17). Our higher aspect is our soul, which mirrors the Intellect and like it is eternal and divine, and our lower aspect is our body, which changes and decays. Here, too, Plotinus is emulating Plato's Divided Line. Our minds are illuminated by the light of the One, which is the only source of the light of wisdom. We partially reflect that light in our thinking.

For Plotinus, like for Plato, our individual souls existed prior to our material birth, and our souls continue after material death, returning to the One. Our bodies are composed of matter. Our body receives form and order from the Forms, but the Intellect and its Forms do not act on our material body. Our bodies are separated from Intellect and the One.

Like Aristotle, Plotinus saw matter as amorphous and characterless, devoid of form. Unlike Aristotle, Plotinus saw matter as deprived of Being. Plotinus justifies this odd characterization with his analogy of the One as the sun. The sun gives off light, but as we know, the farther something is from a source of light, the more diminished that light is and the more in darkness an object is. The One is Being itself, but the farther something is from the source of Being, the more diminished that particular thing is. Plotinus argues that matter is separated from the One, farther from Being than are Soul and Intellect. Having also equated the One with Plato's the Good, Plotinus also implies that matter is deprived of good. It's important to realize that Plotinus is not saying that matter is evil. Plotinus didn't believe in the existence of evil as an entity or force. He saw that just as darkness is the absence of light, what we call evil is merely the absence of good. Matter, separated from Intellect and the One, is absent Being and goodness.

Again, the emanations to which Plotinus refers are not deliberately willed. They simply happen, emanated like a magnetic field emanates from a magnet. This means that reality is not the conscious product of a creator deity. The world and everything in it simply are, and they simply are the way they are. The cosmos *is*, though, based on reason. It has a rational order to which everything in the visible world is subject. Again, Plotinus is adopting Plato's Divided Line.

Part of the rational order in the world is that we humans are divided—part intellect and part body. Our intellect is from the divine Intellect, and with discipline and focus, we can more closely connect with the Intellect. Our material bodies are not evil, but in the order of reality, our bodies have less Being and goodness than our intellect has.

Therefore, we are faced with the choice of whether to focus our attention on our intellect, which is closer to the One, or on our body, which is farther from the One. Our rational part, our better part, wants to be closer to the One—the source of all Being and goodness; and it is to the One that we wish to return. However, our material bodies are an impediment to returning to the One. As Plotinus puts it, we have fallen into the lower material realm because of our vanity and desire for independence. Plotinus likens our arrogant ignorance to the prisoners trapped in Plato's allegorical cave. If we focus on our bodies and the material world, we only strengthen our own chains, and we are alienating ourselves from the higher realm to which we should return.

Plotinus teaches that the more we concentrate on reason, the more we will understand what is real and good, and that understanding will purify us. To not be rational, then, is a sin. This is not a religious idea, because it is not about a need for salvation from a deity or a church. Rather, we can attain our own salvation through our dedication to wisdom and truth. Dedication to reason shall set us free from the darkness of the world.

Plotinus's ideas inspired religious and nonreligious thinkers, philosophers, writers, poets, and scientists for centuries, and they still reverberate today. Although we will not hear the name Plotinus mentioned often, if you pay attention throughout this book, you will see this dualistic view of the universe holding sway over philosophy, religion, science, and culture.

Augustine

Augustine was one philosopher deeply influenced by Plotinus, Augustine (354–430 CE) also began his philosophy from the assumption that reason was the source of all that is real and good. Augustine is often misunderstood and dismissed as being merely a theologian. The truth is that he is one of the deepest and most innovative thinkers in the history of philosophy. Augustine delved into questions that no one before him had considered, and he undertook philosophical explorations and reached fundamental insights not seen again for more than 1,200 years.

Augustine has a bad reputation today because, to be honest, his most famous book, *Confessions*, though containing brilliant philosophy in parts, is mostly a maudlin exercise in self-pity. Also damaging his reputation is that late in his life as a bishop of the city of Hippo, he became a zealous persecutor of nonconformists, suppressing their freedom of thought and religion. His zealotry was largely driven by his strange obsession with the doctrine of original sin, the doctrine that he championed that humans were inherently evil. Despite these realities, Augustine's earlier philosophical thought is deep, insightful, and compelling and could easily fill an entire philosophy course. As I said at the end of Chapter 2, as philosophers we must make discerning judgments about a philosopher's ideas, taking the good and leaving the bad.

Augustine's philosophy, though highly original, was influenced by the cosmopolitan intellectual environment of the late Roman Empire. In his young adulthood, Augustine adopted Manichaeanism, an ideology that, like Plato's and Plotinus's cosmology, was highly dualist. Much starker than the cosmologies of Plato or Plotinus, Manichaeanism taught that the cosmos was divided between the forces of Good and Evil. Regarding our material world, Plato and Plotinus saw an imperfect realm, but Manichaeanism taught that our world is a realm under siege from darkness in which even good people could be devoured by evil as though by wolves. Even though Augustine eventually renounced Manichaean ideology, it seemed to have influenced some of his thinking. For example, Augustine said that he had read Aristotle's book, *Categories*, but that he was not interested in investigating the objects of the world. He became a professor of rhetoric in the Roman style and later converted to Christianity, which greatly influenced his later thought.

Against Skepticism

Like Plato, Augustine was convinced that there is universal truth and that knowledge of that truth is possible. One of Augustine's first philosophical writings, *Against the Academicians*, is a treatise addressed to the philosophers who had taken over Plato's Academy from 266 to 86 BCE. Ironically, Augustine was more true to Plato than were those who ran the school Plato founded. The new caretakers of the Academy had become anti-Plato in being deeply skeptical about the possibility of knowledge. These skeptics held that nothing can be known conclusively and, therefore, that intellectual assent should not be given to anything. Instead, they taught that we can make statements only about what appears to us. We can say, "That appears to be a tree," but we cannot make any statement about whether it actually is a real tree, and we certainly cannot make any dogmatic claims about what the tree is, what causes it, and so on. The Academic skeptics thus reject both Plato and Aristotle and say we should suspend all judgment on all matters and content ourselves with a life without firm beliefs. Augustine could not abide by a life that lacked such certainty.

Augustine's argument against the skeptics turns the skeptics' argument against them. Augustine's refutation of the skeptics can be depicted as follows:

- The skeptics claim that there are no truths that can be known.
- But to deny that we can know truth requires the skeptic to have a definition of truth.
- The skeptics' definition of truth must be either true or false.
- If the skeptics' definition is true, then they do know at least one truth, refuting their claim in 1.
- If the skeptics' definition is false, then it is useless in the defense of skepticism and therefore meaningless.

In other words, the Academic skeptics were trying to have it both ways in claiming that they know that nothing can be known. Academic skepticism was inherently contradictory. If anyone argues for an "all" or "never," all you need to do to refute the argument is to find one contrary example. That is what Augustine did. Augustine showed not only that the Academicians' argument was fallacious but also that there has to be at least one truth that we can be certain that we know.

Augustine takes the issue further than simply disarming the Academic skeptics. In a later work, he advanced the argument that there are things that we can know with absolute certainty. Most important and foundational is the fact that we exist.

> For we both are, and know that we are, and delight in our being, and our knowledge of it. Moreover, in these three things no true-seeming illusion disturbs us ... I am most certain that I am, and that I know and delight in this. In respect of these truths, I am not at all afraid of the arguments of the Academicians, who say, What if you are deceived? For if I am deceived, I am. For he who is not, cannot be deceived; and if I am deceived, by this same token I am. (*The City of God* 11.26)

In other words, the skeptics' argument that we can be deceived by our senses does not apply to our knowledge that we exist. We know this fact directly, and we know that we know it. I cannot have a mistaken belief that I exist because if I have such a mistaken belief, I must be existing to be able to have such a belief. This argument foreshadows a similar one offered by Descartes that we will discuss in Chapter 4. Augustine's argument proves that complete skepticism is impossible. His argument also demonstrates the importance of an individual's power of reason. There are things that can be known, and we *can* know those things. One's quest for knowledge begins with knowing oneself. That is exactly how Augustine proceeds.

The Inner Teacher and Illumination

Augustine adopts Plotinus's teaching that the human intellect is endowed with the power of reason. Unlike Plato, who saw learning as recollection, Augustine held that learning is actively thinking for ourselves. However, to understand truth, we need the divine light of reason. His conception of how our minds see truth is analogous to how our eyes see objects. Our eyes have the ability to see, but they need help to see. Our eyes cannot see objects without light. Augustine thinks of intellectual understanding in the same way. Our minds have the ability to understand truths, but we need help. That help is the light of reason, a divine illumination, that is accessible to everyone.

Certainly, Augustine equates reason with God, but in this context, Augustine considers God in the same way that Plato considers the Good and Plotinus considers the One. Augustine, as a Christian, believes we should love and submit to God, but in matters of philosophy and intellect, his view of God is the God of the philosophers not the God of Christianity. What I mean by this is the "God" of philosophy is a fundamental rational principle, a Beingness like Plotinus's the One, rather than a personal, knowable deity.

Augustine's idea of divine illumination can be difficult to understand. That's because it is too easy to slide into the mistake of thinking Augustine means that God is doing the thinking for us and that we are not actively thinking. Augustine thought the opposite—we *will* (desire) to understand, and our understanding results from our active thinking—with help.

Think of it this way: your eyes can see objects, but only if two things are happening. The first is if light is illuminating the objects so that your eyes can sense them. You are able to see, but only with the help of light. The second is if your eyes are open—you are willing to look. The same is the case, Augustine believed, for your mind. You can think about truth, but your mind can see truth only if there is light to illuminate that truth. That light that illuminates is the divine light of reason. So just like the sun shines and we can see physical objects, the divine light of reason shines, and we can see truth.

Augustine equates that light with the Christian God, but he admits that this light of reason, as a fundamental principle of reality, is shining whether one believes in the Christian God or not. Reason is a part of the universe that every human can experience, Christian or pagan. But we must be willing to use our capacity to reason. Just like we can close our eyes and refuse to look, we can close our minds and refuse to see truth. On that point, Augustine felt that pagans are more closed to letting in the divine light of reason.

It is incumbent upon the individual to discover the truth, and at the heart of Augustine's philosophy is his idea that within each of us exists an inner teacher. To illustrate this idea, Augustine writes his book, *The Teacher*, in the style of a Platonic dialogue, portraying a philosophical conversation between him and Adeodatus, his real-life son. In the opening of their discussion, they deliberate on the questions of what teaching is and what the role of the teacher is. Augustine's answer is that all communication is a form of teaching because it is the speaker attempting to inform others about what is in the teacher's mind. If I say, "I see a tree," I am teaching you about what I am seeing. It is a broad definition of teaching, but Augustine uses it consistently.

Augustine says that we communicate in two ways—by saying and by showing. Augustine, in the first appearance in Western history of a philosophy of language, points out that words are useful only if we already know what the words signify. Before we can say anything, we first have to learn what words mean, and we must be taught these be being *shown* the connection of words to things. If someone says to you the word "walking," but you do not know that word, that person has not communicated anything to you. But if someone stands up and walks, that person is showing you something you don't need prior knowledge of a word to understand. If the person then says the word "walking" and points to the action of walking, you could learn the word "walking" by connecting the word to what it signifies. Augustine says this is how we learn language.

Because all words are learned by showing, Augustine concludes that showing is the only true teaching. He identifies three ways by which we are shown truths—through our senses; by our memories; and, in the case of concepts (such as mathematics), by an inner light of Truth. This inner light is the inner teacher, which Augustine connects with divine illumination. An individual's mind is doing the thinking, though, just like the eye is doing the seeing of the light. The inner teacher is our innate ability to reason that can show us truth, but it is up to us to be open to what it shows us.

Augustine was also the first Western philosopher to develop what is now called a "philosophy of mind." He saw the human mind as a vast, amazing world in itself. In his book, *Confessions*, he writes that his mind is a power of his, and belongs to his nature, but that the paradox of his mind is that he cannot comprehend all that his mind is.

> So speak I to myself: and when I speak, the images of all I speak of are present, out of the same treasury of memory; nor would I speak of any thereof, were the images wanting. Great is this force of memory, excessive great, O my God; a large and boundless chamber! who ever sounded the bottom thereof? yet is this a power of mine, and belongs unto my nature; nor do I myself comprehend all that I am. Therefore is the mind too strait to contain itself. ... A wonderful admiration surprises me, amazement seizes me upon this. (*Confessions* X, 14)

This passage is from Book X in *Confessions* (before the book turns to straight devotional utterances) and is part of a wonderfully expressive description of human mental faculty. Augustine also writes about "the fields and spacious palaces of my memory, where are the treasures of innumerable images" (*Confessions* X, 12). He concludes that these images are brought into memory by our senses and that we enlarge or diminish them through our thinking.

Augustine marvels about how we can remember things about our past, how our memories are a mysterious mixture of order and chaos. What a gift memory is, he writes, and what a mystery. He likens memory to a vast warehouse in which particular memories are stored in wondrous cabinets. Every sensation we experience gets stored in the warehouse and somehow ordered. Our memory connects sights and sounds of past experiences, and names with objects. When we seek to remember something, it is as though we go to the warehouse. Sometimes the memory we ask for comes out, sometimes other memories do. We do not have full control of what we remember and when.

Memory is so important, Augustine points out, because we are completely dependent on it. "But what is nearer to me than myself? And lo, the force of mine own memory is not understood by me; though I cannot so much as name myself without it" (*Confessions* X, 24). What's your name? You say you know your name, but the truth is that you remember your name. All names, words, and concepts that we have learned are in our memory. We can understand the words of other people because we were once shown what those words signify, and we remember what we were shown and apply that memory to our conversations.

Our memory is larger than we can comprehend, overflowing with specific memories and the many associations our minds have made with those memories. Try to remember all at once everything that ever happened to you. You can't; but every one of those memories is within you, part of who you are. Like Augustine, when you look into your mind, you get a glimpse of an infinite realm of truths, leading to the paradox that you cannot comprehend the totality of what you are.

The Human Will

Augustine was influenced by ancient Greek philosophy, but he broke with the Greek philosophers on a principal idea. Almost all Greek philosophers believed that reason is primary to the will. Plato and Aristotle both held that to know the good is to do the good; thus, morality was a matter of teaching people the moral facts. Immorality was the product of ignorance. Once someone understood moral truths, that person would act morally because they would not will to act otherwise.

Augustine rejected this idea, pointing out the obvious that humans are quite capable of committing an act when they know it's wrong. Augustine said that there are three forces within a person—intellect, will, and love. He claimed that the will is stronger than the intellect and that the intellect follows the will. No amount of rational argument can convince the will, he said. A person's will is free, but a person's will is pulled in the direction of what that person chooses to love. "My weight is my love; thereby am I borne" (*Confessions* 8.9). Just as an object's weight pulls it downward if it's heavy, or the object rises if it's light, love is a powerful weight that pulls the will. Wherever we are carried, our love is what carries us. Because love pulls the will, which commands the intellect, Augustine believes that what we love is ultimately the most important indicator of who we are.

Augustine's thought has a pervading tension between on the one hand, the power of God and on the other hand, the power of human intellect and will. Augustine wants to give all power to God, who by definition is omnipotent and omniscient. However, Augustine cannot help but marvel at and acknowledge the power and freedom of both the human intellect and human will. Augustine had to acknowledge that we know what is true only when we allow it. We can deny even that which is obvious before our eyes. The human will accesses (or not) the power of the human intellect.

Humans have free will. This is an undeniable fact. Augustine's discussion of human free will and its implications is deeply thoughtful and perceptive. He gives us a thought experiment beginning with the question, "Does God know which choices I will make tomorrow?" Augustine agrees that, on the one hand, if God is all knowing, then God definitely has to know beforehand which choices I will make tomorrow. But what does that mean? If my choices are already known, does that mean I cannot change my mind and choose differently? That would indicate that I don't actually have free will. God, who knows everything already, knows what I will do, but could I prove God wrong by making a different choice? But if I could, then it would mean my will is more powerful than an all-powerful God, which is a logical contradiction.

To get out of this dilemma, Augustine ingeniously proposes that God is outside of time, while we are within time. Being outside of time, God sees all events, including my choices, as one—there are no future or past events for God. We, who are inside time, must move from past to future and are forced by the passage of time to make choices. God's knowledge of our choices in no way interferes with our ability to make those choices—God is in this sense an observer. We have to make our own choices because we are the time-bound, earthbound beings that we are. Even if you don't accept the premise of an all-knowing God, Augustine's solution is clever and compatible with both Plotinus and Christianity.

The Transition from Antiquity to the Medieval Era

Shortly after the time of Augustine was when the supposed Dark Ages began. There was a relative lack of published material in philosophy between 450 and 1250 CE, but that was not caused by religion. Christian, Jewish, and Islamic scholars were, in fact, the only ones who kept philosophy and protoscience alive. What dark age there was was caused by a loss of social cohesion that caused severe economic and demographic disruption.

The Visigoths sacked Rome in 410 CE—a stunning catastrophe that affected people then far more than the 9/11 attacks affected the early 2000s. Rome was literally the center of the known world and had been for more than 500 years. That the Eternal City would fall to an impoverished, barbarian people was world shattering. Then in 455 CE, the Vandals sacked Rome even more viciously, which gave us the words "vandals" and "vandalism." The military government of the western Roman Empire, rife with corruption and civil strife, finally fell to barbarians in 493 CE. Further waves of peoples invaded significant swaths of Western Europe over a 500-year period. Continual outbreaks of plague also contributed to the strife and anarchy.

These violent disruptions affected the western half of the former Roman Empire more than the eastern half that was based in Constantinople. As social conditions deteriorated, western lands were increasingly isolated from the still vibrant political, economic, and cultural centers in what are now Greece, Turkey, and the southern Balkans. The political and economic structures of the old Latin-speaking western empire were swept away or withered away. Social structures such as law and education were sharply reduced.

Classical Latin learning did not disappear entirely, but it became limited to prominent families who had access to the very few remaining private tutors. These included heads of state, Christian bishops, and their dependents and advisers. Even this education had a limited curriculum compared with that of times past and consisted primarily of grammar and rhetoric.

Philosophy was decreasingly part of that education, even for the elites. This was not because it was banned or frowned on but because it simply was lost to the chaos of the times. The only remaining bastions of learning were isolated Christian monasteries from Ireland in the far west to Persia in the east where the monks kept libraries of ancient scrolls of Greek, Roman, and Christian scholars. The monks' withdrawal from the world was more than a spiritual statement; it was an eminently practical response to the social and political chaos around them.

Accidents of history contributed to the decline in philosophy during the medieval period. Those in the West did not have much Greek philosophy at all because the great works of the philosophers were lost to them and knowledge of the Greek language had all but disappeared. Knowledge of Aristotle in the Latin West survived thanks only to the efforts of Boethius (477–524), who translated into Latin and wrote commentaries on Aristotle's logical works. Thus, the West's supply of Aristotle's genius included only his works on logic that informed philosophical dialogue, producing a very incomplete view of Aristotle.

The loss of most of Aristotle's texts meant that medieval scholars did not know his ideas about observation, objects, biology, change, morality, and politics. That meant they didn't have a counterpoint to the more mystical ideas of Plato and his most notable interpreter—Plotinus.

The one book of Plato that survived in Latin translation, *Timaeus*, is the oddest of Plato's books. In *Timaeus*, a follow-up to *The Republic* and its story of the Allegory of the Cave, Plato tells a story that's a kind of creation myth for the two realms. The story is of a divine Craftsman who created the world and gave it order and goodness. The Craftsman admired the Forms and created the visible realm to resemble it. This idea explains how everything in our world is a copy of the Forms. The problem is that a copy is never as perfect as the original; therefore, our world is composed of imperfect copies of the perfect Forms. Plotinus's thought was largely inspired by *Timaeus*.

What scholarship survived the collapse of the Roman civilization eventually developed into the discipline of philosophy known as Scholasticism—understanding the nature of God and creation by using Aristotle's rigid rules of intellectual reasoning. The whole of Plato and Aristotle, and the rest of Greek philosophy, would not be restored to Western Europe until the 1200s.

The Islamic Renaissance

Philosophy as we know it today exists thanks to Islamic scholars who preserved the knowledge of the ancient Greeks. The Islamic world from present-day Spain in the west, to present-day Uzbekistan in the east, had had access to Aristotle going back to as early as the 800s CE, when they discovered ancient Greek manuscripts kept by Christian monasteries in what is now Syria. Islam eventually recovered much of Aristotle's writings and some more of Plato and other scholars. Islamic philosophy kept alive the tradition of Greek study and learning.

Having access to more of Aristotle facilitated Islamic scholars in their explorations of politics and natural philosophy—the study of the natural world. In a quirk of fate, Plotinus's very Platonic book, *Enneads*, was included in the monastic collections of Aristotle's manuscripts, but it was mislabeled as being a book written by Aristotle. Islamic scholars understandably assumed Plotinus's book contained Aristotle's thoughts about the structure of the universe, a subject on which Aristotle had never actually written, so *Enneads* seemed to occupy that gap. Thus, Islamic scholars spent a great deal of time and effort on the difficult challenge of trying to reconcile Plotinus and Aristotle.

Islamic scholars also diligently tried to show the compatibility of Islam with the ancient authority of Greek philosophy, and that is because Islamic and Christian scholars alike held all ancient texts, not just religious texts, in reverence. They esteemed Aristotle as a great teacher, and they treated his writings as essential wisdom that had to be reconciled with other writings—even the Qur'an had to be shown to be compatible with Aristotle, the great philosopher of antiquity.

There were several dozen notable Islamic scholars who contributed to an Islamic renaissance of learning in natural philosophy, medicine, mathematics, epistemology, and logic. We will look at three Islamic philosophers who had significant influence on later Western philosophy.

al-Farabi

Abu Nasr al-Farabi (ca. 872–ca. 950) lived most of his life in Baghdad, where he wrote extensively on logic; mathematics; physics; music; and, of course, philosophy. He founded a major school of philosophical thought that built on the philosophies of Plato and Aristotle. For centuries after, al-Farabi was referred to as "the Second Teacher," after Aristotle, the First Teacher.

al-Farabi drew on both Plato's theory of the ideal state and Aristotle's writings on biology to craft a comprehensive account of life on earth. In multiple books, he adopted Plato's concept of the well-ordered state led by specially trained leaders, linking it to the idealized city-state governed by the prophet Muhammad at the beginning of Islam. Understandably, al-Farabi found the various subsequent Islamic governments as falling short of this ideal. He was not, however, as antidemocracy as Plato was because he argued that people had an innate disposition to join together with others to work to better their society. He advocated for strong leaders guided by the cosmic Intellect, showing he was influenced by Plotinus, who al-Farabi and others thought was Aristotle.

Building on Plotinus's view of human nature, al-Farabi considered humans to be divided between the physical body and the intellect. The human intellect he divided into a potential for thought and the actuality of thought. He portrayed human thinking as the act of abstracting universal concepts from particular sense perceptions retained in memory. Similar to Augustine, he said that thinking requires the light of reason that illuminates the world and concepts about it. al-Farabi called the light of reason the "Agent Intellect," which is an emanation from the First Cause (his Aristotelian term for Plotinus' the One). We cannot comprehend the First Cause except by negative statements: it is uncaused, indivisible, without beginning or end, and so on. However, we can comprehend the emanations of the First Cause that manifest in the world if we act on our potential to think by using our active mind that is part of the Agent Intellect.

Ibn Sina

Abū-ʿAlī Ibn Sina (980–1037), known in Christian Europe by his latinized name "Avicenna," was from present-day Uzbekistan. He trained as a physician but also wrote about astronomy, logic, and philosophy. Much of Ibn Sina's philosophy was a continuation of al-Farabi's, including the ideas of the emanations from the Intellect, but Ibn Sina put more focus on the nature of Being.

Central to his theory of Being are the three modalities of Being and the distinction between essence and existence. There is, Ibn Sina said, a Necessary being (God or the One) whose essence and existence is one—in other words, it necessarily exists, it cannot *not* exist. Therefore, its existence has no external cause. Every other entity is either impossible or contingent. Impossible entities would be logical contradictions—such as a round square—they cannot exist. All other entities either could or could not exist, and their existence is contingent on an external cause. We can consider the essence of a contingent object, but reason alone cannot tell us whether it exists. To know what entities exist, we need to know the efficient causes that impart existence.

Expanding on Aristotle's theory of change, Ibn Sina said that form and matter cannot interact on their own to create a contingent object; an efficient cause must act to create it. The same is true for contingent objects changing. Other than God, nothing has the power to change itself. An attribute of an object will change only if and when an entity that already possesses the attribute affects the object. For example, for a log to burn there must be a fire that possesses the attribute of burning (it is currently burning) that puts the attribute of burning onto the log. The condition of the log is changed from not burning to burning by the power of the fire affecting it.

Following Aristotle and al-Farabi, Ibn Sina held that God is the First Cause that contains all attributes and therefore is the ultimate source of all change. He isn't suggesting that God is immanently and actively involved in every change (although some other Islamic philosophers did believe that). He held instead that God, being pure Intellect and the necessary being, created the universe according to logical necessity. The idea is that God's logical perfection is such that the creation is a chain of logically necessary events, one efficient cause to the next, from God's creation of the universals to the creation of every particular object. Thus, the universe is as it logically has to be. We can learn about God's creation because our thinking brings about knowledge of the logical mind of God. Ibn Sina means that when we think about the objects of the world, we identify the universal forms that God used to create everything, and we can discern the logically necessary causal chain of events that stems from the necessary being—God.

Ibn Sina offered an interesting thought experiment to explore the question of what we can know and what we are. He asks us to imagine a person suddenly created who is floating in midair and deprived of all physical senses. This newly created person would have absolutely no awareness of any objects, even of its own body, but could perceive its own self-consciousness. The only thing this person could assert is its self, having no experience of anything else. Ibn Sina concludes from this that we can be sure of the existence of the self, or soul, and that the self is something other than the body.

Ibn Rushd

Abū al-Walīd Ibn Rushd (1126–1198), better known in the West by his latinized name "Averroës," was the most prolific and famous of all the Islamic philosophers. In both the Islamic world and Christian West, he was known as "The Commentator" because of the meticulous commentaries that he wrote on every one of Aristotle's many surviving works. When later translated into Latin, his commentaries became central to Scholasticism. Ibn Rushd wrote more than 100 books on nearly every subject studied in his time, including extensive medical texts. Ibn Rushd thought that earlier philosophers, including al-Farabi and Ibn Sina, had distorted Aristotle's philosophy by blending in too much of Plato and Plotinus. Instead of attempting to reconcile Aristotle with Plato, Ibn Rushd wrote about their differences—most significantly, Aristotle's rejection of Plato's theory of Forms.

Ibn Rushd charted a journey of the human intellect from fully passive to fully active that fit with Aristotle's methodology of learning about the visible world. In brief, Ibn Rushd said that when we are fully passive all we do is take in sense perception—we are just like the animals. But when we begin to reflect on what we are seeing, we begin to understand the universals that exist in objects (as Aristotle said), and this, Ibn Rushd said, leads us to understand how ideas such as mathematics work. We become in touch with our own personal active intellect. Rather than stop here, we should, he said, continue to reflect on universals across objects, mathematics, and geometry, which allows us to understand objects, their place in the world, the universals apart from objects, and eventually the universals in the mind of God.

One of Ibn Rushd's many books was a detailed point-by-point refutation of **Abû Hâmid al-Ghazali's** (1058–1111) book, *The Incoherence of the Philosophers.* In that book, the fundamentalist al-Ghazali condemned philosophy, declaring that all Platonist influences amount to nonbelief in Islam. Despite his own objections to Ibn Sina's Platonism, Ibn Rushd had greater problems with al-Ghazali's attack on philosophy itself. To defend philosophy, Ibn Rushd wrote *The Incoherence of the Incoherence.* In it, he quoted the Qur'an frequently in support of his contention that God wants people to study nature (natural theology) and interpret the revelation of scripture (revealed theology) rooted in knowledge, a study that Ibn Rushd said referenced philosophy, the highest method of knowledge. Given his position as a judge, he went so far as to issue a *fatwa*, a legal opinion, that philosophy is allowed for Muslims and is even an obligation for those with the intellectual capability to study it.

In a commentary on Plato's theory of an ideal society, Ibn Rushd offered a social/political theory that was a synthesis of Aristotle, Plato, and Islamic law. Starting from Aristotle's premise that the ultimate functional good of all humans is happiness, Ibn Rushd argued that the ultimate end of religious law and philosophy is to create an ideal political state that will provide for the happiness of everyone in society. He adopts Plato's concept that the ideal state is divided into three groups, but whereas Plato had delineated society on the basis of a division of labor, Ibn Rushd did so on the basis of intellectual capacity. This was his ingenious way of upholding the social and moral necessity of religious law while preserving a special place for philosophy and intellectual speculation beyond religion.

The majority of people, Ibn Rushd said, live by their senses rather than by reason. They can lead productive lives, but they cannot comprehend higher rational principles. Nevertheless, they are God's creations, and they deserve happiness, so God has provided the teachings of Islam to provide the order and structure that they need to be happy. Ibn Rushd criticized Plato for not sufficiently caring about the happiness of the masses. Islam supplied a better solution for society through the theologians who have more intellectual capacity and use it to interpret Islamic law and guide people, increasing happiness for all.

Those blessed with the highest level of intelligence, Ibn Rushd said, can recognize that religious orthodoxy cannot provide all the answers. They are, therefore, unable to be content with the religious law. They are still subject to that law, but they require more to be happy and are drawn to philosophy, the highest method of attaining knowledge. These people Ibn Rushd calls "metaphysicians"—those who go beyond surface explanations—and God has laid a duty on them to use their intellect to seek higher knowledge. They can discover truth directly for themselves, truths beyond the ability of the theologians and common people to grasp. Ibn Rushd even said that the metaphysicians do not have to accept all of the religious doctrines that are meant for the masses.

This led some to accuse Ibn Rushd of a double truth theory, that there are two separate truths, but this is a misinterpretation. What Ibn Rushd means is that some religious teachings are tailored by God to fit the limited intellectual capacities of most people. For example, there are verses in the Qur'an that seem to indicate that God has a physical body. Ibn Rushd says these are simply metaphors that the Qur'an— believed in Islam to be directly written by God—uses to help the masses accept the faith. The higher truth is that God is immaterial, but this is a difficult truth to comprehend. The metaphysicians can understand it, but God, the wise and merciful, provides religious metaphors for the masses so as not to perplex them and lead them astray.

This isn't as elitist or condescending as it may at first sound, and it actually is more egalitarian than most political thinking of the time. Ibn Rushd contended that this is how humanity is, created to be so by God. God has benevolently provided the teachings of Islam for those who need it and the light of Intellect for those who are capable of understanding higher truths. Ibn Rushd naturally prefers that people of higher intelligence be the rulers in government, or at least be advisers to the rulers, but Ibn Rushd stresses that rulers should use persuasion, never coercion, to teach virtue to citizens. He also was one of the first in western history to call for women to have full rights equal to those of men, saying that women had the same nature as men and were fit to share power in government and participate in all professions, even as soldiers and philosophers. It was 600 years before anyone wrote similarly about women's rights in Christian Europe.

William—The Forerunner of Modern Philosophy

William (ca. 1287–ca. 1347) is often referred to as "Ockham" or "Occam." He was born in the village of Ockham, England, but his name is William, so we will call him by his name. William was a Franciscan monk and a radical thinker for his time—so radical he was excommunicated by Pope John XXII. The Church was not concerned about William's philosophy but about his condemnation of corruption and excessive wealth in the Church. He even declared that the pope was a heretic for the un-Christian behavior of attacking the monastic doctrine of poverty.

William's philosophy centered on the principles of nominalism—the idea that universals are just names without reality—and voluntarism—the idea that the will preceded the intellect. On the basis of these principles, he concluded that God's omnipotence is fundamental to the universe, everything in God's creation is contingent, and the human mind is active and able to understand the creation through observation rather than through reason.

William's philosophy was a direct refutation of Scholasticism, a philosophical school that developed in response to the recovered works of Aristotle. Scholasticism emerged from the writings of **Thomas Aquinas** (1225–1274), who synthesized Catholic theology and ancient philosophy. As mentioned, the Western European philosophers had long known about Aristotle's logic, and Thomas demonstrated how Aristotle's natural philosophy, new to Christian Europe, is compatible with Christian philosophy.

Thomas's biggest influence on Scholasticism was his interpretation of Aristotle's idea of a final cause. Like Aristotle, Thomas said that every event, whether it is a stone falling or a flower blossoming, occurs because there is an end toward which it is directed. It was easy for Thomas to synthesize Aristotle's final cause with the sovereignty of the omnipotent Christian God. It is God who designed the hierarchy of creation and imbued all objects with their dynamics of potentialities and actualities with natural purposes.

Scholasticism applied Aristotle's logic to the questions of what objects' final causes were. The assumption was that God had set down the final cause of every object, which human minds could comprehend by contemplating the substance or essence of the object. For example, God created humans to love God, created horses for humans to ride, created stone to be used to make buildings, created wood to be used for fuel, and so on. We need only know what an object is and we know its final cause.

The problem as William saw it was that the Scholastics made no further inquiries, assuming that through logical contemplation they knew enough about the world and everything in it. He sought to replace what he saw as the empty intellectual vanity of Thomist Scholasticism with a more constructive exploration of the world. At the heart of his philosophy was the conviction that knowledge comes to those who go into the world and seek it—ironically more true to Aristotle than was Scholasticism's logic. William's theory of knowledge, being a radical break with the then-dominant Scholasticism, foreshadowed and contributed to modern science.

William's Theory of Knowledge

William stated that all of our knowledge begins in experience; nothing is known unless it is known intuitively. By intuitive knowledge—meaning directly evident to the mind—William referred to both our sense perceptions of external objects and our awareness of our own thoughts and emotions. Any knowledge not directly related to an object of immediate experience is a derivative knowledge, which he also called "abstract knowledge," because this type of knowledge is an abstraction of original experience.

William's impetus for his epistemology (theory of knowledge) was to clarify our thinking. Part of his project was establishing detailed rules of reasoning, a basic logic, but here we will discuss his rules for what it makes sense for us to reason about. The centerpiece of those rules is William's rejection of universals, the idea that goes back to Plato's idea of the Forms, and Aristotelian forms, which still influenced most philosophical thought in William's time. He thought that by eliminating universals from our thought, we can think more clearly.

William's epistemological reasoning is that when we perceive an object, our senses cause an image in the mind. Our minds intuitively and naturally know certain things about our mental image of the object, for example, that this tree exists, that it is green, and so on. What's most important about William's conception is that perceiving and knowing these basic judgments about objects is natural in and of itself. That is what the human mind does naturally and self-sufficiently, without need of universals such as the Forms.

What about universals? William explained that we invent names (words) to refer to our mental images, and each culture invents its own words for them. We invent names to refer to particular individuals, like "Plato," and we invent names to refer to abstract ideas like "tree," "circle," "dog," and "green." We abstract from mental images ideas such as green that we use to describe a characteristic of an object: "that tree is green."

Scholastics in William's day said that greenness is a universal form. William replies that greenness is no more than an abstract mental image to which we have given a name. The abstract idea of greenness is a useful concept, but it exists only in our minds and in our language. William says that abstract ideas seem to be universals because they are indistinct, general representations of qualities or objects of kind (for example, all trees are kinds of tree). These abstract ideas are not universals, William says, because they lack any reality of their own outside our minds.

Put another way, when we say, "That tree is green," we are not saying that there is an additional reality, greenness, beyond that particular tree. The name "green" refers to the mental image that stands for our many experiences of particular objects that have the quality of greenness. William's important conclusion to this line of reasoning is that mental images and the names we attach to them are all that we need to explain our thinking about objects. There are no universals, no Platonic Forms, and we have no need to postulate that they exist. The idea that universals are not entities but merely names, is called "nominalism," from the Latin *nominalis*, meaning pertaining to a name or names. William was the foremost nominalist in philosophy, although his position is now universally (no pun intended) accepted in philosophy.

William's method of reasoning came to be known as "Ockham's razor," although he never used the term. The principles behind Ockham's razor are that the simpler of two explanations is more probably true and that we should not needlessly assume the existence of additional entities. In other words, we cut away with the razor of rational thinking the unnecessary notion of universals. Mental images and our names for them is a simpler explanation for human thinking. The idea of universals is not needed to explain our perception and knowledge, so we cut away the idea.

William went even further to state that universals do not exist even in the mind of God. This was in contradiction to Ibn Sina, who argued that God thought first the universal Forms and used them to create all of the particular objects. William's idea is that in the creation, God had in mind individuals, not humanity. God didn't create humanity; God created particular, individual people. Because we have the reason that God gave us, we think about particular objects by using mental signs or names.

The Contingent Universe

The idea that God created particulars not universals is the point at which William's nominalism connects with his voluntarism—the idea of an active, free will. His conception of voluntarism has significant implications for God, the universe, and us.

Ibn Sina stated that God created the world according to logical necessity, a view accepted by most Christian philosophers, most notably Thomas. In a similar vein, many scholars in William's time had accepted

Ibn Rushd's argument that God could not be said to have decided to create the universe and then perform the act of creation because God being eternal and thus outside of time could not be said to have a gap between decision and action. This means that it cannot be said that God has will or desire as we humans have within time. God, being without limit, also cannot be said to have had once not been the creator and then after acting been the creator; thus, the universe must be an eternal creation of God (think emanation like in Plotinus's cosmology). Thus, the eternal universe is the way that it is by logical necessity.

That view meant that God could not will that things be other than they are; God was limited and subject to what logic dictates, and some Christian philosophers found that unacceptable. John Duns Scotus (ca. 1265–1308) was one of the latter philosophers. He adopted Augustine's conviction that the will precedes the intellect and concluded that this meant that both God and humans are freed from following logical necessity. William agreed that God created as God wanted to create and was not limited by logical necessity. God's creation is not governed by logical necessity; everything is contingent to God's will. Things are the way they are because God chose to create them that way, and God could have chosen to make things be otherwise.

This is no mere theological argument for William. In fact, it has more to do with us than with God. It means that if the universe is not governed by logical necessity, then we cannot understand it through logic. Logic is a separate sphere from the phenomena we perceive in the world. The world is contingent and, therefore, logic tells us *nothing* about the world.

The contingency of creation forces us to give up hope that we can capture the structure of reality through logical deduction. Even causation—that we perceive event x followed by event y and therefore we assume that x causes y—is called into question. William observes that we never experience the supposed causal power within x that causes y, and we also never perceive necessity. There may be a cause-and-effect relation, but we cannot know this for certain because we can perceive only probable relationships. God maintains the uniformity of the universe, but God's will is not limited by logic, so God can act otherwise and has the power to produce y without it coming from x.

William wasn't against logic but warned us to limit logic to matters on which it is sensible to use it. Logic cannot tell us about the world and can only help us construct propositions about our mental ideas. The world is contingent; therefore, the important implication for us is that knowledge of the world can be attained only through experience. You want to understand the world? Get out there and perceive it! The Scholastic notion that we can logically reason to what *must* be the case is a fruitless endeavor. The philosopher must instead observe and catalogue facts about the world. We then act on our God-given potential to reason actively about our observations to understand the world. Logic can help us order our ideas, but logic can never establish facts, not even about God.

William rejected efforts to establish logical proofs of God's existence. He countered that it may be possible to accept God's existence through experience or through faith, but not through logic. Arguments for the existence of God are empty and worthless. William does admit the truth revelation of Scripture on God and morality. What is right and wrong is also contingent on God's will; why couldn't God have decreed that murder is righteous? Similarly, William leaves all questions of theology to divine revelation.

William's contingent universe without universals separates natural philosophy from logically necessary causation. This sets observation over logical contemplation, leading to modern philosophy and science. In William's universe, logic tells us nothing about how the world is; the truth is found by the individual who searches and uses reason to understand sense experiences.

Political Theory

William was concerned over corruption and excessive wealth in the Church. After he was excommunicated, he felt free to develop a radical new view of society. He declared that the Church should not own land, which should belong solely to earthly rulers (the idea in William's time was that land belonged to the king or Church). He said that people had the right to select their rulers and that those rulers were obligated to serve the interests of the people, not their own. William also called for the separation of Church and state. These ideas that are now basic to our conception of a good society were developed by a monk in the 1300s.

Chapter 4

THE "SCIENTIFIC REVOLUTION"

The term "Scientific Revolution" has often been used to describe a series of events in the late 1500s and the 1600s. Like other terms used to describe social movements, it is too glib to be accurate. True, a small number of people in those years started to approach the world in a manner that later came to be known as "science." Before the 1700s, the word "science" meant knowledge in general or what is known. The word "science" took on its current meaning from people who turned knowledge of the natural world into an experimental discipline of theorizing, experimenting, and observing. That movement was more philosophical than anything else, and it took place gradually over many decades, not suddenly, as the word "revolution" implies.

William's ideas were an inspiration to the movement that led to science. William had sought to liberate philosophy from Scholasticism. For those inspired by William's philosophy, replacing Scholasticism's approach became a major priority. William gave natural philosophers important theoretical tools to do just that. William had stressed that logic on its own tells us nothing about the world, meaning that we can't just sit and contemplate how things should logically be, as the Aristotelian Scholastics had done. The universe cannot be predicted on the basis of logic—we have to go out and observe how God made the world. The world doesn't bend to how our logic thinks it should be. Knowledge of the world comes to those who go into the world and discover what's there, said William. He also said that we have an active mind that could reason about our sense experiences.

These ideas were the inspiration for observational science. This is one example of why philosophy has always been and remains so important: philosophy develops ways of thinking that we can use and apply to life that allow us to do everything we do. Even today, science benefits from philosophy.

Montaigne—"What Do I Know?"

Michel Eyquem de Montaigne (1533–1592) was born into a wealthy French merchant family. His father, Pierre Eyquem, acquired nobility from King Francis I in reward for military service, and he served as mayor of Bordeaux. Michel received a rigorous education set up by his father, and his father succeeded in his desire that Michel become a worldly man, familiar with history and multiple cultures. He followed in his father's footsteps of serving the nation in the legal courts. In 1571, he resigned from his civil government positions to devote himself to writing. His end product was a book called *Essais*, which he continued to amend over 20 years, publishing multiple editions beginning in 1580.

The significance of *The Essays* for philosophy is Montaigne's new approach to the questions of knowledge, truth, and human nature and his new style of first-person perspective writing. The French word, *essais*, means "attempt," and to Montaigne, his book was an attempt at understanding, a personal confession of what he thought. Montaigne's *Essais* was the first blossoming of subjectivity, demonstrating an individual's attempt to understand the world. The literary style of the *Essais* is the origin of our word "essay," meaning a literary composition of moderate length on a particular subject.

Montaigne's *Essais* helped move philosophy from a formulaic exposition of past writings to a free process of forming judgments. He accused Scholasticism (still dominating intellectual activity in his time) of pedantry, its philosophers suffering from their thoughts being stifled by their excessive knowledge of archaic dogmas. Montaigne was one of the first to view philosophy as being connected to and a part of our daily life, rather than as an isolated academic pursuit. He did not offer a systematic method of conducting philosophy. He instead wanted to put it into what he saw as its proper role. Practiced with restraint, he said, philosophy is a useful exercise, but in excess, it leads to eccentricity and unsociability. The rational theorizing of the Scholastics will not tell us about human life, Montagne believed.

What will tell us about life, Montaigne said, is experiencing the world. In this vein, he advocated that children be taught through active and playful activities rather than rote memorization and drills. Through playful interaction with others, children will adopt social customs and manners free from coercion and servility.

He saw education as philosophy and philosophy as learning how to live. We never stop learning, Montaigne said, and the most important learning comes from asking questions: "What does this mean?" "Is it true?" and so on. Montaigne's most important question is, "What do I know?" He practiced a positive skepticism, in that he rejected theory and dogmatic certainty and instead continually questioned his own thinking to move toward greater understanding.

Reason alone cannot decide questions; one must practice the skill of making judgments that identify the best choices among many options. Our use of reason should be to ask questions, of ourselves and of the world, consider alternative opinions, and exercise natural judgment to find the best answers for use in our lives. Montaigne's skepticism was not a bitter or dour one but a celebration of open-minded thinking and use of the human mind.

Montaigne did not target his philosophical approach directly on the matters of science, but his rethinking of human reasoning and its limitations and potentials was influential in the development of science. His *Essais* inspired many thinkers, particularly in its expressive approach to life's questions. His method of using skepticism to work toward greater judgment and knowledge directly inspired philosophers of the new scientific method.

Francis Bacon—The Foundations of Science

In the early 1600s, British scholar and royal council **Francis Bacon** (1561–1626) took very seriously William's idea that we learn about the world through observing it. Bacon brought to the forefront the method of diligent observation and the cataloguing of those observations. Bacon's goal was to achieve a total reconstruction of all human knowledge, raised on the proper foundations. Bacon, one of the first to use the term "science" as we use it today, was a significant influence on the ideas of science and scientists that persists to this day.

Bacon wanted to replace what he saw as the vain obfuscation of Scholasticism that was largely based on Thomas Aquinas's interpretation of Aristotle. Thomas had adopted Aristotle's notion that all objects had in their form a final cause. Scholasticism focused on understanding these final causes—the end toward which an object is ordered, has been constructed, or has come to be, and that to which the object is drawn.

Bacon called for philosophical inquiry into natural phenomena to seek not Aristotelian final causes but the material and efficient causes of those phenomena. Scholasticism defined objects in terms of matter and form, but Bacon wanted to dispense with the idea of forms.

> Matter rather than forms should be the object of our attention, its configurations and changes of configuration, and simple action, and law of action or motion; [because] forms are figments of the human mind. (*Novum Organum* I.LI)

The Scholastics, having adopted Aristotle, had focused on form as defining an object's substance—the type of object that it is. Ironically, that meant that, in practice, the Scholastics were closer to Plato than to Aristotle, focusing on disputes over the nature of forms rather than studying objects in the world. William had sought to break that habit, and Bacon followed. Bacon said we should study matter—the changing configurations and actions of objects in the world. When Bacon calls forms "figments," he is thinking similarly to William, who called them merely names.

Bacon described science as the endeavor to discover the unknown, which he contrasted with Scholasticism's method of systematizing logical concepts. He urged his countrymen to sweep away the rubble of medieval tradition and head toward a "new continent" of knowledge, with science being the ship that will guide us to new lands. Bacon's nautical explorer analogies captured the burgeoning optimism bordering on hubris in England in the early 1600s. He was writing toward the end of the "Age of Discovery," the period from the 1470s into the early 1600s when the European powers "discovered" the rest of the world. (The indigenous populations already knew where they were and preferred to be left alone.) Bacon saw the emergence of science, freed from Scholasticism and adopting its own intellectual methodology, as the great hope for humanity (for the Europeans anyway).

It may appear to us today that Bacon's program is secular, but his thinking was thoroughly grounded in religious tradition. He believed science would recover the knowledge that humanity had once possessed in the Garden of Eden but had lost because of the fall. In Eden, Adam and Eve had dominion over all of the earth. Because of their disobedience, God rescinded Adam and Eve's authority over nature and set nature at odds with their descendants, who were now required to toil by the sweat of their brows to survive. But, Bacon believed, by God's grace and Providence, humanity was being granted an opportunity to recover this dominion. "The true ends of knowledge," Bacon wrote, are "a restitution and reinvesting of man to the sovereignty and power which he had in his first state of creation" (*Novem Organum* III, 222).

The new sciences are not just the endeavor to increase human knowledge and power; they are the means of righting an ancient mistake and partially restoring humanity's rightful relationship with nature. This was not mere lip service by Bacon to keep from running afoul of religious authorities. There is no reason to doubt that Bacon, like nearly all of the intellectuals of his era, sincerely believed that the biblical narrative of the creation and fall were history. In Bacon's system, science was in no way contrary to the established doctrines of Christianity.

The Idols of the Mind

Knowledge is power, Bacon said, but not all experience leads to true knowledge. Yes, we can have *false* knowledge if we think we know something is true but it isn't. Bacon understood that the way we approach the world affects how we perceive what we experience. We see what our knowledge tells us we see. Therefore, it is important that we have true knowledge, not false knowledge. False knowledge comes from what Bacon calls the corruption of our minds by idols.

"Idol" was originally a religious term that morphed into a general term for anything foolishly worshiped—like singers on reality TV shows. In his book *Novum Organum* (1620), meaning "New Instrument," Bacon observed that people don't think clearly because they are distracted by four types of idols of the mind that still apply to this day.

1. The Idols of the Tribe. Here, the idea of tribe refers to humanity as a whole, and these idols are part of human nature. When we assume that the universe should conform to our expectations, we are being distracted by this idol.

> The Idols of the Tribe have their foundation in human nature itself, and in the tribe or race of men. For it is a false assertion that the sense of man is the measure of things. On the contrary, all perceptions as well of the sense as of the mind are according to the measure of the individual and not according to the measure of the universe. And the human understanding is like a false mirror, which, receiving rays irregularly, distorts and discolours the nature of things by mingling its own nature with it. (*Novum Organum* I.XLI)

Our human inclination is to want the universe to make sense in the way we think it should make sense (like the Scholastics did). Our desires affect how we perceive things, especially, Bacon says, how we assume there is more order in the universe than is really there. We all tend to make the facts fit our preferred conclusions. We see what we want to see, and what we think we see is a mirror of ourselves, not a true picture of reality. It is a human tendency we need to overcome, Bacon says, if we are to think clearly. To overcome this idol of wishful thinking, we need a disciplined approach of objective observation and reasoning about what actually is.

2. The Idols of the Cave. The first idol pertains to the false mirror in humanity as a whole. Bacon uses the cave metaphor from Plato's allegory to describe our own personal false mirrors of understanding. Bacon says that each one of us dwells in our own unique "cave" of beliefs that we think are true. These beliefs, formed by our dispositions, education, experiences, and the authorities we admire, limit our perception of the world. Beset by the idol of our personal cave, our philosophy follows our personal history more than it follows reality, so it distorts our perceptions. A pessimist sees the cup as half empty; the optimist sees the same cup as half full. Bacon says we need to guard against our natural idiosyncratic prejudices.

> Generally let every student of nature take this as a rule—that whatever his mind seizes and dwells upon with peculiar satisfaction is to be held in suspicion, and that so much the more care is to be taken in dealing with such questions to keep the understanding even and clear. (*Novum Organum* I.XLII)

In other words, we should always question ideas, *especially* our own ideas that we find attractive. That an idea feels right doesn't make it true.

3. The Idols of the Marketplace. Today we read "marketplace" and think of economics. Bacon is using the term in the 1600s sense of the market square as the hub of civic life. In that market, you would have found people gathering to buy; sell; and talk, talk, talk. The cacophony of voices in the marketplace was Bacon's analogy for the problems of language that interfere with our pursuit of truth. "Words plainly force and overrule the understanding, and throw all into confusion," he says (*Novum Organum* I.XLIII). Words can deceive us. For example, we have names for things that do not exist, like "luck," but the existence of these names can deceive us into believing in their existence and using their names to explain events incorrectly. More problematic is our use of abstract terms that are vague and ambiguous. Today, we might complain about a "heavy" cell phone even though it weighs less than a "light" backpack. And "heavy" is one of those words that have many different meanings. You can say you have a heavy heart because of your heavy course load, so you listen to heavy metal music, none of which can be measured objectively. The point that Bacon is making is that we need to be careful not to let words lead us into empty controversies and distract us from perceiving the world clearly.

4. The Idols of the Theater. Bacon lived in the time of Shakespeare. No, Bacon didn't write Shakespeare's plays, but Bacon uses the Shakespeare-like metaphor: "All the received systems are but so many stage-plays, representing worlds of their own creation after an unreal and scenic fashion" (*Novum Organum* I.XLIV). What Bacon means is that there are various dogmatic systems of philosophy, such as those of Plato and Aristotle. These systems created large, internally coherent systems of connected concepts that told a story about how the world is. But like a world created in a fictional plot, these intellectual unreal worlds have no connection to the real world. We need to hold in suspicion any intellectual system that claims to explain the world, no matter its origin. Bacon means not only philosophical systems but also the axioms of science that by tradition, credulity, and negligence have come to be received knowledge. His answer is to reject all dogmatism and ideology and instead learn by observing the world and gathering facts.

The Foundation of the Sciences

Bacon, like many before him, assumed that the universe had a unified rational order. To learn how that order works, we need to conduct observations to gather facts about the world, properly catalogue those facts, and then look for the forms within those data. Bacon used the term "forms" in different way than did Plato or Aristotle.

> For when we speak of forms, we mean nothing else than those laws and regulations of simple action which arrange and constitute any simple nature, such as heat, light, weight, in every species of matter, and in a susceptible subject. The form of heat or form of light, therefore, means no more than the law of heat or the law of light. (*Novum Organum* II.XVII)

Bacon rejected Aristotle's theory of final causes but saw the forms as the supreme causes of objects and their motions. We learn about the forms of nature by collecting particular facts and inductively reasoning to discern where forms are present and where they are absent. Bacon's forms are the fundamental laws of nature that we come to know as the result of a methodical procedure.

One example of Bacon's method was learning about the form of heat by observing where heat is present and where it is absent and when heat increases and decreases; then we correlate those data with other data to find relationships among phenomena. His method led him to conclude that the form of heat is an expansive force that travels through material bodies, which is an accurate assessment as far as it goes.

Bacon's primary contribution to science was to establish the foundations of science as a collective enterprise. He proposed the creation of committees of scientists working to discover the forms of nature. The areas of science would be divided into specialties. He specified 128 distinct specialties, from the study of astronomical bodies to the study of machines. Within each specialty, he called for the creation of two groups of scientists. One group would engage in observational research, conducting experiments and collecting empirical data. Another group would analyze the data by using a method he called "inductivism"—what we now call "inductive reasoning." Using inductivism, scientists would identify positive and negative relationships in the data and infer from their sample the forms that exist across nature within that scientific specialty. Across all specialties, another group of scientists would take the findings of all the specialties and use induction to identify positive and negative relationships among the areas of science. Bacon confidently predicted that such a structural method would lead to "the power and dominion of the human race itself over the universe" (*Novum Organum* I.CXXIX).

Bacon placed great faith in our capacity to gain knowledge through disciplined observation and the recording of our sense experiences. He therefore believed that science properly conducted would, in only a short period of time, discover all that could be discovered. Such was Bacon's optimism that, although he never finished it, he wrote a book, *New Atlantis*, in which he imagined the future world as a utopian society transformed by science and technology. It would be a new age of religious tolerance and progress in the arts and sciences.

Bacon's positive contributions to science were diminished by some serious blind spots in his thinking. He was so enamored with his new observational method that he rejected as obsolete and unnecessary all theoretical thinking. He therefore rejected the theories of **Mikołaj Kopernik** (1473–1543, latinized as "Copernicus") and **Johannes Kepler** (1571–1630) on planetary motion, as well as any other theory that he saw as reasoning from principles. Bacon established the empiricist movement in philosophy and pioneered the notion of systematic science, but his failure to appreciate the essential contribution of legitimate theorizing in science prevented him from developing a full scientific method.

His shortcomings aside, Bacon was lauded for his accomplishments and inspired generations of thinkers. In 1660, a group of scientists established the Royal Society of London for Improving Natural Knowledge. The Royal Society was founded on Bacon's dream of a collaborative scientific enterprise and dedicated itself to acquiring knowledge through experimental investigation. The members of the Royal Society made it very clear that their inspiration was Bacon's philosophy. In 1665, they began publishing an academic journal, *Philosophical Transactions of the Royal Society*. For at least the next 200 years, the Royal Society was one of the world's leading organizations in promoting science. The society and its journal are still active today.

René Descartes—The Methodical Scientist

Frenchman **René Descartes** (1596–1650) is one of the few philosophers who is a household name. He is best known for the most famous quote in philosophy: "I think, therefore I am." That quote, and his most famous book, *Meditations*, have inspired the picture of Descartes as a dreamy thinker detached from the world. This view is understandable, but it's very far from true.

The real-life Descartes was a diligent scientist and mathematician thoroughly grounded in the world and the history of scholarship. His concerns were meticulously practical and devoted to how we can better understand science and mathematics so that we can better comprehend the world in which we live. His interest in how to think about science brought him to philosophy. Descartes claimed to have discovered a philosophical method of guiding his reason that was highly effective in helping him make significant discoveries in his scientific research. His method, and the philosophical conclusions to which his method led him, were immediately influential in science and philosophy and remain so.

It has become habit to describe Descartes's method as a method of doubt. True, the willingness to doubt ideas which we take for granted is in Descartes's method, but doubting is only a tool in service of his higher goal. His overarching purpose was to discover an ultimate truth—a certainty on which he could base all thought. Rather than being a method of doubt, his methodical philosophy is a method of avoiding error. Descartes was not a skeptic. He believed that knowledge was possible. In fact, he believed that the human mind, when engaged in the proper method, is incapable of making an error of knowledge.

Descartes proceeds from two fundamental assumptions. His first assumption is that there are objective truths that can be known (again, Descartes is not a skeptic). His second assumption is that every human being is equally well endowed with reason and possesses the power to know the truth. What people need is an effective method by which they can discipline their power of reason and guide it to success. People have different opinions about the truth, Descartes thinks, not because some people are better equipped with reason than others but because different people have varying degrees of success in applying their reason.

He proposes his method of reasoning not as a set of rules that all must follow but as a description of the path he has followed in the hope that others might similarly profit from it. Descartes's method is a strategy for self-instruction, a do-it-yourself method for learning about the world. Descartes firmly believed not only that individuals could think for themselves but also that they should do so.

The Cartesian Method

Descartes's method marks a complete break from the classical and medieval focus on the philosophers of antiquity. Coming from a well-connected family, he received the finest education of his time—Scholasticism, but he roundly rejected it.

> From my childhood, I have been familiar with [the books by ancient scholars]; and as I was given to believe that by their help a clear and certain knowledge of all that is useful in life might be acquired, I was ardently desirous of instruction. But as soon as I had finished the entire course of study, at the close of which it is customary to be admitted into the order of

the learned, I completely changed my opinion. For I found myself involved in so many doubts and errors, that I was convinced I had advanced no farther in all my attempts at learning, than the discovery at every turn of my own ignorance. (*Discourse* I.4)

Leaving behind the stilted education of his time, Descartes resolved to learn instead from "the great book of the world." He decided to travel, choosing the unusual path of serving in several armies in the 1620s. Being a gentleman of means, he didn't have to be involved in much of the fighting of the Thirty Years' War; mostly, he had time to think, of which he took full advantage.

He wrote *Rules for the Direction of the Mind* sometime in those years, but the manuscript was only published in 1701, years after his death. In 1637, he published an expanded version of his ideas as *Discourse on the Method of Rightly Conducting One's Reason and of Seeking Truth*, known by the shorthand, *Discourse on Method*. That book contained chapters on science and on philosophy, linking the subjects to show that philosophy provided the foundation for success in science. His famous book, *Meditations*, published in 1641, is a more poetic version of the philosophical content in *Discourse*.

Also in 1637, Descartes published the book, *Geometry*, in which he set forth the principles of coordinate geometry and algebraic equations, like $x + y = 5$, for defining circles and lines. Descartes's interest in and love for geometry inspired his approach to science and philosophy. He saw the continuing disputations among the philosophers of his time as only increasing the level of doubt and confusion. He sought for all knowledge the certainty he found in mathematics and geometry. For example, if I ask you what two plus two equals, you almost automatically say, "Four." You didn't require extensive reasoning to come up with the answer. You clearly and distinctly knew the answer. That's the type of knowledge that Descartes was seeking.

To reach that level of clear and distinct knowledge about the world, Descartes sought a way to get past arguments over definitions, disputes in which the Scholastics were bogged down. Descartes's revolution was to construct philosophy based not on any external authority, such as ancient books, but on the internal authority of the mind.

> For since God has endowed each of us with some light of reason by which to distinguish truth from error, I could not have believed that I ought for a single moment to rest satisfied with the opinions of another [person], unless I had resolved to exercise my own judgment in examining these whenever I should be duly qualified for the task. (*Discourse* III.5)

Because we have been born with the ability to reason, Descartes urges us to question and withhold assent to all external authorities, even the authorities of our own senses. Once we have cast off all of our traditional authorities, we come to the position of accepting the only authority we can fully trust—our own reason. Descartes believed that our rational mind is capable of finding and employing a method that makes it incorruptible to all manipulations of external sources. When we think clearly, we can discover specific principles that we can use to understand our experiences and gain knowledge.

In constructing his method to gain knowledge, Descartes saw it as more important than anything else not to fall into error, even if it meant advancing slowly.

> But like one walking alone and in the dark, I resolved to proceed so slowly and with such circumspection, that if I did not advance far, I would at least guard against falling. I did not even choose to dismiss summarily any of the opinions that had crept into my belief without having been introduced by reason, but first of all took sufficient time carefully to satisfy myself of the general nature of the task I was setting myself, and ascertain the true method by which to arrive at the knowledge of whatever lay within the compass of my powers. (*Discourse* II.5)

The true method of gaining knowledge must be disciplined, and its fundamental principle must, of course, be reason. Nothing should be believed unless it is approved by reason.

But on what should we base this rational discipline? Descartes considers the candidates that the Scholastics had given as methods for knowing truth with certainty—logic, geometry, and algebra. He agrees that the true method should use the advantages of these three fields of learning: they have the ability to construct, by means of deduction, knowledge of the truth. These three fields use deductive reasoning to proceed from a self-evident axiom that is known to be certain and proceed carefully, step-by-step, to a new conclusion that is just as certain as the starting point.

The problem with logic, geometry, and algebra, though, is that they are insufficient in our investigations of the unknown. As William had, Descartes admits that logic is valuable only in better communicating what we already know. Geometry, Descartes says, is so exclusively restricted to the consideration of abstract figures, that it can exercise understanding only on condition of greatly fatiguing our imagination. While valuable to a point, the numerous rules and formulas of algebra hamper the mental faculties and result in confusion and obscurity. These condemnations come from Descartes who invented coordinate geometry and proved that the figures of plane geometry can be represented in algebraic equations. He saw the value in logic, geometry, and algebra, but he accepted that they cannot be the basis of a useful method by which we can learn about the world. As William had said, logic tells us nothing about how the world is.

New scientific knowledge is what Descartes is interested in discovering. He had the same mission as Bacon, believing that science is about exploring the unknown, venturing into uncharted territories to shine the light of reason on new discoveries and separate the true from the false. Descartes conducted his explorations in physics, anatomy, optics, and other observational sciences to learn about the world and come to understand it. Rather than the multitude of laws of logic, geometry, and algebra, Descartes said that we need a simple set of rational rules that can be rigidly applied.

Descartes's Four Rules

To that end, Descartes proposes four fundamental rules that he has found to be perfectly sufficient in his scientific exploration. He sets down four short, simple rules with "the firm and unwavering resolution never in a single instance to fail in observing them."

> The first was never to accept anything for true which I did not clearly know to be such; that is to say, carefully to avoid precipitancy and prejudice, and to comprise nothing more in my judgment than what was presented to my mind so clearly and distinctly as to exclude all ground of doubt.
>
> The second, to divide each of the difficulties under examination into as many parts as possible, and as might be necessary for its adequate solution.
>
> The third, to conduct my thoughts in such order that, by commencing with objects the simplest and easiest to know, I might ascend by little and little, and, as it were, step by step, to the knowledge of the more complex; assigning in thought a certain order even to those objects which in their own nature do not stand in a relation of antecedence and sequence.
>
> And the last, in every case to make enumerations so complete, and reviews so general, that I might be assured that nothing was omitted.
>
> The long chains of simple and easy reasonings by means of which geometers are accustomed to reach the conclusions of their most difficult demonstrations, had led me to imagine that all things, to the knowledge of which man is competent, are mutually connected in the same way, and that there is nothing so far removed from us as to be beyond our reach, or so hidden that we cannot discover it. (*Discourse* II.7–11)

Notice the rules' repeated emphasis on self-discipline. That is the key to Descartes's method. We can summarize Descartes's rules as follows and see how the bottom line of each rule is to avoid precipitancy, meaning not rushing to judgment.

Rule one: "Never to accept anything for true which I did not clearly know to be such." Avoid precipitancy and reserve judgment until we have all the facts.

Rule two: Break down what we are examining into manageable parts. Avoid the precipitancy of trying to solve the entire complex problem in one go.

Rule three: Begin with the simplest part of the problem and progress step-by-step through to the complex. Avoid precipitancy by methodically building our knowledge from simple ideas to more complex ideas.

Rule four: "Make calculations throughout so complete that I might be assured that nothing was omitted." Advance cautiously and thoroughly, leaving no step unconcluded. Avoid precipitancy by never jumping ahead in the step-by-step process.

Descartes teaches that we must continually rein in our reasoning. We are all prone to accept ideas as true without properly weighing all considerations. Often, we are not even consciously aware that we are doing this. We frequently accept ideas without exercising due critical inquiry, and this leads us into error. Instead, we should not too easily accept quick judgments or surface definitions.

Descartes has complete confidence in this methodology because he has complete faith in the power of the human mind. Following the views of such philosophers as Augustine and William, he agrees that the will can control the intellect, although Descartes insists that can also be otherwise.

> Whence, then, spring my errors? They arise from this cause alone, that I do not restrain the will, which is of much wider range than the understanding, within the same limits, but extend it even to things I do not understand, and as the will is of itself indifferent to such, it readily falls into error and sin by choosing the false in room of the true. (*Meditations* IV.9)

When our will runs ahead of our intellect which is what Descartes means by precipitancy—we fall into error. Descartes therefore views controlling the will as the key to discovering truth.

Like other philosophers before and after him, Descartes believes we need to be devoted to reason and follow the dictates of reason. Descartes argued that our senses alone cannot lead us to knowledge about the world. Our senses can be deceived and are not beyond doubt, so we need something more to gain knowledge. When we explore the world through disciplined reason, we cannot err. Descartes contends that when he avoids precipitancy by restraining the will and following the proper method of reasoning, it is quite impossible for him to go wrong.

> As often as I so restrain my will within the limits of my knowledge, that it forms no judgment except regarding objects

which are clearly and distinctly represented to it by the understanding, I can never be deceived. (*Meditations* IV.17)

Rigorously following his four rules will make our minds incorruptible and immune to the manipulations and distractions of the world. Or so Descartes claims.

Descartes's philosophical project is to establish a method of science to empower us to discover all of the truths about the physical world. Similar to Bacon, Descartes had an unbridled optimism about what science with the proper method could accomplish.

Doing Science beside the Fire

Having provided us with the four rules for directing our minds, Descartes then gives us several thought experiments to demonstrate what applying those rules can do for us. In *Meditations*, Descartes gives us a dramatic reenactment of how he claims to have come to his philosophical methodology. He gave a shorter but more difficult-to-read version in his earlier book, *Discourse*, but in *Meditations* he tries to reach a more general audience by making his story more flowery. In *Discourse*, he says he was stuck sitting in a cold military barrack in front of a stove (probably a historically accurate portrayal of a night during his time in the army). In *Meditations*, he portrays himself in his own home, in his dressing gown in front of his fireplace (a case of literary license).

Sitting comfortably by the fire in *Meditations*, he resolves to find the firm and permanent structure in the sciences that can lead us past doubt to intellectual certainty. First, he needs to clear away any thoughts that don't contribute to this goal. He resolves to doubt anything that can be doubted, because if an idea could possibly be false, then it lacks the certainty required to be part of the firm and permanent structure in the sciences. He embarks on a scorched-earth policy toward all of his beliefs, whatever they are, declaring he will at length apply himself earnestly and freely to the general overthrow of all his former opinions. By demolishing everything he had believed before, he hopes that what remains will be the unassailable truth of which he can be certain.

He considers in turn beliefs of which he had previously felt certain: that the world exists around him, that he has a physical body, that there is a creator God, even that two and three together always equals five. Perhaps, he wonders, every belief we have was simply acquired from long and familiar customs that deceived us into believing as true what is actually false and imaginary. Or, he wonders, perhaps some being with godlike powers is deceiving him. Descartes can't immediately disprove this fantastic possibility. He has to admit that every belief he has could be a false belief caused by a malevolent force. He will therefore suppose that the sky, the air, the earth, all external objects, colors, figures, sounds, even his own body, are nothing but illusions.

As radical as is this program of doubting everything that can be doubted, it's only a temporary suspension of his beliefs. Always for Descartes, the purpose of his doubts is to clear the way for more certain beliefs. Anything that has deceived us, even once, cannot be trusted. Our senses have frequently deceived us in the past and led us to untrue beliefs, so we should not trust them completely. He therefore suspends belief in every thought that comes from sense experience.

Where does that leave him? He has to consider the possibility that he alone exists—that there is actually no external world, no other people, no God. He has to consider the possibility that he has no physical body and that he is mistaken to believe that there is anything material. All of these beliefs could be caused by a deceiver, a very powerful and very cunning being that employs its great power to deceive him into believing as true what is actually false.

At this point, Descartes borrows (without attribution) Augustine's argument against the skeptics that he exists and knows that he exists. Augustine said, "If I am mistaken, I exist." Descartes's formulation is only slightly different: "If I am deceived, I exist."

> Doubtless, then, I exist, since I am deceived; and, let him deceive me as he may, he can never bring it about that I am nothing, so long as I shall be conscious that I am something. So that it must, in fine, be maintained, all things being maturely and carefully considered, that this proposition "I am, I exist," is necessarily true each time it is expressed by me, or conceived in my mind. (*Meditations* II.3)

"What Am I?"

But being a true philosopher, knowing that he exists is not enough for Descartes. He next asks *what* he is. A person? A body? A thing that senses? All of these thoughts can be doubted because perhaps the various bodily sensations he has are because he is dreaming. In dreams he "sees" and "hears" things that are not real. How can he tell when he is dreaming or awake? It's not so simple to tell the difference. But of one thing he can be certain:

> Thinking is another attribute of the soul; and here I discover what properly belongs to myself. This alone is inseparable from me. I am—I exist: this is certain; but how often? As often as I think; for perhaps it would even happen, if I should wholly cease to think, that I should at the same time altogether cease to be. I now admit nothing that is not necessarily true. I am therefore, precisely speaking, only a

> thinking thing, that is, a mind, understanding, or reason,
> terms whose signification was before unknown to me. I am,
> however, a real thing, and really existent; but what thing?
> The answer was, a thinking thing. (*Meditations* II.6)

He concludes that he is not a body; he is "a thinking thing." "But what is a thinking thing?" he asks. "It is a thing that doubts, understands, [conceives], affirms, denies, wills, refuses; that imagines also, and perceives" (*Meditations* II.8).

I mentioned at the beginning of this chapter that Descartes is a household name because of his statement, "I think, therefore I am," or in Latin, "*Cogito, ergo sum*" (*Discourse* IV.1; *Principles of Philosophy* 1.7). The common misconception about this statement is that Descartes's purpose is to prove his existence. Instead, his purpose is to demonstrate what sort of being he is. In the argument, "I think, therefore I am," Descartes assumes the "I"—his existence—prior to the exercise. He immediately proceeds from affirming his existence to affirming that "I am therefore, precisely speaking, ... a thinking thing" (*Meditations* II.6). The end goal and conclusion are to know what sort of being he is.

That is what we humans are—thinking things. That's what Descartes claims distinguishes us as humans from all other things. The essence of being human is thinking. There is an element of Aristotelianism in Descartes's conclusion. If the essence of being human is to be a thinking thing, then our purpose is to think as excellently as possible. But more important for Descartes's purpose is the conclusion that his essence is a thinking thing. He is a mind, not a body, whether or not he has a physical body. Descartes's first bedrock of certain knowledge is that he is a thinking thing. On this thought he cannot be mistaken.

The Wax Example

Descartes then turns to the question of corporeal (physical) things. He cannot stop believing that there are corporeal objects. His bodily senses continually feed him information that such things exist. As he showed before, however, the existence of corporeal things can be doubted (we can imagine that what we think we perceive are not corporeal objects) despite how real they seem to be. He remarks how strange it is that we say we know and understand distinctly these corporeal objects the existence of which is dubious. What can we know, and how can we know and understand these alleged corporal objects?

Descartes explains how we can understand the physical bodies we perceive and interact with in his thought experiment, the wax example. It's one of the great thought experiments in the history of philosophy.

> Take, for example, this piece of wax; it is quite fresh, having
> been but recently taken from the beehive; it has not yet lost

the sweetness of the honey it contained; it still retains somewhat of the odor of the flowers from which it was gathered; its color, figure, size, are apparent (to the sight); it is hard, cold, easily handled; and sounds when struck upon with the finger. In fine, all that contributes to make a body as distinctly known as possible, is found in the one before us.

But, while I am speaking, let it be placed near the fire—what remained of the taste exhales, the smell evaporates, the color changes, its figure is destroyed, its size increases, it becomes liquid, it grows hot, it can hardly be handled, and, although struck upon, it emits no sound. Does the same wax still remain after this change? It must be admitted that it does remain; no one doubts it, or judges otherwise. What, then, was it I knew with so much distinctness in the piece of wax? Assuredly, it could be nothing of all that I observed by means of the senses, since all the things that fell under taste, smell, sight, touch, and hearing are changed, and yet the same wax remains. (*Meditations* II.11)

Think about the problem that Descartes is putting before us and imagine yourself in a similar situation. You are sitting beside a fireplace, and you have poured the honey from a honeycomb into a cup of tea. You like your honey the old-fashioned way—straight from the beehive, not from bear-shaped plastic bottles. You identify that it is a honeycomb because of the qualities you perceive: its shape, color, size, smell, feel, taste, and sound. You realize you forgot the cookies to have with the tea, so you set down your wax honeycomb next to the fireplace and go into the kitchen. But when you return with your cookies, you discover to your horror that your honeycomb has vanished. Where you had placed it near the fire, there is no longer your wax honeycomb but a puddle of goo. What is your first thought? Do you think someone broke into your home, stole your honeycomb and left in its place this puddle of goo? No, your first reaction, without hesitation is, "Oh no, my honeycomb melted."

The point to this thought experiment is that we automatically assume that the honeycomb and the puddle of goo are the same object even though they differ in every quality. They are not different objects but the same object that has changed qualities. Descartes's question is this: what are we doing when we think this way? How is it that we can make the connection that these two sets of sense impressions with different qualities are from the same object?

Descartes's answer is that we can make the mental connection because we understand that what the wax honeycomb *is*—its essence—is not its sense qualities (sweetness of honey; the scent of flowers; its color, shape, or sound). The essence of the honeycomb is a material body that we perceived first in one form and then in another form. Descartes concludes that what belongs to the wax itself is nothing except something extended, flexible, and movable.

Therefore, when we recognize that the wax has changed form, we understand that underlying all of its qualities that we perceive through our senses is something that can be defined only as extension in space. In other words, the essence of the object is that it takes up space—it has height, depth, and width and is flexible and movable. The piece of wax was the same extended thing when it was a wax honeycomb and when it was a puddle of goo, but, Descartes concludes, we don't comprehend that fact through an act of vision, touch, or any other physical sense. We were fooled by our senses into believing that the wax was a set of qualities, but instead it is through an intuition of the mind that we understand what the wax is in essence—extension in space. In terms of you leaving the room and returning, you know that the wax honeycomb and the puddle of goo are the same object because in both instances it is taking up space in the same location, only its qualities have changed.

What Descartes is showing us with this thought experiment is that the physical senses give us information, but it is only with the mind's rational judgment that we understand what our senses are presenting to us. He follows with this short example.

> [When looking from a window and saying I see people who pass in the street], I do not fail to say that I see the people themselves, just as I say that I see the wax; and yet what do I see from the window beyond hats and cloaks that might cover artificial machines, whose motions might be determined by springs? But I judge that there are human beings from these appearances, and thus I comprehend, by the faculty of judgment alone which is in the mind, what I believed I saw with my eyes. (*Meditations* II.13)

Returning to the wax example, if we were limited to knowing only what our senses told us, we would be unable to make the judgment that the honeycomb had melted into the puddle of goo. We would remain stuck with the false idea that there are two unconnected objects. Left to sense impressions alone, we'd be fooled into thinking they were two different objects, not a single object that had changed.

Our senses can deceive us. Fortunately, we aren't reliant solely on our senses. We can perceive what objects truly are because we are a mind, a thinking thing. This is the second bedrock of certainty for Descartes: being thinking things, we have the power to understand the world rationally, despite the unreliability of our senses. Using Descartes's method for rightly conducting our power of reason, we can gain knowledge of the world.

The Clear and Distinct Idea and the External World

Using his thought experiment of doubting all that can be doubted, Descartes has affirmed that his mind can know that something is true if and only if it presents to his mind clearly and distinctly.

> There is nothing that gives me assurance of its truth except the clear and distinct perception of what I affirm ... and accordingly it seems to me that I may now take as a general rule, that all that is very clearly and distinctly apprehended [perceived] is true. (*Meditations* III.2)

Descartes has now achieved his ultimate bedrock of certainty: he can accept as true those ideas that are clear and distinct. He has established the unassailable idea that he exists. He knows with equal certainty that he is a thinking thing and that his mind is capable of making judgments about external objects. He is aware that to have a method for success in science he still needs to establish a reliable connection between the ideas in his mind and the external world.

Descartes says there are three types of ideas in the mind—ideas innate or inherent to the mind, ideas invented by the mind, and ideas caused by external forces. Innate ideas cannot be doubted because we cannot think of them without at the same time thinking that they are true. That a circle is round is an example. Ideas we invent cannot be doubted because if you imagine a purple unicorn, that idea exists only as *your* idea, so it is neither true nor false; it simply is.

Ideas caused by external forces, what Descartes calls "natural impulses," can be doubted. The natural light of reason, Descartes says, only illuminates innate ideas such as the idea that he exists; it does not illuminate natural impulses like the idea that there is a tree over there.

Here is the dilemma. I can be certain that I think I see a tree, but how can I be certain that the content of my idea is an accurate description of what exists outside my mind? I cannot doubt that I exist or that I can imagine fictitious animals, but how can I believe beyond doubt that my natural impulses are of an external world that exists more or less as it appears to my senses?

It may seem odd that Descartes is returning to the doubt that he may be deceived about the external world after his wax example confidently showed that his mind is capable of knowledge. But that's his point. His mind is reliable, but his senses can still be deceived. The wax thought experiment works whether or not there actually are honeycombs and fireplaces in an external world. That's why you can think accurately about the thought experiment even though you are not presently experiencing any honeycombs or fireplaces.

In his thought experiment by the fireplace, Descartes showed that the existence of external objects can be doubted and that a deceiver could deceive him about the existence of an external world even though it cannot deceive him about his own existence. Descartes needs to escape the trap of the skepticism called "solipsism"—that the only things he can prove are that he exists and that he has ideas. But Descartes is not a skeptic; he believes that there is an objective external world and that we are endowed with reason capable of knowing the truth about that world. Now he has to prove how he can have reliable certain knowledge about the external world. If we cannot have confidence in our ability to perceive the external world, then science is not possible.

Knowledge is a relation between a knower and what is known. Descartes has proven that he can be certain of the knower side of the equation, that he is a thinking thing who has clear and distinct ideas, but what he is much less certain of is the cause of any of his ideas about the external world. The problem facing Descartes is that what exists in his consciousness are his own ideas about external objects but not what causes those ideas. He cannot deny that he has many ideas about objects that seem to exist in the world external to him. These ideas of external objects that are given to his mind by his senses sometimes seem to be clear but later prove to be false. So, he still needs to solve the big problem of the unreliability of sense perception before he can reach the experiential form of cognitive understanding that we call "science."

This is where God comes in for Descartes, but in no way does he mean the God of religion. He uses the idea of God only as a prop in service of his larger argument. His idea of a perfect, supreme being is the key to being able to have certain knowledge about the external world and, thus, success in science.

His argument is that he has a clear and distinct idea that there is a sovereign God that is eternal, infinite, all knowing, and all-powerful; that possesses all perfections, including ethical perfection; and that is the creator of all things beyond itself. I will make the rest of his long argument short: Descartes contends that God, being all knowing and all-powerful, could be the deceiver he mentioned earlier who could deceive Descartes into falsely believing that there is an external world. But, because God has all perfections, including being perfectly good, God would never so deceive us or allow a powerful and cunning being to do so. Therefore, we can be confident that there is an external world and that the natural impulses that cause ideas in our minds about external objects are in truth caused by real external objects.

What does all of this mean? Descartes is inserting the idea of God as an answer to our general systematic doubts. Descartes is not saying that he cannot be mistaken about particular propositions such as "that tree looks safe to climb" because he knows his will can overreach and lead him to error. But God being perfectly good is not a deceiver and the all-powerful God would not allow us to be deceived into believing in a world that does not exist. Because Descartes knows he is a thinking thing who can use the power of reason and because he knows God is not an evil deceiver, then it's possible to derive knowledge from observing the external world. Thus, if he can reason correctly (his four rules for directing the mind), then his mind is incapable of error because he can reason from clear and distinct ideas to truth. We still must be continually on guard to avoid precipitancy so we do not make mistakes about our sensory perceptions of the world, but we can rely on the knowledge that an external world does exist more or less as it appears to exist, and that means that science is possible. Establishing the validity of the nascent observational science of the 1600s was Descartes's primary purpose. Descartes's argument can be questioned on a number of its premises, but it is not circular reasoning.

Descartes's Influence

The methodology of science that Bacon and Descartes helped establish came to dominate intellectual inquiry. Aristotle had established the four causes to explain objects in the world. The new science narrowed investigation of the world to efficient causes. It sought to reveal the regularities of events in the world—objects fall to earth, fire heats, hearts pump blood, and so on. Identifying and cataloguing these regularities empower us to know the efficient causes of natural phenomena and be able to predict future events better.

Despite Bacon and Descartes having basically the same objectives, historians of philosophy often say that Bacon and Descartes started two separate branches of philosophy based on two very different theories of how we gain knowledge. That view is that Bacon began a trajectory in philosophy known as "empiricism" (we'll meet more empiricists in Chapter 5), and that Descartes began a trajectory known as "rationalism." The traditional way of describing this split is that the empiricists believe that all knowledge comes from sense experience, whereas the rationalists believe that our rational analysis of propositions reveals truth. There is some truth to this characterization, but it oversimplifies the complexities and nuances of the philosophers' ideas. Descartes certainly believes in the value of rational analysis, but he never denies the value of sense experience. We will see similarly how the empiricists never denied the value of reason.

Descartes's most enduring influence is what has come to be known as the "Cartesian subject." This idea comes from a reasonable interpretation of what Descartes means by his method of discovering truth. Descartes doesn't appeal to the external authorities of experts or institutions but to the internal authority of the mind's clear and distinct ideas. Descartes is seeking mental clarity—not a dogmatic definition but an intuitive (direct) experience of the objects in the world. That means that his experience and his alone determines what is true. The view that Descartes seems to leave us with is that we are a mind detached from the world that makes pure rational judgments about the world.

Descartes's method also leads him to the conclusion that he is a mind, not a body. Even though in his thought experiment he eventually determines that he does have a body, his idea remains that what he is is a thinking thing not a bodily thing. This conclusion leads to what has come to be known as "Cartesian dualism," the idea that a human being is composed of two separate substances—mental and material. Descartes certainly subscribes to that idea, but it was not his invention. The idea that the physical human body is accidental to the immaterial human psyche, soul, or intellect was an old and widely held idea long before Descartes. Nevertheless, it is Descartes's version of mental/material dualism that philosophers still debate today.

As we will see, most philosophers today reject the idea of the Cartesian subject as a mind independent of the world, arguing that it ignores the influences that embodiment and culture have on people and their perceptions and thinking. In the years since Descartes, many philosophers have been influenced by his ideas and have taken them into account in their own philosophies, either agreeing with Descartes or reacting against him.

Chapter 5

THE RISE OF MODERN EPISTEMOLOGY

By the mid-1600s, some people questioned the new methodology of observation. They weren't against science, and they certainly weren't against gaining knowledge. What people questioned was the assumption that observational science was a direct path to certain knowledge. Bacon, Descartes, and others had been boldly optimistic about what science could achieve through disciplined observation. Was that optimism justified? Discoveries in astronomy, anatomy, physics, chemistry, and biology seemed to indicate it was.

Philosophy always questions, but not always in opposition to ideas. The questioning of the assumptions of science that began in the mid-1600s, and continues to this day, has attempted to improve science, not oppose it. If we are to investigate the world through observation, then we should be clear about what observation means, how it works and what knowledge is possible through observation.

Epistemology (from the Greek word for knowledge, *episteme*) is the study of the origins and limits of human perception and knowledge. The core question of epistemology is, "What can we know?" Philosophers since ancient times have considered some issues pertaining to perception and knowledge, but the dedicated study of epistemology truly flowered in England in the 1600s, mainly because of the influence of Bacon. These philosophers are known as the empiricists, advocates of empiricism, the theory that knowledge comes from observation. In reading about their ideas, it is important to keep in mind that the philosophers in the era of English-language empiricism were prone to using their own definitions of certain terms.

Thomas Hobbes's Materialist Epistemology

English philosopher **Thomas Hobbes** (1588–1679) is best known for his political theory (see Chapter 6), but his empirical theory of epistemology is also important in the history of philosophy. Both Hobbes's political and epistemological theories were founded on his belief that there exists nothing but matter, a view he discussed in his primary book, *Leviathan* (1651). Hobbes was an uncompromising materialist and determinist who insisted that the universe is nothing but material bodies in motion. He was and still is often mistakenly considered an atheist because he said even God was material and subject to material causation. He was not hostile toward God or religion, but he did think of them in terms of his radical materialism.

Hobbes's epistemology was influenced by the emerging science of his time, and he personally knew several major scientists. He worked for a time as a translator and secretary for Bacon. He met with Italian scientist **Galileo Galilei** (1564–1642) and with a number of French philosophers, perhaps even with Descartes. Descartes invited Hobbes to write a reply to *Meditations*, which Hobbes did, respectfully disagreeing with Descartes on several points. However, Hobbes didn't share the scientists' enthusiasm for the new observational methods. He admired Galileo's work on motion of physical bodies, but he didn't agree with Bacon's empirical and inductive methods, so he tried to steer the new science in a different direction.

Hobbes was, to a fault, a very straightforward thinker. He believed it was important to reduce the many phenomena in the world to a few simple, basic principles. He adopted the deductive logic of euclidean geometry as opposed to the inductivism of Bacon—a method that Hobbes dismissed as speculative and inexact. Hobbes argued that science should be conducted deductively like geometry—by reasoning from first principles to logical conclusions. Once we understand the first principles of the visible world, we can understand all knowledge.

Hobbes's Physics of Knowledge

Hobbes's physics was a natural philosophy of the motion of bodies. Hobbes took to heart Galileo's conception of the universe as bodies in motion and saw the laws of motion as basic principles that can explain all physical phenomena. Hobbes fought a losing battle with other English scientists of his time over the new observational scientific method of Bacon. Hobbes fervently believed that observations made by the easily mistaken senses could not be a foundation for science. Instead, science must proceed from first principles. He believed that an economy of thought was essential to physics; therefore, he rejected what he saw as extraneous ideas. Hobbes's application of Ockham's razor was to say that nothing existed except matter.

The central idea of Hobbes's physics is that the only things that exist are material bodies. It was an idea compatible with, if not inspired by, the corpuscular (atomic) theory of matter of **Pierre Gassendi** (1592–1655), a Catholic priest and philosopher who had embraced the new science. Gassendi thought that reality is composed of the primary elements of matter and void. These exist within a universe of absolute space and time, within which material bodies move. He likens the universe to a floor plan within which there are furniture. Material bodies—the furniture so to speak—are made up of a-toms (indivisible particles) that exist in space and time, possess qualities, and are the substrata of all the objects that we perceive. Material substance, Gassendi thought, explains all of the qualities that we perceive in objects.

Going further than Gassendi, Hobbes argued that the concept of "immaterial substance" was a contradiction; for something to be a substance, it must be material. If a spiritual thing exists, then it must be made of something material, even if that material is very fine, even finer than a fog. We ourselves are only material, Hobbes claimed. We do not have a separate spiritual substance apart from the material body, as Descartes, among many others, had said. Hobbes said that what we call a mind or soul is a part of our material existence that is made of finer particles of matter. In turn, all qualities of objects are also material. Colors, sounds, and odors are all to be explained as matter in motion. Our perceptions of external objects are caused by particles impinging on our material sense organs. This in turn is a cause of our ideas, which are also particles in motion.

The corpuscular theory of matter seemed to confirm, to Hobbes, the importance of first principles. From this principle that everything is material, he could proceed to the second level of practical science— particular observations of particular bodies, such as the study of planetary bodies or earthly bodies. The world is a world of bodies in motion. Period. Hobbes assumes that nothing moves itself but moves because it has been caused to move by another body. All motion is caused by material contact (collisions) with other bodies; there is no action at a distance (an idea considered by some in Hobbes's time and later confirmed by Isaac Newton in his theory of gravity). All motions and collisions are governed by material laws that exist eternally and unchangingly and presumably were set down by God.

The Basis of Perception

Hobbes insisted that all knowledge comes to us through sensory perception. This means that all of our thoughts have their origin in sense perception, and we can only know what comes to us through our senses.

> There is no conception in a man's mind which hath not first, totally, or by parts, been begotten upon the organs of sense. The rest are derived from that original. (*Leviathan* I.2)

This denies notions, such as Plato's, that the human mind has stored within it innate knowledge. Hobbes is thus an empiricist—one who believes that knowledge comes from sense experience. Hobbes taking a view of absolute empiricism, that knowledge comes *only* from experience.

Hobbes derived his conclusion of our complete dependence on the senses from his notions that (1) everything is causally determined and (2) everything is material. Hobbes described bodies on macro and micro levels. Although objects may appear to be at rest on the macro level, they are in fact composed of smaller particles at the micro level that are in motion (a truth later confirmed by Albert Einstein). The motion of some micro particles off an object collide with our sense organs, and that is the cause of our sense perceptions. Particles of light cause vision, particles of sound cause hearing, and so on.

The particles collide with the organs of sense and produce what Hobbes called a "seeming" or "fancy." If a particle enters our eye, it causes a visual fancy; if a particle enters our ear, it causes an auditory fancy; and so on. By the word "fancy," Hobbes meant a kind of conception, like how we would say something is "a flight of fancy." He did not mean that it's something unreal but that it's something that is a mere copy caused by the pressing of external things on the organs of sense.

The fancies in our mind are copies, a mere semblance, of the objects in the external world. They are only impressions on our mind—and I'll use the word "impressions" from now on, which sounds less weird today. The total of all of the impressions within a human mind makes up our realm of impressions. This realm of impressions is separate from the external world and the objects themselves. What we directly experience within our mind are different things from the objects that cause them. It is important to remember, however, that the impressions are still real; they are mere semblances, but they are not illusions. All of the impressions are actually material bodies and are caused by material processes. Think of a shadow. We know that a shadow is caused by a material object, and we know that a shadow is not as substantive as the material object that causes it. Nevertheless, we would admit that the shadow is a real thing, not an illusion.

The impressions in the mind are the cause of all other mental processes. To Hobbes, the mind works in a very straightforward manner. Mental events are material motions no different from motions of bodies in the world. The senses produce impressions in the mind, and what we call "thinking" is the associations of those impressions among each other that more or less mirror the associations of bodies in the world. What we call "reason" Hobbes defined as "nothing but reckoning—that is, adding and subtracting—of the consequences of general names agreed upon, for the marking (to our selves) and signifying (to others) of our thoughts" (*Leviathan* V.2).

Our mental reckonings are dependent on our memories, but Hobbes had a very different view of memory than Augustine did. Our memories are what Hobbes called a "decaying sense" of original impressions. They are like the fading echoes that bounce back from the impressions created by sense perception or the fading ripples on the water when a stone is thrown in. Imagination is what arises from the motions of the impressions—just as material objects in the world move and collide, so do the impressions in our mind. The results of these motions and collisions are the new thoughts that we call "imagination." However, our imagination can do no more than add or subtract the existing impressions in the mind; it cannot create anything truly original. What we imagine had to first be present in sensation. For example, the idea of a unicorn is simply the combination of the existing impressions of a horse and of a horn added together.

Hobbes's view of the human being is quite unromantic. The universe is *dis-agree* nothing but bodies in motion. Our thoughts, feelings, and imagination are nothing but particles in motion. We have no real creativity or self—our beingness is just ripples on the surface of a pond. We will see a very different philosophical perspective beginning with Immanuel Kant in Chapter 8, but between Hobbes's time and then, the notion of a passive mind dominated empiricist philosophy.

Hobbes's radical materialism had an interesting implication for his religious beliefs. He believed in God and did not question Christianity, but, like many in his day, he was critical of religious institutions. However, his materialism meant that he had to believe that God is made of matter, which he did. He reasoned that either something is matter or it is void. God could not be immaterial because immateriality is nothing. God exists; therefore, God must be material. Of course, God is a different kind of matter than what rocks, plants, trees, and our bodies are made of. Hobbes saw God as a rarefied matter, like a very fine mist, but still matter.

Not surprisingly, Hobbes's theory met with great criticism in his time—and not just from religious authorities but also from other philosophers and intellectuals. Hobbes could find few to agree with him that observation should not be the foundation of scientific inquiry. His idea that there is nothing but matter was not intellectually palatable and seemed to contradict common sense, especially the reality of our human mind. The preferred notion was from Hobbes's contemporary, Descartes, who reasoned that there were two types of substance—mental and material. Mind and consciousness have no extension in space and thus could not be material. The same argument for a material God would have to be made for a material mind, and, not surprisingly, Hobbes thought that mind was nothing but matter. But if mind is matter, then what is consciousness, which has no extension in space? Would Hobbes's theory require us to deny the existence of consciousness?

Newton Captures the Universe

Hobbes's *Leviathan* was published in 1651. Over the next decades, Hobbes saw his political desires fulfilled (we'll cover that in the next chapter) but not his scientific desires. Although the corpuscular theory of matter was being widely accepted, being rejected was his fervent belief that science must be based on first principles of logic and geometry and not on the new method of experimentation advocated by Bacon and his followers.

The growing number of observational discoveries greatly increased enthusiasm for the observational method. One significant development was **Robert Hooke's** (1635–1703) book, *Micrographia* (1665), that detailed his microscopic observations. It opened a window into the unseen world of the microscopic and showed a whole new reality all around and within us. It seemed proof positive to many that truth would be found by increased observation rather than logical speculation.

There were some philosophers and other intellectuals who looked for an approach that combined observations with mathematics. One who adopted this approach was **Isaac Newton** (1642–1726). Science as we know it today began with Newton. In a letter to John Trumbull, Feb. 15. 1789 (Jefferson 1789), **Thomas Jefferson** wrote, "Bacon, Locke and Newton...I consider them as the three greatest men that have ever lived, without any exception, and as having laid the foundations of those superstructures which have been raised in the Physical & Moral sciences." As we have seen, Francis Bacon invented the scientific method and inspired the formation of the Royal Society, the driving force of British science for centuries. John Locke's contributions to epistemology and political philosophy you will see shortly.

Newton fulfilled the hope that had begun with William of a true natural philosophy—what we now know as "science." Newton brought to science two innovations: mathematics can explain motion, and reality can by understood through theoretical modeling. Newton didn't discover gravity—people did know that bodies fell to earth—but he gave us a method of describing not only gravity but the motion of all physical bodies. He did this by realizing that the motion of bodies can be modeled mathematically through the use of calculus—which he "borrowed" from German mathematician–philosopher **Gottfried Wilhelm Leibniz** (1646–1716) and pretended he invented it. Newton's mathematical modeling confirmed the idea that there are rational laws of nature like gravity that govern all material objects and that can be defined by mathematical formulas. Take any set of bodies—real or hypothetical—plug their qualities into the equations that describe natural forces, and you can describe how these bodies have moved in the past and predict how they will move in the future. The Newtonian universe was a clockwork universe that was easily understandable and predictable. All we needed to do was do the math. At least, that was the dream.

John Locke's Epistemology

The earlier quote from Thomas Jefferson mentions **John Locke** (1632–1704) with good reason. Locke was an intellectual giant within his own lifetime and remains one of the most important philosophers. He is equally well known for his political philosophy (see Chapter 6) and his epistemology. Locke talks more about beliefs than knowledge because, as he correctly observes, every idea we have is a belief—an idea we believe to be true. Locke was concerned primarily with establishing the limits of human understanding and the grounds of our beliefs. Locke was, therefore, interested in understanding how it is we come to our beliefs.

Locke's main philosophical influences were Descartes, Bacon, and Newton. This is part of why I stressed the importance of Descartes's scientific method. Locke didn't see Descartes as a dreamy meditator. He understood that Descartes's rules for clear thinking and forming justified beliefs were a way forward for science. Locke, like Descartes, was interested in helping clarify and strengthen science. But Locke was so much more cautious than Descartes or Bacon about people's ability to know about the world. He believed on the one hand that if one reasoned correctly one could have knowledge but on the other hand that it was easy for one to fall short of knowledge. We fall short because all of our beliefs are based on our sense experiences and our senses are limited.

In trying to understand how it is we come to our beliefs, Locke had the benefit that Descartes had not had of the tremendous innovations of Newton. Locke wanted to develop a Newtonian view of our minds, meaning a physics of how ideas are caused by the motion of bodies in ways that can be modeled and predicted. He wanted to find out how external bodies created ideas in our minds, and he wanted to understand why certain of our thoughts were often found together as though attracted to each other by a kind of mental gravity.

How Our Minds Work

Locke's word for our beliefs is "idea." You need to lose your preconception of what "idea" means to understand fully Locke's use of the term. For Locke, an idea is anything in the human mind—not just something we create, as in "I have an idea—let's order pizza." See? I put the idea of pizza in your mind because you had the experience of reading "pizza." You didn't invent the idea, it came to you from reading the word, which you associated with your prior experiences of pizza, both past and present experiences becoming ideas in your mind. So now we all have the idea of pizza, which is usually connected with the idea of wanting pizza. I really want pizza now.

Locke insists that we had no innate idea of pizza or of anything else. Innate ideas are ideas that are inherently known by the mind prior to any sense experience—these are a priori ideas, literally meaning prior to and separate from experience. In Locke's time, the debate over whether we have innate ideas dovetailed with the dispute between what can be known a priori versus what can be known via experience. It's a debate that still goes on today with significant relevance to how we think, what we can know, and what kind of claims we can make.

Plato's Forms are examples of innate a priori ideas. A Platonist would say we recognize a particular pizza because we have the innate idea of Pizzaness; Locke says we only know about pizza because we have had the experience of delicious, hot, savory, pizza. OK, I will stop talking about pizza to avert further cravings in my readers.

Other examples of alleged innate ideas are the basic concepts of logic, mathematics, and moral laws. The theory of innate ideas claims that everyone universally possesses these basic bits of knowledge. Locke counters that even if some ideas are universally known, that doesn't prove they are innate. The ideas could be universal because human experience is universal. He also rejects the idea that logical and moral ideas are universally held by people, pointing to the ample evidence that there are illogical and immoral people and that beliefs and morals differ among cultures.

Locke said that if a person had been blind since birth and had only been able to identify objects by sense of touch, if that person suddenly gained sight, that person would not be able to identify objects by sight. That's debatable, but Locke is stating a rational conclusion of his idea that we know nothing except through sense experience. If so, then we know an object only by the direct sense experiences we have had of it and cannot extrapolate from one sense to the other—in his example case, from touch to sight.

Locke's claim is that we have ideas only because we have experienced objects in the world. For example, we have the idea of a tree from our experiencing sensations furnished by external objects that we have come to know as "tree." Locke says that when we are born, our minds are like blank sheets of paper on which experiences make their marks. The only ideas in our minds have been put there by our sense experiences. Locke also likens our minds to a camera obscura (Latin for "dark chamber" and, yes, where we get the word "camera"). The camera obscura was a well-known device in Locke's time, a small hole in a wall through which light would pass and shine an image onto a wall or canvas. It was used primarily by artists as a drawing or painting aid as shown here. The artist could trace the image shown by the light shining on the canvas.

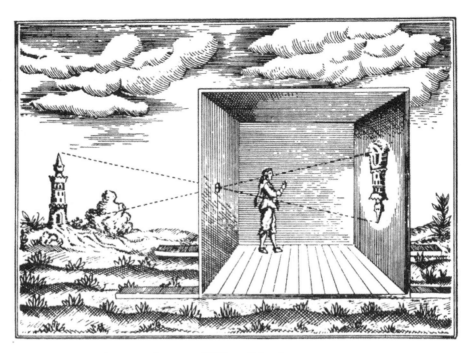

A camera obscura, c. 1600s, artist unknown.

The camera obscura of our mind is a dark box with holes (the senses) through which sensations enter. Inside the dark chamber, the mind begins life as a tabula rasa (Latin for "blank slate") on which sensations make their mark. As we have experiences in life, we gather more and more ideas, which Locke calls "simple ideas of sensation," which are ideas such as green, flat, smooth, hard, tall, hot, sweet, and so on. That is all our senses give us—simple minute qualities presented to the mind as sensations. Our senses do not show us a tabletop; they give us the simple sensations of flat, smooth, and hard.

What happens in the mind to these simple ideas of sensation? Clearly, the human mind is more than a dark box into which simple sensations pour. Locke says that the human mind is also aware of its operations, and this awareness is "the other fountain from which experience furnisheth the understanding with ideas" (*Essay* II.I.4). This set of ideas is our internal sense. These ideas come not from external objects but from our own "thinking, doubting, believing, reasoning, knowing, willing, and all the different actings of our own minds...[ideas] the mind gets by reflecting on its own operations within itself" (*Essay* II.I.4). Locke calls ideas of our internal sense "ideas of reflection." For example, the simple ideas that enter our mind of an object that is flat, smooth, and hard are simple ideas of sensation; being aware of and thinking about these simple ideas of sensation are simple ideas of reflection.

Locke contends that together with the simple ideas of sensation, the simple ideas of reflection are the only ideas that are ever present in the mind. "External objects furnish the mind with the ideas of sensible qualities, which are all those different perceptions they produce in us; and the mind furnishes the understanding with ideas of its own operations" (*Essay* II.I.5). That's it. Those are the entire contents of the human mind, and because the mind can reflect only on ideas of sensation furnished to it by external objects, Locke concludes that "the mind thinks in proportion to the matter it gets from experience to think about" (*Essay* II.I.22). The contents of our minds, then, are strictly products of our experiences—initially of external objects, then by reflecting on our experiences of external objects. Our minds, Locke says, can neither create nor destroy ideas.

What, then, can our minds do, according to Locke? Locke says that the mind has the power to process ideas; it can repeat, compare, and unite the simple ideas. In so doing, the mind creates complex ideas. Locke identifies three mental operations that we use to process simple ideas into complex ideas: compounding, comparing, and abstracting. For example, if we have the simple ideas of flat, smooth, and hard, we can combine these simple ideas into the complex idea of a tabletop. The simple ideas of green and tall can be combined into the complex idea of a tree. Much of our thinking uses this activity of compounding simple ideas that come to us through our five senses. We don't think "that's flat, smooth, and hard"—we think "that's a tabletop." Our dealings with the world are mostly in terms of complex ideas like "tabletop."

The second activity we use is comparing. Exactly as it seems, we compare ideas. It's hotter today than yesterday, that tree is taller than that one, and so on. Comparing also includes relations such as mother and son, over and under, cause and effect—ideas that you don't experience but determine from comparing relations between things.

The third activity is abstracting, the process that gives us abstract or general ideas. Locke sees these as an important set of ideas. Compounding gives us the complex ideas of a particular tabletop and a particular tree, and abstracting gives us the *general* ideas of tabletops and trees. This is Locke's answer to the age-old problem of whether universals exist. Treeness doesn't exist, either as a Form or in particular objects. The complex idea of trees is a general idea that comes from the process of abstracting. Locke says that from our experiences of a number of trees, and in thinking about trees in general, we hold in our minds an abstract idea of "tree" without a particular size, color, or other qualities. Our minds abstract all of the qualities that particular trees have in common and ignore individual differences. What remains is the general abstract idea of trees. An abstract idea, therefore, is a general combination of qualities we have experiences of as external objects. One of the examples Locke gives of an abstract idea is the notion of infinity—a notion others, including Descartes, believed was an innate idea. Locke countered that the idea of finite, in both space and time, is a simple idea. Through the process of compounding, we can imagine a repeating without end of a finite length of space or time. This is all the abstract idea of infinity is, Locke claims. Our idea of infinity is not innate but determined by a mental process—a faculty of our mind. Our idea of infinity is vague because our minds are finite, but then all of our abstract ideas are vague, not definitive, something to which George Berkeley would respond, as we will see in Chapter 7.

Primary and Secondary Qualities

Locke gives us an interesting vision of the human mind as almost completely passive. Experiences happen to it, and external objects cause the mind to form ideas. Therefore, you have nothing in your mind that is not formed by something else, and all we know are our own ideas. This leads to the conundrum of how we can know that what's in our mind corresponds to the external world. Locke was aware of this problem and tried to solve it by dividing the external causes of simple ideas of sensation into two types of qualities. By "qualities," Locke refers to a power to produce ideas in our mind.

Primary qualities exist in the objects themselves. Primary qualities include solidity, extension, shape, motion or rest, and quantity—qualities found objectively and manifestly in the object. These qualities, such as height or weight, can be objectively measured. Like Galileo and Descartes, Locke sees nature and the motion of bodies as mathematically describable. Primary qualities are entirely independent of the observer, and they are inseparable from the object. Descartes had defined material substance as extension in space, and Locke held the same view. An object has a certain size, shape, motion, and so on whether or not a person is observing it. Primary qualities cause our ideas of them. For Locke, then, the simple ideas of sensation that we have of the primary qualities are representations of the primary qualities themselves that exist in objects. Therefore, we can trust that our ideas of those primary qualities are natural representations of the objects.

Secondary qualities are powers that external objects have to produce ideas in us, but these qualities do not exist in the objects, and the ideas they produce do not resemble the qualities in the objects. That these qualities exist in the perceiver, not in the objects themselves, is shown by the fact that they cannot be objectively measured and can differ subjectively among individuals Included in secondary qualities are colors, sounds, tastes, odors, warmth, or coldness, all of which are subjectively experienced by particular people. Secondary qualities are mind dependent—only existing within the mind. Color is a secondary quality, meaning that color is not part of the object but only an idea that has been caused to appear in our mind. Colors are not part of an object's primary qualities. This can be demonstrated by shining a red light on a red object which makes the color disappear. Also, objects change color on the basis of the light around them and are colorless at night. All of this points to the reality that colors do not exist in objects themselves.

Taste is another secondary quality that is not in the object itself but in the experiencing of it. If I detest pickles, but you love pickles, I have two choices in trying to understand this contradiction. Either you are ignorant, perhaps delusional, or a pickle somehow changes substance when you taste pickles versus when I taste pickles. It is easier to believe that taste is a secondary quality of an object, meaning that the quality exists in the perceiver's experience of the object, not in the object itself. That means that the power of secondary qualities in the food creates different sensations in different people and that explains why some people like a food while other people do not: they are different people whose bodies are experiencing the food differently. Locke said that we need to know only the primary qualities of an object to have scientific knowledge of what that object is.

Locke's theory of epistemology still has a big problem. Despite his argument that our ideas of objects' primary qualities are true representations of those objects, our mind is still a sealed chamber, and we can never leave that chamber to compare its contents with the object in the world. We can never know how well the contents of our mind correspond to the external world. Locke admits that we do not perceive objects themselves; we perceive only our sense impressions of objects, and we do not ever know for sure if our ideas of objects match the objects in themselves. That we cannot know what lies behind our perceptions does not mean that there is nothing beyond our perceptions. Locke said that there must be material substance that objects are composed of. This substance, he said, this "something-I-know-not-what," must be what has the power to create the simple ideas of sensation in our minds. But we can't confirm that—it's beyond our perceptions.

Another problem is that Locke can't explain how the motion of material bodies can cause our subjective experiences of secondary qualities. This remains a problem in philosophy, although Berkeley (see Chapter 7) thought he had the solution, as we will see.

Summary of Locke's Epistemology

Locke's influential epistemology can be summed up as follows. Sense perceptions furnish simple ideas of sensation to the mind, and the mind's awareness of sensations furnishes simple ideas of reflections. All simple ideas are products of experience of external objects and mental processes. The mind processes simple ideas into complex ideas through compounding, comparing, and abstracting. Complex ideas about the primary qualities of external objects are representations of those objects

Our idea of "tree" is a complex idea that was created in our minds through a combination of simple ideas like height, width, color, and so on.

Simple ideas of sensation in our mind are connected to primary qualities of shape, size, and color. In other words, when we walk by trees, they produce simple ideas of brown, green, shape, height, and so on, which create the complex idea of "tree" in our minds—no Platonic Forms required. Trees are probably too complex an idea to help easily grasp what is going on here, so try a blank sheet of paper. We have the sensations of whiteness and rectangular shape, which cause the simple ideas of those qualities in our minds. Put together, the simple ideas of white and rectangular form the complex idea of a sheet of paper. Our personal judgments are complex ideas of reflection: "It's a nice day." This is a judgment made from the sum of simple ideas—the sunshine, the warm breeze, the birds singing—it is an idea of reflection based on experience.

Very important for Locke is that every idea we have can be traced to an original sensation and that nothing exists in the mind that cannot be so traced. He thought this conception provided a firm foundation for scientific observation because it describes all activities of the mind in terms of a Newtonian physics of the mind. This physics he describes as the basic activities of compounding, comparing, and abstracting that create complex ideas.

If the qualities in objects cause perceptions in the mind, then we can know only the qualities of the objects, not the reality of the objects themselves. William had said that logic tells us nothing about the world; now Locke was saying that our scientific observations can tell us nothing about the substances behind the objects we perceive. We are not perceiving the objects themselves; we are perceiving only the sensations they create in us. We cannot ever step outside the sealed camera obscura of our mind and compare the simple ideas in our minds with the objects themselves.

Locke's insistence that all human knowledge can be explained by a causal chain of qualities to simple ideas to complex ideas is unconvincing. There has to be some sort of consciousness that is making the deliberate mental activities of judgments that generate knowledge. A collection of mere representations of objects cannot arrange themselves into knowledge. Portraying the mind as entirely passive, as Locke does, leaves no room for human free will, despite Locke elsewhere in his philosophy accepting the reality and importance of free will. Locke's epistemology is innovative and insightful, but incomplete.

Chapter 6

THE RISE OF MODERN POLITICAL PHILOSOPHY

We all have a sense of what politics means, and that it tends to be full of ugly arguments and manipulations. But when we talk about political philosophy, we strangely aren't talking about *politics*. Political philosophy, like all branches of philosophy, is looking at the deeper, fundamental issues that lie behind the phenomena that we see in human social interactions. The philosophy of the political sphere of society analyzes what lies beneath the political phenomena that we see in human societies. Political philosophy is the exploration of the principles on which we can build better communities and a better society at large.

Political philosophy has ancient roots. **Plato** and **Aristotle** had each set forth their visions of how they thought society should be structured. Their thinking about society understandably was shaped by the time in which they lived. When Aristotle said a state should be no larger than the distance a person can view from atop a hill, he was reflecting the social reality of his time. Ancient Greece was a collection of city-states, like Athens. The Greek word for city, "polis," is the root for our words "political" and "police" and can be a suffix for the name of a city "-polis," like "metropolis." The word "political" has come to mean a number of things, but its foundation remains the idea of community or society. For the ancient Greeks, society meant the city. As societies changed over time, philosophers had to develop new political philosophies to reflect new social realities.

Shortly after Aristotle came the empire of **Alexander the Great**. Later came the Roman Empire that dominated the Mediterranean region for centuries. Augustine's political philosophy responded to this new reality of massive autocratic states with his view of how imperial states should be. His view was that God moves the events of history and the rulers are those whom God has chosen to rule. **Augustine's** view of the de facto legitimacy of political authority came to be known as the "divine right of kings." The Roman Empire dissolved into many smaller states, but Augustine's view influenced political thought for centuries to come; it understandably found favor in the minds of many rulers. As Europe transitioned into the feudalism of the medieval era, the predominant thinking was that the king, put in place by God, owned the land and by extension the people who lived on it.

For centuries, wealth had been an issue of the ownership of land. Gold and jewels were fine, but land produced food and other natural resources. Control of land had long been the basis of power arrangements in much of Europe. The aristocracy were the landowners, often granted rights to the land by the monarch in exchange for pledges of fealty (loyalty with duties attached). It was never an absolute system; the landed nobles were never totally loyal to the monarch, but they did rule almost absolutely over the peasants who were tied to the land and bonded to their noble lord.

By the middle of the 1500s, colonialism had changed the dynamic among the landed nobles and the monarchs because the exploitation of natural resources in the colonies changed the sources of wealth and economic power. The nations of Europe conquered and exploited other lands and their resources and fought each other for control of those lands and resources. How to acquire, control, and distribute resources had long been a concern of rulers, but in the modern colonial era, the economic dynamics took on new breadth and dimension as a global economy began to emerge. The rise of the business corporation posed new challenges and opportunities for the crown heads of Europe. Governments were forced to deal with mercantile interests in new ways, and economics itself was changing as raw materials became more diverse, widely available, and cheaper. Economics became far more of a political issue than ever before and forced the state to view its political power in new ways. The bureaucracy of the state expanded to deal with the economic changes and needed to develop new means of asserting sovereignty.

By the middle of the 1600s, the question for philosophers was identifying the fundamental principles behind the nation-state. How should the state be governed? What is the role of the individual within the state? Should the state have absolute authority or do individuals have rights, and if the latter what rights? In this chapter, we will look at different ways of thinking about political society and acting within political society. What they have in common is the realization that governments and nations are human creations rather than having been instituted by divine forces.

Hobbes's Social Bargain

We looked at **Thomas Hobbes's** epistemology in Chapter 5. Now we turn to his political philosophy that he discussed most notably in his book *Leviathan* (1651). Hobbes's philosophy of government and society derived from two major influences. One was his own extreme material determinism; the other was the political debates of his time. Believing he had identified the fundamental principles of human nature and the world, he developed a prescription for how to build a better society: a draconian social bargain to protect the peace. His solution is harsh but, he felt, necessary.

Individual and Political Bodies

Hobbes's political philosophy is consistent with his materialist epistemology. He believed that reality is composed of two types of material bodies: natural bodies (including people) and political bodies (nations). Material forces act on and determine the behavior of both types of bodies and thus every event in the universe is necessarily determined by prior causes. Hobbes believed he could apply the methods of his physics of natural bodies to human society. After all, if a human was a material body governed by physical laws, and a human society was then simply a collection of human bodies, then the laws that govern human social interactions could be formulated in the same way Galileo formulated the laws of motion. The more we understand the laws of motion, Hobbes thought, the more we can predict the movements of material bodies, including human beings and nations. Societies and nation-states are collections of human beings. Each individual person is like a single stone, and a society is like a collection of stones. Just as physical laws of nature govern the movement of stones, those same physical laws of nature govern the movements of people.

Human bodies may seem to act purposefully and independently, but this is not true, Hobbes said. Human bodies are governed by two endeavors: desire and aversion. Desire is the compulsion humans have to move toward something pleasurable, and aversion is the compulsion humans have to move away from something unpleasurable. In other words, humans desire pleasurable experiences and are averse to unpleasurable experiences. Hobbes said that these two simple endeavors govern all human actions. When humans seem to reason and deliberate between choices of possible actions, what is really happening within the human is the conflict between competing desires and aversions. The human is being pulled and pushed, and whichever force is the stronger at that moment will prevail and cause the human to move in a certain way. Each human body is like a cork on the surface of the ocean buffeted by winds and currents, mechanically determined in its motions by the collection of forces acting on it.

Because Hobbes believed in this deterministic view of human behavior, he believed that all of human society is similarly determined. Because he believed that the endeavors of desire and aversion govern all human beings, he assumed that human society as a whole is governed by the endeavors. Therefore, to create an orderly society, one needs to control the forces affecting the human bodies in it, and that will translate to controlling the larger body that is society. In terms of politics, Hobbes saw there being two primary endeavors in action. Humans desire peace and stability and are averse to chaos. These two endeavors underlie all of the other many endeavors that act on humans, such as desires for food, water, and shelter and aversions to discomfort and suffering. All of human society, Hobbes believed, can be reduced to actions caused by this material determinism of conflicting endeavors of desire and aversion.

The Political Arguments in Hobbes's Time

As we see throughout this book, philosophers respond to the current events in their time. Throughout Hobbes's life, English people debated the source of human rights and the proper structure of society. It wasn't always a deeply intellectual, philosophical debate; it more often was an angry argument over power. How much power should the king have over the nobility? What rights do the nobility and freemen of the kingdom have? Peasants were not included in this discussion.

In the early 1600s, the kings of England and France gained in power and wealth, and they felt emboldened to centralize power and made more demands on their nobility. Unsurprisingly, some in the nobility resisted. Growing tensions escalated into open civil war in England (1642 against Charles I) and in France (1648 against Louis XIV). Hobbes was a firsthand witness to both rebellions, having been born in England, then having had to flee to France in 1647. Hobbes served a noble family connected to Charles I, who had lost the civil war with the nobles and had been executed. Hobbes and other royalists chose exile in France over suffering probable reprisals in England, which was now ruled by Oliver Cromwell, leader of the revolt against King Charles I. In Paris, Hobbes was mathematics tutor to the son of Charles I—the later king Charles II—and was in the company of other royalist exiles. All of these developments helped inspire Hobbes's political philosophy.

For Hobbes, the conflicts among the noble factions were further proof of the prevailing assumption that social diversity was dangerous. It was widely believed that uniformity of language, ethnicity, social practices, and ideas were necessary for social stability. Difference of any kind was suspected to be a threat to society. In the early 1600s, as for many years before and after, a prevailing feeling was that a society was best when it had one ruler ruling over one homogeneous culture. This sentiment extended to all aspects of human society, including the religious loyalty confession, which in the 1600s was being either Catholic or Protestant. This basic assumption was practiced by nearly all European states: If the ruler was Catholic, everyone had to be Catholic. If the ruler was Protestant, everyone had to be Protestant. Diversity was dangerous. England's king was a Protestant; therefore, to not be Protestant was to be suspected as an enemy of the state. Hobbes was Protestant, but mostly out of a sense of loyalty to his monarch. He was not strongly anti-Catholic. For Hobbes, the subject must always be loyal to the sovereign; let's see why he so passionately believed that.

Hobbes's Thought Experiment

To understand how best to govern society, Hobbes asked us to imagine how life would be if there was no government. This hypothetical situation he called the "state of nature," living without any laws or social conventions. In the state of nature, there are not the class distinctions that were a given in English society at that time. No one has any rank or status or any of the associated rights, privileges, or restrictions. Hobbes's purpose in this thought experiment is to understand what forces are at work on humans prior to social conventions being created. Hobbes is not necessarily saying that there actually was a "state of nature" from which human society emerged, but thinking about what it would be like is illustrative of human nature and society.

In the state of nature without social conventions, everyone is equal, and life consists only of material facts and forces. There are no laws and rules to guide or stop behavior. Everyone has "a right to every thing," Hobbes said, "even to another's body." Hobbes's use of "right" is discordant to us today because we think in terms of moral and civil rights. By "right," Hobbes means a "freedom based on power." In other words, if I want your food, I have a right to take it if I have the power to do so. Of course, you have a right to stop me, if you have the power to stop me. The power in question includes physical violence. In the state of nature, there are no laws and no police to stop us from wounding or even killing each other as we struggle to take for ourselves nature's finite resources.

Hobbes's view of human nature is that we are inherently selfish. We are governed alone by the endeavors of desire and aversion and we have no inherent sentiment for others. He did not believe that altruism is natural. Buffeted like corks on the ocean by desires and aversions, we think and feel about our own needs. In the state of nature, humans are bodies moving and colliding, their desires and needs coming into constant conflict, each particular human compelled by the endeavors to survive by whatever means necessary. Like a postapocalyptic movie, everyone in the state of nature is seeking advantage over others, even dominance. Those with superior physical strength have an advantage, but they have no guarantee of safety because, as Hobbes pointed out, even the strongest person can be overcome when weaker people combine their power to take down the stronger.

It comes as no surprise then that the state of nature is a miserable existence dominated by fear and chaos without peace and stability. Hobbes summed it up this way:

> In such condition, there is no place for Industry; because the fruit thereof is uncertain; and consequently no Culture of the Earth; no Navigation, nor use of the commodities that may be imported by Sea; no commodious Building; no Instruments of moving, and removing such things as require much force; no

Knowledge of the face of the Earth; no account of Time; no Arts; no Letters; no Society; and which is worst of all, continual fear, and danger of violent death; And the life of man, solitary, poor, nasty, brutish, and short. (*Leviathan*, I.XIII.9)

The state of nature would be, Hobbes said, a war of all against all, in which nothing is unjust and thus nothing is off-limits. If anyone thinks this portrayal of how humans would behave without laws and conventions is exaggerated, Hobbes points out that we already know this is how people are. We lock our doors at night and lock away our valuables, and this is when we know there are laws and police. Our behavior shows our true opinions of our fellow humans, Hobbes said. How much worse would other people be without laws and police?

Fortunately, there is a way out of the vicious chaos of the state of nature. This is why Hobbes gives us the state of nature thought experiment: to explain the existence of human society and government. The natural forces of the endeavors led humans to form a government. The first endeavor in all humans is the desire for peace—the absence of conflict. This, Hobbes said, is the first natural law: to seek the peace and follow it, or, failing that, be prepared to defend oneself by any means necessary to restore peace. This desire for peace is present even in the strongest human, because no human is so powerful that he or she cannot be overcome by others. Peace and safety cannot be ensured by individual strength or craft.

When Hobbes said, "seek the peace," he didn't mean some flower power love and understanding sentiment. He was thinking in terms of his belief that people are governed by desires and aversions. We want to be left alone in our shelter with our food. We don't want to have someone break in and steal our food. We certainly don't want to be beaten or killed. We want to be left in peace. Simple as that. Hobbes called it our desire for ease, and we can understand this. We want life to be easy, and we desire to be at ease, without strife and conflict.

The first law is to seek the peace, and the second law follows from it: To achieve peace, one ought to surrender all of one's rights, provided that everyone else does the same. Remember that this is Hobbes's definition of "rights" as meaning "freedom based on power." In other words, Hobbes's second law is: "I will give up my freedom to do whatever I want if you agree to give up yours. I won't steal your stuff if you won't steal my stuff. I won't kill you if you won't kill me. This way, we can have peace rather than constantly fighting over resources." This agreement, in its essence, is a cease-fire between warring parties. This bargain of necessity is one of self-interest—again desires and aversions.

But what would stop someone from breaking the agreement to surrender all rights? There is no honor among thieves, it is said with much truth. If, as Hobbes said, we care only about our own desires and aversions, why would we keep any agreement to limit our freedom? Wouldn't we still seek advantage over others? Sure, I can agree to not take your stuff, but when your back is turned I can still grab your stuff if I think I can get away with it.

Hobbes is aware of this problem, and he provides a solution:

> There must be some coercive power to compel men equally to the performance of their Covenants, by the terror of some punishment, greater than the benefit they expect by the breach of their Covenant. (*Leviathan*, I.XV, 3)

Remember that for Hobbes, humans are just material bodies in motion. Whatever force is the strongest at that moment will cause the human to move in a certain way. Thus, you control human actions by exerting force on them, just as you control any other material object. Control the endeavors that compel humans to move, and you control the situation. An individual human's actions are manifestations of that human's power, so a stronger power is needed to control that human. All humans are averse to suffering, so to prevent them from breaking their agreement to surrender their rights, we need to put in place a force strong enough to make breaking the agreement painful.

This coercive power, Hobbes said, is a particular form of government that wields absolute power. The only way to compel others to obey their agreement is when everyone agrees

> to confer all their power and strength upon one man, or upon one assembly of men, that may reduce all their wills, by plurality of voices, unto one will. (*Leviathan*, II, XVII, 13)

Hobbes adopted the ancient Roman idea of the "body politic" and interpreted it literally. A nation is a political body made up of all of the particular humans living in it. A human body could not survive if the various organs and bodily parts were at war with each other. The body politic of the nation is the same. Hobbes declared that only by reducing all of the wills of all of the humans to a single will personified by one man, the sovereign, can the nation survive. The sovereign is the absolute ruler of the nation, one human who is granted all power and all freedom to act on behalf of all of the humans within the nation.

Title plate of Leviathan

Hobbes took the idea of the sovereign as the body politic quite literally as shown in the title plate of his book *Leviathan*. Looming over an English town and its surroundings is the sovereign, whose body is made up of the bodies of all his subject humans (look closely and you can see people in the sovereign's body). Their will and voices are subsumed in him. He speaks and acts for them. His word is law, and he is the coercive power that will compel humans to live up to their agreements.

Hobbes's proposed political arrangement has come to be known as a form of "social contract." The contract is between all particular humans. Everyone gives up all of their rights and freedoms and confers them on the sovereign. In return, the sovereign, as the source of the law of the land, guarantees peace and stability, which, Hobbes thought, is what everyone wants more than anything. Anyone who acts contrary to the social contract by breaking the laws of the land will be dealt with by the sovereign who also acts to protect the nation form foreign invaders.

The sovereign is outside the contract that created him, so he does not have to give up his rights. He has absolute power to compel men to the performance of their agreement. What prevents the sovereign from abusing his power? Hobbes never said. Like Plato long before him, Hobbes believed that those in power will act according to reason and natural laws and, thus, act only in the interests of the nation. Plato understood that people have free will but believed that no one would choose to do bad deeds if they knew they were bad. Hobbes denied free will, but he seemed to assume that the force of the common power of the social contract would compel the sovereign to act only to benefit the body politic.

If all of this seems far-fetched to our current way of thinking, remember that Hobbes was thinking in the 1600s. This was the age, on the one hand, of monarchism and absolute government and, on the other hand, of sectarian violence and rebellion by elements of the aristocracy against the monarchs. Political chaos was a constant threat, and Hobbes, among other like-minded thinkers of his time, thought that the only way to stop the fighting among the aristocracy for power was to concentrate all power in one man—the king.

Hobbes saw as his model the Kingdom of France in the mid-1600s. Louis XIII had consolidated political power and elevated France to a world power. After a 33-year rule (1610–1643), his son, Louis XIV continued his father's program of absolute monarchy and ruled as sovereign for an amazing 72 years (1643–1715; his successor, Louis XV ruled another 58 years). Hobbes wrote *Leviathan*, his book on political theory, in France while exiled from England during its civil war. The English civil war resulted in the fall of King Charles I and his execution, while Louis XIV successfully squashed the rebellion in France and restored peace. Hobbes's thinking in the early years of Louis XIV's rule was no doubt influenced by experiencing the Kingdom of France on the rise, sheltered from the turmoil taking place in his English homeland.

Locke's Theory of the Divine Right to Change Kings

Government at the consent of the governed. It is a principle we assume today and demand. It was not always so. Hobbes's philosophy of the sovereign bears strong similarities to the "divine right of kings"—the idea dating back to Augustine that the monarch held a sacred right to be monarch and was above the law because the monarch was the law. It was the principle held by Charles I. A generation after Hobbes's *Leviathan*, England didn't have the absolute sovereign Hobbes had prescribed as the antidote to political chaos. Charles II had, as Hobbes had hoped, ascended to the English throne in 1660, but it didn't end the strife over who should rule England. There was another removal of a monarch, James II, and another civil war, again over the balance of power in the nation-state between the nobles and the monarch.

John Locke was an ideas person, a kind of a 1600s think tank fellow who advised politicians and governmental officials. He himself was not a politician or governmental official, but he did work for Lord Ashley, the first Earl of Shaftesbury. His boss was very involved in government and politics, late in life, as a staunch opponent of the king, James II—a cause Locke wholeheartedly supported. It was the principle of the right of political opposition that captured Locke's attention. The need to philosophically justify the removal of the rightful monarch, James II, moved Locke to develop his theory of political philosophy. His magnum opus on political philosophy, *Two Treatises of Government*, was likely written while he was evading capture and prosecution for his association with Shaftesbury. Locke had to go into exile in Holland beginning in 1683.

The Political Background for Locke's Philosophy

Locke was writing his political philosophy about 50 years after Hobbes had written his. The political situation was much the same, including the perceived Catholic threat. In 1685, French king Louis XIV revoked the 1598 Edict of Nantes that had granted tolerance and rights to French Protestants. Louis—who had been king of France when Hobbes was in France tutoring Charles II and writing *Leviathan*—was a keen proponent of the theory of absolutism. Louis found the idea that all citizens of a country were not of the same religious confession as their king disruptive to the unity of the country. Louis' revocation of the Edict made loyalty to the king's views on religion compulsory. The king was Catholic, so the state and you had to be Catholic.

Also in 1685, the openly Catholic brother of Charles II, James, became king, Charles II having no heir on his death. James was not an exclusionary Catholic like Louis XIV, but English fears, real and imagined, of a Catholic king were strong. Earlier, forces in parliament, including nobles such as Shaftesbury, had unsuccessfully tried through legislation to prevent James from becoming king. Anti-Catholic forces attempted several rebellions shortly after James's coronation. James responded with excessive force that, along with his restructuring of the army and local governments, further stirred up distrust of James's intentions among both the English aristocracy and the common people.

In 1688, a group of English nobles reached out to the Dutch nobleman William of Orange, a Protestant and fierce enemy of Louis XIV. William was married to James's daughter, Mary. The English nobles invited William to become coruler, with Mary, of England if he would raise an army to depose James. William, recognizing a great opportunity, did raise an army to invade England, and James, correctly seeing that he didn't have enough support to stay in power, fled the country. Parliament, members of which plotted the whole thing, declared that James had abdicated the throne, and William and Mary were named co-monarchs.

The victors named it "The Glorious Revolution." The aristocracy in Parliament restructured English law to decrease the power of the monarch and increase the power of Parliament. It settled the political power struggle that had led to so much strife earlier that century, and the political arrangement of a constitutional monarchy remains the governmental system in the United Kingdom to this day. Locke, who played a small part in the revolt against James, crafted his political philosophy to justify a right of people to revolt against a king they saw as a threat to their well-being.

Locke's Natural Right of Property

Despite the strife over the Catholic question, Locke was largely unconcerned about religious issues, like Hobbes had been earlier. By all accounts, Locke was motivated by a desire for religious tolerance. He displayed it when he was a university student at Oxford and wrote that most religious disputes were over matters of no great import and should not disturb peaceful coexistence. He displayed it when he published his first major work, *A Letter Concerning Toleration* (1685), in which he argued for restraint from political leaders instead of trying to dictate the personal religious beliefs of the people. It is certainly possible that Locke's opposition to James II was motivated by a desire for religious peace within England. But in his major work on political philosophy, *Two Treatises of Government* (1689), he didn't present religious tolerance as a major argument.

Instead, Locke's primary concern in the *Two Treatises* is the question of what rights people have, especially in resisting authority. Locke had earlier argued that individuals had the right to believe however they wished on matters of no great import. Locke now extended that idea to who should rule a country, which was clearly a matter of very great import. He felt the people had the power, at least to a degree, to choose who their leader should be. His argument for the right to rebel was made by establishing individual rights within a framework of property rights. That sounds like an odd approach, but Locke's argument is ingenious and takes into account philosophical and political history.

Locke accepted as natural law what almost everyone accepted—that acts such as murder and stealing are wrong. Where Locke broke with the social conventions of his time was on his theory of property, primarily "real" property, or land. (Still today we use the idea of "real property" or "real estate.")

The prevailing idea in the 1600s about what justified ownership of land was the notion of the divine right of kings. Expressed best philosophically by the Dutch natural law philosopher **Hugo Grotius** (1583–1645), the argument was that the earth was created by God who granted ownership of various pieces of land to particular rulers. The king thus owned the land and could do what he wanted with it, including granting it to whomever he wanted. It wasn't really biblical, but that wasn't the point, really. It was an explanation of how things had worked for a very long time. It was "natural." The monarchies of both Britain and France operated in this way, as did most European states. The entire realm was considered to be owned by the king, who granted parts of it to various lords and barons, and people who lived on the land effectively belonged to the lord or baron who owned that land. This was how the feudal system worked. Grotius gave the philosophical explanation and defense of this reality, expressing it in terms of natural law.

Locke argued against Grotius that property was, in reality, something that humans earn through their own efforts. Locke made a distinction between natural rights and legal rights. Legal rights are granted by a government's authority, and the government can take them away. But natural rights are not subject to governmental authority. It would be wrong for a government to try to take away any of our natural rights.

The theory of the divine right of kings and Hobbes's theory of the sovereign both assume that the monarch possesses the original natural right of use of the land. Locke disagreed. Nature and all of its resources are given to humanity as a whole by God, Locke says, repeating a view first proposed by William of Ockham. Locke's innovation was to extend the idea of natural rights to the property held by individuals.

Locke's labor theory of property holds that when people mix their labor with the land, they create property that is theirs alone. One's labor, the work of one's own hands, is one's own property, and one acquires a right to it as one's own property. Locke lists hunting, gathering, and cultivating the ground as examples of how a person acquires the right to the material that the person's labor has produced.

It makes some sense. God made all the trees in the forest for human use, so if you go into the forest, chop down a tree, drag it back, and build something out of it, your labor gives you the right to the product of that labor. The apples on a tree may belong to everyone, but by going and picking the apples you make them yours. This is the condition of human life, Locke says. To survive, we need to mix our labor with the raw materials in nature to provide ourselves with food and shelter, and this necessarily introduces private possessions.

Earth's natural resources are humanity's common property, free to everyone to use as they need. The king has no inherent entitlement to the land over anyone else, Locke said. When I mix my labor with a part of nature, it becomes my property. Sounds great, but his view was not quite egalitarian. As Locke puts it:

> Thus the grass my horse has bit; the turfs my servant has cut...become my property, without the assignation or consent of any body. The labour that was mine, removing them out of that common state they were in, hath fixed my property in them. (*Two Treatises of Government*, II.V.28)

If you are paying any attention at all, something in Locke's passage should jump out at you: "the turfs my servant has cut become my property." Locke talks about the power of the people, but he is operating under 1600s assumptions about who "people" are. He still considers the lord of the manor to be the one who owns the land by virtue of the labor his servants expend on it because the servants belong to the lord. Locke's passage places the horse and the servant on the same level.

Nevertheless, for Locke, human labor is what distinguishes what belongs to all from what belongs to one; as long as that one person is of the aristocracy, thus, of course, excluding working people. Regardless, the philosophical point is that obtaining property is a natural product of living, and property properly acquired through one's labor is one's own by natural right.

Locke's State of Nature Thought Experiment

Having established property as a natural right, Locke engages in a thought experiment similar to Hobbes's. He also imagines a state of nature without government, but Locke had a very different view of human nature. Hobbes thought we are inherently selfish, and without coercive control, we would be in a constant state of war. Locke saw human beings as individuals with free will and rational capacity who also possessed sentiment for their fellow humans and were capable of altruism.

From this different view of human nature, Locke imagined the state of nature quite differently than did Hobbes. He thought a life without government would be one of general peace, goodwill, and mutual assistance. Most humans would act based on reason and benevolent sentiments and get along with each other, respecting each other's property and personal natural rights.

The problem would be the minority of people who acted contrary to reason and natural law. To preserve the peace, we would have to deal with those miscreants who ruin it. How do we deal with those who do harm to others? In a Wild West situation of the state of nature, we'd have to do it ourselves, resorting to vigilante justice. This is possible, but inconvenient and chaotic. Besides, Locke says, even though we could live in the state of nature without society, we humans are naturally inclined toward living in an ordered society.

This is Locke's social contract: We agree to form and live within a government that establishes and enforces laws that make our lives better. Locke's idea of government is one based on the principles of natural law, which are written down and enshrined in civil law, to resolve controversies among individuals. From a written law and constitutional government, individual human bias will not enter into judgments concerning individual cases. Rather than force each individual in the state of nature to enact justice and punish wrongdoing, a government can officially appoint indifferent judges who can apply the laws of the land in a manner more equitable than can a person whose interests are at stake.

A crucial element of Locke's social contract is that it is between the citizenry of a nation and their government. This is different from Hobbes's social contract which is among the people that creates a sovereign outside of the contract. For Locke, the government is bound by the contract. Locke's social contract is like when you hire someone to do work for you. You dictate the terms, and the people hired to do the work perform based on the terms of the contract. Government serves the people in Locke's social contract. We agree to hand over some of our rights and freedoms to the government in exchange for the convenience of having government administer justice and handle the running of daily life on our behalf. The role of government, then, is to defend people's natural rights. Locke was blind to the rights of working people, women, and minorities to be involved in government, but he did state that one role of government was to protect the powerless from abuse. Ensuring social stability for the working class was essential to peace and stability for the nation.

Locke's Right to Revolt

How does the labor theory of property relate to the right to revolt against a king? It transforms the idea of government. For Locke, government is a convenience. It is not necessary, and it is not divinely ordained. Rational people established government because they find it preferable to live in a society rather than in a state of nature. Hobbes viewed the social contract as among the people—"I surrender my rights, if you surrender yours, and we hand over all rights to the sovereign." Locke viewed the social contract as between the people and the government—"we appoint you to rule as long as you serve our interests." This difference in vision explains why Locke can accept revolt against the monarch, but Hobbes cannot. For Locke, if the monarch, or government in general, breaks the terms of the social contract, they have lost any right to remain in government. The people have a right to replace them. In fact, Locke argued that, to preserve society, revolt against tyranny was not only the right but also the duty of every person.

Locke was no anarchist. He believed in morality, laws, and that people should obey authority and keep the peace within a society. Nevertheless, he asserts that there is a right to resist unjust authority and in the last resort to rebel against and overthrow that authority. Just as you would fire someone you hired who proved to be corrupt or incompetent, a people should fire rulers who proved to be corrupt or incompetent. The basis of sovereignty is the law. A ruler is not above the law; therefore, a ruler can be fired. People have a right to change rulers when they see fit.

Locke wrote *Two Treatises of Government* in response to the Glorious Revolution of 1688. This revolution was purely political and served the interests of a group of wealthy British landowners. Locke was part of that group, as an employee of Shaftesbury. Locke's primary purpose in his book was to provide philosophical justification for the act of treason committed by his allies. This is why he uses his labor theory of property to explain why the king has no inherent rights to the land but does not extend the right of property to the people lower in social class than the aristocracy. It is also why Locke's formula of the primary law of nature is that no one ought to harm another in his life, liberty, or *possessions*. Only later, in the United States, was this formula changed from "possessions" to "pursuit of happiness."

To be fair to Locke, his political philosophy contains more than a rationale for revolt. He was genuinely interested in how government can be structured to be stable and serve the interests of the people. The government, in Locke's conception, should have a separation of powers split into three branches, the roles of each being clearly delineated by a written constitution. The legislative branch had supreme power and had the ultimate authority over how the force of the state should be used. The executive branch was in charge of enforcing laws and how they are applied to specific cases. The federative power was to act internationally according to the law of nature. The United States, in establishing its form of government ninety years later, patterned its basic structure after Locke's ideas; this, after justifying its revolt against the king by referencing Locke.

Locke's faults and blindness aside, we can't dismiss the importance of his political philosophy. The basic ideas that there is a social contract between the people and their government, that government exists to serve the people, that government should be divided and limited by a constitution, and that government should enforce the laws on behalf of the powerless are ideas that are now central to our notion of a democratic society. Locke is an example of how terms such as "liberal" and "conservative" are relative to their time and place. Locke's ideas were, for his time, liberal. For our time, because they do not extend rights to the working class, women, and minorities, his ideas would be considered conservative.

Radical Political Critique

The social contract theories of Hobbes and Locke established the template for political philosophy for the next few centuries. That does not mean that some philosophers didn't step outside of the template to develop philosophies that radically challenged the prevailing assumptions of philosophy and wider society. Two very different philosophers of the 1700s—Jean-Jacques Rousseau and Mary Wollstonecraft—each in his or her own way fiercely critiqued society. We'll also look at the philosophical issues that underpinned the radical experiment in government known as the United States of America.

Jean-Jacques Rousseau's General Will

Frenchman **Jean-Jacques Rousseau** (1712–1778) gets short shrift from many, but his philosophy was incredibly influential. His influence was mostly in France, however, which partially explains why he gets little attention in the English-speaking world. The other reason for the lack of attention is that his political philosophy was more or less a disaster when it was put into practice.

Rousseau has been called a "militant lowbrow" because he railed against what we consider "highbrow" culture. Rousseau's targets included science, religion, the arts, education, government—basically everything we would call "civilization." Others, like Thomas Paine who we'll meet later in this chapter, described the 1700s as "The Age of Reason" and "The Enlightenment," denoting their self-satisfaction with what they saw as humanity's progress in the modern age. Rousseau vehemently disagreed and offers us a challenge: Who are we? Why do we assume that our progress in philosophy, science, and technology is an improvement?

The quick version of Rousseau's philosophy is summed up in his book, *The Social Contract* (1762):

> Man is born free; and everywhere is in chains. One thinks himself the master of others, and still remains a greater slave than they. How did this change come about? I do not know. What can make it legitimate? That question I think I can answer.... But the social order is a sacred right which is the basis of all other rights. Nevertheless, this right does not come from nature, and must therefore be founded on conventions. (*The Social Contract*, I.I.1-2)

(Note: Rousseau's use of "man" excludes women, whom he thought should remain "passive and weak.") By the "social order," he meant what Hobbes meant by "social conventions": the class structure of society and the many related expectations of how people should behave. France was a hierarchical society in Rousseau's time; a king, a small aristocracy, and the masses of common people. Everyone knew their place in the hierarchy because social recognition norms taught people what was expected from them and what to expect from others (we'll talk more about recognition norms in Chapter 17). That set of social relations was what made France a civilized society. But Rousseau saw civilized society as a prison. Its structure of social norms chained people, restricting their true expression.

Rousseau complained that social norms encouraged people to obsessively concentrate on the approval of others to maintain their social status. This social pressure created in people the artificial state of *amour-*

propre. Rousseau picked up the concept of *amour-propre* (literally "self-love") from the French moralist **François VI, Duc de La Rochefoucauld** (1613–1680). François, a contemporary of Descartes, was also raised on Thomist Scholasticism and was familiar with Augustine, who had condemned love of self, "*amour de soi,*" as the vice of making oneself more important than God. François added to Augustine's *amour de soi* the idea that, motivated by love of self, people seek the approval of others. We are, in fact, so desirous of the approval of others that we put up a public front to cast ourselves in a flattering light, highlighting our positives and hiding our negatives, to win that approval. Being familiar with the French royal court, François saw how courtiers would go to great lengths to gain prestige and status.

This pursuit, despite being motivated by self-interest, actually causes people to forget their true nature and misjudge their behavior. "We are so used to disguising ourselves from others that we end by disguising ourselves from ourselves." (François, Duc de La Rochefoucauld, *Maxims*, Maxim 11). This excessive desire for esteem, François terms "*amour-propre*." The concept helps him explain why we behave as we do and why we are blind to why we behave as we do.

Rousseau took the concept further and defined *amour propre* as our constant desire for the approval and esteem that must come from others. This, he argued, was not natural self-love, or *amour de soi*, which Rousseau, in sharp contrast to Augustine, saw as positive. Rousseau claimed that *amour-propre* was an artificial creation of civilization that caused in individuals a false need to compare themselves with one another to gain social status. He claimed that *amour de soi* was compatible with happiness but that *amour-propre* corrupted individuals and led to misery and vice. Rousseau saw *amour de soi* as difficult, if not impossible, within civilized society, which is dominated by the pressure to conform to social norms.

Civilized man is born and dies a slave, Rousseau wrote in his book, *Emile, or On Education* (1762). All his life, man is imprisoned by institutions. Man is naturally good, and in the state of nature we can live organically in unity with each other and ourselves. In nature, we are savage but noble, happy and with goodwill toward others. Civilization is harmful; its nature is corrupt. Imprisoned within it, we are forced to compete with others for esteem and status. We are deceitful to each other and to ourselves, alienated from our true nature. Our greatest evils, Rousseau says, flow from ourselves. Trapped together in society, alienated and confused, we are all in chains.

You may ask (as you should), how does this convert into a political philosophy? Well, that was the problem. As much as he'd like to see civilization swept away and ended, he understood it was not that simple. He settled for a lesser evil. The short version is that Rousseau, like Hobbes and Locke, adopted the concept of a social contract. Rousseau, however, had no tangible concept by which he could unite society under a contractual bond. So, in his book, *The Social Contract* (1762), he put forward the tenuous concept of the "general will"—a difficult combination of total political freedom with strong authoritarianism.

Rousseau's version of the social contract also begins with the state of nature. He believed that in the state of nature, which he meant more literally than did Hobbes and Locke, an individual's will would be allowed to express itself freely. Society was a prison; nature was freedom. Rousseau pointed to an idealized vision of the indigenous populations of North America, whom the French had come to know in their explorations of what is now Canada. Indigenous societies seemed to the French explorers to be less rigidly structured than was French society, its people more at peace with the land and with themselves. It was the myth of the "noble savage," a person of dignity free from the social constraints of class hierarchy and war. Rousseau thought that if we were more free, as the indigenous peoples of North America are, we would be happier. This was his rough idea of the state of nature.

People in the state of nature desired a higher moral freedom, Rousseau claimed, so they agreed to give up all of their powers to the community, so that the superior general will could emerge. The general will is the abstract expression of what is best for all, as if the society were one individual. The idea is similar to Hobbes's sovereign as the embodiment of all. Rousseau, however, does not reduce the will of all to one man but considers the body politic as the sovereign. (*The Social Contract,* I.VII.3) Also like Hobbes's sovereign, the collective general will is the sole source of sovereignty to which each individual must subjugate himself or herself. The general will produces a higher moral freedom because it transcends special interests to establish a moral framework that serves the community as a whole.

Because the general will is not one man, as Hobbes proposed, Rousseau adds that the general will is determined by individual participation—no elected representatives. That is because any legislative body would create a false general will of its own, separate from the whole community's will. Good laws make for good citizens, but good laws can be willed only by good citizens, and laws are legitimate only if they are agreed on by the common assembly of citizens. Rousseau believed that through public debate and voting, disagreements that arose from individual opinions would cancel each other out. What is left is the general will. Everyone was required to obey that general will as the law of the land. In this way, everyone develops within a framework of equality under the law.

It did not work. Rousseau's basic idea of the general will was implemented in the early years of the French Revolution but was beset by multiple difficulties. Rousseau said that individuals are still free to pursue their own desires as long as they continue to obey the general will, but where that line was between individual freedom and the sovereignty of the general will was unclear. The question of who decided what the general will of the people was also unclear. The French Revolution, at first so confident that it would improve the lot of humanity, slid into a morass of self-serving petty disputes. A bloodbath ensued, which came to be known as the "Reign of Terror" (1793–1794). In a few years, Napoleon grabbed power and plunged all of Europe and most of the world into decades of total war. It would be unfair to blame it all on Rousseau, but in contrast, the American Revolution was philosophically based on Locke's version of the social contract, and that turned out a bit better. These revolutions weren't entirely about philosophy, but philosophy did have a part in them both.

Mary Wollstonecraft and the Birth of Feminism

A woman! Yes, finally we are discussing a female philosopher. Not because we are now censoring female philosophers but because women were censored back then. In many countries, prior to the 2000s, women were legally forbidden from publishing books. So, although women were every bit as intelligent and thoughtful as men (perhaps more so), we do not know about them. Women's voices were silenced throughout history (and still today are not as fully accepted as are men's voices).

Mary Wollstonecraft (1759–1797) was vividly aware of these facts. She refused to accept the secondary status to which society had relegated women. Wollstonecraft's central idea was that all human beings have God-given abilities and rights and, *very* importantly, that these abilities and rights are shared by *both* men and women. Yes, feminism is the radical idea that women are human beings (see Chapter 18). And I am not being funny. That is an accurate description of what Wollstonecraft was doing with her 1792 book, *A Vindication of the Rights of Woman.*

The dominant idea then and since the beginning of civilization had been that women lacked the capacity to be rational and therefore could not do philosophy or be leaders. Aristotle was a big believer in this idea—women were lesser humans too weak-minded to reason. One of the few philosophers who thought otherwise was Descartes, who had a long intellectual correspondence with Princess Elisabeth of Bohemia, and he supported her efforts to publish her ideas on philosophy, which she did. (Elisabeth, despite her talents, made no significant contributions to the history of philosophy, so she is not included in this book—we can only cover so many—and hundreds of male philosophers are left out for the same reason.) Wollstonecraft was adamant that women have every bit the rational capacity that men have.

Wollstonecraft's political philosophy matches well with Locke's, and she was greatly influenced by him. Locke wasn't as anti-woman as most philosophers were, but he was no feminist. Neither was **Edmund Burke** (1729–1797), who was also influenced by Locke but took a different direction to which Wollstonecraft objected. Burke is known as the father of conservatism as a political philosophy. He believed in natural law, as did Locke and Wollstonecraft. What Burke did with natural law, though, is to say that what happens in the world is an expression of how things should be. One of Burke's arguments is that we should not question tradition because if society has been doing things a certain way for many years it must be because people long ago figured out that is the best way to do things. That is basically why Burke opposed the French Revolution and its efforts to change society.

Wollstonecraft's fame and reputation began with her 1790 book, *A Vindication of the Rights of Men* (in a gender inclusive sense), a critical response to Edmund Burke's *Reflections on the Revolution.* Burke had launched a conservative attack on the French Revolution and its calls for radical social and political change, including eliminating the monarchy. He defended social tradition and custom in general, and specifically the institutions of the monarchy and aristocracy. Wollstonecraft was of exactly the opposite opinion about the French Revolution, mainly because of its idea that women should be equal to men. Wollstonecraft saw the French Revolution as a necessary rational response to the corruption of the French absolute monarchy. Wollstonecraft embraced the new ideals of progress and social reform. She turned Burke's arguments back on him and exposed the inconsistencies in his position. For example, she pointed out that logically, because Burke is such a staunch defender of tradition, he should be opposed to Jesus, a radical who broke with Jewish tradition. Similarly, she noted that Burke, a Protestant, should oppose the Protestant Reformation that rebelled against Catholicism. Furthermore, she observes that the American war for independence, which Burke supported, could not be supported if he was true to his stated principles.

Wollstonecraft adopted the then emerging view that humans have natural, God-given rights:

> It is necessary emphatically to repeat, that there are rights which [people] inherit at their birth as rational creatures, who were raised above the brute creation by their improvable faculties; and that, in receiving these, not from their forefathers but, from God, prescription can never undermine natural rights. (*A Vindication of the Rights of Men,* ¶31)

These natural rights precede the social conventions of rights obtained through inheritance or the privileges of one's place in the social structure.

Throughout *Rights of Men*, Wollstonecraft condemns the tradition of hereditary privilege and the inequalities of the class system and social structure of England. She argues that people should be judged on their individual merits rather than on who their family is. Following Locke's labor theory of property (that ownership of land and products is acquired through one's own labor) and against Burke's justification of inherited wealth, Wollstonecraft says,

> The only security of property that nature authorizes and reason sanctions is, the right a man has to enjoy the acquisitions which his talents and industry have acquired; and to bequeath them to whom he chooses. (*Rights of Men*, ¶62)

Burke's central argument was that political traditions of England had been tested for centuries and thus should be accepted and that radical social and political change should be rejected. Wollstonecraft countered that no government or constitution was above rational reassessment because all human institutions are unavoidably imperfect.

Wollstonecraft followed up in 1792 with her most famous book, *A Vindication of the Rights of Woman*. This book extended her ideas and responded to Rousseau's. One of Rousseau's themes is the question of nature versus nurture: How much of our character and behavior are produced by nature and is inherent to us versus how much of our character and behavior are nurtured and learned through our upbringing and socialization? Pretty much everyone in the 1700s believed that there were fundamental, inherent differences between men and women (and upper and lower classes). This assumption, coupled with the concept of natural law, presupposed that it was simply natural for women to be kept in a status subordinate to men.

This assumption of a natural order of the sexes is the object of Wollstonecraft's strongest ire. She argues that women have the same human nature as men and that women should aspire to the same standard of virtue.

> But I still insist that not only the virtue, but the knowledge of the two sexes should be the same in nature, if not in degree, and that women, considered not only as moral, but rational creatures, ought to endeavor to acquire human virtues (or perfections) by the same means as men, instead of being educated like a fanciful kind of half being. (*A Vindication of the Rights of Woman*, 3.4)

Wollstonecraft argues that the differences between men and women are strictly the artificial result of men keeping women subordinated and preventing women from fulfilling their potential, a potential that was the same as that of men. The issue was how women are socialized and deprived of education and opportunities.

Wollstonecraft condemns the view of Rousseau and others as believing that woman "was created to be the toy of man, his rattle, and it must jingle in his ears whenever, dismissing reason, he chooses to be amused." (*Rights of Woman*, 2.58) She also chastises women for accepting the male-created false ideal of femininity that dictates who and how women are supposed to be. Wollstonecraft decries how "Gentleness, docility, and a spaniel-like affection are...consistently recommended as the cardinal virtues of the [female] sex." (*Rights of Woman*, 2.58) Girls are from birth indoctrinated to embrace these ideals, even by older women: "The civilized women of the present century, with a few exceptions, are only anxious to inspire love, when they ought to cherish a nobler ambition, and by their abilities and virtues exact respect." (*Rights of Woman*, Introduction.1) Women, Wollstonecraft said, are the equals of men in their natural capacities and should claim that as their God-given right.

Wollstonecraft sees reason as what defines human beings. On this point, she agreed with most philosophers, but in sharp contrast to them, she sees women and men as possessing equal capacity for reason. Since men and women have the same natural human nature, any social structure that prevents women from fully and freely developing their talents is irrational and unjust. Wollstonecraft declares that women deserve full equality and that society harms itself by depriving women of equality in education. She points out that women are the primary educators of children and, therefore, it is important to educate all mothers. She further calls for a reform of marriage. Women, she says, should not be mere ornaments or property of men. Educated women should be equal companions of their husbands, and, in this, both spouses would benefit.

One of Wollstonecraft's ideas was to challenge everyone that if we as a society treated girls the way we treat boys—teach girls like we teach boys that they can reason—women would equal or surpass men. Wollstonecraft argued that women should not be restricted to particular professions; with the proper education, women can contribute to society in traditionally male professions such as medicine, business, politics, or farming. This issue of occupational fairness is a challenge that even today our society has not fully met. For example, less than one-quarter of philosophy faculty in the United States are women. It is better in Europe, but women are still underrepresented. It is worse in many areas of science and engineering with women constituting as low as one-tenth of faculty. It is because, as Wollstonecraft said more than 200 years ago, we raise girls differently than we raise boys. In the language of today, we raise everyone to be sexist.

Alas, not surprisingly, Wollstonecraft's arguments were rejected by the men who dominated society. Nevertheless, her arguments on the social benefits of the rights of women were taken up years later by John Stuart Mill and his wife Harriet (see Chapter 10). Oh, and worth mentioning: Mary Wollstonecraft had a daughter, Mary, who became the author of a famous novel called *Frankenstein*.

The American Experiment

Hobbes and Locke had considered the question of whether it was acceptable to rebel against the monarch. Hobbes had said almost never, and Locke had said yes, if the circumstances justified it. Locke's position was known to a number of well-to-do intellectuals in the American colonies, and they took it to heart. Locke provided an intellectual justification for the colonies' rebellion against the British Empire, its monarch, and its parliament. The movement toward independence of the United States of America from the British Empire had multiple influences, but we can pick out, in addition to Locke, two major philosophical influences and one significant philosopher who directly inspired the revolution.

Colonialism had altered the economic dynamic and resulted in increased tensions between nobles and monarchs and the growing importance of trade between the colonies and the home nations. These changes were intensified in the North American colonies for two reasons. These colonies were far removed from the seat of empire, and they were far more populated than other colonies with European, mostly British, settlers who took not just resources but land from the natives. These two factors developed in the colonial settlers an attitude that eventually was called "Manifest Destiny"—the idea that providence had ordained that all of North America should become the property of European settlers.

The attitude of destiny fueling settler colonialism tied in with the second philosophical influence. We have seen in previous chapters the gradual move toward accepting the ability of individuals to reason to truth independently. By the 1700s, this acceptance was commonplace among the learned middle class, which was growing as a result of the economic changes. The idea grew of the "self-taught man" (women were still excluded) who could learn for himself, think for himself, and rule himself.

Thomas Paine (1737–1809) had his finger on the pulse of these changes. A strong advocate for American independence and a sharp-witted writer, he wrote "Common Sense," an appeal to individuals to reason for themselves. His assumption was that anyone who could think clearly could realize that the American colonies should be independent from England. In "Common Sense," Paine presented philosophical arguments directed at the common person.

Paine was clearly influenced by Locke's political theory and similarly argued that government was a convenience established by rational people who find it preferable to live in a society than in a state of nature. He also adopted Locke's notion that people had a right to rebel against the government if the situation justified it. Given these two notions, Paine's task was to show that the situation justified the colonies rebelling against England. Simply stated, he portrayed George III and the English nobility as rulers who contributed nothing to the people. The very idea of a monarchy is false, he argued, because all men are created equal (as long as they were white). The colonies must declare independence and elect their own government that would serve the common interests of the people. The American revolt against England came about predominantly for economic reasons, but there is no denying the philosophical underpinning for the movement for greater self-determination. These three philosophers inspired not only their eras, but political philosophers in more recent times, as will see in later chapters.

Chapter 7

QUESTIONING EPISTEMOLOGY'S ASSUMPTIONS

By the 1700s, the optimism of modernity, or the Enlightenment, had taken hold in Europe and the United States. Loosely defined, the Enlightenment worldview is that there is one true picture of reality that humans can know through reason and science. This is a worldview that originated in the 1600s with people like Francis Bacon, but especially with René Descartes and this concept of the rational knowing mind as the source and ultimate judge of all ideas. Both Bacon and Descartes had optimistically predicted that once human beings start to think perfectly, rationally, and deliberately they would know everything, literally everything—all human problems would be solved, all knowledge of the universe would be understood—all through the use of calculated logic, reason, and the scientific method. A large number of scientific discoveries and technological advancements gave credence to the optimism of the Enlightenment, but not everyone was completely convinced that science and observation were so easy.

George Berkeley—Matter Doesn't Matter

As you are reading this, are you sitting down? On what are you sitting? A chair, probably. Of what is the chair made? Wood? Plastic? Metal? A combination? And what does science, and common sense, tell us that these things we call "wood," "plastic," and "metal" are? We say that all of these things are matter. Wood, plastic, metal, and things like chairs that are made from them, we say are all made of matter. Since Aristotle and on through Locke, everyone has believed in matter, and not just philosophers; everyone assumes that the objects of the world are made of matter. Irish thinker **George Berkeley** (1685–1753) asks a simple and surprising question: why do we assume matter exists?

The philosophy of George Berkeley (pronounced BARK-lee) is often misunderstood and unfairly mischaracterized. Because he was a cleric, eventually a bishop, some people who are hostile to religion irrationally dismiss Berkeley's argument as religious nonsense. Such dismissal is intellectually dishonest. Berkeley's argument is solid and important philosophy that presents us with a dilemma that we cannot easily dismiss.

His argument strikes at the core of our assumptions, calling into question how we perceive the universe and what it actually is.

Exposing Our Unthinking Assumptions

Berkeley took Descartes's method of questioning and turned it on Locke's empirical philosophy. His first target was Locke's theory of general ideas. Berkeley agrees with Locke that all of our knowledge comes from ideas that come from experience. As mentioned in Chapter 5, British empiricist philosophers used terms slightly differently. Berkeley uses the term "ideas" similarly to how Locke used it, but because Berkeley's focus was on what lay behind our experiences, "ideas" in his writing refers to experiences rather than concepts. For example, when Berkeley writes about our idea of fire, he refers to our experience of the light and warmth of fire not our concept of fire. That is important, as we shall soon see.

In the introduction to his book, *A Treatise Concerning the Principles of Human Knowledge (1710)*, Berkeley first dismisses the Platonic idea that Forms exist separate from objects.

> It is agreed on all hands, that the qualities or modes of things do never really exist each of them apart by itself, and separated from all others, but are mixed, as it were, and blended together, several in the same object. (*Principles* Introduction, 7)

On that point, he agrees with Locke. Berkeley then takes on Locke's concept that we have abstract ideas and that we can hold in our minds the quality "green" or "motion" abstracted from any particular object.

> But we are told, the mind being able to consider each quality singly, or abstracted from those other qualities with which it is united, does by that means frame to itself abstract ideas. . . . Not that it is possible for color or motion to exist without extension: but only that the mind can frame to itself by abstraction the idea of color exclusive of extension, and of motion exclusive of both color and extension. (*Principles* Introduction 7)

We saw Locke make this argument that qualities exist only in, not separate from, objects but that we can think about them as abstract ideas. Locke claimed that we experience a number of green objects and abstract from those experiences the idea of "green." Similarly, we experience a number of dogs, and in thinking about dogs in general, we hold in our minds an abstract idea of "dog" without a particular size, color, or other qualities.

Locke's mistake, Berkeley said, was in deriving the objective existence of primary qualities through a principle of abstraction. This principle,

Berkeley argued, was false. Berkeley critiques Locke's account of abstract ideas with two arguments: we can't do it, and we don't need to do it.

The first argument, that you can't think of an abstract idea, is simple: try thinking of the abstract idea of "dog." If you are honest with yourself, what comes to your mind is not an abstract dog of no particular size, color, and so on, as Locke had said. What comes to mind when you think of "dog" is a particular dog; maybe a dog you have or once had or one you saw recently. You focused on an image of a particular dog, which stands as a general idea for all dogs. This may seem a subtle distinction, but a general idea differs from an abstract idea. A general idea is a particular idea that stands as an example of a type of object. Whenever we think of such concepts as "tree," "dog," "person," or "green," Berkeley said, we are holding in our minds a particular idea that stands for all other similar objects.

We can really see Berkeley's point when we think of broad concepts like "animal" or "color." We can't hold in our minds an idea of an animal that abstracts all of the qualities that particular birds, fish, lizards, mammals, and so on have in common and ignore their many individual differences. How many wings and legs would this abstract animal have, and what size would it be? Similarly, how can we think of color as having no particular color? We can't; we think of a particular animal or a particular color.

Berkeley points out that the very idea of an abstract idea is inconsistent. He quotes Locke's abstract idea of a triangle, an idea that "must be neither oblique nor rectangle, neither equilateral, isosceles, nor scalene, but *all and none* of these at once" (Locke, *Essay* II.IV.7). Berkeley counters that such a thing is inconceivable because it is contradictory. A triangle is equilateral, isosceles, or scalene. It can't be all of them. It can't be none of them. To be a triangle, it has to be one of those three.

Where Berkeley seems to make a mistake is to assume that if we have an idea without specifying a particular quality—such as the idea of an animal of no specific color—that means we are thinking of an object that lacks that quality—an animal with no color. True, an animal with no color is nonsensical, but is that what we are doing when we think of what is common among all animals? Are we ever denying that animals have color? What Berkeley does not take into account is that we can have a concept about objects that is separate from a particular idea of a particular object. For example, we can think of the idea that animals are life-forms that possess specific qualities that differentiate them from plants, without needing to think of a particular animal with a particular color.

Berkeley's stronger second argument, that we do not need abstract ideas, harkens back to William's nominalism. As almost everyone did by that time, Locke believed that only particulars exist, not universals, Platonic Forms having been widely dismissed. Berkeley says that we only ever encounter particular entities, never abstract entities. As he showed in his first argument, we think in terms of particular ideas. These particular ideas can function as general ideas, but they are always particulars. What, then, are words? Berkeley says that "it seems that a word becomes general by being made the sign, not of an abstract general idea but, of several particular ideas, any one of which it indifferently suggests to the mind" (*Principles*, Introduction 11). Words like "tree" or "dog" stand in general for all the particular ideas we have for trees or dogs in general. The principle of Ockham's razor holds that the simpler of two explanations is more probably true. Following this principle, Berkeley holds, as William had, that words are signs that we use to denote objects or kinds of objects; they are not entities that exist outside our minds. There is no need to postulate that there are abstract ideas.

Rethinking Primary and Secondary Qualities

Armed with his disproof of abstract ideas, Berkeley turned his sights on Locke's theory of primary and secondary qualities. Locke had said that primary qualities exist in objects themselves, whereas secondary qualities are powers that external objects possess to produce ideas that reside in us. This, Berkeley argued, was a fiction. Berkeley offered multiple arguments demonstrating that both primary and secondary qualities exist only within the perceiving mind. For brevity, we'll look only at two—the perceptions of pain and of color.

Locke had argued that pain and pleasure were secondary qualities because these sensations existed in the perceiver, not in the objects. A fire can cause us pain if we stick our hand in it, but we would not say that the pain is first in the fire; the pain is only in our perception. Pleasure is the same. Food gives us feelings of pleasure, but we would not say those feelings are present in the food, only within us. Berkeley answers that pain and pleasure must exist only when they are perceived, only when they are experienced by a mind. That means that every quality that is experienced as a pain or pleasure (temperature, smell, taste) exists only when it is perceived.

You can reply with the reasonable objection that heat exists in the external object and that this causes pain in us. Berkeley's equally reasonable response is that heat does exist external to us, but the many responses it produces in us exist only within us, the perceiver. We experience temperature as a range of sensations corresponding to a range of pain and pleasure—too hot, too cold, and just right. That includes the distinct sensation of intense heat *as* pain.

Berkeley also examines our perceptions of color, which Locke and others had labeled a secondary quality. Berkeley uses color to argue that we cannot separate our ideas of primary and secondary qualities because we always perceive them together. We never perceive green all by itself. We perceive green grass, green leaves, green shirts, and other green things. If, as Locke says, color and other secondary qualities are mind dependent and do not inhere in objects themselves, then the same must be the case for primary qualities we perceive like size and shape. Here's an example.

Consider this black circle. How wide is it? Width is a primary quality, right? You can measure it, and it is an objective quality of the object, yes? So how would you measure the width of the circle? You'd need a measuring device—a ruler, but how would you use that ruler to measure the circle's width? You say you would place the zero mark on your ruler at one edge of the circle and measure to the other edge, yes? Great! So how do you know where the edge of the circle is? The edge would be where the color changes, correct? The edge is where the black stops. But color is a secondary quality. It's mind dependent, Locke says. But if the only way we can perceive the width of the circle is by the secondary quality of color, how is width not also mind dependent?

The same is true of every object we perceive through the sense of sight. Look at the walls of the room you are in. This example has long worked well for me in classrooms, which invariably are uniformly painted a dull off-white. I ask the students where the corners of the room are. They can see where one wall ends and another begins by the subtle differences in shading of the off-white color. You can see this is the case in any room. Even if we accept the explanation that those differences are caused by the different ways that light reflects off the walls, we still are judging where the walls meet on the basis of color. Our experiences of colors and, thus, of walls and ceilings, and circles, and every object are mind-dependent secondary qualities. At least, that's Berkeley's argument, and it's difficult to say he's incorrect.

When we analyze our concepts in our minds and our language, Berkeley argued, we will see that the "curtain of words" deceives us. Like Bacon did (see Chapter 4), Berkeley holds that we put too much faith in our language and that our words obscure what is going on behind them. In the case of Locke's abstract ideas, the words used to stand for those ideas, like "color" and "texture," seem to indicate a reality. Berkeley counters that when we remove the idol of the words, we see that there are really no distinctions between primary and secondary qualities and no such things as abstract ideas.

Well, if we accept Berkeley's claim that there is no distinction between primary and secondary qualities, we can still trust that our ideas of primary qualities are representations of the objects, right? Here, too, Berkeley has a compelling argument to refute Locke's argument. It's actually Locke's argument, or rather Locke's admission, that Berkeley justifiably leverages against Locke. We saw in Chapter 5 that we cannot leave the sealed chamber of our mind to compare our ideas with objects in the world. Berkeley correctly points out that if we can perceive only our own ideas, then Locke has no basis for claiming that our ideas resemble the primary qualities of objects because he cannot compare the two.

Matter Doesn't Matter

Having exposed our assumptions about abstract ideas and primary qualities, George Berkeley asks a simple question. Why do we assume matter exists? Matter had always been assumed. Locke equated matter with the abstract idea of substance. Substance is a definite weak spot in Locke's philosophy, and Locke was aware of it. He said that objects must be composed of a something-I-know-not-what that we cannot perceive but must be the real essence of an object and its primary qualities that cause the simple ideas of sensation in our minds. Locke assumed this something-I-know-not-what was matter. Locke had to concede that we never have an experience of matter but only of the effects of matter on us.

As we've seen, Berkeley argued that both primary and secondary qualities exist only when they are perceived. Not surprisingly, then, Berkeley also argues that all external objects that people assume to be composed of matter exist only when they are perceived.

> It is indeed an opinion *strangely* prevailing amongst men, that houses, mountains, rivers, and in a word all sensible objects have an existence natural or real, distinct from their being perceived by the understanding. But with how great an assurance and acquiescence soever this principle may be entertained in the world; yet whoever shall find in his heart to call it in question, may, if I mistake not, perceive it to involve a manifest contradiction. For what are the forementioned objects but the things we perceive by sense, and what do we *perceive besides our own ideas or sensations*; and is it not plainly repugnant that any one of these or any combination of them should exist unperceived? (*Principles* 4, emphasis his)

Yes, the only things we perceive are our own ideas. Locke said as much. Berkeley is willing to accept the full consequences of this, even though they lead to an extreme conclusion: matter does not exist.

Berkeley argued that Locke's idea of substance was a conclusion relying on an abstraction that close scrutiny would reveal to be a mistake.

Locke held that there is a "real" tree with primary qualities and material substance that cause simple ideas of sensation in us, but we cannot perceive this "real" tree. Berkeley responds that if substance is a something-I-know-not-what, then why should we assume its existence? We can't say that our sensations of the tree correspond to a "real" tree because we can't compare our ideas with external objects. Instead, Berkeley states that our ideas of a tree are not representations caused by a "real" tree beneath appearances. Our ideas of the tree are the real tree. He asks how an idea could resemble something that is not an idea.

Where does our idea of matter come from? Berkeley asks. We have no sensations of matter, something to which Locke has to agree. We also have to agree. **Samuel Johnson** (1709–1784), a learned man of the time, said he refuted Berkeley by kicking a stone, making the assumption that his material foot kicked a material stone thus proving matter exists. But that's a specious objection. Johnson can say no more than that he has an idea of a foot and an idea of a stone and an idea that they interacted. If you kick a stone, what does that prove? You experience the idea of solidity of the stone in your foot and the idea of the stone moving. Ideas. A series of sensations. It doesn't at all disprove Berkeley's philosophy. All we have are ideas and beliefs about our ideas. We can't demonstrate otherwise.

We never, ever experience matter, and, in fact, we have no need to assume that matter exists. Nowhere is Berkeley suggesting that there is no mind-independent reality. He is questioning the philosophical conception of matter, not the existence of a world outside our mind. However, Berkeley says the idea of substance is a mistake as are the ideas of universals. You probably dismissed Plato's idea that universal Forms exist, right? Here's why we should dismiss the idea of matter. Berkeley argues that the essence of objects is that they are perceived.

> Attend to what is meant by the term "exist," when applied to sensible things. The table I write on I say exists, that is, I see and feel it; and if I were out of my study I should say it existed—meaning thereby that if I was in my study I might perceive it, or that some other spirit actually does perceive it. There was an odor, that is, it was smelt; there was a sound, that is, it was heard; a color or figure, and it was perceived by sight or touch. This is all that I can understand by these and the like expressions. For as to what is said of the absolute existence of unthinking things without any relation to their being perceived, that seems perfectly unintelligible. Their ESSE is PERCIPI (their essence is being perceived), nor is it possible they should have any existence out of the minds or [of the] thinking things which perceive them. (*Principles* 3)

The essence of any object is not composed of material substance, as Aristotle had assumed and everyone since had gone along with. The essence of any object is to be perceived or known. "All those bodies which compose the mighty frame of the world, have not any subsistence without a mind, that their BEING (ESSE) is to be perceived or known" (*Principles* 6). Thus, Berkeley concluded that "*esse est percipi*"—"to be is to be perceived."

Think about this. If you are in a classroom, think about your bedroom at home. If you are at home, think about your classroom. If you are not in a room, why do you think that room and the things in it exist? What basis do you have to believe that any particular thing exists if you are not currently perceiving it? You would reply "because when I go to that room, I can perceive those things" or "because other people can perceive those things when I don't." That's correct, and you prove Berkeley's point. We believe that something exists only if someone perceives it. (Yes, even nonmaterial things, but that's another topic.) You go home because you believe that you will perceive home once you get there. You come back to a classroom because you believe you will be able to perceive what is in that room once you are there. The essence of existence is being perceived. Matter doesn't matter; being perceived does.

What Causes Our Ideas? Berkeley's Simple Solution

Here's the thing. If matter doesn't actually exist, but something nonmaterial is causing these ideas we have of objects, how would our experiences be different? The answer is—not at all. You are reading this, either as a paper book or as an e-book on a screen. Either way, all you have are your perceptions of these words. All that exists for you are your ideas about these words. You don't know what, if anything, exists behind the appearance of words.

The same is true for everything. Take a table or desk. Why do you believe it exists? Well, to simplify things, let's take the top of a table. You believe it's a tabletop because when you perceive your hand touching it, you perceive qualities like flatness and hardness. But that is *all* you perceive—ideas of those qualities. You don't perceive what causes those ideas. What that cause is does not matter; the sensations you experience would be the same.

Interestingly, unlike Hobbes and Locke, Berkeley believes we have an active mind. One knows that one causes some of one's own ideas, Berkeley says (*Principles* 28), and that is important for Berkeley: minds create ideas. However, the mind is also passive when perceiving external objects, so there are ideas that one's own mind does not cause. But ideas can exist only within a mind—to be is to be perceived. Therefore, Berkeley concludes, only another mind can be a cause of objects that exist outside of our mind. "There is therefore some other will or spirit that produces them" (*Principles* 29).

This, for Berkeley, is where God comes in. It's not an argument like Descartes using the idea of God as a prop for a larger argument. It's more akin to the arguments of Plato, Plotinus, and Augustine—God as the source of all existence and understanding. Everything that exists is ideas in the cosmic mind. Berkeley's basic principle of "*esse est percipi*" ("to be is to be perceived") requires a "first perceiver" or cosmic mind to be the cause of all existing objects that we can experience. It oversimplifies things a bit to say that we are all living inside the mind of God, but that's not too far off. Your bedroom exists even when you are not there because God is everywhere and is continually perceiving everything, keeping everything in existence. God's perception is different from ours, of course. Berkeley drew on two by then widely accepted notions—(1) the primacy of will over intellect and (2) that any will or choice must have a cognitive component, an idea, that gives content to the will or choice. Thus, Berkeley can assert, compatible with the philosophy of his time, that God in willing the world is holding an idea of the world, thus creating it and everything in it.

Berkeley's idealism (everything is thought) perhaps sounds weird, but it shares the same foundation with quantum mechanics, which posits that reality is dependent on the observer. We will see a similar philosophy from Johann Gottlieb Fichte in Chapter 9. A current philosophical conundrum is the suggestion that we are all living in a simulation created by a gigantic computer. It is a clichéd science fiction trope, but some philosophers and physicists discuss the idea seriously. This conundrum is just a technology-based version of Berkeley's argument, replacing the concept of God with the concept of a computer simulation.

It is important to remember that Berkeley is not at all denying that there is an external reality. His theory is an attempt not to multiply entities needlessly, according to Ockham's razor. The application of his theory works in two ways—in categorizing reality and in explaining human perception. Descartes had concluded that there exist two types of substances—mental (our mind) and material (our body). Berkeley is saying that there exists only one type of substance—mental. He is thus simplifying the explanation for reality, a legitimate scientific and philosophical practice.

Berkeley sees the prevailing assumption about our perceptions as also needlessly complex. Berkeley argues that Locke's epistemology theorizes that there is an immaterial God who created material objects that are perceived by a material human body and understood by an immaterial human mind. If we apply the principle of Ockham's razor, Berkeley's theory of perception is simpler. There is an immaterial God who created immaterial objects that are perceived and understood by an immaterial human mind. There is still an external reality that causes our perceptions of ideas; Berkeley just offers a more elegant explanation for it.

The science of Berkeley's time was based on the assumption that matter exists, and Berkeley was upending the basis of that science, yet Berkeley was not denying science. His books, *An Essay towards a New Theory of Vision* (1709) and *The Analyst* (1734), were scientific works of high quality. Whether it's matter or a cosmic mind that causes our perceptions, everything about our science remains the same. Scientific experimentation and observation are nothing more than our perceptions—ideas in our minds. Scientific instruments do not alter this fact because, again, their measurements and readings are simply perceptions—ideas in our minds. Again, matter doesn't matter. Our ideas or perceptions are all we have.

All of this contradicts our "commonsense" assumptions of matter, so it's difficult to take in. If you think Berkeley is being irrational, keep in mind that we see a seemingly opposite but actually quite similar reasoning by materialists today. Whereas Berkeley assumes ideas, the materialists assume matter. And it is an assumption—there is no perception of matter, only sensations caused by something-we-know-not-what. Any criticism you can make of Berkeley's argument applies equally to any argument for matter.

We cannot disprove Berkeley's theory. No one has, even centuries later. Some philosophers have criticized elements of Berkeley's argument, and as with all philosophies, there are some weaknesses in Berkeley's, but his uneasy conclusion remains that we may be making more assumptions about reality than we can rationally prove. We can correctly say that Berkeley is making an assumption that he can't prove, and Berkeley admits this. His motive is not to prove God but to challenge our assumptions, although Berkeley certainly wouldn't mind if you accepted that God created everything.

David Hume—The End of Philosophy?

David Hume's (1711–1776) philosophy was the culmination of the trajectory of British empiricism. He took the philosophies of Locke and especially Berkeley very seriously and responded to them. Hume's shocking conclusion was that philosophy had reached no true understanding at all. Descartes was not a true skeptic because he did not doubt that knowledge is possible. Hume was a true skeptic in that he genuinely doubted whether knowledge was possible. Is scientific and philosophical knowledge possible? Does it make a difference in our lives? Yes and no, is what Hume's philosophy tells us.

In Hume's time, science was rebuilding the structures of knowledge, but he was disturbed by the looseness he saw in those structures. Similar to Descartes, Hume thought that all was not well with the foundations of science and knowledge, as he stated in *A Treatise of Human Nature* (1739):

> There is nothing which is not the subject of debate, and in which men of learning are not of contrary opinions. The most trivial question escapes not our controversy, and in the most momentous we are not able to give any certain decision. Disputes are multiplied, as if every thing was uncertain; and these disputes are managed with the greatest warmth, as if every thing was certain. Amidst all this bustle 'tis not reason, which carries the prize, but eloquence; and no man needs ever despair of gaining proselytes to the most extravagant hypothesis, who has art enough to represent it in any favorable colors. (*Treatise of Human Nature* Introduction 2)

Hume claimed that debates in science and philosophy were based on flowery language more than on reason, something that perhaps is still the case today. Rather than wading into the lingering, tedious scholastic skirmishes at the periphery, he resolved to march to the center of all the sciences—human nature.

Hume states that all of the sciences are related to human nature but that we have little understanding of human nature. Hume decided that philosophy needed to establish the foundations for all other disciplines, the science of humanity being the foundation of all other sciences, and the application of experimental philosophy being the only useful method of understanding human nature. Hume sought to lay down the foundations of the physical sciences, but in the end, he destroyed all hope for certain scientific knowledge.

Hume's Epistemology

Hume, being Scottish, was educated in the British empiricist tradition, so his exploration of human nature began in epistemology. He respected Locke's epistemology, but because he took Berkeley's critique of Locke seriously, Hume thought he needed to begin again with an analysis of our perceptions and consciousness. Hume uses terms differently than philosophers before him did, although the concepts are largely the same. You need to keep straight his particular usage of terms. The main difficulty is Hume's use of "ideas," a term he said we wanted to restore to its original sense, "from which Mr. Locke had perverted it, in making it stand for all our perceptions" (*Treatise* I.I.I, footnote 1).

Hume said that introspection shows us that our perceptions of the world fall into two classes—impressions and ideas.

> By the term "impression," then, I mean all our more lively perceptions, when we hear, or see, or feel, or love, or hate, or desire, or will. And impressions are distinguished from ideas, which are the less lively perceptions, of which we are conscious, when we reflect on any of those sensations or

movements above mentioned. (*An Enquiry Concerning Human Understanding* II.12)

Locke talks about simple ideas of sensation and reflection, but Hume labels the former "impressions" and the latter "ideas." Take that into account, and Hume and Locke are similar in their epistemology. They agree that everything in the mind can be traced to sense experience and every idea in the mind is a representation of the objects of sense impressions.

In Hume's epistemology, impressions may be either sensations (seeing a tree) or the immediate and original contents of our own thoughts (oh, hey, it's a tree) and our psychological states (I feel happy seeing that tree). For Hume, when we experience anything, either an object or our own thoughts or feelings, those are impressions, but they immediately become ideas or memories. Our ideas are copies of impressions that become increasingly faint over time. There is a direct one-to-one correspondence between impressions and ideas. Every one of our ideas directly comes from an impression. Hume says this:

> Every idea which we examine is copied from a similar impression. Those who would assert that this position is not universally true nor without exception, have only one, and that an easy method of refuting it; by producing that idea, which, in their opinion, is not derived from this source. (*Enquiry* II.14)

Our thinking, Hume says, is a processing of ideas that come only from original impressions.

Hume is more pessimistic than Locke is about the powers of the human mind. In fact, Hume was rather cynical about human beings and life in general. Hume adopts the model of the passive mind. For him, the creative power of the mind amounts to no more than combining, resizing, and switching around ideas provided by impressions. For Hume, all ideas originate from impressions, each of which is distinct and exists only for a brief moment, disconnected from any other. The human mind is just a kind of theater where ideas come and go. As we shall soon see, this belief of Hume's has profound consequences.

A Science of the Mind

On the basis of his conception of impressions and ideas, Hume wanted to create a science of the mind. Locke had offered one, but Hume believed, with good reason, that Locke had failed to explain fully how simple ideas became complex ideas. Hume sought to identify the "bond of union" or a "gentle force" that constituted a kind of mental gravity that brought together particular ideas into association. For example, the idea of touching fire is associated with the idea of pain, not pleasure. A certain shade of green is associated with grass but not cows, and so on. Hume thought that because particular sets of ideas introduce each other with a certain degree of method and regularity it was evident that we could identify three principles of the association of ideas: (1) resemblance, (2) contiguity, and (3) cause and effect.

Hume's first principle is resemblance. Ideas with similar features tend to be associated with each other. A cartoon caricature reminds you of someone real because they share similarities. Different particular trees resemble each other, and you compare and contrast their appearances. Second is the principle of contiguity. If you look at a building, you see the rows of windows, and these impressions lead to ideas that behind the windows are rooms that are connected to other rooms in the building. We frequently move from one idea to another in this way, just as we would bodily move from one room to another. The third principle, and one that will become especially important for Hume, is causation, or cause and effect. Certain pairs of impressions follow one another frequently. Whenever we touch fire, we shortly afterward feel pain. When one impression regularly succeeds another, we associate the former with causing the latter.

These "gentle forces" of association operate entirely without any conscious willing on our part, which is why Hume is not interested in asking why our ideas become associated. In his view of the world, there is no reason behind anything—things just happen. Ideas are not something that we control, Hume says. Ideas just happen to us, controlled by mental forces like natural objects are controlled by the force of gravity. Hume does not quite go to the extreme of saying we entirely lack free will, but he implies it.

Reasoning about Our Ideas

Hume adopted the conception that there are two types of reasoning. He took the concepts from **Gottfried Leibniz** (1646–1716), the German polymath who invented calculus. Leibniz's labels of "analytic" and "synthetic" for these two types of reasoning are what survive, thanks to Immanuel Kant, as we will see in Chapter 8, but Hume's labels describe the same concepts.

> All the objects of human reason or enquiry may naturally be divided into two kinds, to wit, *Relations* of *Ideas*, and *Matters of Fact*. Of the first kind are the sciences of geometry, algebra, and arithmetic; and in short, every affirmation which is either intuitively or demonstratively certain.
>
> . . .
>
> Matters of fact, which are the second objects of human reason, are not ascertained in the same manner; nor is our evidence of

their truth, however great, of a like nature with the foregoing. The contrary of every matter of fact is still possible; because it can never imply a contradiction, and is conceived by the mind with the same facility and distinctness, as if ever so conformable to reality. *That the sun will not rise to-morrow* is no less intelligible a proposition, and implies no more contradiction than the affirmation, *that it will rise.* We should in vain, therefore, attempt to demonstrate its falsehood. Were it demonstratively false, it would imply a contradiction, and could never be distinctly conceived by the mind. (*Enquiry* IV.20–21, emphasis his)

Relations of ideas are propositions that must be true because their negation leads to a contradiction. An example of that is the proposition "all unmarried men are bachelors" whose negation "all unmarried men are not bachelors" is a contradiction of the two ideas, unmarried men and bachelors. In the same way, all of the necessarily true propositions of logic, geometry, and algebra are relations of ideas. We can be absolutely certain of the truth of relations of ideas.

Unlike relations of ideas, matters of fact are not ascertained through reason but are based on our previous observations of the world—impressions that are now ideas in our minds. Matters of fact are propositions the contrary of which are still possible because their negation can never imply a contradiction. Hume's example is this: "*That the sun will not rise to-morrow* is no less intelligible a proposition, and implies no more contradiction than the affirmation, *that it will rise.*" (*Enquiry* IV.21, emphasis his) If the sun does not rise tomorrow, although it may surprise you, it would not be a logical contradiction. It is not logically *necessary* that the sun rises tomorrow in the same way that it is logically necessary that a triangle has three sides.

Matters of fact are very different kinds of propositions from relations of ideas in that we can't be absolutely certain of any matter of fact. A good litmus test is this. If you can imagine the opposite of a proposition, it is a matter of fact; if you can't, it's a relation of ideas. You can't imagine a triangle without three sides, so the proposition "triangles have three sides" is a relation of ideas. You can imagine the sun not rising tomorrow, so the proposition "the sun will rise tomorrow" is a matter of presumed fact.

Another example might clarify what's going on here. There is a table in this room. It is a fact because of the impression we have in our mind of the presence of a table. But the opposite possible fact, that there is no table in this room is not logically impossible. Of course, a room could be without a table. No amount of logic can determine whether there is a table in the room because there is no logical necessity for there to be a table in the room. You cannot know a priori whether there is a table in the room. You have to observe the world to gain knowledge of the facts. Will the sun rise tomorrow? You don't know! You have to wait to find out. And, as we shall see Hume tell us, your thought, "but of course the sun will rise again because it has always happened before," is not a guarantee that it will happen again.

The point is that it is not *logic* that tells us about tables and sunrises. Hume completely agrees with William of Ockham's contention that logic tells us nothing about the world. Matters of fact have to be discovered through observation and experience. Hume used the literary example of the first human, Adam, to illustrate the need for experience.

> Adam, though his rational faculties be supposed, at the very first, entirely perfect, could not have inferred from the fluidity and transparency of water that it would suffocate him, or from the light and warmth of fire that it would consume him. No object ever discovers, by the qualities which appear to the senses, either the causes which produced it, or the effects which will arise from it; nor can our reason, unassisted by experience, ever draw any inference concerning real existence and matter of fact. (*Enquiry* IV.I.23)

We know that water drowns people only because humans have drowned in water. Thinking based on experience can explain this association of the ideas of water and drowning, but it could not have told us prior to experience (a priori) what effect it would have on us. Hume's point is that there is a gulf between the realm of reason and logic and the realm of experience. Proof of his point that reality does not conform to the ideas in our reason is that since Hume's time, scientists have learned that euclidean geometry does not always work to explain facts of the universe (and let's not even start on quantum mechanics).

Hume's empirical epistemology states that impressions are the strong and vivid originals of experience and therefore have priority in our knowledge. Impressions literally force themselves on us. Sights and sounds happen to us, and Locke was correct that we passively receive them. Ideas are different in two ways. First, they are feeble and derivative copies of impressions, but second, we seem to think actively about ideas.

Hume wants to establish the rule that every one of our ideas must be tied to a corresponding original impression for it to be valid. Any idea, and especially any philosophical term, that cannot be traced to an original impression is empty and useless. It does not have even the faint content of a legitimate idea. Using this rule, we can "banish all that jargon which has so long taken possession of metaphysical reasonings and drawn disgrace upon them" (*Enquiry* II.17).

Hume never asks why or how allegedly empty ideas arise in our minds. On the one hand, he says that ideas come only from impressions, but on the other hand he insists that there exist empty ideas that do not come from impressions. Despite this contradiction, Hume places great importance on these empty ideas that he thinks should not be thought.

Two Empty Ideas—Substance and Self

Hume says we need to consider every idea as to whether it is a relation of ideas or a matter of fact and discard as empty any idea that fits into neither category. This may seem a simply academic enterprise, but "Hume's fork" (the fork in the road between relations of ideas and matters of fact), as it has come to be known, reveals interesting things.

The first target of Hume's fork is the long-held philosophical idea of substance. Locke had argued that substance must be assumed, even though we could not experience it, because there must be something, we know not what it is, in which the qualities of objects inhere. But this idea failed under Hume's fork: the notion of substance could not be tied to an original impression or found as necessary in logic, so substance was neither a reaction of ideas nor a matter of fact.

Hume accepted Berkeley's critique of Locke's primary and secondary qualities distinction and agreed with Berkeley that the idea of material substance has no basis in our experience. Therefore, Locke the empiricist is believing in something his empiricism forbids him from believing. Hume is also an empiricist in that he argues that we know anything only through experience; however, Hume thinks that to be consistent he needs to reject the idea of substance. All that we can know about the world is the flow of impressions we receive. We have impressions but never any perception of what causes those impressions. Again, we perceive no proper identity that we can ascribe to anything that could be substance. Hume is not denying that there is a reality beyond our perceptions, only that we have no evidence to justify that belief fully.

Also falling to Hume's fork is the idea that we have a self. This is the most difficult of Hume's ideas to grasp, but he is on solid ground. Hume writes this:

> It is certain there is no question in philosophy more abstruse than that concerning identity, and the nature of the uniting principle, which constitutes a person; [however], it is evident these ideas of self and person are never very fixed nor determinate. It is absurd, therefore, to imagine the senses can ever distinguish betwixt ourselves and external objects. (*Enquiry* IV.II.6)

Why do you think you are a self? A self, meaning a distinctive "I." This is a different question from "why do you think you exist?" Descartes—well, Augustine before him—had conclusively proven that if thinking is happening then that thinking thing exists. Hume gives us a different conundrum: awareness of impressions and thinking about ideas are happening, but why do we think this means there is an "I," an enduring self underneath these impressions and ideas? Hume correctly states that "there are some philosophers who imagine we are every moment intimately conscious of what we call our SELF; that we feel its existence and its continuance in existence" (*Enquiry* IV.VI.1). Descartes and Berkeley are two of those philosophers, and almost everyone would tend to agree that we think we are conscious of a self that is the "I."

Hume concludes that there is no self, no "I," because he has no impression of it. "I never can catch myself at any time without a perception, and never can observe any thing but the perception" (*Enquiry* IV.VI.1). Oddly, Hume here is taking Descartes's "I think, therefore, I am a thinking being" more literally than Descartes did, for Hume is saying that our existence is simply the collections of perceptions (thoughts or ideas), and we never perceive a self that is connected to those perceptions. We are *nothing* but perceptions:

> [We perceive] nothing but a bundle or collection of different perceptions, which succeed each other with an inconceivable rapidity, and are in a perpetual flux and movement. Our eyes cannot turn in their sockets without varying our perceptions. Our thought is still more variable than our sight; and all our other senses and faculties contribute to this change; nor is there any single power of the soul, which remains unalterably the same, perhaps for one moment. The mind is a kind of theatre, where several perceptions successively make their appearance; pass, re-pass, glide away, and mingle in an infinite variety of postures and situations. There is properly no simplicity in it at one time, nor identity in different; whatever natural propension we may have to imagine that simplicity and identity. The comparison of the theatre must not mislead us. They are the successive perceptions only, that constitute the mind; nor have we the most distant notion of the place, where these scenes are represented, or of the materials, of which it is composed. (*Enquiry* IV.VI.1)

Let what Hume is claiming sink in. Your mind is a series of perceptions—impressions and ideas, but there is no "you" behind them; your mind isn't even a stage on which these perceptions occur. There are only the flickering of images or shadows. This constant variation and interruption of perceptions means, he says, that there is no proper identity that we can ascribe to anything that could be called a self. Thoughts happen, and there isn't even an "I" to which they happen; they simply happen like so many other motions in the world. That is what Hume claims.

Because we cannot tie material substance to an original impression of it, we have no evidence to justify belief in the idea. The same applies to the idea of a self. This is the case whether we call the self a mental or spiritual substance or simply a human "me." Your instinct is to say that of course you have a self. Well, when do you ever experience a self? Oh, sure, you have ideas of confusion (like now), feeling disturbed (also like now), and all the other emotions and thoughts you have, but analyze deeply every one of those thoughts and feelings and you will not find a self. You experience only those surface impressions just like you experience only the surface impressions of the qualities of objects. You never experience the objects themselves, and you never experience a self itself. Hume claims that there is no privileged "I" different from any external object. Hume's theory of the mind says that there is no coherent self that underlies the stream of consciousness, which is itself just a bundle of impressions. And you never experience a "me" that is having these impressions. Or at least that is Hume's claim.

Interestingly, John Locke's definition of a person can stand as a refutation of Hume's denial of a self. Locke says that a person is "a thinking intelligent being, that has reason and reflection, and can consider itself as itself, the same thinking thing in different times and places" (Locke, *Essay* 2.27.11). Today, you can reflect back to five years ago, ten years ago, and so on and remember events that you perceived. Using reason, you can connect past events that you have experienced as a sequence in time, the common element of which is your experience of them. You can remember where you were, what happened, and how you thought about it. Locke says that you are the same self now as you were then, and it is that same self now that reflects on what happened then. Hume's theory of a bundle of completely different perceptions does not coincide with the reality that our perceptions and ideas about them do have a consistent quality—the sameness of our consciousness. Locke goes as far as to state that if a person's consciousness could somehow be transferred into the body of another, we would have to identify the person before us as according to the one whose consciousness and memories is present rather than according to the body's external appearance.

Causality and Science

The third victim of Hume's fork is our idea of causation, a critique that strikes at the foundation of science and knowledge. Hume's most challenging arguments are against science. He was in no way against science, but he became aware that science is based on assumptions that are on shaky ground. Like Berkeley's argument against matter, Hume's arguments against scientific reasoning have no easy refutation.

Hume's critique exposes three assumptions that underlie all of science—that the present and future behave like the past, that we have impressions of causation, and that we can reason from effect to cause. We will see how he relates science's three assumptions to his three principles of the association of ideas—contiguity, cause and effect, and resemblance.

On the first assumption, our default, unthinking way of dealing with the world is to assume that, if the impression of the table in the room today is similar to the impression of the table the last time we saw it in the room, it is the same table. Hume points out that we have no solid rational reason for our assumption that similarity of impression equals similarity of identity. Someone could have switched tables that look the same. This may seem a silly argument, but science is based on such an assumption, and Hume points out that it has no rational basis. The problem for science is that all scientific beliefs in laws assume that the objects and forces operated the same in the past as they do now and will continue to operate the same in the future. What if this is not the case? Hume points out that if gravity started operating differently tomorrow, this would not violate logic. Gravity is not an a priori idea. Many of Hume's arguments in the mid-1700s were directed at the still lingering belief in the logical approach of Scholasticism, of deciding what "has to be" the case.

Science's second assumption is the target of Hume's most devastating critique—causation. Science depends on the notion that there are cause-and-effect relationships—that one or more things happen as a result of a cause. A great deal of scientific activity is seeking to identify the causes and effects of events. The problem that Hume identifies is that we never have an impression of causation itself and therefore have no justification for cause-and-effect relationships.

Hume's argument is that the reason that you concluded the hammer caused the pain in your thumb is because you had an impression of the hammer hitting your thumb and immediately afterward you felt an impression of pain in your thumb. But this is correlation not causation. We have not experienced the actual causation of the impression of the hammer on the impression of pain. As another example, if we conditioned someone by shining a light before we secretly flipped a switch opening a door. The person, not seeing us flip the switch, would come to conclude that the light switching on is what caused the door to open, but this would be an incorrect assumption.

Here's an example that Hume uses that I will describe more fully. Consider a game of billiards. In the game, we experience three separate impressions, as shown here.

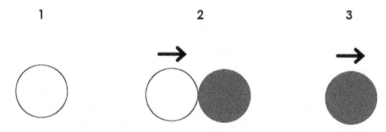

We (1) see a white ball moving in a straight line across the billiard table toward a red ball. Then we (2) see the white ball appear to come in contact with the red ball. Then we (3) see the red ball move.

We assume that the white ball has caused the red ball to move. Why? Hume asks where we find the impression of *causality*. That the red ball moved is not the question—*why* the red ball moved is. It's actually a complex set of imagined assumptions on our part that the white ball caused the red ball to move. We are not only assuming that the three distinct impressions are connected, we are also assuming that the white ball has the power to move the red ball. In the case of establishing scientific knowledge, such as "white calls colliding with red balls cause red balls to move," we are also assuming that there is a necessary connection between the three distinct impressions.

This is a difficult argument to grasp, but work with me here. Let's briefly return to Hume's earlier sun example. Hume says we have observed the sun rise every day, so we have come to expect that the sun will rise tomorrow. But the relation between the fact "the sunrise has always happened" and the proposition "the sun will rise tomorrow" is not a necessarily true relation of ideas. That's because the proposition "the sun will not rise tomorrow" is not a logical contradiction. It would not be contrary to reason if the sunrise did not happen tomorrow. Obviously, that would be a surprise to us, but that's Hume's eventual point.

Back to the billiard balls. If we saw the white ball come in contact with the red ball and the red ball did not move, would that be a logical contradiction? Well, remember our litmus test. Can we image the red ball staying still when the moving white ball comes in contact with it? Of course, therefore, it is not logically *necessary* that the white ball will make the red ball move. We will find the same to be true about every single cause-and-effect relation in which we believe.

"Wait a minute," you might say, "we can demonstrate that a white ball striking a red ball will cause the red ball to move." Hume would say you are making a mistake of reasoning. You appeal to science, thinking, "Can't we prove this scientifically?"

OK, let's construct a scientific experiment. We'll conduct 100 trials of white balls striking red balls and record the results. We do this, and we record the data that 100 times the white ball struck the red ball and 100 times the red ball moved, and you feel this vindicates your proposition that white balls striking red balls causes red balls to move.

All right, I say, what if we did a 101st trial. Would you say the red ball will move again? "Of course!" you reply. Can you imagine the red ball not moving? Yes, you can. It would not be a logical contradiction for the red ball not to move when the white ball strikes it. Therefore, our experiment has not established a *necessary* causal connection. We have recorded a pattern only of past behavior. We have never observed causation, or a cause-and-effect relationship. In each trial, we saw only three separate impressions. We saw a white ball moving toward a red ball; we saw the white ball come in contact with the red ball; we saw the red ball move. That's all we observed. We did not observe the necessary connection between these separate impressions that establishes causation. It's no more than the influence of habit or custom, Hume said, to believe with certainty that on the 101st trial, the red bill will move again.

Hume said that we imagine causation on the basis of our experiences. We can imagine it, so causation is *possible*, but that doesn't mean it is *necessarily* true. We imagine causality because we experience contiguity between certain events; in this case, the white and red balls appear contiguous in space. We also experience priority in time. We experience impressions in a certain order; in this case, we always experience the order as 1, 2, and then 3 in our graphic, never another order. We also experience the impressions in constant conjunction, meaning that we have witnessed the impressions 1, 2, and 3 conjoined repeatedly. These are real matters of fact, we have experienced them, and Hume says we add to these impressions the further idea that there is a necessary connection between these events. We observe *x* followed by *y*, so we infer that all similar occurrences of *x* will be followed by similar occurrences of *y*. We infer it, but we cannot *prove* it as a certain relation of ideas. It is, at most, a probable correlation, but as any good scientist should know, correlation is not causation.

Hume's argument about causation has enormous implications for science. Everything in science is predicated on cause-and-effect relations, from the motions of the planets to the workings of cells. But if we have no rational basis for our belief in causation, what faith can we place in our science? Is our faith in physics, chemistry, biology, and all of the other sciences misplaced?

This is a big problem because, as we can see in Hume's arguments, science not only assumes causation without a rational basis but also makes arguments that depend on the assumption that we can reason from observable effects to their causes. This is science's third assumption—that we can infer a previous event from an existing matter of fact. For example, when a paleontologist finds fossil bones, he or she tries to determine what caused the bones. The paleontologist looks at other bones, including from animals alive today, and tries to infer what animal in the past created the fossil bones. The paleontologist is doing science and is relying on three assumptions: causation (that we can know that a particular something caused these bones), that the past behaved like the present (that we can reason from present examples to what happened in the past), and that we can reason from an effect to a cause (that we can infer from this bone [the effect] what caused the bone). All other sciences make the same assumptions and operate similarly. It is the basis of observational science as set down by Bacon and Descartes—collecting observations of what has happened and inferring from those effects what the physical laws are that caused them.

Intertwined within that reasoning from effect to cause is science's assumption that the future will operate as it has in the past. We've touched on this point previously, but it is worth mentioning that there is absolutely no reason to believe, on the basis of either reason or experience, that even the most fundamental laws of physics will continue to operate in the future as they have in the past.

Hume is not suggesting that we give up on science. He is suggesting that our science is based on assumptions born of *habit*, not reason, and that this should concern us. We have become accustomed to certain patterns of impressions, and we have developed habits to expect those patterns to continue. Reason cannot prove our most fundamental beliefs about how the universe operates. We must give up the pretension that our reason and science give us perfect knowledge. Instead, we must accept that human knowledge is inference based on inexact ideas of fleeting impressions.

Why then do we continue to believe in causation, in continuity of objects, in inferring the existence of one object from the appearance of the other? All of our inferences from experience, Hume says, are the effects of custom, not of reasoning.

Custom, then, is the great guide of human life. It is that principle alone which renders our experience useful to us, and makes us expect, for the future, a similar train of events with those which have appeared in the past.

> Without the influence of custom, we should be entirely ignorant of every matter of fact beyond what is immediately present to the memory and senses. We should never know how to adjust means to ends, or to employ our natural powers in the production of any effect. There would be an end at once of all action, as well as of the chief part of speculation. (*Enquiry* V.I.36)

We are creatures of habit. We have to be. We develop customs as a means to function in the world because logic can tell us nothing about the world. Hume says that this way of thinking not by reason but by custom is an operation of our soul, our natural instinct. Our collective natural instincts create social customs, and our individual thoughts are molded by social customs and personal habits. None of this can be justified by reason, but it is how we humans live.

The Dead End for Philosophy and Science?

Let's tally what Hume has done. In seeking a science of the mind, he has instead found that reason tells us nothing about the world, we are nothing but a collection of customs and habits based on fleeting impressions, we have no basis for believing in material substance or mental substance, we have no basis for believing we are a self, we have no basis for believing in causation, and therefore all of science is without foundation.

Perhaps philosophy is at a dead end. Hume seems to think so, as he writes in the conclusion of his *Treatise*:

> The intense view of these manifold contradictions and imperfections in human reason has so wrought upon me, and heated my brain, that I am ready to reject all belief and reasoning, and can look upon no opinion even as more probable or likely than another. . . . I am confounded with all these questions, and begin to fancy myself in the most deplorable condition imaginable, invironed with the deepest darkness, and utterly deprived of the use of every member and faculty.

> Most fortunately it happens, that since reason is incapable of dispelling these clouds, nature herself suffices to that purpose, and cures me of this philosophical melancholy and delirium, either by relaxing this bent of mind, or by some avocation, and lively impression of my senses, which obliterate all these chimeras. I dine, I play a game of backgammon, I converse, and am merry with my friends; and when after three or four hours' amusement, I would return to these speculations, they appear so cold, and strained, and ridiculous, that I cannot find in my heart to enter into them any farther. (*Treatise* VII.9)

Give up philosophy and play backgammon? Well, that's not exactly Hume's answer, but he is admitting he sees no way out. Rational philosophy and empirical philosophy have both reached dead ends. Science, too.

We can't just dismiss Hume's conclusions—his arguments are valid. He took earlier philosophers seriously, and he drew their work to their rational conclusions. A philosopher who took Hume seriously was Immanuel Kant, whom we will discuss at length in the next chapter.

Chapter 8

IMMANUEL KANT'S REVOLUTION

Immanuel Kant (1724–1804, rhymes with "want") is the single most influential philosopher in history, even though you have probably never heard of him. How we in the Western world think of the universe and how we think about how we perceive the world around us comes from Kant's philosophy.

Philosophy is a long conversation. Immanuel Kant is a significant turning point in that conversation. And Kant was inspired by Hume, who was inspired by Berkeley, who was inspired by Locke, who was inspired by Descartes, who was inspired by Augustine, who was inspired by Plotinus, who was inspired by Plato. It really has been a long conversation.

There are two eras of philosophy: before Kant and after Kant. Again, and I can't emphasize this enough, how we think about human perception is based on Kant's philosophy. All subsequent continental philosophy is based on Kant, and he inspired the field of psychology. You will see why as we explore his insights into the structure of the human mind.

Now, if Kant's philosophy is difficult to understand, it is because he is revealing the foundations of our perceptions and thinking, concepts so fundamental that they are difficult to put into words. Kant's more complicated ideas are off-the-charts complex and obtuse. We won't deal with those here. You're welcome. But we will deal with Kant's basic philosophy, which is still complicated, but you've made it this far, so you can grasp this, too.

Kant's Way out of Hume's Dead End

Kant became so influential because he listened to and took part in the long conversation of philosophy that preceded him. Kant was educated in Prussia, which is significant, because that meant he was taught 1700s German language rationalist philosophy. That school of thought, which rejected the British empiricism of Locke, took no small amount of inspiration from Plotinus and was dominated by the grand system of Gottfried Leibniz and philosophers who extended his system.

In a nutshell, Leibniz created a rational system that claimed to explain all of reality. He based his system on his assumption that all truths can be known through applying the basic logical principles of mathematics. Philosophy, he claimed, was the project of reducing all truths to elementary units that would serve as a logical language that would correspond to the logical structure of the world (we'll see more of that approach in Chapter 16).

Leibniz pointed out a mistake that Locke and the other empiricists (see Chapters 5 and 7) had made. Leibniz said that, yes, there's nothing in the intellect that was not put there by the senses with one very important exception—the intellect itself. This was an important point because it meant that the mind's ability to process sensations of the external world must be present in the mind prior to experience. However, Leibniz assumed that this meant that all the eternal laws of logic were innate within the mind and that learning was a process of awakening those innate ideas, a throwback to Plato.

Leibniz's rationalist approach was steeped in his distinct view of the knowledge of history. The example he used was the historical fact that in 49 BCE, the Roman general Julius Caesar crossed the Rubicon River with his army, starting a war. That he did is a fact frozen in time; it has happened and therefore cannot be changed. That was the kind of certain truth that Leibniz wanted. He therefore claimed that although it was not logically necessary that Caesar acted as he did, Caesar crossed the Rubicon because he would not have acted otherwise. That was the only choice true to his nature. Leibniz claimed that we can be certain about all events past and future because everything that is the case must be the best it could possibly be. God, in infinite wisdom, had created everything to have a specific nature. God had created Caesar such that it is absolutely certain that Caesar would have made the choice that he did. Leibniz declared that because God in infinite goodness would create only the best of all possible worlds, everything and everyone was given natures from which actions would certainly take place to contribute to the best of all possible worlds. The world we live in is that best of all possible worlds, and of that we can be certain. That means we can also be certain that every event past, present, and future could not be otherwise than it is. It also means that what we call evil are just unavoidable imperfections of no real consequence.

Oh, and Leibniz said that logically, all of reality must be made out of fundamental particles he called "monads," which are like little atoms of perception, each unique but mirroring the entire universe; which are not located in physical space or time; and which do not interact with each other but appear to interact with each other because everything was preordained by God to act the way it does—the best of all possible worlds. Leibniz was the most famous philosopher of the rationalist tradition and was completely devoted to the notion that if a proposition makes rational sense to us within our minds it therefore must be true. Truths, like everything, are monads, and we need simply to apply logic to understand how the world is.

Kant was trained in the Leibnizian rationalist system but managed to get ahold of Hume's books. Kant wrote that Hume "interrupted my dogmatic slumber and gave my investigations in the field of speculative philosophy quite a new direction" (*Prolegomena to any Future Metaphysics* Introduction 9). He referred to Hume's critiques as the most decisive to date for philosophy; he thought that, although Hume's investigations were incomplete, they deserved further concentrated attention. Kant explained how seriously he took Hume's critique of causation.

> [Hume] demonstrated irrefutably that [causation] was perfectly impossible for reason to think a priori and by means of concepts a combination involving necessity. We cannot at all see why in consequence of the existence of one thing another must necessarily exist, or how the concept of such a combination can arise a priori. Hence he inferred that reason was altogether deluded with reference to this concept, which she erroneously considered as one of her children, whereas in reality it was nothing but a bastard of imagination, impregnated by experience, which subsumed certain representations under the law of association, and mistook the subjective necessity of habit for an objective necessity arising from insight. (*Prolegomena Introduction*, 9)

What Kant means is that Hume was correct: We have only the belief that causation exists, but we never actually witness it. We believe in cause and effect only because we have developed habits from our experience to believe that certain events are connected. For example, we have developed a belief that flipping a light switch turns lights on or off because we have experienced the sensations of flipping the switch and the lights turning on or off. Habitually, we now believe that switches turn lights on and off, but we do not *know* that this is the case. In fact, we do not know with absolute certainty that anything causes anything. We have just developed the habit of believing that specific things we do create specific results, and we believe that causation exists. Kant agreed with Hume that this calls all of our knowledge and science into question.

Like Hume, Kant is talking about the *justification* for believing in causation, not whether it exists. Key to Kant's philosophy is the understanding that we think *in terms of* causation and that no amount of reason or experience proves causation. This does not mean we completely ignore the idea that certain actions cause certain effects, but it does demand that we not blindly assume our theoretical beliefs are full understanding. This insight requires us to look into how our own minds are contributing to our experiences of the world.

Kant's Copernican Revolution

Kant's philosophical revolution was a new critical reflection on what we contribute to our experience. The result Kant achieved shifted the center of epistemology from external objects to the human mind., which is why Kant's philosophy has been compared to Copernicus (Kopernik) shifting the focus of astronomy's view of the universe from the Earth to the Sun.

Since Plato, the unanimous assumption in philosophy had been that our senses create copies—images—of external objects in our minds. Think of Locke calling the mind a camera obscura: the world creates images in our minds of external objects. Thus, philosophers also unanimously had to answer the question of how well the impressions in our minds connect with how external objects actually are. The main problem facing epistemology was how we can know whether our minds contain accurate images of the external world.

Hume had cast doubt on the possibility that the ideas in our mind are accurate representations of objects in the world. Kant's solution to the doubts Hume raised was to recognize that our minds are not entirely passive, as Hobbes, Locke, and Hume had thought, but are active in shaping our knowledge. Now, be sure not to misunderstand: Kant does NOT say that we create ideas or knowledge out of nothing. It is much more complex than that.

The foundation for understanding Kant begins with understanding this sentence:

> That all our knowledge begins with experience there can be no doubt. . . . But, though all our knowledge begins with experience, it by no means follows that all arises out of experience. (*Critique of Pure Reason* Introduction, I.1–2)

What Kant is saying here is that both empiricism (all knowledge comes from sense experience) and rationalism (all knowledge comes from reason) offer incomplete views of epistemology and the mind. Neither alone provides us with understanding of the world, but both have a grain of truth in how they approach philosophy and the world. Everything in our minds begins with experience, BUT our minds contribute to our understanding.

Kant's Copernican revolution means that instead of looking to see how objects form images in our minds, we should be looking at how our mind depicts objects. Kant realized, what Hume and others had not, that what we have in our minds are *depictions* of objects, not *copies* of objects in the world.

Our minds are not completely blank prior to experience, as Locke had assumed. Our minds come with abilities to process sense perceptions into knowledge, as Leibniz had said. Kant also connected with William on the latter's teaching that logic tells us nothing about the world—only experience does. Kant agreed but also understood that experience alone cannot tell us about objects in the world. Our minds are active in our perceptions.

Instead of the passive mind theory of perception (Hobbes, Locke, and Hume) that said that the mind conforms to external objects, Kant's active mind theory says that objects conform to the mind's rational structure. What that rational structure is and what it does will take a lot to explain in this chapter, but at its most basic, Kant is saying that the human mind contributes to our experience by imposing a form or structure on the contents of sense experience that enables knowledge about objects.

Locke had said that we can never step out of our mind to compare its contents with the objects in the world. What Kant says is that we can never have an experience that has not been processed by our mind's rational structure. Kant realized that the external world that we perceive through our senses is not completely separate from the human mind; therefore, the human mind can have a priori (prior to experience) knowledge about the structure of the external world. Kant's theory is that the human mind constructs the world of appearances by combining impressions provided by the senses with a priori concepts supplied by our mental faculties.

This is the heart of Kant's Copernican revolution. Hume was correct that concepts like causation are not derived from experience, but, Kant says, we know concepts like causation by "a completely reversed kind of connection which never occurred to Hume, not by deriving them from experience, but by deriving experience from them" (*Prolegomena* 30.2). These concepts of the understanding in the human mind do not give us absolute knowledge of the sensible world. But because our mind does contribute to the structure of the world as we perceive it, we can have real knowledge about the sensible world, and we are not left with Hume's dead end.

The Varieties of Judgments

Kant's goal was to identify the necessary conditions for understanding. Kant is convinced that we do have knowledge of the world and that reason does have power, but speculative rationalism, for example Leibniz's logical conjectures, is not knowledge, and Hume had shown that passive empiricism can't explain how we can know anything about the external world. To explain how we can gain knowledge of the world, Kant first needs to show what power reason does and does not have to gain understanding and, specifically, what concepts in the mind can extend our understanding of the world.

For Kant, knowledge is a judgment about a belief or proposition. To say that a proposition is true or is false is a judgment. Kant clarifies the varieties of knowledge judgments that are possible by identifying two types of judgments—analytic and synthetic. To understand Kant's philosophy, we need to delve briefly into a bit of logic.

Analytic judgments, Kant says, are when a predicate B belongs to the subject A. His example is Descartes's idea that we saw in Chapter 4 that physical bodies are defined by extension in space. The quality of extension (B) belongs to the definition of bodies (A). In other words, the meaning of bodies includes that they are extended. The judgment "all bodies are extended" does not amplify our concept of body but has only analyzed it. Analytic reasoning is the analysis of the meaning of terms that we already know. Analytic judgments are mostly empty tautologies; although they may clarify propositions by confirming the relations of terms, this type of reasoning tells us nothing about the world.

Synthetic judgments are when a predicate B can be connected to, but lies outside, the subject A. Kant's example is the judgment, "all bodies have weight." The quality of weight (B) does not belong to the definition of bodies (A) but "it amplifies my knowledge by adding something to my concept" (*Prolegomena* 2.2). A synthetic judgment combines (synthesizes) two different concepts. Synthetic judgments tell us something about the world because instead of just linking terms we already know, we gain new connections beyond what we already knew.

Kant also identifies the two types of knowledge—a priori and a posteriori—both terms from Latin, literally meaning "prior to" and "after," respectively. Knowledge that is a priori is known by us prior to and separate from any experience; these are innate ideas or ideas that are self-evident to analysis.

All analytic judgments are a priori knowledge independent of experience. Knowledge that is a posteriori is learned through experience—our observations of the world. A priori judgments are justified by reason and need not be verified by experience; we know them independent of our experience. A posteriori judgments cannot be verified by reason; they can be verified only by experience, thus "after experience." Most of our knowledge is of this type of learning through experience, such as "there is a tree in the yard" and "the Twins won the World Series in 1991."

Kant's Four Propositions

Kant combines the two types of judgments and the two types of knowledge into four kinds of possible propositions, shown here.

Knowledge	Analytic Judgments	Synthetic Judgments
A priori (independent of experience)	Logic/Math/Geometry	?
A posteriori (derived from experience)	Impossible	Science

We are already familiar with two types. Analytic a priori propositions are what Hume called "relations of ideas"—propositions that are intuitively or demonstratively certain based on an analysis of terms. Synthetic a posteriori propositions are what Hume called "matters of fact"—propositions learned through observations of the world. Analytic a posteriori propositions are impossible; if a judgment is analytic, it is not based on experience, and if it was derived from experience, then it is synthetic, not analytic.

That leaves the fourth type of proposition, synthetic a priori judgments. Everyone before Kant believed such propositions were impossible contradictions as are analytic a posteriori propositions. But Kant claimed that there are propositions that are independent of experience *and* that give us certain knowledge about the world. His example is this: "all events have a cause." We don't derive this proposition from experience; we bring this knowledge to our perceptions. Hume pointed out that the concept of cause does not belong to the concept of event and that we do not perceive causation in experience. Kant agrees but counters that universal causation is a synthetic a priori proposition that gives us knowledge by structuring our perceptions. We perceive events *in terms of* the proposition "all events have a cause." Propositions like these give us a kind of knowledge that goes beyond the analysis of terms or the collection of experiences. A priori propositions can explain how the ideas in our mind can be accurate representations of objects in the world.

The Transcendental Method

The challenge for Kant is to demonstrate how synthetic a priori propositions are possible. To accomplish this, Kant engages in what he calls the "transcendental method." It's *transcendental* in that the method transcends any particular experience to explore the universal nature of experience to uncover the universal and necessary conditions for understanding. If we cannot imagine experiences without a specific feature, then that feature must be a universal and necessary condition of our experiences. This was Kant's method to identify the concepts in the mind that can extend our understanding of the world. His method is possible because he accepts that our experiences are mental depictions of external objects, not copies of them. Our active minds contribute to our experiences and our understanding.

Kant's transcendental method is difficult to grasp because it explores a reality beyond words: it is the mode of thinking before we put thought into words. Also, we don't use the word "transcendental" much anymore, which is a shame. By "transcendental," Kant means what is always present in consciousness—it transcends any particular thought or experience. So, his transcendental method is to uncover what is present in all thoughts and experience. What he's basically doing is asking, "when I see a tree, when I think about going for a walk, when I listen to music, and so on, what is present in my consciousness in every one of those experiences?"

Time and Space

The transcendental method uncovers the most fundamental structure of our experiences—space and time. Grasping time and space is so difficult because we never actually experience them, yet we never experience anything without them. Kant writes the following:

> Space is not a conception which has been derived from outward experiences. For, in order that certain sensations may relate to something [external to me] . . . the representation of space must already exist as a foundation. Consequently, the representation of space cannot be borrowed from the relations of external phenomena through experience; but, on the contrary, this external experience is itself only possible through the said antecedent representation. Space then is a necessary representation à priori, which serves for the foundation of all external intuitions. We never can imagine or make a representation to ourselves of the non-existence of space, though we may easily enough think that no objects are found in it. It must, therefore, be considered as the condition of the possibility of phenomena, and by no means as a determination dependent on them, and is a representation à priori, which necessarily supplies the basis for external phenomena. (*Critique of Pure Reason* I.I.2.2–3)

We do not perceive space—we perceive things *in terms of* space. The same is true with time. Kant adds the following:

> Time is not an empirical conception. For neither coexistence nor succession would be perceived by us, if the representation

of time did not exist as a foundation à priori. Without this presupposition we could not represent to ourselves that things exist together at one and the same time, or at different times, that is, contemporaneously, or in succession. Time is a necessary representation, lying at the foundation of all our intuitions. With regard to phenomena in general, we cannot think away time from them, and represent them to ourselves as out of and unconnected with time, but we can quite well represent to ourselves time void of phenomena. Time is therefore given à priori. In it alone is all reality of phenomena possible. These may all be annihilated in thought, but time itself, as the universal condition of their possibility, cannot be so annulled. (*Critique of Pure Reason* I.II.5.1–2)

Space and time are the intuitions that make our understanding of objects possible. They are the conditions to which all of our experiences conform. Try to imagine the color green. You cannot imagine "just" green; you can only imagine a green something that has qualities of both space and time. Remember Berkeley's argument that we can't conceive of abstract ideas? We can add to it that we cannot imagine green in the abstract, and we cannot imagine it outside of space and time.

Kant refers to space and time as "the pure elementary notions of the Sensibility" (*Prolegomena* 39.4). Time and space are forms of inner sense that structure our mental depictions of objects. We derive all of our experiences from them. Without their structure, the contents of our minds would be no more than what Hume called the flux of impressions. Time and space are synthetic a priori judgments that structure our perceptions and allow us to have sensible experiences. We do not experience space or time in and of themselves—only objects within space and time. Space and time are intuitions that make experiences possible, but we do not learn them through experience; they are always there, prior to any experiences. Human perception is impossible without them.

The Categories of Understanding

Space and time are just the beginning of what the transcendental method uncovers. Kant also says that our mind has a set of further categories that structure our mental depictions of external objects. He calls them "Pure Concepts of the Understanding," or "Categories." The Categories are, like space and time, conditions by which our understanding is possible. Our mind's depictions of objects are structured and made sensible in space and time, and the Categories do what Kant describes as a synthesis

by which alone the elements of our cognitions are collected and united into a certain content. . . . a blind but indispensable function of the soul, without which we should

> have no cognition whatever, but of the working of which we are seldom even conscious. (*Critique of Pure Reason* I.III.6.1)

The Categories are the concepts that turn mere collections of sensations into depictions of things. We never experience the Categories because they are a priori—they are independent of experience because they are a necessary precondition of experience. We don't experience what the Categories do; we experience only their effects.

Kant's bold claim is that the Categories are synonymous with all possible logical functions and judgments. In other words, they are how we think, and we cannot think otherwise than through their a priori synthesis. Kant says he calls these pure conceptions "Categories" after Aristotle's Categories (see Chapter 2) because his purpose is identical with Aristotle's but executed differently.

Kant's Table of the Categories of Understanding

Quantity	Quality	Relation	Modality
Unity (Measure)	Reality (Affirmative)	Inherence and Substance	Possibility— Impossibility
Plurality (Quantity)	Negation (Negative)	Causality and Dependence	Existence— Nonexistence
Totality (Singular Whole)	Limitation	Community and Interaction	Necessity— Contingence

(Critique of Pure Reason I.III.6.8; Prolegomena 21, 2)

The concepts in this table are rational concepts that the human mind contains a priori. They are not what we think about; they are *how* we think. They are thinking at the most basic level, the rational, synthetic a priori judgments by which we understand anything and everything. They are literally how we make sense of our mental depictions that we perceive in terms of space and time.

Kant said that objects are given to us by the faculty of *Sensibility* (sense experiences) and space and time, and the Categories are the faculty of *Understanding*. Knowledge is the product of these two faculties of the mind, and we need both to have knowledge. The understanding can comprehend nothing without sense experience, and the senses themselves can think nothing.

Kant's discussion of how the Categories give us understanding is complex—so complex he had to write a second book (*Prolegomena to Any Future Metaphysics*, published in 1783) to explain his first book (*Critique of Pure Reason*, published in 1781) on the subject. For our purposes here, a simple example can show how the Categories unite our depictions into one conscious understanding of objects.

Imagine a dot. Just one dot. Right away you are using the logical judgments of the Categories, to understand that you are considering the Totality of one dot. You didn't need to think hard at all; your mind possesses that capability prior to any experience. Now imagine a second dot. That's using Plurality to go beyond one dot to a plurality of dots. If I draw seven dots and ask you how many dots there are, you can answer because you can count the Quantity of dots as equaling seven. If I then ask you to draw a circle around three of the seven dots, you can do that because you logically Limit the Reality of the dots, choosing (Affirming) three while Negating the other four dots. If this sounds very simplistic, that's the point. This is *the* most basic level of human thought. We don't learn this—we know this a priori—but we can use these judgments to gain knowledge of the world, so these propositions are synthetic propositions.

The Categories of Modality are also basic forms of thought. They are logical modes by which we judge objects and ideas. They come in pairs, and each pair of modalities underlies substantial questions that philosophers have debated for centuries. We never learned these modalities through experience; we think in terms of them. To think that something is possible or impossible, that it exists or does not exist, or that it is a necessary or contingent occurrence means to think in terms of synthetic a priori judgments of the Categories.

The Categories of Relation deserve special attention because they answer several of Hume's serious objections. Kant agrees that we do not have sense experience of substance or causality, but the Category of Inherence and Substance forms a unity out of our various perceptions of qualities that enables us to form universal concepts such as "tree," "dog," and "human." True, we cannot say what the reality beneath these qualities is, but that's not the point. Substance is a logical function and judgment that orders the flow of sensations into coherent objects in our mind. Perhaps the idea of "tree" is, as a skeptic could say, nothing but an idea in our mind, but that's all we have to work with, and it's how we think about our sensations.

Hume said our idea of necessary causality is simply a product of habit. Kant replied that causality is a logical, a priori synthetic judgment by which we understand the succession of events that we perceive. In the billiard ball example, Hume said that we do not witness causation; we witness only three distinct impressions. Kant agrees and says that our mind contributes the concepts of Causality and Dependence (Cause and Effect) to the impressions given to us by the senses to understand the events that we witness. We cannot imagine a world in which there is no causal order and no interaction between objects (Leibniz's bizarre theory of monads aside)., These a priori concepts structure our experiences and enable understanding. The Categories are how the human mind is structured. Kant says that all human beings have the same Categories and thus experience the world in the same basic way.

What does all of this mean for us in our daily lives? Kant's Categories of Understanding helps us see how we perceive objects and think about them. Think of Kant's a priori concepts more as knowledge gained *separate* from experience rather than prior to experience. In Kant's philosophy, it's not about priority in time, but about knowledge we have prior to *any* experience. He means the rational knowledge we have that can be expressed in the Categories of Understanding. This is the structure of our mental understanding of our sense experience. This is a central element of his philosophy, so it's important to get it correct. In the light switch example, it's not that we know prior in time that light switches work to turn lights on and off, it's that we know causation, and this allows us to understand the impressions we have of light switches and lights turning on and off.

Kant's Active Mind

Kant views the human mind as an active mind. The intuitions of space and time and the Categories of Understanding provide structure to our thoughts, but we do actively think thoughts through that structure. We perceive what Kant calls a "manifold of phenomena" (*Critique of Pure Reason* III.3.B4) always in succession; but although we passively perceive that manifold in a particular order of succession, we can actively think about it in different ways.

As an illustration of what Kant said about the mind's active capabilities, imagine listening to a piece of music. Music is a succession of notes that your mind perceives as a succession of perceptions. Your mind is performing multiple tasks as you do this. First, you are separating the notes of the music from all other sounds in the background, isolating the notes as the concept of a song. Kant refers to this with the clunky term "synthesis of apprehension in intuition," which means that your mind is synthesizing out of the manifold sensations a particular thread of phenomena and considering them together as one experience. Your mental capability allows you to listen to a song in your car, despite everything else going on while you are driving.

As you listen to the succession of notes, you can remember the previous notes in the sequence. To switch the thought experiment briefly—if I said a sequence of numbers to you and then asked you what the second number was, you can, using your memory (what Kant called the "synthesis of reproduction in imagination") repeat what that second number was. Note what's happening here. Your mind is more than an app that records and plays back sounds. You can do more than merely repeat a sequence of sense impressions. Kant gives the examples of drawing a line in your head or thinking of the amount of time from one hour to another hour. You need reproduce in your imagination what you have learned and synthesize new ideas from it.

Back to the piece of music. You are more than simply a perceiver; you can think about the music to which you are listening, and using what Kant calls the "synthesis of recognition in a concept," you can think about the piece of music in terms of its melody, its rhythm, its genre, what instruments are being played, and so on. These examples of how our mind works are possible because of the intuitions of space and time and the Categories of Understanding, but you are actively thinking about what you experience, and objects conform to your mind. You not only have memories, you have the ability to do things with your memories— reproduce them, analyze them, compare them, and so on.

The Three Transcendental Ideas of Pure Reason

Kant considers the mind as also having a faculty of *pure* reason, which produces its own concepts different from those produced by the intuitions of space and time and the Categories of Understanding. The concepts of pure reason relate to the most difficult quandaries about the nature of reality that transcend all possible experience. They are, Kant said, questions, that human reason must necessarily encounter. Kant discussed three concepts of pure reason—self, cosmos, and God. We have no experience of these concepts, but they are important because, Kant argued, we must hold these concepts to make sense of the universe.

Self

Hume said that we never experience a self, which is a very challenging claim. Basically, what Hume means is that we have no impression of the self within our sense impressions but only the sense data themselves. Kant agrees with Hume that we never experience the self in our thoughts just as the eye never sees itself in visual perception.

But does Hume not make a mistake here? Do we believe we do not have eyes because we do not see the eye when the eye sees? And what is seeing without an eye? What is gathering sense impressions and having ideas if not a self? Finally, and most damning to Hume's argument—if he is correct that we have no idea that is not linked to an original impression, from where, then, comes the idea of a self?

Kant said that the self is not a thing we experience but is another necessary condition for experiences to exist. Kant does not agree with Descartes and Berkeley that the self is a substance because Kant sees substance as a Category of Understanding within experience. We do not think of our self in the same way that we think of a particular object, through the Categories of Understanding. Instead, we intuit our self as an abstract idea of pure reason.

Concepts of pure reason stand behind experience. The self is transcendental to all experience and underlies all experience. We can't experience the transcendental self just like the eye can't see itself, but we do think of our experiences as being experienced by a unified self, the subject of all our experiences.

Hume unwittingly showed this in his objections to the idea of a self. He said, "I never can catch myself at any time without a perception" (*Enquiry* IV.VI.1). He can't construct that sentence without the words and concepts of "I" and "myself." We always assume the self and need the concept of self, even when we try to deny the self. The self is a logically necessary idea for us to be able constitute our past experiences and believe they are our experiences.

Although Kant affirms that we must have a self, he states that we can have no real knowledge about it. "I have therefore no knowledge of myself as I am, but merely as I appear to myself" (*Critique of Pure Reason* I.I.21). In other words, we can look inward and see the undeniable signs that there is a self, but what that self is we cannot say.

Cosmos

The ancient Greek word "cosmos" meant the entirety of everything. The school of speculative philosophy in which Kant was educated made bold dogmatic claims about the nature of the cosmos and statements about it such as "the world has, as to time and space, a beginning." This seems like a reasonable claim to knowledge, but, as Kant points out, the opposite or contradiction, "the world is, as to time and space, infinite," is equally reasonable. Another set of antinomies is "every event is determined" and "some events are not caused because we have free will." These two statements cannot both be true, but both are logically possible.

He brings forward these conflicting propositions, and two other similar pairs, to demonstrate that our reason can go beyond what it can prove and can reach dogmatic propositions that are nonsense. What he means by "nonsense" is that the propositions have an opposite proposition and that these pairs of contradictory propositions cannot both be true, but neither side of the antinomy can be proved true or false. The proposition and its opposite can be held only dogmatically, without evidence or rational argument, and that is nonsense.

Kant's purpose in stating the antinomies is that reason has certain proper bounds within which it must stay. He means something different than Descartes meant about restraining the will. Kant is declaring that reason has its own limits and, disagreeing with Bacon and Descartes, that we can go wrong with our use of reason. We cannot reason to propositions about the cosmos as though it were a finite object. Synthetic a priori judgments are acceptable in mathematics and physics because they make sense of our experience. But the entirety of the cosmos is beyond our experience and beyond our reason. We do not and cannot experience the totality of everything.

To help understand what Kant is getting at, consider a more finite example of the same basic idea. Our knowledge of the world is limited by what we can perceive in space and time; therefore, there is a limit to our sense experience and our reason. Remember that Kant's transcendental method found that our minds actively form and structure our sense impressions. That means that what our minds perceive is appearances of objects as our mental categories structure them. We do not have direct experience of the objects themselves.

This means that there are for us two aspects to the world. There is a phenomenal world (a world of phenomena) that contains objects we can perceive within time and space. There is also a noumenal world—the objects in themselves—a world independent of our sense of it. When we perceive an object, we can perceive the object as it appears to us, but we cannot perceive the thing-in-itself, the noumenon that is beyond our perception and the noumenon is not structured by the Categories of Understanding.

Accepting the reality of the noumena seems to be a logical necessity. If there are limits to our capabilities of perception and understanding, then there must be a realm of reality beyond the reach of our knowledge. The noumenon is that which is beyond what we can perceive. Kant agreed with the British empiricists that we don't really see the tree-in-itself; we see sense impressions caused by the tree. Kant postulates the noumena as a logically necessary reality because we do not and cannot experience the things-in-themselves.

Similarly, the cosmos, the entirety of everything, is independent of our sense of it but is a logically necessary reality. This is partly an answer to Berkeley. Yes, there is a cosmos that persists independent of our perception of it. We cannot prove that through either perception or reason; however, it makes sense to assume that there is a cosmos and that all that we can perceive is within it. We need to restrain our reason within its proper limits and not engage in dogmatic propositions beyond those limits. We cannot say whether the cosmos is finite or infinite or whether every event is determined. Such universal statements are beyond our rational powers to assert. The cosmos is a logically necessary idea for us to believe that there is a reality.

God

I have said nothing in this book about the various rational "proofs" for the existence of God. Even when I teach philosophy of religion (a very enjoyable course because human thinking about God and religion is beautiful), I leave out the alleged proofs. That's because I take seriously Kant's admonition that God is neither provable nor disprovable. One of his antimonies about the cosmos was the pairing of "there is a necessary being (God)" and "there is nothing necessary; all is incidental." These two statements cannot both be true, but both are logically possible.

Kant believed in a supreme creator, but he thought that attempts to argue for it rationally are nonsense, for the same reasons he thought propositions about the cosmos are nonsense. Kant systematically refutes the well-known arguments that allegedly demonstrate God's existence— ontological, teleological, and cosmological—exposing them as the rationally baseless, dogmatic assertions that they are. Similarly, any and all arguments against the existence of God are also nonsense. Atheism is just as dogmatic an assertion as is theism. Interestingly, Kant does not say that God's existence is a matter of faith. He's not against that, but that's not the conclusion at which he aimed. What he states is that, like the concept of self and cosmos, the concept of God is a logically necessary idea for us to think about why there is something we can call morality. We can say nothing more about God.

Kant's rejection of the dogmatic propositions of speculative philosophy serves the purpose of, on the one hand, keeping reason within its proper limits, and, on the other hand, establishing a positive role in philosophy for these unprovable concepts of self, cosmos, and God. We cannot prove that we have a self; that there is a coherent, enduring cosmos beyond our perceptions; or that there is a God, but it is helpful if not essential to think that they are true. They are important regulative concepts that give us reference points to help us make sense of what we can experience. One quick example is that it is only because we think that there is a coherent, enduring cosmos beyond our perceptions that we can explore new territory or plan for the future. After all, if we assume that all that exists is what we have already perceived, how could we discover new things? What reason would we have to think that there will be a tomorrow?

Kant's Legacy

In a real sense, the whole rest of this book (save one chapter, as we shall see) is Kant's legacy. Most philosophers since Kant have adopted Kant's admonition against dogmatic rational speculation and his realization that the mind actively contributes to perception. Kant changed everything in philosophy and by extension in all of the sciences. The German poet **Heinrich Heine** (1797–1856) said that Kant's philosophy was world destroying, world crushing. It's difficult for us to understand that today because we have grown up in the Kantian world. We have no experience of the world that Kant destroyed. Every way that we look at our world and every way in which we understand our world as Westerners is Kantian.

One huge implication of Kant's philosophy is that our minds are not purely passive perceivers. Think of a motion-sensitive spotlight that simply reacts. It has no consciousness of what it's doing; it turns on only in response to stimulus. Locke and others had more or less reduced the human mind to that level of mere passive reaction. Locke would say that he did believe we are aware of our ideas of sensation, but that's just a second layer of passivity—sensations cause ideas of reflection. Hume agreed with that model of the passive mind—objects cause impressions, impressions cause ideas, there is no self, there is no active mind.

Kant is saying that our mental content is limited because we have a limited number of experiences but that our mind has the ability to process those ideas and go beyond simple experiences and have a level of understanding. Kant's realization that the human mind is active in structuring perceptions solved some of the problems present in the epistemologies of Locke and Hume. Our minds join different mental ideas, and we comprehend their diversity and their connections in our faculty of understanding. We can have knowledge. However, there remains the issue that the phenomena in our minds are not copies of the objects themselves, so there remains the issue of the noumenon—the thing-in-itself that is beyond our perception.

Kant's philosophy increased the contribution of the human mind to our understanding but at the same time limited its reach. Kant leaves us with a world that we perceive through our intuitions of space and time, on one side of which is the unknowable noumenal self and on the other side of which is the unknowable noumenal world. On the one hand, Kant believed in human free will, that the will is in its every action a law to itself, and he believed that we can freely use our reason to make decisions. On the other hand, Kant also said that our perceptions and thoughts about them conform to the structure of our mental faculties. The Categories of Understanding are how all human beings perceive the universe, and all human beings have the same mental structure. Perception and understanding, therefore, are determined by a one-size-fits-all structure. He also said that we can't go beyond the Categories of Understanding— they determine how we can perceive and think about our perceptions.

A group of philosophers accepted Kant's idea that the mind is active in perception but disagreed with Kant's restrictions on human possibilities. We meet them next in Chapter 9.

Chapter 9

GERMAN IDEALISM

At certain points in philosophical history, someone opens a conceptual door and others walks through it. Immanuel Kant opened such a door with his revolutionary insight that our perceptions conform to our mental structure, including the Categories of Understanding. The implication of Kant's new doorway toward understanding human perception was that reality conforms to our minds and our minds are more than purely passive perceivers. Our minds are active in our experiences, and the structure of our mind structures our experiences.

In the early 1800s, a philosophical movement arose as a direct reaction to Kant's philosophical system. The movement came to be known as "German idealism." "German" because it was discussed by a circle of German philosophers and artists, and "idealism" because the movement argued that everything must be understood as being dependent on mental or spiritual reality, though don't confuse this with Berkeley's idealism. The Kantian Copernican revolution places the human mind at the center of philosophy. Even more important to the German idealists, this worldview positioned human individuals as the engines of creativity. Kant opened a door, and the German idealists barged through it with glee. The German idealists developed a unique philosophical movement that synthesized multiple earlier ideas into an approach to reality that greatly influenced the arts and, by extension, much of human society.

Going Beyond Kant

In the late 1700s and early 1800s, German-speaking culture was awakening to a fresh view of human expression inspired in large part by the polymath **Johann Wolfgang von Goethe** (1749–1832), who was opening up new possibilities for literature. The thinkers in the German idealist movement were also open to new possibilities, and they were willing to take in Kant's insights about human understanding and reassess everything in human experience.

These thinkers asked a number of penetrating questions. If, as Kant showed, the mind is active in experience, then the question is how active it is. If our perceptions conform to our mental structure, then does that structure ever change? Do people in different cultures have different mental structures? Kant said we can't go beyond the Categories of Understanding in our perception and thinking, but is perception outside their limits really impossible? Are the Categories really the same for every individual human being, as Kant says? Can we willfully change the way we experience the universe by changing our approach to it? The German idealists, each in his own way, explored these fundamental questions about the way we approach the universe.

The various thinkers in the German idealism movement crafted new philosophical approaches to the questions of what the universe is and what we can know about it. The essential theme within German idealism is the thought that reality is dependent on the mind of the perceiver; therefore, when the perceiver changes his or her approach to the universe, that changes his or her understanding and perhaps even his or her reality. This opens us up to the big question of which approach will best reveal reality to us. Philosophers and artists gravitated to the German idealism movement to talk about the possibilities of new approaches that could lead to new perceptions and realizations.

The German idealist thinkers rejected the limits that Kant had placed on human knowledge. The first limit is Kant's belief that human perception is limited to the unchanging Categories of Understanding. The second limit rejected by the German idealists is Kant's idea that there is a noumenal realm—the ultimate reality of the things-in-themselves that is beyond our sense-based and rational knowledge. If there are limits to our sense perceptions of objects in the world, then there must be a realm of reality beyond our knowledge. The only way around that sound reasoning is to believe instead that human perception can transcend the limitations of the senses and Kant's Categories of Understanding. Along this line of thinking, the German idealists largely rejected the scientific approach to knowledge. They saw that approach as reductionist—reducing all phenomena to simplistic, categorical explanations. Such a limited approach to the universe was exactly what the German idealists wanted to transcend.

There is a large area between the limits of scientific knowledge and perfect knowledge, and the German idealists each staked their own claim in that territory. They each believed that our minds have the power of intuition that can transcend the limitations of science and reason and reveal the deeper reality of the universe. They argued that Kant and those who followed his system were limiting their understanding, believing they were cut off from reality beyond sense perception. The German idealists argued that what Kant called the noumenal realm is not actually beyond our reach.

Common to the German idealists was their belief that the path to greater knowledge was to accept the inseparability of thinking and being. The German idealists saw reality as essentially mental, not like Berkeley's immaterialism (see Chapter 7), but reality as dynamic processes in which one's mental paradigm plays an active part. Thus, they were interested in overcoming the idea that thought and being are separate. They sought to connect self-consciousness with the rest of reality. Some German idealists even flirted with the idea that our human understanding is, at least in theory, unlimited.

To varying degrees, the German idealists rejected scientific and rationalist approaches to the universe and instead adopted an intuitive, passionate, and artistic approach. In this way, they shifted the focus of philosophy to the personal. The artistic movement, known as "Romanticism," was burgeoning in the 1790s, and armed with Kantian philosophy, the German idealists gave Romanticism intellectual power. Romanticism and German idealism both celebrated personal experience and supplemented, if not supplanted, rationality with emotional and spiritual experience. They combined the emphasis on personal experience with a spiritual view of nature as a living force to be encountered with a sense of wonder rather than with science's dispassionate approach. It's easy to see how this personal approach encouraged creativity and individual expression.

Johann Gottlieb Fichte

We see in **Johann Gottlieb Fichte** (1762–1814) another philosopher who sought to discover the foundations of human knowledge. Fichte led the charge through the door that Kant had opened. Fichte and several other German thinkers were impressed with Kant's approach to knowledge as being structured by the mind but thought it incomplete. Fichte's conviction was that Kant had only indicated the truth but had neither fully explained it nor proved it. Fichte certainly had great respect for Kant as a person who had a power for divining truth, but he also thought that Kant was not conscious of the grounds on which he stood.

Fichte applied Kant's critical philosophy to the contents of the human mind and its ideas and came to conclusions beyond what Kant accepted as our minds' limits. Kant's philosophy is critical in that he says that all of our beliefs are open to analysis. You should be responding to that sentence with the thought, "but wasn't every philosopher before Kant also analyzing our beliefs?" True, but what Kant changed in philosophy (and our culture) was accepting that our minds actively contribute to our perceptions and beliefs. Look back at Locke's epistemology (see Chapter 5). Locke saw the mind as completely passive—sensations happened to the mind. Hume, too, saw the mind as no more than a "stage" on which ideas caused by the outside world appeared and disappeared. Kant said that the human mind not only actively structures its sense impressions by means of the Categories of Understanding but also is active in and of itself. That means that we are capable of critically analyzing our perceptions and ideas by focusing our rational capability on particular ideas. Fichte and the other German idealists took that idea and ran with it.

Kant held that there is only one set of categories that structured human understanding that is universal to all people in all times and places. Fichte challenged that assumption. Fichte claimed that there is more than one way to perceive and make sense of the world. Kant had made the human mind the new center of epistemology by declaring that objects conform to the mind's rational structure. Fichte went further than Kant's Copernican revolution by saying that the categories each person uses are what make the world meaningful. Philosophy, Fichte said, was not a dead piece of furniture but something animated by the soul of the person who wields it. The world is my world. *I* structure it. That means that my thoughts and values structure my experience.

This thinking also leads to the possibility that I can change the categories through which I understand the world. Fichte unfolded Kant's insights by centering his philosophy on the idea of freedom. In Fichte's view, freedom is a presupposition not only of human actions (choosing to eat out or cook at home, for example) but also of human cognition. Our experiences of the world, of events happening beyond our control, are accompanied by the feeling of necessity (that events happen inevitably in a causal order.), Fichte said, but there is also always the practical certainty of human freedom. Our decisions affect how we perceive and understand our world.

Fichte asks, What is the ground and meaning of our experience? He postulates that there are two alternatives. The first he calls "dogmatism," an approach to the universe that assumes that the foundation of experience is in an independent external reality. This approach interprets our inner experience as being determined by the outer world beyond our perception (the Kantian noumena). This approach of dogmatism is assumed by the scientist and by both the rationalist and empiricist philosophers. In sharp contrast, Fichte advocates "idealism," which finds the ground of experience in our own nature, our own self. This approach interprets the outer world in terms of our inner experience. Fichte argues that if we limit ourselves to scientific knowledge, as the dogmatist does, we will see ourselves only as passive objects subject to the deterministic necessity of the material world that science assumes.

For Fichte, the self is the foundation of experience. We have to begin with the self, he says, because we know our inner world of consciousness better than the outer world. Exactly the opposite of Hume's argument, Fichte's argument is that the objects of perception come and go, but behind all of our mental impressions is the constant activity of the self that stands behind all appearances of the world. Fichte argued that we cannot help but experience objective reality through self-positing. We begin from the certainty that we have an empirical consciousness—I am an "I" who asserts "I am" and can perceive and think about the world. The I is a self-positing activity that in its self-positing connects thought and being. That is Fichte's bedrock of certainty and why he asserts that we have no thoughts and no actions that are not grounded in our continual activity of self-positing. To illustrate this idea, Fichte reportedly once said to his students, "Gentlemen, think the wall," then, "Gentlemen, think him who thought the wall." What he meant is that in addition to every object that appears to you is your individual self that grounds those appearances.

How we should view ourselves and our world is, for Fichte, an intensely important and practical question. Like the later American pragmatists whom he influenced (we will meet them in Chapter 12), Fichte thought that our beliefs cannot be proved by rational arguments. He said that what makes a belief viable is whether it positively affects our lives and our interests. We choose our beliefs on the basis of their perceived value to us. The scientific method is not a given and not the only possible or best approach to the world. "Facts" are not beyond interpretation. Of course, people are free to choose to approach the universe scientifically, but those who choose this approach are doing so because they believe it serves their interests and makes the world meaningful to them. Even science is based on subjective commitments and acts of practical faith.

The conclusion that Fichte wants you to draw from his argument is that the world you live in is always a world structured by the way you approach it. The world that you experience is not a collection of meaningless bits of sense data that you take in passively like Locke's idea of a camera obscura. Quite the contrary, Fichte says—the world you experience is structured by your interests and values. Your world is a dynamic place in which you make choices. Our philosophy, thus, must move from understanding our self toward an understanding of the outer world. If we, as the dogmatist does, approach the universe as though it is nothing more than a plurality of matter in motion, we will never be able to discern our unified mind and consciousness. Only if we begin with our inner experience of being a unified, creative self will we then have the basis for giving meaning to everything else.

According to Fichte,

> The Nature on which I have to act is not a foreign element, called into existence without reference to me, into which I cannot penetrate. It is molded by my own laws of thought, and must be in harmony with them; it must be thoroughly transparent, knowable and penetrable to me, even to its inmost recesses. In all its phenomena it expresses nothing but the connections and relations of my own being to myself, and as surely as I may hope to know myself, so surely may I expect to comprehend it. (*The Vocation of Man* 125)

Thus, the "external world" is not so external after all. Through sense perception, you encounter many sensations that make up your experiences. However, you will encounter meaningful objects only when you creatively make those objects a part of your world. However you experience the world, it's always a world you have made in your own image. The world is not a world of dead objects but is a dynamic, spiritual process in which we participate.

Late in Fichte's philosophical career, his philosophy morphed into a transcendental speculation that came to be known as "subjective idealism." Fichte taught that all of our individual thoughts are avatars of a universal intellect he called the "Absolute Idea." There are shades of Plotinus in Fichte's later philosophy, although it is also strongly reminiscent of Berkeley's philosophy. Fichte said that we *are* experience and that we cannot raise ourselves above experience. He therefore rejected Kant's idea of the noumena because the idea of the thing-in-itself beyond experience is, Fichte claimed, a pure invention with no reality whatsoever.

For an object to be objectively real, Fichte said, means it possesses possible experiences. In other words, a tree is real because it can be perceived by a potential observer who can interact with the tree in many ways—look at it, sit under it, paint a picture of it, cut it down, and so on. Those experiences are what the tree is, and its reality is summed up by all possible experiences of it. In Fichte's later philosophy of idealism, all of these interactions are thoughts because thought is an interactive act, not a passive reflection on something apart. In this way, everything is thought, connecting thought and being, and everything is mind dependent, like in Berkeley's philosophy. This idealism perhaps sounds weird, but it shares the same foundation with quantum mechanics in that reality is dependent on the observer.

German Idealism and Romanticism

Contemporary with, and stimulated by, the philosophy of German idealism, was the artistic movement of Romanticism. This movement was an artistic expression of the active mind that can connect thought and being. At the heart of Romanticism was the vital importance of the artist's free expression. This expression was not a rational one but an emotional one. The artist's feelings are a law to themselves, and artistic creation should be free from rules dictating art's content or form. What the artist thinks and feels is what the artist creates.

The initial nucleus of the Romantic movement was two brothers in Jena (pronounced YAY-na), Germany—**August Wilhelm von Schlegel** (1767–1845) and **Friedrich von Schlegel** (1772–1829). Beginning in 1798, they published a philosophy of literature journal, *Athenaeum*, which, although it only published six issues over three years, was influential in establishing Romanticism as an intellectual movement. *Athenaeum* was the centerpiece of a circle of philosophers and artists in Jena, many of whom were professors at the city's university, who discussed and wrote about philosophy, religion, science, literature, and art. Notable members of the circle include Fichte; natural philosopher, **Friedrich Wilhelm Joseph** von Schelling (1775–1854); philosopher of religion, **Friedrich Ernst Daniel Schleiermacher** (1768–1834); poet and philosopher, **Friedrich Hölderlin** (1770–1843); **Georg Wilhelm Friedrich Hegel** (discussed at length later in this chapter); and literary critic, **Caroline Schlegel** (1763–1809), who was married to August Schlegel until she divorced him in 1803 to marry Schelling when she became Caroline Schelling.

After the circle in Jena dispersed in 1804, the center of the Romantic movement shifted to Coppet Castle, in Switzerland, where **Germaine de Staël** (1766–1817), commonly referred to as Madame de Staël, held court. Madame de Staël had been educated in the writings of Rousseau (see Chapter 6) and legal theorist **Charles-Louis Baron de Montesquieu** (1689–1755) by her mother who hosted an influential Parisian salon (a regular gathering of intellectuals). She followed in her mother's footsteps, holding her own salon and writing about political philosophy. She used her social and political connections (her father was the French minister of finance and her husband the Swiss ambassador to France) to urge dialogue and moderation among the adversaries in the years of chaos (1794–1799) amid the French Revolution. She opposed Napoleon, publishing a book of political philosophy and then a novel that argued against his absolutist ideology. Napoleon responded in late 1803 by banishing de Staël from France. That was the impetus for her setting up a new salon at Coppet Castle, where she conversed with many dozens of intellectuals and politicians (including Napoleon's brother), many of whom were or became leaders in academia, literature, or government.

In her Coppet salon, de Staël learned about German idealism and Romanticism, and she became a patron and disseminator of both. She published the French-language book, *De l'Allemagne* ("On Germany"), in 1810, coining the term "Romanticism," which we still use today. The first printing of the book was destroyed by order of Napoleon, who objected to de Staël's philosophical theories, but she managed to get it republished in London in 1813, after which it became popular. In the book, de Staël introduced German idealism and Romanticism to the rest of Europe, and she advanced a progressive vision of society combining Lockean limited government, individual expression, freedom (á la German idealism and Romanticism), and liberal Christianity. Her views influenced modern ideas of religious liberty and tolerance within a secular society.

Romanticism found natural expression in literature and music. Poets **William Wordsworth** (1770–1850), **Lord George Byron** (1788–1824), **Samuel Taylor Coleridge** (1772–1834), and **John Keats** (1795–1821) were among the writers who immersed themselves in Romanticism. Many people are not aware that **Ludwig van Beethoven's** (1770–1827) tremendous musical innovation was in part influenced by the incredible innovations occurring in German philosophy at that time. Beethoven knew several German idealist philosophers and corresponded with them. That's not to say that Beethoven was himself a philosopher. He produced no philosophical literature, preferring to do his thinking and being through music. Nevertheless, he was certainly influenced by the philosophers whom he knew and read. The cool thing about Beethoven is that he was the punk rocker of his day. Yes, really. His *Fifth Symphony* is famous not only because of its sublime beauty but because it shattered previous musical forms. In this and other compositions, Beethoven willfully disregarded convention and wrote music that expressed his emotions. In this, he captured the spirit of German Romanticism and German idealism.

G.W.F. Hegel and His Grand System

It's an exaggeration to say that in the last 200 or so years there has been a war in philosophy. But if we can describe the long "analytic/continental" divide in philosophy as a war, it was **Georg Wilhelm Friedrich Hegel** (1770–1831) who started it. That was not Hegel's intention, but he produced an all-encompassing system that still incites passionate debate among philosophers. To call someone a "Hegelian" has been, depending on who is saying it, high praise or an insult. Few, if any, today are true followers of Hegel's system, but his philosophy has influenced much of what is called "continental" philosophy. Understanding Hegel helps understand some of the issues in continental philosophy that developed in response to Hegel.

Hegel was a Prussian philosopher who followed in the footsteps of Kant but took Kant's ideas in a different direction. Some say Hegel is even more difficult to understand than Kant. I don't agree with that, which is not to say that Hegel is a walk in the park, but if you break Hegel's philosophy down into three main components, it's more manageable. The first part is to see his epistemology as an extension of Kant's in Hegel's phenomenology of mind. The second is to understand Hegel's philosophy as a historicist system sees human freedom in terms of history and the political state. The third part is his theory of interpersonal relations, centered on the concept of recognition.

Hegel's Phenomenology of the Mind

To learn about human understanding, Hegel uses a method he calls "phenomenology." He means the study of the phenomena of the mind, which is not an entirely new approach to epistemology, but Hegel places it at the center of philosophy as a full-fledged approach and discipline. He believed that we learn about ourselves and the universe best by starting with an analysis of the phenomena we perceive within our mind. Hegel's phenomenological approach inspired a new school of philosophy, which we will discuss in Chapter 14.

Hegel's phenomenology reveals human understanding to be a three-step process. The first is sense perception, which provides direct sensory information. This level of perception he calls "sense certainty" because it is direct experience without the mind contributing any content or concepts. This is a level of experience Kant would say is not possible, but Hegel says not only that it is possible but that this pure but empty and abstract experience shows us our need for concepts to interpret it.

The conscious mind must take the information given by sense certainty and place it under universal concepts. This second level, which Hegel calls "perception," shows that our minds are actively interpreting sense information about objects. We begin to see patterns and connections in our experiences, but we still do not have knowledge.

That requires the third level, "understanding," in which we conceive of objects in the context of the logical physical forces of the universe—specifically for Hegel, Newton's physical laws. At this level, we understand the unity of the object and how its qualities can change or endure. These three levels of consciousness work in sequence to give us conscious understanding of objects.

Continuing his phenomenological study of the mind, Hegel says that the next mental activity is self-consciousness, the level of awareness that the physical laws within understanding are attributed by our own minds. The mind is actively cocreating our understanding. This is similar to Kant's idea of the Categories, but for Hegel, our minds engage in a more conscious and dynamic process. Hegel sees the theories and models of science as products of the mind that are internal mental concepts by which we understand objects at the level of perception. When we aren't self-conscious, we mistakenly think these laws are external to us. When, using the phenomenological approach, we are self-conscious (that is, conscious of ourselves), we can see how we are creating the structures of theory, formulas, and interpretation by which we understand objects.

Hegel was also Kantian in that he believed the human mind is structured by "concepts"—the term he preferred over Kant's Categories. He rejected Kant's theory that all humans had the same set of Categories and instead said there are a variety of ways that peoples in different times and places can experience the world. This idea that concepts change over time led him to adopt historicism.

As early as 1797, Friedrich von Schlegel was lecturing at the University of Jena on the idea of historicism, the idea that philosophy should stress historical development and, in particular, how historical and cultural context affects ideas. This approach is in keeping with German idealism's concept that the structures of perception differ in different people, as opposed to Kant's idea that all people have the same, unchanging Categories of Understanding. This approach also reflected the growing belief in the reality of cultural, if not biological, evolution, meaning that ideas are products of their time and place.

People in the 1790s could see that a new era was upon them. The medieval era was long gone, the so-called Enlightenment had happened, and society was now morphing into something else. The United States had rebelled against England, and the French Revolution had toppled the long-standing French monarchy. James Watt's new steam engine (patented in 1769) had ignited the first Industrial Revolution. Change was happening. More than change, there seemed to be progress. The growing belief was that an old era was being replaced by a new, better era, just as the previous era was better than the one before it.

Almost hand in hand with German idealism was the idea of progress as a historical inevitability. The new era was progress over the Enlightenment, which was progress over the Renaissance, medieval, and classical periods. The challenge for philosophers and indeed all intellectuals was to understand earlier writers and their works in their historical contexts. Increasingly in the 1800s, writers portrayed human civilization in terms of historical progress and interpreted past writings according to their place within the unfolding development of humankind—in other words, how those past writers fit within the greater totality of progress. One of the biggest proponents of historicism and progress was **Karl Marx** (1818–1883), whom we will meet in Chapter 10. He was a follower of Hegel, although, as Marx himself said, he turned Hegel on his head. First, we need to understand Hegel's approach and his motives for adopting historicism.

Hegel's goal was to encapsulate in a philosophical system the unified rational totality of everything. Hegel saw Fichte and other German idealists as advocating idealism as a personal choice. Hegel wanted to establish idealism as an objective reality. He therefore did not agree with Fichte's dichotomy of idealism versus dogmatism. Hegel was a rationalist in that he believed that the universe had a rational order that could be understood through human reason. He was Kantian, however, in also believing that reason alone cannot bring us knowledge. Our reason needs sense experience to provide us with details about reality. Hegel's program is to gather information about the world, put that information into context, and then use reason to discern patterns and synchronicities in the information to understand the rational order of the universe. Hegel saw all of world history as an expression of a unified, rational process. He therefore believed that to understand any particular thing, we need to understand it within its place in the rational historical process. We are also a part of that process, so understanding the process of history is one part of understanding ourselves.

Hegel is saying two things about understanding and knowledge. The first is that our theories about the universe are the framework by which we understand the universe; our knowledge tells us what we perceive. The second is that the framework we have right now is the product of many centuries of human development. Humanity is evolving and has been doing so for a very long time, and the mental framework of our understanding is a product of that evolution. Philosophy and science have evolved as humanity has evolved. This is a vital aspect of Hegel's historicism—we are continually progressing. Of course Kant had a more advanced epistemology than Aristotle did. Of course Newton had a more advanced science than any of the ancient Greeks did. Later scholars built on the achievements of the past. All ideas are products of their time and place and need to be viewed within their historical setting. The larger point is that human understanding is evolving and growing as it interacts with the world and with previous understandings. Hegel's idea that understanding is a result of active cocreation also applies to an individual's consciousness. We learn through experience and by applying reason to our perceptions, learning from the experiences of others and ourselves. What we understand today is a better understanding than we had in the past.

Hegel noted that much of philosophy's history has been spent arguing about the correct criterion or method on which we must base all of our reasoning. Hegel says this is the wrong approach. We must begin where we are, not wait to find the perfect method. Hegel says that in starting to try to understand the universe, we find that our own consciousness provides the criteria we need. Hegel's view of knowledge is that it is through the continual act of investigating, questioning, and reasoning that we learn. We begin with a partial understanding of what we investigate, and as we gather more and more information, we develop greater and greater understanding. Thinking, for Hegel, is a continual process of self-correction, progressing from limited to more complete understanding. This is true no matter what we investigate, including the operation of our own minds.

Despite Hegel's acknowledgment that different times and places have different understandings, he still believed in absolute truth. His rejection of Kant's ideas about the limitations of human reason extended to his rejection of Kant's antinomies. Kant had said that we cannot use reason to decide between conflicting propositions about the cosmos. Hegel claimed that the seeming contradictions of Kant's antinomies can be resolved by going beyond personal subjective perspectives into an objective idealism. As mentioned earlier, the German idealists sought to overcome the distinction between thought and being through connecting self-consciousness with the rest of reality. Hegel interpreted this notion as overcoming the opposition between subject and object, knower and known. But although most German idealists celebrated individualism, Hegel rejected individual subjectivism and embraced the notion of absolute idealism—one absolute Idea that is truth itself. It is a philosophical view similar to that of Plotinus (see Chapter 3). One advances, Hegel says, toward self-consciousness through a continuing process of positing not the self but of positing the absolute object. As we shall see in our discussion of the second and third parts of Hegel's system, he connected thought and being, the subject and the object, by stating that the individual person will find identity only in objectivity.

Hegel's Historicist System

The second part of Hegel's philosophy is his system that attempts to show how people find freedom within the march of reason through history. One way to look at what Hegel is doing is that he is telling a story about human history. As we explore this story of history, it will seem difficult to see that his focus is on freedom. It is, but not in the way we understand freedom today. Perhaps we have evolved further? We'll see. It is, for him, all about reason.

Hegel believed that the human framework of thought was a true expression of the objective reality and that the evolutionary progress of human thinking was connected to the evolutionary progress of the divine Intellect, which he called "*Geist*." His philosophical system was his phenomenology of the march of reason through history as the expression of *Geist*.

Hegel's historicist system has four main ideas that we will go through in rational sequence.

History is the dialectical process by which *Geist* comes to know Itself and realize Its Idea.

Yes, *Geist*. It's a German word that has no exact translation into English (this is a problem for English speakers, especially in trying to understand German-language philosophy), so I will leave it untranslated, as I will do for several of Hegel's terms. *Geist*, as Hegel uses it, means mind, spirit, and culture simultaneously. Remember when I said that Plotinus is the most influential philosopher in history? Here is part of the reason why. *Geist* is Hegel's name for what Plotinus had called "*Nous*." Hegel sees *Geist* as Intellect that is active in the world, and the world is an expression of *Geist*. Hegel thinks that everything, and I do mean everything, is *Geist* trying to understand itself.

Don't mistake *Geist* for the monotheistic conception of a God with whom we interact and who cares about us. *Geist* is doing its own thing and is not a knowable deity. However, we are living in *Geist's* universe. Berkeley's philosophy made it seem as though we are living in the mind of God. Hegel's philosophy is that the universe *is* the rational mind of *Geist* manifesting Its thought in a material and spiritual reality. For Hegel, "God" or "Intellect" is not an entity separate from the universe; it *is* the universe, and the universe *is Geist*. We are all parts of a cosmic matrix that is a mind trying to understand itself.

As *Geist* engages in its rational process of understanding, it literally creates the universe, and the evolution of *Geist's* understanding creates the evolution of rationality in the world in which we live. Hegel's philosophy of history is based on the idea that *Geist's* reason directs the world through universal rational laws, and when we look back at history, we can discern this march of reason through history as the development of rationality. The purpose of the universe is *Geist* trying to understand Its Idea, Itself. We are part of that purpose. In Hegel's philosophy, Idea is not a mental entity, but the full actualization of a concept, of its "truth." An Idea, for Hegel, is continually making itself present in reality.

Freedom is the idea of *Geist*, and *Geist* is reason in and for itself.

Geist is Intellect; it is rationality. Because *Geist's* rational activity is the cause of everything, rationality is what is real, and all that is real is rational. Freedom was the final cause (in the Aristotelian sense) for Kant, but Hegel didn't believe in individual freedom as we would understand it. The final cause of the universe is for Geist to realize Itself as Reason Itself, and this realization gives It freedom. That's freedom for Geist, and we can only find our own freedom within that because...

The realization of freedom is the passionate individual as subject and object of history, and Its expression is the nation-state.

This is a very interesting aspect of Hegel's thought and is less "out there" than the previous two ideas. You are the subject and object of history. This is true whether or not you agree with the existence of *Geist*. You are the subject because you are an active participant in history. Your actions contribute to the unfolding of events. You are the object of history in that history happens to you, and you are a part of that matrix of historical events that, in Hegel's opinion, is *Geist* trying to realize Its Idea. Like *Geist*, we all have a drive for self-realization—to understand who we are and what our greatest potential is. Self-realization is true freedom. For Hegel, rationally realizing your role as a cog in the machine is the realization of your freedom, and the fullest realization of this is understanding your role in the political nation-state. Yes, your freedom is realized in your nation; if you are an American, your freedom is realized by being a passionate American. That's about culture, not politics.

Hegel wrote about "the I that is We, We that is I" (*Phenomenology of Spirit* § 177). This is an important concept for Hegel and has remained so for a number of subsequent philosophers. What Hegel means is that you are who you are in the context of your society. This makes sense when you think about it because, although you are an individual with your own mind and thoughts and feelings, you are defined more than anything else by your relations with others and the society around you. Your life history of friends, family, community, and learning and your reactions to them define who you are. This idea from Hegel, inspired by Kant (inspired by Hume, inspired by Berkeley, and so on...) is accepted today by every academic worth anything. What is distinctive about Hegel is that he thinks this interconnectedness is primarily expressed as the nation-state. Your freedom and identity are realized in being a good patriotic member of your nation and its culture.

The national *Zeitgeist* is a moment in history as world *Geist*.

The German word "*Zeitgeist*" is best translated as "the spirit of the time." Hegel applied the concept of *Zeitgeist* to the nation-state as a whole, and he believed we can discern its *Volksgeist*, or "national spirit." Hegel accepted Kant's idea that the human mind was active in cocreating its experiences, but he placed individual human minds within the nation-state, which is within the absolute mind of *Geist*. We aren't exactly cogs in the machine, but we are parts of a whole, and the whole is what is significant. Hegel believed that nations are the only real individuals in history. You are insignificant. The nation is significant. And *Geist* works out Its Idea on the grand stage of interactions of nations. History is the progressive working out of that idea. What Hegel called "the march of reason" through history is *Geist* learning and developing through history as it manifests its reason through nation-states. Hegel further said that on earth at any given time, there is one nation that most exemplifies *Geist* and Its Idea. That nation's *Volksgeist*, was the greatest current flowering of culture and reason. It once was ancient Greece, then the Roman Empire, and so on. In Hegel's time, he saw first Napoleon and later the Prussian Empire as that manifestation of *Geist*. It seems that Hegel believed that at any given time the most powerful nation-state in the world was leading the march of reason.

Hegel's Recognition Theory

All of that fits well with the third main component of Hegel's philosophy—recognition. Hegel uses a German word, "*Anerkennung*," that does not have an exact match in English but is translated as "recognition." In English, "recognition" has two meanings. The first is to identify something—"I recognize that object is a tree" (*Erkennung* in German). The second is to acknowledge, value, and respect something—"I recognize you as a student and treat you as a student deserves to be treated" (*Anerkennung* in German). It is this latter definition, to respect and value something, that is the sense Hegel means.

Hegel realized that recognition is crucial in social life. You are defined by your relations with others. To have successful, healthy relations with others, you need the acknowledgment and approval of others. Hegel realized that we are all dependent on recognition from others. Think about any role or idea by which you can identify yourself—friend, student, citizen, and so on. You cannot meaningfully be that unless others acknowledge you as that; therefore, you are dependent on other people and social institutions for your identity. You are not a friend unless someone recognizes you as a friend. You cannot say, "I am a student at

State University," unless the university recognizes you as such. You are not a citizen of a country unless that country legally recognizes you as one. Every single relation you have, every social identity you have, has a similar requirement. This includes even simple things like being a nice person or being attractive. You are not such unless others think you are. That's why we stress out so much about how we appear to others.

The positive side of recognition is that, when we receive it, we become part of a community. The negative side of recognition is that, because people need it, they compete for it. Remember **François VI, duc de La Rochefoucauld** and **Jean-Jacques Rousseau's** discussion of *amour propre* in Chapter 6. People often become obsessed with the need for approval and recognition from others. This obsession drives them to act according to how society tells them to act, and people become untrue to themselves in order to curry favor with others.

Hegel doesn't share Rousseau's antisociety position—he sees social norms as positives because he sees our freedom as realized within our nation-state. We are members of a society, and that society has a system of social norms that inform people how to act and how to treat others. When we act in accordance with those norms, we receive recognition from others, which includes social authority. Hegel believed that recognition is essential for providing the conditions in which individual people can form an identity. Hegel said that an individual develops as a person through the guidance of recognition norms. Through our actions, some successful, some not so, we receive approval and disapproval, and we learn how to behave and be a part of our society. Recognition also gives us social roles and responsibilities by which we come to self-realization of who we are as a passionate individual and member of our society. Recognition is the means by which we actualize our various freedoms through becoming a good member of our social community and of society as a whole.

Hegel acknowledges that recognition can also be a negative burden. His position is that recognition is more of a problem within interpersonal relations. Because we are defined by others and need recognition from them to know how we are and thus be autonomous, Hegel thought that we will fight against another person to affirm our own freedom by proving that our status is of more importance than that other person's. We are trying to express our freedom through elevating ourselves over another, but this conflict cannot achieve the mutual recognition that is essential to our freedom. Hegel's example is the master–slave relation, which needs to be interpreted more as an analogy than as literal. Someone is a master only if a slave acknowledges that mastery. So, Hegel says, the master is actually dependent on the slave for his own autonomous identity. This creates a conflict that neither can ever win. In Hegel's harsh assessment, the conflict ends only when one of them dies. The master–slave analogy illustrates how the irony of freedom is that we cannot be free except in terms of our relations with others and our place in a society. The theory of recognition based on Hegel's ideas became a topic in social philosophy, as we will see in Chapter 15.

Hegel's Influence

For several decades in the mid-1800s, Hegel and his philosophical system were very popular in Europe, especially in German-speaking lands. Hegel captured the *Zeitgeist* of the time in seeing everything as a continually improving rational order. It fit with the bourgeois optimism of the Industrial Revolution of the early 1800s. Hegel had many devoted followers—Hegelians—who developed his basic system in different ways. Karl Marx (1818–1883) is the most famous and influential of the Hegelians, although he strongly opposed certain aspects of Hegel's philosophy. Hegel also inspired fierce opposition to his system and its implications, and the most famous and influential of these philosophers is **Søren Kierkegaard** (1813–1855). We will meet Marx and Kierkegaard, respectively, in the next two chapters.

As mentioned earlier, Hegel is at least partly responsible for the analytic/continental divide in philosophy. Hegel's acknowledgment that human thinking and perception are relative to time and place and his call for a contextual study of ideas compose much of the foundation of what is now known as "continental philosophy." This approach to philosophy accepts that the ideas of philosophy and science are not eternal objects but are expressions of people living within historical and cultural contexts. The continental approach to epistemology is similar to Hegel's—gathering sense information, placing it in context, and using reason to identify the physical and social forces at work. Granted, recent philosophers have taken contextual studies far beyond what Hegel would have accepted, as we shall see in later chapters. Marx is an example of how one can be inspired by Hegel but take Hegel's ideas in a new direction. We'll see several branches of continental philosophy in the rest of this book. It's quite different from the approach of analytic philosophy, which focuses on logical analysis of language and scientific data, largely separated from their context.

Chapter 10

POLITICAL PHILOSOPHIES
OF SOCIAL REFORM

Politics has always been influenced by philosophers, and political change has frequently been inspired and informed by philosophical ideas. Philosophers are likewise influenced by the events of their time, and their political and social philosophies are usually responses to current events. The 1800s was a period of tremendous activity and change in philosophy, and these changes affected and were affected by large-scale social and political changes in Europe and the United States. In this chapter we look at two philosophical movements with rather different approaches to how we should improve society. The first is the British reform movement, a general term for the efforts to institute social, economic, and political reforms in the United Kingdom in the 1800s. The second is the philosopher Karl Marx (1818–1883) who called for fundamental change to society's economic and political structures. Both of these movements broadly affected society, including philosophy.

British Reform Movement

Significant developments in social philosophy and social reform took place in the United Kingdom in the 1800s. The Parliament of the United Kingdom passed a progressive series of laws beginning in 1802 regulating working hours and requiring basic safety and sanitation for people working in the country's factories. By 1847, factories were not allowed to employ children under the age of nine, and for other laborers, the work day was limited to 10 hours and the work week to 63 hours. These working hours seem unacceptably high to us today, but they were significant reforms in favor of workers' right for the time. The sentiment was growing in British society that working people deserved legal protections from exploitation and abuse. Throughout this period, philosophy and society were progressively moving toward awareness of ways that society can be reformed to benefit more people.

Social Reform Theories

British social reform philosophy remained firmly within the empiricist conception that the mind was passive and that all aspects of a human were formed by experience. These thinkers were influenced by both Hobbes and Locke, taking elements from each. A tension that was difficult to reconcile arose between the doctrine that all human character is formed (determined) by external circumstances and the conviction that one must be allowed freedom to act in one's self-interest.

That men (in the gender-exclusive meaning) act primarily on the basis of self-interest was popularized by **Adam Smith** (1723–1790) who argued that government must address itself to men's self-interest and not interfere unduly in men's freedom to act on it. Smith is often misinterpreted as believing men act *only* out of self-interest, but Smith also stated that men feel benevolence for others and have genuine interest in the good fortune of their fellow man. Smith's writings demonstrate the tension in human nature between the desire for oneself to be happy and for others to be happy. This tension translated to the question of how best to govern; how do we best structure society such that it funnels human nature into appropriate acts without interfering with individual self-interest?

Adding to this tension was the ethical philosophy of utilitarianism. Its inventor, **Jeremy Bentham** (1748–1832), used the term "utility" to mean a quality within any object whereby it tends to produce pleasure, good, or happiness or to prevent pain, evil, or unhappiness. Utilitarianism is a social ethical system based on the principle of utility, meaning that happiness should be maximized for the greatest number of people. We will not, in this book, go into the details of the ethical system of utilitarianism. For our purposes, we need only understand that (1) a number of the social reform theories were guided, at least in part, by the principle of utility, and (2) the principle of utility was considered in terms of the good of society as a whole.

The common remedy for the tensions between individual freedom and the determined human character was education. From Locke's epistemology, British philosophers saw the human mind as a tabula rasa, a blank tablet on which experience writes. If individuals are determined by external circumstances, good circumstances will make them good and bad circumstances will make them bad. Thus, we are wise to fill the individual with good circumstances that mold the individual's character. Hence, reform-minded philosophers advocated for public education—filling people with the good circumstances to make their "free" actions conform to appropriate standards of propriety. Proper education would develop an enlightened public that would act rationally—at least, that was the theory.

Another key element in social reform that intended to enhance utility was the expansion of the franchise—meaning the right to vote for representatives in government. John Locke had proposed the liberalization of government by expanding power beyond the monarch, but only extended political power of choosing who is in government to landowners. In the early 1800s, reform-minded philosophers urged a further liberalization of who was allowed to vote for members of the British Parliament. Their argument was firmly grounded in the idea that giving more people a voice in government would increase social utility. Utilitarian philosopher **James Mill** (1773–1836), in his essay, "Government" (1820), argued that all men are moved by self-interest and the only way to secure good government is by making the interests of elected representatives identical with those of their constituents. He therefore called for expanding the voting franchise to all men (he thought's women's interests were involved in that of their fathers or husbands),

The United Kingdom had an arcane system of electing members to Parliament that was uneven and too easy to corrupt. Desire for fairness led to Parliament's passage of the Reform Act of 1832, which reapportioned the distribution of Parliament seats and standardized voting eligibility rules across the United Kingdom. This was in no way universal suffrage. The Reform Act still limited voting rights to men of a certain level of wealth measured in terms of land owned or leased. However, it increased the number of eligible voters from around 366,000 to 650,000. That was still only 18 percent of the total adult male population. Even so, it was the first step toward full democratic participation in government.

The reluctance of reformers to include unpropertied working people came from their belief that such people were not sufficiently rational to make good political decisions. Education was proposed as a remedy for this, but the prejudices associated with the British class system—that one was either a "gentleman" or a "peasant"—meant that all but the most radical thinkers were disinclined to suggest that the working man should have a voice in government. Only male humans were thought to be capable of rational voting, and the Reform Act of 1832 put into law what had previously been custom—that only men were allowed to vote.

The doctrine of self-interest inclined John Stuart Mill, son of James Mill, to reject any socialist or communitarian political reforms, as they relied, he claimed, on what he called the "inferior" efficacy of feelings for one's fellow persons. The younger Mill wanted to expand the franchise, but he wanted to put in place systems that would ensure that the "very *élite* of the country" would be elected to and exercise influence within government.

John Stuart Mill

John Stuart Mill (1806–1873) is literally a second-generation British philosopher of social reform. His father, James Mill, was a colleague of Jeremy Bentham, and the elder Mill raised the younger in utilitarian social philosophy. The younger Mill had interests in the philosophies of science, epistemology, and logic, but his most influential work was in social philosophy. Mill cowrote several essays with his wife, **Harriet Taylor Mill** (1807–1858), whom he considered his friend and equal, although most people ignored her because she was a woman working in a very sexist time. In his social philosophy, Mill was primarily motivated by the central principle of maximizing social utility. Suffice to say that Mill thought that political philosophy should be guided by what is good for society as a whole and that what is good is the collective happiness of the society as a whole.

There is a tension in Mill's thinking between the interests of the individual and society as a whole. Mill does not think like Hobbes and Hegel that the individual should give his or her all to the state, but Mill also does not think like Rousseau or Marx that the state and the individual are at odds. Instead, Mill believed that the state should be interested primarily in ensuring the welfare of its citizens, especially their liberty. In 1859, he wrote *On Liberty*, in which he advocated for all people to have complete freedom as long as they acted responsibly toward other people.

Central to Mill's social philosophy was that "over himself, over his own body and mind, the individual is sovereign." In this idea, Mill was not celebrating the individual as did Rousseau, Kierkegaard, or Nietzsche (the latter two we will meet in Chapter 11). Mill's reasoning is that diversity and innovation lead to greater social utility; therefore, "the despotism of custom is everywhere the standing hindrance to human advancement, being in unceasing antagonism to . . . the spirit of liberty, or that of progress or improvement" (*On Liberty*, 132). It's not that greater individual liberty doesn't benefit the individual, it's that what matters is what is good for society as a whole.

Mill was conscious of the problems that Rousseau's concept of the general will created, in particular what Mill termed the "tyranny of the majority." A totalitarian government is almost by definition tyranny of the minority over the majority. If the government is democratic, it's possible that the majority can tyrannize the minority. To protect those in the minority, Mill introduced the "harm principle."

> The sole end for which mankind are warranted, individually or collectively, in interfering with the liberty of action of any

of their number, is self-protection. That the only purpose for which power can be rightfully exercised over any member of a civilised community, against his will, is to prevent harm to others. His own good, either physical or moral, is not a sufficient warrant. He cannot rightfully be compelled to do or forbear because it will be better for him to do so, because it will make him happier, because, in the opinions of others, to do so would be wise, or even right. These are good reasons for remonstrating with him, or reasoning with him, or persuading him, or entreating him, but not for compelling him. (*On Liberty*, 17)

By establishing the principle that government should interfere in human lives only to prevent harm, Mill is prohibiting the exploitation of the few by the many. Government should not exert any power of coercion on people, even when public opinion calls for such coercion.

The harm principle intends to accomplish several things. It denies the utility of exploitation of labor, even slavery, which a strict utilitarian could argue is justifiable if the pain caused by the enslavement of some is less than the pleasure of those who benefit from the products of slavery. It provides a delineation between permissible and impermissible speech. One can express an opinion critical of others, but one cannot incite a mob to physically attack others. The harm principle also expressed Mill's strong belief that an individual's personal tastes and habits are the concern of only that individual. As long as an individual doesn't harm anyone else, the public has no business interfering. This has led to concept of the "victimless crime," the usual examples being drug use and prostitution. Mill was not endorsing these practices but simply making the point that social morality has bigger, better concerns. Social utility is not increased by compelling people to act in certain ways unless their actions are harming others.

One of Mill's social concerns was eliminating poverty, which caused disease, a sense of worthlessness, unkindness, and other forms of suffering that diminished society's overall utility. He agreed with Adam Smith that businesses should be unhindered to engage in commerce but thought that government had a responsibility to ensure equal access to commercial opportunities. He further believed that government should intercede when market forces are not sufficiently providing for the needs of the people. Mill advocated for progressive taxation—the system that places greater tax burden on the wealthy who can better afford it.

Mill also thought that government should regulate working conditions to create a structure that would increase happiness in the working class. Like Karl Marx and Friedrich Engels (whom we meet later in this chapter), Mill criticized how the labor market pressured workers to accept working terms that were against their own self-interest (*Principles of Political Economy* 1848, the same year that Marx and Engels published

The Communist Manifesto). In language remarkably similar to that of Marx and Engels, Mill said that the system created competition among workers that incentivized workers to concede to capital, meaning they had to work for less money. This concession by the worker drives down wages and makes all workers worse off. Unlike Marx and Engels, Mill thought the rational solution to this wage exploitation was not revolution but government intervention and regulation.

Mill was a leading influence on what has come to be known as "social democracy." As Mill put it, the role of government is to represent the public interest, serve society, and be answerable to it. Mill emphasized the preventive and supportive roles of government. He believed that government was obligated to provide for the general welfare of all of its citizens, including providing sanitation, safe food and water, roads, and other infrastructure. To protect the innocent, the government must take precautions against crimes before they have been committed and must detect and punish criminals afterward. He agreed with the death penalty for aggravated murder but said that the legal system must be constrained to following the harm principle. Mill said that punishment of offenders must reform more than harm the offender, otherwise it is counterproductive to society. Consistently, Mill supported actions that would increase social utility.

Mill became a well-known and respected author and politician, and he leveraged his fame to argue for the legal equality of women in his book, *The Subjection of Women* (1869). His arguments were similar to Mary Wollstonecraft's arguments (see Chapter 6) decades earlier, but Mill's book, because he was a man and famous, was more widely read and respected. Mill took up Wollstonecraft's observations that society systematically discriminates against women, subjecting them to a lower status, and that this subjection was harmful to women and to society as a whole.

Interestingly, Mill's argument for equality of the sexes was not based on equal human rights but on the grounds of the passive mind doctrine that all human character is a result of education and circumstances. Yes, he said, treat women the same as we treat men, but because we can mold women in the same way that we mold men. Legal and political institutions should be impartial toward all people, Mill argued, and the legal subordination of one sex to the other should be abolished. He advocated for ending discrimination against women even though his rationale was simply to enhance social efficiency and utility.

Regardless of Mill's motivations, he did much to inspire the first wave of feminism (which we will discuss in Chapter 18). In *The Subjection of Women* (1869), he called for women to have control over their own bodies, to be allowed to own and control property, to have solo legal custody of children, and to be able to engage in occupations outside the home.

Mill ran for public office and served a term as a member of the British Parliament. During his tenure there, he was a leading progressive voice, most notably being the first member of Parliament to advocate for women's suffrage. He also called for reform of laws on marriage to give women legal equality with their husbands, including legally suing for divorce, on the grounds that society should be impartial toward all people.

Karl Marx—the Misinterpreted Diagnostician

Pretty much everything you think you know about German philosopher **Karl Marx** (1818–1883) is wrong. A century of misinformation about what Marx actually wrote and advocated for has given people false impressions. Much of that false information about Marx came from those who claimed to be instituting his ideas but, in fact, were not. There has never been a truly Marxist society. No, the "communism" of the Soviet Union and China were not true to Marx's philosophy. Another huge chunk of that false information about Marx came from the capitalists whom Marx opposed and who wanted to stamp out Marx's critique of capitalism.

Marx studied law then switched to philosophy, earning his PhD 1841. His outspoken radical politics led to him being exiled from Prussia in 1843 and then France in 1845. He took refuge in multiple cities before moving to London in 1849 where he lived until his death. He supported himself by working as a journalist, including as a London correspondent for the *New-York Daily Tribune*. His passion throughout his life was the liberation of the working class from their oppression by the upper classes. He wanted to change the world for the better, he said. In a number of essays and books, several published only after his death, Marx developed his philosophies of class struggle and historical materialism.

The Era of Revolutions?

The path to understanding Marx begins by understanding this excerpt from *The Communist Manifesto*:

A spectre is haunting Europe—the spectre of Communism. All the Powers of old Europe have entered into a holy alliance to exorcise this spectre. . .

Where is the party in opposition that has not been decried as Communistic by its opponents in power?. . .

The Communists disdain to conceal their views and aims. They openly declare that their ends can be attained only by the forcible overthrow of all existing social conditions. Let the ruling classes tremble at a Communistic revolution. The proletarians have nothing to lose but their chains. They have a world to win.

WORKING [PEOPLE] OF ALL COUNTRIES, UNITE! (*The Communist Manifesto*, Preamble, emphasis theirs)

Whoa, dudes, that's intense. Marx, with **Friedrich Engels** (1820–1895), wrote *The Communist Manifesto* in 1848. In it, they famously predicted a worldwide workers' revolution. They were incorrect, but they had good reason to believe that what they predicted would transpire. That very year, 1848, came to be known as "The Year of Revolutions" because, across Europe, six different peasant or worker revolts took place against local or national aristocratic rulers. Everything seemed to be coming to a head. For Marx, it seemed to be the case that workers were realizing their state of alienation and were rising up against their oppression. He applauded this because, unlike John Stuart Mill, he saw revolution as the only possible response to the alienation and other harms caused by capitalism. Marx thought that the purpose of philosophy was to change the world. That's why he wrote.

As the manifesto's text shows, the idea of communism already existed—Marx didn't invent it. "Communism," after all, comes from the Latin "*communis*," which means "communal," so the idea of communism is the idea of a communal society, variously interpreted, in contradistinction to a hierarchical society dominated by an elite class. Marx and Engels were discussing an emerging philosophical idea that, on the basis of contemporary events, they thought was about to become the major political philosophy in Europe. Marx's goal was to understand both the movement he thought he saw coming and the broken sociopolitical system that the movement was opposing.

How did Marx and Engels come to the conclusion that revolution was inevitable? They based it not only on then current events but also on then current philosophy.

The dominant philosopher in Europe in the 1840s was Hegel. A split had developed among Hegel's followers into a conservative, or right-wing, interpretation of Hegel, and a radical, or left-wing, interpretation of Hegel. The split was predominantly based on whether the followers focused on the transcendent or the earthly interpretation of Hegel's system.

Here is the central example. Hegel had written that the real is the rational and the rational is the real, by which he meant that rationality is reality and vice versa. Right-wingers linked this concept to the hierarchical philosophical systems of the past. "The real is the rational" harkened back to Platonic ideas of the Good and Aristotelian ideas of final causes and essences. These Right Hegelians saw the Hegelian system as a fulfillment of that historical progression of human thought guided by a higher force. It was certainly a reasonable interpretation of Hegel, who saw human progress in terms of a march of reason through history (European history and thought, of course).

Marx was one of the left-wing Young Hegelians who agreed with the Hegelian idea of historicism (the notion that there is a pattern to historical development) but who believed that human society is not rational and not guided by a higher rational force. If the "rational is the real," then history is still evolving and not yet fully real. In brief, Marx saw the central contradiction of European society as, on the one hand, thinking it embodied the ideal of individual reason and liberty but, on the other hand, being in denial about the lived reality of irrationality and the lack of freedom caused by industrialization and poverty. Marx believed that working people were waking up to these contradictions and were rebelling against the elite class that was oppressing them.

The March of Class Struggle

Armed with the Hegelian notion that history has a pattern and that history is developing along rational lines, Marx believed he saw that pattern.

> The history of all hitherto existing societies is the history of class struggles. Freeman and slave, patrician and plebeian, lord and serf, guild-master and journeyman, in a word, oppressor and oppressed, stood in constant opposition to one another, carried on an uninterrupted, now hidden, now open fight, a fight that each time ended, either in a revolutionary re-constitution of society at large, or in the common ruin of the contending classes. (*The Communist Manifesto* I.1-2)

History shows, Marx and Engels claimed, that the rich exploit the poor. Always have. Society has always been divided into a small wealthy elite and the poorer masses. In Marx's time, that divide was between the capitalists who owned the means of industrial production and the workers who owned nothing and were therefore forced to sell their labor to survive. The capitalists were profiting from the labor of the workers—the rich exploited the poor.

Similar to Hegel, Marx thought that when we look back at history, we can discern a rational evolution through successive epochs. Marx said that he had turned Hegel on his head, replacing Hegel's *Geist* as the force that determines history with economic determinism, a concept that Marx, along with Engels, invented. The epochs of history rise and fall as a result of economic determinism. All human activity is determined by inescapable economic necessities. Individual humans are powerless to escape or affect these material macroeconomic forces that determine the nature of what they are and their lives.

Human history is, therefore, economic history for Marx. Humans need to satisfy their material needs; therefore, they are dependent on the forces of production that satisfy those needs. As history evolves, the forces of production are altered by economic necessities and technological changes. What never changes are human material needs and the uninterrupted struggle between the ruling class of elites and the working class over control of the forces of production. History is, therefore, the history of the class struggle.

In the economically determined epochs of history, according to Marx, there was first the epoch of slavery when the elite directly owned other people, then the epoch of feudalism when the elite owned the land and tied the people to it, and now the epoch of capitalism when the elite own the industries and tie the people to them. In each epoch, the elite own and control the means of production, including farm fields, mines, and factories from small to large. In each epoch, the system of economic exploitation grew until its rational contradictions meant that the economic structure could no longer maintain the forces of production and circumstances forced an evolutionary change to a new system. So, slavery morphed into feudalism and feudalism morphed into capitalism. Next, capitalism will collapse from the weight of its rational contradictions, which make it unsustainable. This collapse of capitalism will usher in the next epoch—communism—when the class divide will finally end and society will be without rational contradictions. At least, that's what Marx predicted.

The Problem with the Bourgeois Class

Why will capitalism collapse? What did Marx see as its rational contradictions? Capitalism is an economic system defined by bourgeois property ("bourgeois" from Middle French, roughly meaning "merchant class"). Marx and Engels write in *The Communist Manifesto* that "modern bourgeois private property is the final and most complete expression of the system of producing and appropriating products, that is based on class antagonisms, on the exploitation of the many by the few" (*The Communist Manifesto* II.11). It's crucial to understand what Marx and Engels do *not* mean by bourgeois private property. They say this:

> We Communists have been reproached with the desire of abolishing the right of personally acquiring property as the fruit of a man's own labor, which property is alleged to be the groundwork of all personal freedom, activity and independence. Hard-won, self-acquired, self-earned property! Do you mean the property of the petty artisan and of the

small peasant, a form of property that preceded the bourgeois form? There is no need to abolish that; the development of industry has to a great extent already destroyed it, and is still destroying it daily. Or do you mean modern bourgeois private property? But does wage-labor create any property for the laborer? Not a bit. It creates capital. (*The Communist Manifesto* II.13)

You should note that Marx and Engels are referring to John Locke's labor theory of property (see Chapter 6), pointing out that the bourgeois capitalist system does not create property for the laborer. The system creates capital for the bourgeois class. Capital is money, but it's more than that—it's power. Capital is not a personal but a social power. The problem with bourgeois society is that its private property is capital. Capital is independent and has individuality, while the living person (the laborer) is dependent and has no individuality.

Marx and Engels refer here to the corporation, a social institution that was developed in the 1600s with the express purpose of creating capital for its investors. Corporations proliferated in the early 1800s, and Marx and Engels were prescient in their description of capital having individuality because 18 years after *The Communist Manifesto* in 1866, the United States ratified the 14th Amendment to the Constitution. That amendment, affirmed by multiple Supreme Court decisions, recognized a corporation as a "natural person," giving corporations as many rights as, if not more rights than, individual people naturally have (Congress.gov, "U.S. Const. XIV Amend."). Marx and Engels were also prescient in that today, the power of corporations dominates economic, social, and political life.

The bourgeois system is the private ownership of the means of production that splits society into the classes of bourgeois and proletariat (from the Latin, *proletarius*, meaning the lowest class of society). Members of the bourgeois capitalist class own the means of production at which workers produce commodities to be sold for the personal profit of the bourgeois class. Driven by the combination of greed and competitive pressures from other capitalists, the capitalists need to keep costs low, and labor is the biggest cost to production. Yes, there are fixed costs, such as the costs for raw materials and the running of a factory, but the lower the wages the capitalist can pay the worker, the more profit the capitalist makes. Capitalism has an inherent need to keep wages low.

Regardless of the level of wages, the capitalist business model is inherently corrupt and exploitative, said Marx. All profits, Marx argues in his book, *Das Kapital* (1867), are made by exploiting wage labor. *Das Kapital* is a dense book devoted to exposing economic contradictions of capitalism, but Marx's basic philosophical argument is simple and eloquent and shows one of the differences between capitalism and free enterprise.

Capitalism is the exploitation of the surplus value produced by labor. Here's what that means. In free enterprise, where the worker—for example a blacksmith or a tailor—owns the means of his or her own production, the worker also owns the goods that are the products of his or her own labor and can sell those products and keep all of the revenue. In capitalism, the bourgeois capitalist owns the means of production but does not work, hiring others to perform the labor needed to produce goods. The workers do not own the products of their labor, the capitalist does, who then sells the product and keeps all of the revenue. But to make a profit, after subtracting other fixed costs, the capitalist has to pay the workers less than the value of their labor. In a twelve-hour workday (common in the 1800s), the worker is paid wages, but only the equivalent value of eight hours of work. The value of the other four hours of work is pocketed by the capitalist as profit.

This is why the capitalist work relationship is not equal. Because you as a worker do not own the means of production, your only way of surviving is to sell your labor at a discount to the capitalist. Because they own the means of production, the capitalists hold much more power in the labor-for-wages transaction. The wages you receive from the capitalists are not a fair exchange for the value of your labor. Marx claims that in the capitalist system, instead of working only for yourself, you work only partially for yourself. You mainly work to make profits for the capitalist. The worker doesn't receive a fair wage for his or her labor, and in the capitalist system, never will. This is one principal corruption of the capitalist system, and a major reason why capitalism is doomed to failure, Marx claimed.

Capitalism's Greatest Harm: Human Alienation

For Marx, the injustice of capitalism is far deeper than "I don't get paid enough." The capitalist system harms human beings. Even the capitalist, who benefits from the exploitation of the proletariat, is harmed. The capitalist is trapped by the system, Marx says. The capitalist is in continual competition with other capitalists—business competitors—and is driven to make more profits so that the profits can be invested to grow the means of production to make more profit to grow more, and so on, and so on. "Accumulation for the sake of accumulation, production for the sake of production," characterizes the bourgeois capitalist, Marx says. This, along with its inherent need to exploit labor, is why Marx sees capitalism as an irrational system doomed to collapse.

But, of course, it is the worker who suffers the most.

> It is true that labor produces for the rich wonderful things, but for the worker it produces poverty. It produces mansions, but for the worker, shacks. It produces beauty, but for the worker, deformity. It replaces labor by machines, but it

throws one section of the workers back into barbarous types of labor and it turns the other section into a machine. It produces intelligence, but for the worker, stupidity, ignorance. ("Economic and Philosophic Manuscripts of 1844")

For Marx, the central question is the relationship of workers to production. Among other things, capitalism is a particular system of production, and all production is dependent on labor, so capitalism has a particular relationship of workers to production. Workers suffer not just economic deprivation but also a kind of spiritual alienation. In Marx's early writings, now known as the "Economic and Philosophic Manuscripts of 1844," he explains the forms of alienation suffered by the proletariat. It is unfortunate that Marx did not publish these manuscripts (they were found years later) because they show another side of his philosophy about which few people know.

Marx said that the irrational nature of the capitalist system causes estrangement or alienation for the worker in four ways, all of which stem from the fact that in capitalism's system of production, labor is *external* to the worker. When one works for oneself, one's work is a personal expression. Marx, more than 150 years ago, was much more familiar than we are with independent craftspeople who owned their own workshops, producing their own goods to sell. Marx said the work of such belongs to their intrinsic nature and their work affirms who they are. The opposite is true in capitalism. Work is a job that is external to one's intrinsic nature. You go to your job at which you are unhappy because the labor is neither an expression of who you are nor an activity that develops you mentally or physically. These facts cause the first two forms of alienation.

Workers are alienated from the product of their labor.

We've covered much of this idea already, and it's central to Marx's philosophy. Craftspeople, because they own their means of production, own the products they produce. Workers in capitalism do not own the means of production. They work at the bourgeois property owner's factory, producing goods that are owned by the factory owner. The products of the workers' labors are owned and controlled by the factory owner, who is free to sell and profit from what the labor of others produces. The workers have no control over or ownership of the product of their labor. Yes, the workers receive a wage, but as Marx explained earlier, that wage is not fair compensation for the workers' labors.

Workers are alienated from the process of production.

Workers have no say in the process of production; they are merely used by it. The process is fully external to them. To manufacture products, factories require the commodities of raw materials, the commodities of the machinery that processes the material, and the commodity of workers to run the machines. On the job, workers are not people; they are interchangeable parts—commodities. Still today, businesses refer to their "human resources," showing that workers are just so much fungible raw material to be used by the company as it sees fit and for its sole benefit.

Workers are alienated from their own human nature.

Workers are human beings, but capitalism does not treat them as human beings. Marx says that the nature of human beings is to be free and consciously active. As other philosophers have acknowledged, we each have our own will, and Marx says that our conscious life activity distinguishes us from the animals. Animals act only to satisfy their own immediate needs, but we humans can create for purposes beyond our immediate needs, and we see ourselves in the world we create. The capitalist system of production strips this creative activity away from workers. The capitalist system objectifies workers, turning them into mere beasts of burden, but actually making them lower than beasts of burden because the capitalists spend no effort to care for and feed the workers. The bourgeois property owner feeds and takes care of his horses but expects his workers to fend for themselves. Workers are forced to work to sustain their physical bodies—they work to eat. Work, therefore, is forced labor that is merely a means to satisfy needs external to that work. The height of the workers' servitude is that it is only as workers that they can maintain themselves as material beings and that it is only as material beings that they are workers. They are no longer human beings.

Workers are alienated from each other.

Workers not only are degraded below being human but also are forced to see other workers as degraded to that level. In their servitude, they are alienated from their employers, but they are also alienated from their fellow workers. Because capitalism reduces them to fungible commodities, they don't see their fellow workers as allies but as competitors for the finite number of jobs available. As John Stuart Mill had observed, Marx also saw that the capitalist system of production created competition among workers that incentivized workers to work for less money than their peers thereby driving down wages and making all workers worse off. Far worse, in Marx's mind, is that this competition turns workers into mutual threats to each other. The other worker could be willing to work longer hours and/or for lower wages; therefore, one's fellow workers are potential adversaries.

Marx was hardly the only person aware of the dehumanization of the working class. James Mill, not a radical by any stretch, had bemoaned in an 1813 essay ("Essays on the Formation of Human Character,") the plight of the factory worker. The elder Mill almost poetically sympathized with the workers whose eyes were exclusively fastened day after day upon one and the same narrow circle of objects and operations, while their minds had access to an even smaller number of ideas. Marx and Mill were describing the patently obvious effects of the capitalist system of mass production.

The Structure of Society

Marx defined three large-scale structures in society. These structures delineate capitalist society, but similar structures can also be found in precapitalist epochs. The first is the forces of production, which are the means of production—industry and the raw materials, machinery, and labor that it consumes. The second is the relations of production—the social institutions and practices that regulate the forces of production. To differentiate them from the third structure, Marx refers to these first two structures as the combined economic substructure. At a social level above the economic substructure is what Marx calls the superstructure—the social institutions and norms involved in the production of ideas. Marx's use of "ideas" is not the same as the epistemologist's limited uses of the term but is the broader sense of the term "idea" common to us today. Therefore, the superstructure contains all of our social ideas—moral, political, legal, cultural, philosophical, religious, and linguistic.

Superstructure: the political system and its cultural expressions
|
Relations of production: economic institutions and practices
| } Economic
Forces of production: material means of production   substructure

The superstructure is the way in which people think about themselves and their world, and includes everything we would consider a society's culture. Marx believed that the superstructure rose out of the economic substructures. The superstructure is an expression of the economic substructure and, therefore, changes over historical epochs and is subject to economic determinism. The superstructure's foundation is the economic forces to which the superstructure corresponds, which affects society as a whole.

From this point on, Marx's philosophy gets complex and even more controversial. Marx claims that because society is defined by class struggle, the ideas produced by the superstructure serve the interests of the ruling class. Those who control the economic substructure also control the superstructure, and they use the superstructure to rationalize the current social system. The ruling class—in capitalism, the bourgeois property owners, including corporations—creates a false consciousness that hides or justifies the irrationalities and injustices of the exploitation of workers. Marx calls this illusionary consciousness "ideology." In the capitalist system, the superstructure pushes the ideology that creates the false consciousness that capitalism is rational and good.

Marx claims that in every epoch of history, every society is ruled by the ideology created by the ruling class. This is Marx's most influential and controversial idea. The debate is not whether he has identified a real feature in human society but how complete the reach of ideology is in affecting societal and individual thinking. Marx and a large cadre of his followers claim that reach is complete—that ideology inescapably permeates every aspect of human life and is used to enforce the capitalist system's exploitation of the proletariat. In this view, all social institutions are tools of the ruling power structure, and the primary purpose of all social expressions is to perpetuate the class structure. It is this interpretation that that has inspired the more radical expressions of Marxism.

Marx further claims that ideology is always false and therefore always harmful. All ideology deceives people into seeing their circumstances as opposite of how they really are. Ideology justifies social and economic inequities as natural and even beneficial to exploited people. Examples of these false ideological justifications are such ideas as "colonization benefited the primitive colonized people" and "capitalism serves the interests of the working class." Even philosophers and scientists, who think they are discerning truth and leading the way to positive social change, are active ideologists, Marx says. All social institutions and all human consciousness are social products that have no history and no development aside from being tools of ideology. It's easy to see how much paranoia is created by a full embrace of these ideas.

Working People of the World Unite?

We come full circle to where we began this section. The working class has nothing to lose but its chains, Marx and Engels claim. Workers of the world must unite and rebel against the ruling capitalists. Marx, for all his analytical skill, has a very black-and-white conception of how to deal with the inequalities and injustices of capitalism. There is only one solution: capitalism must be ended because capitalism dominates every aspect of both the superstructure and the economic substructure; therefore, it cannot be reformed. All of society must be upended to destroy capitalism. Many small-minded, bitter people have ever since latched onto that idea and acted accordingly. Much hate-filled violence has been rationalized by appealing to Marx.

Marx thought that the workers' revolution was inevitable, what he thought he saw immediately about to transpire. He was wrong. As mentioned earlier, he had some good reasons for thinking that capitalism's breaking point was imminent, but his primary reason was theoretical. His economic determinism told him that change happens when the material forces of social development come into conflict with existing relations of production. The resulting tensions within that society will eventually spark a social revolution and usher in a new epoch. He thought this had happened before when slavery changed to feudalism and when feudalism changed to capitalism. Marx didn't describe how and when these changes happened, probably because there are no clear signs of exactly when and where these changes occurred. Nevertheless, Marx was certain that economic determinism would force the next social revolution to happen soon, sweeping away capitalism and ushering in a new postcapitalist epoch.

Marx's vision of the workers' revolution has much in common with religious eschatological predictions of a final judgment. Evil is in control of the world, but the die is cast that the great evil will be destroyed and humanity liberated. First, though, the current epoch must run its full course until a breaking point is reached, a climactic final battle is waged, and humanity's liberation happens.

In its simplest terms, Marx's prediction is that capitalism is doomed because of the system's inextricable needs to exploit labor and have competing companies engage in cutthroat struggles with each other. Capitalism will accelerate toward its doom as competition eliminates less efficient companies, increasing the consolidation of economic power. Fewer companies competing for the same number of workers gives more economic power to the surviving capitalists and throws more workers (including new workers from the now bankrupt capitalist companies) into competition for the fewer remaining jobs. This further drives down wages in addition to capitalism's inherent pressures to keep wages low. As the numbers of the working class increase, and as their misery increases, they will reach a breaking point, and desperate workers will explode into revolution. Marx describes this no differently than a chemist would describe a reaction of ingredients because Marx thought this entire process was governed by economic determinism.

So, what happens after the breaking point, according to Marx? Violence will inevitably ensue because the only way to end capitalism is through the forceful elimination of capitalism—what Marx ominously calls "the dictatorship of the proletariat." Chaos is unavoidable but will be contained when leaders of the revolution form a temporary state to take over the means of production. This intermediate stage Marx called "socialism" (we'll discuss non-Marxist theories of socialism in Chapter 12). The state's only purpose in this stage is to manage the redistribution of the means of production to the workers. After this redistribution is accomplished, the leaders of the state will willingly dissolve the state and work for themselves alongside the other workers.

The revolution having eliminated class divisions, there remain only the people. Working for themselves rather than for others, they are no longer alienated from their labor and the products of their labor. No longer being exploited by capitalists, they are no longer alienated from their own human nature and each other, so they have no cause for struggle and can express themselves freely. All people are now equal and free, and the people can collectively control the political and economic life of society. This is the final stage of the epochs of human history, which Marx calls "communism," which simply means a communal society. In the epoch of communism, Marx thought, there will be no more class struggle, thus it is the end of history—humanity has reached the most advanced stage of economic determinism. Human society will be rationally and economically ideal because workers will control the means of production. Beyond that, Marx has little to say about what communism is.

Marx's Blindness

Obviously, there are multiple problems with this vision, like the overarching optimism of the sequence of events, for starters. Marx, like Rousseau, believes that greed and selfishness are not a part of human nature but are emotions created by society. When capitalism is destroyed, human behavior will change because the capitalist economic substructure and superstructure will no longer determine human behavior. Instead, people will naturally work together for the greater good. This is why Marx assumes that after the revolution has finished eliminating capitalism, the temporary state will efficiently perform its tasks of redistributing all ownership of the means of production back to the workers and will dissolve itself.

History shows us that human nature is not as communally minded as Marx had hoped. The world has never seen a communist society. The revolutions that claimed to be communist—in the Soviet Union, China, Cuba—were quickly hijacked by leaders who remained permanently stuck in the stage of the temporary state. They called their states "socialist," but they were never dedicated to the good of society, and, thus, their states were political dictatorships, not socialist societies. They clung to power continually claiming the revolution against the capitalists was not yet over, so they had to keep control of the means of production a little longer . . . and a little longer . . . and. . . . The fault in these failed states wasn't communism or socialism because those states never got to those points; they were ironically more capitalist than anything in their exploitation of workers. Marx didn't seem to consider this a possibility. Like Hobbes, Marx didn't take into account how much power corrupts.

Another problem is that Marx never explains how his projected idyllic communist society would actually work. Marx said the motto of the communist society would be "from each according to his ability, to each according to his needs," but he didn't explain how we determine individual abilities and needs or how we prioritize conflicting abilities and needs.

His other basic principle of the new communal society is that workers control the means of production. OK. How? To say that workers will now make political and economic decisions doesn't explain the mechanism by which they do so. Marx seems to be relying on his assumption that, absent class struggle, everyone will be eager to cooperate. Soviet propaganda films played heavily on the theme of happy peasants joyously working, but these expressions of ideology never dealt with the realities of life. How do worker-run farms, mines, and factories govern themselves? How do they conduct business? How do these separate communities interact and work together? Worker ownership is a good idea, but how does the communal society not slip into the mode of businesses competing against each other that is part of capitalism? How can these worker-owned businesses avoid being taken over by selfish and exploitative people?

We need not be as pessimistic as Hobbes was about human nature to realize that people are capable of selfishness and hostility. Locke was correct that some form of government is necessary to preserve the peace. Also, reality is complicated, especially social interactions; some sort of political mechanism guided by a set of social norms is needed to work out every day logistical issues among communities. Marx claims that communism is the solution to the riddle of history and the salvation of humanity, but his conception of a communal society is very poorly defined. This is surprising, considering how impressively detailed and thoughtful his historical critique of capitalism is in *Das Kapital.*

Evaluating Marx

Some philosophers argue that the concept of alienation outlined in his 1844 writings ("Economic and Philosophic Manuscripts of 1844") is the driving force behind Marx's thought. Their reading of Marx (the psychological reading) is that the plight of the proletariat, the workers of the world, is his central concern and that understanding workers' alienation is the key to understanding the rest of Marx's ideas about capitalism, revolution, and communism.

The other primary reading of Marx (the scientific reading) is that Marx's primary concern is macroeconomics. This reading by analytic Marxist philosophers (who we will discuss in Chapter 16) focuses on Marx's later book, *Das Kapital,* which details the excesses of capitalism in the mid-1800s and his theory of economic determinism throughout history. The scientific economic reading sees Marx as interested in detailing the evils of capitalism to show the need to revolt against its ideology and oppressive superstructure. Advocates of the psychological reading counter that the economic and political content of *Das Kapital* is best understood in terms of human alienation.

The primary reason for this divergence in readings of Marx is another accident of history. His views on alienation are contained in the 1844 manuscripts and not explicitly referred to in *Das Kapital.* The 1844 manuscripts were not rediscovered until the 1930s, and by then many people had entrenched ideas about what Marxism is; they were not open to reassessing their opinions. The Soviets had, in their gross, self-serving perversion of Marx, poisoned generations against Marx's ideas. Decades of relentless anti-Marx propaganda by capitalists didn't help. Academic study of Marx was all but censored in the United States, and it's only been in the past few decades that there has been rational, objective study of his philosophy—not that any consensus has yet emerged about how to think about Marx's philosophy, good or bad.

So, what should we think about Marx and his ideas? I have long felt that Marx was a brilliant diagnostician but a lousy prescriber. He knew what was wrong with society but had a wrong idea about how to fix it. His analysis of the alienation of labor in capitalism remains incredibly accurate today. Anyone who has ever held a job working for a company rather than for himself or herself can relate to the four alienations. Marx's accounts of the excesses of capitalism in the mid-1800s are also accurate, pulled as they were from official government records. Marx's conclusions about how capitalism has distorted society, creating an ideological superstructure that maintains the status quo of the class structure, is arguably accurate and highly useful for a wide range of scholarship.

No matter how accurately Marx may have described our world, his predictions and preferred solutions fell well short. One reason why is that Marx focused only on those facts that supported his preferred narrative and ignored historical facts that contradicted his theory. Another reason is that Marx assumed that human actions are fully determined by external forces and that all external forces boiled down to economic concerns. He failed to take into account that individual people could act in ways contrary to the dictates of their class expectations and the ideological teachings of their society. He also failed to consider that people could act for reasons other than economic ones. These omissions are glaring given the time and place in which he lived and learned—a culture influenced by German idealism, among other individualistic and passionate expressions of thought and culture that he could have drawn on to oppose capitalist ideology.

Marx's predicted rise of the proletariat never occurred. No, the Russian Bolshevik Revolution in 1917 was neither pro-proletariat nor Marxist, despite the propaganda they used to justify it. Same for Mao's takeover of China in 1949 and every other so-called communist government. As we will see, the lack of a successful worker rebellion and capitalism not collapsing were quandaries for some philosophers.

Marx's insistence that the complete destruction of capitalism was necessary to improve the plight of the working class was also wrong. Marx could not foresee, because he was a determinist, that workers and capitalists could come to agreements to improve working conditions and pay. Marx believed that economic determinism forced an eternal conflict between the bourgeoisie and the proletariat. Marx did not foresee the possibility of organized labor unions that could take actions to better their lives short of violent overthrow of governments. Marx also could not imagine some capitalists having concerns for workers' well-being and being willing to work together with their employees. Rather than war, cooperation is possible. Marx did not understand that, and neither today do some of his hard-core followers.

Chapter 11

THE EXPLOSION OF INDIVIDUALISM

The German idealists inaugurated a new method of philosophy, opening the discussion about what the individual contributes to his or her experiences and ideas. Hegel had adopted idealism but had woven it into an absolute system in which everything is explained in terms of the one Spirit or mind. Hegelianism quickly became the dominant philosophy of Europe, especially in German-speaking countries. Many people, then and now, like a totalizing, monist philosophical system that explains everything through one foundational idea—knowledge; morality; perception; and the structure of the universe, society, and history.

Into this environment strode the Danish philosopher **Søren Kierkegaard** (1813–1855, pronounced "sorn KEER-ke-go") and the German philosopher **Friedrich Nietzsche** (1844–1900, pronounced "FREE-drick NEE-tjeh"). On the one hand, these two philosophers are drastically different, but on the other hand, they share a fundamental approach to the world, and it is that philosophical approach that is their important contribution to philosophy. Today, we know this approach as "existentialism," although neither of them used that term. It was **Jean-Paul Sartre** (1905–1980, who we will meet in Chapter 14) who coined the term because he, inspired by Kierkegaard and Nietzsche, defined the approach as existence preceding essence. Existentialism is the approach that puts the nature of our existence as a conscious being at the center of philosophical inquiry. It is similar to phenomenology (which we will discuss in Chapter 14) in its emphasis on the contents of consciousness, but existentialism reaches beyond the analysis of the contents of consciousness to the questions of what it means to be a consciousness in a world.

The starting point for Kierkegaard and Nietzsche was the reality that one exists as a particular, individual being. Since Plato and Aristotle, philosophy, and to an extent all of Western culture, even the new science, had defined objects in terms of their universal essences. An object was defined as a type of thing—a tree, a human, and so on—therefore, the particular object must have the characteristics that defined that type of thing. In practice, this meant that all particular things—trees, humans, and so on—are basically the same and do not vary or change much if at all. So, if you understand the universal essence of a type of thing, then you understand all particular objects of that type. That approach looks at everything in the world from the top down; we first understand universal essences, and from those standard types we consider particulars. Even though science had, strictly speaking, rejected Aristotelianism, it still reduced particulars to universal definitions.

This top-down approach to the world through essences is particularly problematic when it comes to humans. It encourages stereotypes about humans in general and groups of humans. This type of thinking says that all women are alike, all Blacks are alike, all Germans are alike, and so on. It leaves little room for individuality because individuality is assumed to be an aberration; to be distinctive is to go against type. If you look at human history, you will see how much that approach has affected human interactions.

Kierkegaard and Nietzsche turned that approach around. They each said that we are not determined by some universal definition. We are all individuals. We are free to make choices, and our choices define who we are. Kierkegaard and Nietzsche thought of this primarily in terms of values—what we find important. Sartre, who considered values to be some kind of imperialist tool of oppression, thought of individuality only in terms of raw existence. Sartre also thought that freedom was something fearful—a horrible burden on us. That says more about Sartre than anything else. Kierkegaard and Nietzsche thought that freedom was a positive thing, although certainly not always easy. We are individuals, and we are free to make choices, and the biggest choice we have to make is what moral system we will follow. These are the main themes of their philosophies.

Kierkegaard was philosophy's first great rebel, and Nietzsche was its second. They ushered in philosophy as an expression of the personal rather than an attempt to capture objective rationality. In that, they took things further than the German idealists like Fichte and Schelling did. The idealists had talked about how individuals experience things differently. Kierkegaard and Nietzsche contemplated the full implications of that realization.

Søren Kierkegaard

Kierkegaard was a brilliant thinker who could take any question and look at it multiple different ways. Unlike most philosophers, he tried to reach nonacademic people. He was a clever writer who used words to try to encourage people to reflect on who they are and change their way of being so they can lead a more authentic life.

Kierkegaard chose to reject much of what his society taught him, especially the Hegelian system. Hegelianism, following Hegel's philosophy (see Chapter 9), taught that humans are nothing more than a part of a historical process. That rankled Kierkegaard. It went against every fiber of his being. The question of being—who he was and who he should be—was central to Kierkegaard's life and, by extension, to his expression of what philosophy should be.

While the fervent followers of Hegel reveled in the perception of human progress, Kierkegaard vehemently dissented. The Hegelians were proclaiming a golden age; Kierkegaard was warning of a coming collapse. Kierkegaard saw himself as a kind of gadfly trying to wake up his people. His master's dissertation was *On the Concept of Irony* (1841) with constant reference to Socrates. In it, he analyzed the conversational method Socrates had used to steer people into questioning their own assumptions. Kierkegaard's interpretation was that Socrates was trying to awaken in them their subjectivity by forcing them to take responsibility for their thinking and beliefs. Kierkegaard was attempting to follow this path; to do so, he used his written words, quite often laden with irony—intentional ambiguities to motivate people to think beyond what they were taught and think for themselves. Like Socrates, he was irreverent toward authority and tradition, and Kierkegaard was at times deliberately shocking to try to jolt people out of their passive obedience to tradition and force them to look inward and reflect on who and what they are.

People bigoted against religion reject Kierkegaard because he was Christian, despite the fact that very few Christians would ever accept Kierkegaard as one of them (and Kierkegaard would agree he wasn't). That's the problem rebels have—so few want to be associated with them. All that said, Kierkegaard is fun but agonizing at the same time. He is like that friend who makes us laugh at times but also often makes us cringe at how darkly negative he or she is.

We Are Beings Who Must Choose and Act

Primary to Kierkegaard's philosophy is the place of the individual. Kierkegaard saw some value in Hegel's philosophy, but he brought Hegel's philosophy of progress in consciousness from the level of nations down to the level of the individual. We inherit the value system of the society into which we are born, but unlike the Hegelians, Kierkegaard said we are free to choose whether to accept this system or not. What's more, we are free to make our own moral choices all the time. We do not have to conform to what we are told. This is a very important issue for Kierkegaard because our decisions shape who we are.

Kierkegaard saw human beings as alienated from their own nature. He came to this conclusion around the time, the 1840s, that Marx was coming to a similar conclusion about human alienation. Also like Marx, Kierkegaard saw the purpose of philosophy in general, and his life purpose in particular, to be to change the world for the better. After that, the similarity between Kierkegaard and Marx ends. Marx saw economics as the driving force of history and to a large extent denied human free will. Kierkegaard saw human choices as the driving force of history and stressed above all the vital importance of our free will. Marx said capitalism is the cause of our alienation; Kierkegaard said *we* are the cause of our alienation.

Like Kant and Hegel, Kierkegaard had as his main concern the concept of freedom, but Kierkegaard railed against the empty freedom about which previous philosophers talked. Fichte and Romanticism were closer to what Kierkegaard had in mind—the concept of freedom as personal expression. But Kierkegaard realized that freedom was more than expression. Freedom was a beingness.

Beingness. Existence. We exist.

Obviously, you say? Maybe. Kierkegaard would reply that your existence is so obvious that you never think about it or the implications of it. Existence means you have the freedom to choose who you are, and this means having a life of commitment. Most people usually ignore questions about the meaning of their lives and prefer to escape into some kind of trivial routine. Today, people blame television, the Internet, and video games, but people have always found various meaningless tasks to occupy themselves to avoid dealing with the questions of who they are and what their lives mean.

People—including you, yes, you—prefer meaningless routine and immersing themselves in the objective environment around them that we call society. You—yes, you—do this to avoid your own subjectivity and freedom and the need to commit to them. Everyone does this, Kierkegaard says. This goes way back, he says, and only a few brave souls fight against it. In *On the Concept of Irony*, he argued that Socrates used irony to force people to abandon their pat answers to Socrates's annoying questions. They had to begin to think for themselves and to take individual responsibility for their claims about knowledge and values.

Hegel had placed individual human minds within the absolute mind of *Geist*. According to the Hegelian system, we can and should actively engage in reasoning about philosophical questions, but the goal of our critical reflection is to understand the mind of *Geist*, which is the logical structure of the universe. Kierkegaard rejected this totalizing narrative that through logic we can understand the cosmic mind and everything in it. He saw it as hubris. He understood the limits of human knowledge and thought it our duty to accept the reality that there are things we cannot understand. And, as is always present in Kierkegaard, he wants the emphasis to be always on the individual, something he noted was sorely lacking in Hegelianism.

Kierkegaard dismissed Hegelianism as being futile and irrelevant to the concrete real-life issues that all individuals must face. For Kierkegaard, philosophy is about life and how to live it. One analogy he uses is that seeking life guidance from Hegelianism is like traveling in Denmark with a tiny map of Europe that shows Denmark only as a dot. In other words, it's impossible. No abstract system, no matter how logical, can address the concrete features of my life. Only I can do that.

In blindly following the traditions and systems of the world, we are avoiding the reality that we humans are beings who must choose and act. Our day-to-day lives are filled with dilemmas that require us to make decisions. Some of these dilemmas are relatively insignificant—what will I have for dinner tonight? Others are life changing—should I marry this person? We agonize over big decisions, worried we will make the wrong choice. Kierkegaard wrote in his book, *Either/Or* (1843), that if you marry, you will regret it; if you do not marry, you will also regret it. What he means is that we are always capable of reflecting on and seeing the negatives of any choice we make. The point is that we should not reduce our lives to a series of binary choices because life is more dynamic than that. Part of that dynamic is that we will always be aware that we could have made different choices. We could have lived our lives differently, and we still can in the future.

> It is really true what philosophy tells us, that life must be understood backwards. But with this, one forgets the second proposition, that it must be lived forwards. A proposition which, the more it is subjected to careful thought, the more it ends up concluding precisely that life at any given moment cannot really ever be fully understood; exactly because there is no single moment where time stops completely in order for me to take position [to do this]: going backwards. ("Journalen JJ:167," vol. 18, p. 306)

Objective Knowing versus Subjective Knowing

Throughout history, philosophers believed that the primary problem of epistemology was how to rise above individual subjectivity to acquire objective truth. Kierkegaard completely reverses this. For him, the primary task in our life is how to become more aware of our own subjective life. He proposed the radical notion that our natural tendency is to hide under the cover of objectivity. We do this, he says, to avoid the difficult crisis of making our own decisions. He makes the stark distinction between following the crowd and being self-directed. We can come to truth only when we are self-directed, arriving at decisions through our own experiences and values.

Kierkegaard declared that truth is subjectivity. He does not deny the possibility of objective truth, but any objective facts are *truth* only when they are taken in and *owned* by an individual. The word "subjective" has two meanings. Most philosophers, and people, focus on the bad kind of subjectivity when personal interests and biases corrupt one's ability to perceive and judge matters correctly. In many matters, for example, grading students' assignments, we want people to make objective decisions rather than biased ones. We often associate "objective" with "fair" and "subjective" with "unfair."

The good meaning of "subjective" is "related to a subject," and philosophers often use the word "subject" to refer to a human as a being who perceives and acts. This is how Kierkegaard uses "subjectivity"—related to a subject, or person. An objective fact becomes truth, he says, when it becomes related to a person by that person's choices and actions. The statement "2 + 2 = 4" is an objective fact, but you could be forgiven for saying, "Yeah, so?" The statement, "Someone got an F in the philosophy class," may be another objective fact, but it would be a very different fact if the statement was, "You got an F in the philosophy class." The difference is whether a fact is related to you in a manner that means something to you. Facts such as "2 + 2 = 4" and "České Budějovice is the administrative seat of the South Bohemian region of the Czech Republic" probably have little direct relation to you, so they don't mean much to you.

When facts do relate to you and you care about them, they become subjective facts and a part of your conscious being. Consider the difference between hearing someone say "I love you" to someone else and hearing someone say "I love you" to you. These are different facts and different experiences. Consider also the difference between understanding that cheating is wrong and actually deciding, "I will not cheat." Someone can objectively know a moral truth but not be subjectively living in that truth. However, someone could be without a grand rational moral theory but still have empathy for others. A large part of Kierkegaard's philosophy was his shift away from philosophy's focus on objective rationality to focus instead on the importance of individuals living their beliefs.

Kierkegaard's Christianity was in keeping with this sentiment. He didn't care at all about objective doctrine. For him, genuine Christianity is subjective being—living a life of passionate inwardness. When Kierkegaard talks about inwardness, he is not at all meaning selfishness. He means a kind of freedom. His conception of freedom is not that far off from that of the German idealists who inspired him. For him, an individual is free when he or she chooses his or her own path in life. The free individual expresses his or her self-activated self in who he or she is and what he or she does. In this context, when Kierkegaard talks about inwardness, he means focusing on one's self-activation of one's potential to voluntarily choose and act.

Philosopher **Isaiah Berlin** (1909–97 who we will discuss in full in Chapter 15) explained that there are two concepts of liberty ("Two Concepts of Liberty," 1958). There is "negative liberty," which means the absence of constraint and coercion, and there is "positive liberty," which means the ability to pursue and accomplish one's goals. Over a century before Berlin, Kierkegaard's view of freedom has both of these concepts. On negative liberty, he saw Christendom—the institutional church—as a source of constraint and coercion. He targeted the People's Church of

Denmark, which functioned as the state religion in his time. He saw the church as effectively dead, mired in dogma and ritual, made all the worse by its leaders enthusiastically adopting Hegelianism. Doctrine was a constraint and coercion on individual freedom, Kierkegaard argued. He called doctrine the way to power for the teacher but for the learner it is indolent aping and mimicking.

Social institutions provide people with valuable ethical guidelines, Kierkegaard said, but institutions also serve to normalize people into stereotyped social identities, which produces the pseudo-individuals making up the crowd of bland, normal, acceptable society. Social stereotypes constrain the ability to realize and actualize one's genuine self. Kierkegaard's critique was directed primarily at Christendom, but he clearly included all social and political institutions. His consistent theme throughout his writings was to champion the individual in the face of forces that constrained the individual.

Kierkegaard also was consistent on the individual's need to cultivate positive liberty through passionate inwardness. This inwardness for Kierkegaard is not an abstract concept; the more passionately subjective one is about one's own path, the more free one is. He calls for us to engage in a deeply subjective focus on discovering and activating who we are meant to be. Rational contemplation about doctrine or philosophical universals cannot tell us who we should be. You are not the universal human; Kierkegaard exhorts you never to forget that you are an existing individual. You are you, and you are in the continual process of becoming. Objective truth is, he says, a chimera of abstraction. Subjective truth is what is true for you, and you need to win an understanding of who you are meant to be.

And that is where Kierkegaard sees Christianity as vital. Again, not Christendom and its artificial doctrines and rituals, but *Christianity* and its passionate inwardness of coming to know who we are meant to be. That's because Kierkegaard sees God as the source of who we are each meant to be. He wrote that he sought to understand himself and to see what God really wished for him to do. That is the truth that is true for him and the idea for which he could live and die. Like many philosophers before him, Kierkegaard equated God with Truth. Unlike most philosophers before him, he does not equate truth with rational objective systems or logic. Truth is subjectivity. The subjective individual, not an objective universal, exists, so the individual must understand what is true for himself or herself. God is the source of all things, so he reasons that God must also be the source of what we are meant to be. That truth becomes actualized when we hold it with passionate inwardness.

Previously, in discussing John Locke's epistemology, I talked about how our every thought is a belief. Kierkegaard challenges you not to rationalize your beliefs with conformity to what others are doing but to *own* your beliefs. Yes, you can believe the same as others do, but if you believe and do things only because you are supposed to, that is false belief. True belief is when you are committed to that belief as *yours*. You have to experience things for yourself, relate those experiences to the values you have chosen, and make those experiences and beliefs yours.

This is where Kierkegaard perhaps goes a bit overboard, talking about owning your beliefs to the point of it being the only type of act that matters and the need to be willing to die for your beliefs in fear and trembling, reflecting on what God may require of us. He called for subjectivity at all costs. His passion scares some people off. Well, it scares almost everyone off. He was intense. But his basic idea is correct. If you do not feel and own your own subjective existence, if you do not contemplate the meaning of your life and are not willing to leap into that continual struggle to know who you are and what your purpose is, how meaningful is your life? Ultimately, you cannot escape the freedom and responsibility that Kierkegaard is talking about. You interpret everything that happens to you through your beliefs and values, and you choose your beliefs and values, whether or not you do so consciously and actively. So, your life and who you are is your creation and, therefore, your responsibility. So own up to it.

The Spheres of Life

Which leads us to Kierkegaard's spheres of life—also translated as stages of life or spheres of existence. Kierkegaard said that life must be lived; it can't be understood through abstract philosophy. He saw life as a journey traveled in terms of one's commitments. He taught that every individual chooses, mostly subconsciously, from among three fundamental kinds of commitments. He described these commitments as three spheres of life—the aesthetic, the ethical, and the religious. That last is very inappropriately named, as we shall see. He variously refers to these spheres as "existential categories"; "modes of existing"; "stages on life's way"; and, most illustratively, "existence-spheres." Kierkegaard says we are unavoidably in one of the three spheres, although we can move between them. Each sphere of existence is a way of life based on the fundamental commitment we have to life and others. One is either an aesthetic, ethical, or "religious" person, depending on which sphere one is living within.

Kierkegaard's first existence-sphere is the aesthetic. He uses the word "aesthetic" to describe people being driven by their senses. This is a person who lives based on sense experiences and animal impulses and emotions. The aesthetic person is similar to how Hobbes described all human beings—ruled by endeavors of desire and aversion. For such a person, things are either interesting or boring, and naturally, such people prefer interesting things. They are driven to go from one vicarious sensation to the next, chasing fleeting, shallow pleasures, like the person mindlessly flipping through Instagram or TikTok, searching for a mindless, mildly interesting picture, until they are bored with it and swipe to the next mindless mildly interesting picture.

Our age of memes, social media, and short videos capture Kierkegaard's concept of the aesthetic sphere in ways he could never have imagined. The aesthetic person believes he or she is pursuing pleasure, but Kierkegaard says such people are simply staving off boredom. They are trapped in an ongoing cycle of looking for the next cheap thrill. Their life is no more than a collection of fragmentary, spasmodic moments. Aesthetic people do not have a self. Their choices are determined by their environment, which feeds them sense experiences to which they can only react according to their fleeting moods and impulses. They constantly need more stimulation, driven by the restless urges to consume more. They have no real values, no real self.

If the aesthetic person wakes up to this predicament and listens to an inner knowing that he or she can be more, this person can choose to move to the ethical sphere of life. It is in this sphere when one can begin to make choices. The aesthetic person is like an addict, addicted to drink, cheap thrills, drugs, video games, or the need to fit in with a group of pseudofriends, but because aesthetic people are determined by their environment, they have no commitments and, therefore, no self. Kierkegaard taught that only when a person decides to make commitments to others and live according to an ethical code, can that person achieves the possibility of gaining a history.

For example (feel free to insert your own preferred gender labels into this example), a womanizer jumps from one woman to another, constantly seeking the next interesting sexual encounter. This man has no real history because he has no actual commitment to anyone. When this man stops using women for his own pleasure and forms a committed relationship with a particular woman, Kierkegaard says, he develops a history with her and a lasting mutually fulfilling relationship that enhances his life and his self. Kierkegaard says it is only in the existence-sphere of living within ethical commitments that one can become a self. One now interacts with the world and other people in it through ethical considerations—recognizing others as full human beings who deserve respect and consideration. Others are no longer just things to be used for pleasure. Similarly, the ethical person can have real pleasure because he or she interacts with the world in terms of what is edifying to himself or herself, not simply in terms of base sensual pleasure.

Kierkegaard said that, although the ethical sphere is a welcome improvement to the senselessness of the aesthetic sphere, the ethical sphere is still somewhat empty. The ethical person is summed up by the series of universal ethical norms that clothe him or her. The ethical person is no more than a set of social roles and corresponding social commitments. These people are no longer ruled by endeavors of desire and aversion, which is good, but their choices are still determined by their environment. They are now ruled by social ethical constraints. They are defined by society as a man, woman, mother, father, student, citizen, and so on, and on, and on. The ethical person is comfortably situated within the ethical sphere and is content to do only what is morally required. Because this person is defined by external norms, such a person is still not a fully self-aware individual. When one realizes that's the case, one can make the difficult but deeply meaningful leap to a new existence-sphere where self-authenticity is possible.

Here is where Kierkegaard's label of this existence-sphere as the "religious" sphere is so strange and unhelpful. Kierkegaard, who rejected all forms of institutional religion as being trapped within the ethical sphere, should have found a different label—"fervent," "spiritual," or "transcendent" perhaps—because he steeps this existence-sphere in language of spiritual communion with God and the universe above and beyond the social world. Better would be the "self-actualizing sphere," similar to what psychologist **Abraham Maslow** (1908–1970) discussed.

For Kierkegaard, even the most fully developed ethical person, who clearly perceives the ethical ideal, will, paradoxically, be painfully aware of his or her ethical shortcomings. The realization of one's chronic inadequacy to live up to social ethical demands produces a despair that must be resolved. Kierkegaard taught that fully pursuing the ethical produces a tension that leads one to the existence-sphere beyond it. The only escape from the tension of the ethical sphere is through a leap to another stage of existence. The religious or self-actualizing sphere is described by Kierkegaard in the religious language of his time. He uses the following example.

In his book, *Fear and Trembling* (1843), Kierkegaard explores the scriptural story of Abraham, who hears the voice of God calling on him to sacrifice Isaac, his son. Kierkegaard retells the story from multiple perspectives to get at the heart of Abraham's experience. Abraham's dilemma is that murdering his son is obviously an ethical wrong but that disobeying an order from God is also wrong. He is caught between choosing to obey the demands of the ethical norms or to serve God. Abraham chooses to believe there has to be a higher purpose for God's command beyond the universal ethical law against murder.

Kierkegaard uses the story to show the sharp contrast between the ethical and religious spheres. Abraham must choose and act, but he can't follow the universal, ethical law, which tells him to love and protect his child. He must instead take on what Kierkegaard calls the "teleological suspension of the ethical." He must suspend his commitment to the universal ethical sphere for the sake of a higher goal—specifically, his individual relationship to God. Kierkegaard concludes from this that there is an existence-sphere higher than the ethical laws of the world.

We need not use biblical stories to understand what Kierkegaard is getting at with the "teleological suspension of the ethical." "Teleological" means living according to a design or purpose. To suspend the ethical teleologically means to go beyond social ethical constraints in pursuit of a higher purpose. We can understand this as the movement a person makes when he or she refuses to obey an unjust law or refuses to conform to social pressures and instead does what he or she believes is correct and life-affirming. Kant declared that the ethical and the religious never conflict—that reason makes plain the commands that are binding upon us and that there are no higher goals than duty to those commands of reason. But Kierkegaard's view of both God and us is akin to William's philosophy that the will guides the intellect (see Chapter 3). Kierkegaard wants us to reject Kant's idea that God's will and the moral law can be collapsed into one. By giving us an example where the two are in tension, Kierkegaard is pointing out that the individual's relationship to God is a higher priority than a rationally based universal ethics.

The religious or self-actualizing sphere is, for Kierkegaard, the existence-sphere in which an individual is willing not to be determined by his or her environment and instead to do what he or she knows is right. This person is willing to be an individual, willing to find the type of person he or she is meant to be and *be* that person. Only in this way can you be a full self.

Friedrich Nietzsche

Nietzsche is one of the few philosophers frequently mentioned in popular culture. As with most things, popular culture gets Nietzsche wrong. Nietzsche was not a nihilistic antimorality monster, as some portray him, and he wasn't the hostile bigot as others portray him. He was cynical, yes, but his was the cynicism of the idealist, of one who believes that life and society can be better than they are, and he is bitterly disappointed that they are not. Nietzsche's negativity was primarily a despair over how people throw their lives away on false and harmful beliefs.

Toward a New Concept of Truth

Nietzsche thought about beliefs in a manner similar to Kierkegaard's thinking. He downplayed the importance of rational objective truth and elevated the personal and subjective. Nietzsche went beyond Kierkegaard in stating that what was important was subjective interpretation, not just subjective experience. We put our own personal stamp on things. This is what is real—not "facts." As he said:

> In opposition to Positivism (which we will discuss in Chapter 13), which halts at phenomena and says, "These are only facts and nothing more," I would say: No, facts are precisely what is lacking, all that exists consists of interpretations. We cannot establish any fact "in itself": it may even be nonsense to desire to do such a thing. (*The Will to Power* §481)

Nietzsche would say that uninterpreted "facts" or "truths" are a fantasy. We never encounter such things. What we do encounter is our interpretation of experiences because everything we experience is seen from one perspective or another. Nietzsche calls this his theory of "perspectivism." Perspectives are unavoidable because they are all we have. All of our perspectives are false, compared to the phantasms of objective truths, yet these "false" perspectives are highly useful.

Here is how it works in Nietzsche's conception. He says that "there is only a perspective seeing, only a perspective 'knowing.'" Each individual, because he or she *is* each an individual, has a different perspective on things, and as we have learned from previous philosophers, all that individuals have are their ideas in their minds caused by their sense impressions. So what each individual thinks about and communicates to others are his or her own ideas, all of which, Nietzsche points out, are ideas influenced by each individual's own past experiences, circumstances, values, and purposes. When he says, "there are no 'facts-in-themselves,'" he means that an interpretation must always be projected onto ideas before they can be facts. Individuals are thus creators of their own facts. They can't help it. It's what human minds do, and we can see here how Nietzsche is influenced by Kant.

But these "facts" created by individuals may or may not be true depictions of the world. Actually, they almost certainly aren't, Nietzsche would say, because what an individual thinks and feels is a product of his or her mind. So, by the age-old standard of objective truth, all we think and speak are false ideas, false beliefs. Nietzsche at one point says that all words are lies because they express how we think and feel, not how things are. Furthermore, once spoken or written down, words are no longer part of us but exist outside of us, and everyone, including ourselves, view these words through perspectives, and the words must be reinterpreted. We suffer the delusion that we capture reality through our words, but we don't. Everything is perspective, even science. Physics, too, is only an interpretation and belief about the world, Nietzsche insists.

Despite our ideas being inherently "false," they are useful. Loosely speaking, how that works is like this. To make sense of our experiences and ideas, we compare them to similar experiences and ideas and apply labels to these groupings of concepts. These labels become words that stand for universal concepts. We use these words to communicate with each other, and these words become grounds for our interpretations of the world.

Nietzsche considers that interpreting the world by means of a perspective is the basic condition of all life. Our ideas are false and our words are lies because they are perspectives that do not perfectly depict reality itself. Regardless, our ideas are needed and useful because they are all we have. Our perspectives create a world that is calculable, simplified, and comprehensible for us.

Here again, we see Nietzsche using Kant's ideas, this time Kant's response to Hume that the human mind imposes order on the jumble of impressions the senses give to it. However, although Kant thinks this gives us a kind of knowledge about the world, Nietzsche takes Kant's insight of the active, ordering mind into an entirely other direction.

Truth, Nietzsche insists, is not defined by our ideas corresponding to the world. Instead, "Truth is that kind of error without which a certain species of living being cannot exist. The value for Life is ultimately decisive" (*The Will to Power* §493). Of any belief anyone has, Nietzsche asks, "Is it useful to us?" It doesn't really matter if a belief is true if it is useful. A belief can be a condition of life and nonetheless be false, Nietzsche says. If a false story protects people from harm, then it serves a useful purpose. All of our human ideas are just that, anyway—fictions that are useful. The most useful fictions become widely adopted and part of our common wisdom. As long as a belief continues to be useful, it survives within society. When a belief is no longer useful, it often, but not always, is replaced by new, more useful, beliefs.

If this sounds weird, it shouldn't. This is, after all, how science works. Scientific theories are created by individuals imposing their perspectives to create ideas that are calculable, simplified, and comprehensible. Scientific theories are accepted until they are no longer useful. Scientists then create new theories that are more useful.

Toward a New Humanity—Nietzsche's Rewriting of Ethical History

Armed with this new perspective on truth and how it functions, Nietzsche called for us to move beyond tradition and forge a new path. Whether we want to or not, Nietzsche says, we must forge that new path because the old ways are dead. He is infamous for declaring that "God is dead" in his 1882 book *The Joyful Wisdom* (¶125). Often quoted, but almost never in context, this is not a declaration about the existence of God but about something he found much more relevant. Nietzsche understood that whatever truth Christianity may hold, its tradition was integral to European culture. What he was announcing as being dead was everything that was built on and sustained by this Christian tradition, especially the whole of European morality.

In this book, I have not discussed ethics and moral philosophy so as not to duplicate the material covered in other courses. I make an exception with Nietzsche because his analysis and discussion of morality is a critique of society and human nature and paves the way for his declarations of how humanity should be. One of Nietzsche's books was *Beyond Good and Evil* (1886), and it could be argued that it is his most important work. Its title is certainly a good motto for his philosophical project.

The European moral system was his real target, and this system, he was convinced, was destined for collapse. Worse, Nietzsche claimed, the Christian moral system that had evolved in Europe was harmful to human beings. Humanity must abandon the old foundation, leave the dead and crumbling structures built on it, and create a new morality that is beyond the old categories of good and evil.

Yes, beyond good and evil is where we must go. Nietzsche correctly understands that morality is foundational to and intertwined with all other aspects of how we are and what we do. He saw 1800s European culture and society as being in crisis because the European moral system was dead; it's just that people did not realize it. Therefore, his critique of European culture had to be a critique of European morality.

What exactly was so wrong with European morality? Nietzsche argued in his book, *Beyond Good and Evil* (1886), that the prevailing moral law based on good and evil was an artificial creation that replaced a more natural morality. His claim is that we lie to ourselves through our philosophy, laws, and religion that our definitions of good and evil are objective, universal realities. They aren't. We Europeans invented a moral law to constrain ourselves and others—a moral law, he claimed, that was born out of resentment. There are echoes of Marx's critique of class struggle and the superstructure in Nietzsche's ethical history, although there is no evidence that Nietzsche was familiar with Marx's writings.

Nietzsche's radical argument is that in humanity's distant past, a social order emerged with a higher class and a lower class. This arrangement spawned a pair of evaluative terms—"good" and "bad." Over time, he argues, the idea of goodness came to be associated with character traits that those of the privileged higher class saw in themselves and by which they distinguished themselves as superior to the masses, who were "bad." Traits such as strength, power, courage, pride, willfulness, and wealth were good and noble virtues. Traits such as weakness, cowardice, timidity, and humility, associated with the lower class, were considered bad. The rulers of the ancient Mediterranean societies, Nietzsche claims, were self-directed, their only justification for their actions being their own judgment. They practiced self-mastery and thus mastered their domains and others. This is why Nietzsche, in *Beyond Good and Evil*, calls good/bad "master morality." Nietzsche is oversimplifying, but ancient history, a field he knew quite well, does support his basic idea.

He goes on to claim that the good/bad evaluative terms were gradually replaced with the concepts of "good" and "evil." This pairing focuses on judging violations of the well-being of others as evil and, therefore, judging altruism for others as good. Nietzsche grants that altruism has some common sense to it, and he is not against feeling love and care for others. Nietzsche's problem with good/evil thinking is its focus on evil to the exclusion of good.

What Nietzsche thinks happened is that people who lost out when the noble higher classes exerted their power came to resent those with power and wealth. Feeling powerless, downtrodden, and uncertain of themselves, and having no value within the good/bad morality, they revolted against that thinking. They engaged in what Nietzsche, in *Beyond Good and Evil*, provocatively calls "slave morality." In his theory, weaker people feared and resented stronger people; to express their bitterness, they invented the moral concept of evil. The values that the higher class had called "good," the slave morality now condemned as "evil." The values that the higher class had called "bad," the slave morality now called "good." He further claims that the drive for social equality, an increasingly common demand in Nietzsche's time, was born of the resentful slave morality. He saw the push for equality as mediocre people demanding that noble, exceptional people be dragged down to mediocrity so that no one is allowed to surpass anyone else.

Nietzsche argues that demanding that no one be made lesser condemns those who assert their self-interest. All of the traits that are good in the good/bad evaluative pairing—strength, power, courage, pride, willfulness, wealth, and so on—are condemned as evil in the good/evil evaluative pairing. That means that the good/evil evaluative pairing declares traits such as weakness, cowardice, timidity, and humility as being morally good. It is a reversal of the original social order, and this Nietzsche saw as the problem.

Historical evidence for Nietzsche's theorized sea change in morality is at best sketchy, but he points blame for it at a reasonable target—Christianity. He saw the Christian morality of "turn the other cheek" and "the meek shall inherit the earth" as a slave morality. He claimed that they turned the qualities of the slave—humility, abstinence, patience, resignation, and submissiveness—into virtues, condemning the opposite qualities. Lacking tangible power, the slaves revolted in the only way they could—through telling and retelling the story of good and evil. This was the revenge of the slaves—to condemn their masters as evil. The Christian good/evil morality has the appearance of gentleness, kindness, and goodness, Nietzsche claims, but it is a mask for bitter resentment and antipathy for the strong and successful.

Nietzsche's summation of slave morality is as follows: "I dislike him."—Why?—"I am not a match for him" (*Beyond Good and Evil*, IV.§185). Because most people lack tangible power in the world, the slave morality of good and evil has enjoyed popularity. When stronger or superior people surpass us and grab what they want, we can condemn them as evil. We have created the categories of good and evil and use them to judge people and actions.

Moving Beyond Good and Evil—The Will to Power

OK, so supposing we accept this explanation of ethical history, how do we forge a new path beyond good and evil? A good first step, Nietzsche says, is to acknowledge that our primary interaction with the world is in terms of our likes, dislikes, experiences, and lack of experiences, all driven by our instincts. The high-minded notion of the philosophers, theologians, and scientists—that we interact with the world through reason—is a big lie, Nietzsche says. We are human animals, and instinct, not reason, is at the center of human behavior. We have drives, but not so much a drive to knowledge as the learned want to believe. "The greater part of the conscious thinking of a philosopher is secretly influenced by his instincts," Nietzsche says (*Beyond Good and Evil*, I.3). Human instinct is just another drive that is disguising itself as thinking. That drive, a centerpiece of Nietzsche's philosophy, is the will to power.

Nietzsche's concept of the will to power has been horribly misunderstood. This is partially because the Nazis misappropriated the concept to justify their hateful and murderous regime. For example, the infamous 1935 propaganda film *Triumph of the Will* was commissioned by Adolf Hitler to glorify himself as the personification of the will to power. The Nazis shamelessly misappropriated Nietzsche as though he were a protofascist, despite the fact that Nietzsche would have vehemently opposed the Nazis and their bigotry.

The truth is that Nietzsche's will to power is not at all a will to dominate others. Nietzsche is not Hobbesian in thinking that we are driven by selfish desires. Yes, we are attracted to pleasure and averse to pain, but not in a brutish and destructive way as Hobbes thought. The will to power is a different truth.

> The will to truth is a process of establishing things, it is a process of making things true and lasting, a total elimination of that false character, a transvaluation of it into being. Thus, "truth" is not something which is present and which has to be found and discovered; it is something which has to be created and which gives its name to a process, or, better still, to the Will to overpower, which in itself has no purpose: to introduce truth is a *processus in infinitum*, an active determining—it is not a process of becoming conscious of something, which in

itself is fixed and determined. It is merely a word for "The Will to Power." (*The Will to Power* §552, emphasis his)

In simplest terms, the will to power is the will to overcome circumstances and make something true.

For Nietzsche, the will to power is about rejecting determinism, both material and cultural, in favor of believing in our own power to make and preserve our being. As long as we believe that something other than ourselves is responsible for our happiness, we corrupt our ability to establish our own truth and become ourselves for ourselves.

Life itself is the will to power, he says, the will to create and the will to self-preservation. Our basic drive is to overcome obstacles and discomforts and create truth—a truth for us. Yes, we are averse to pain, so we want to overcome it and be free from pain. It can be as simple as we don't like to be uncomfortable, so we are driven to soothe our discomfort. If we are cold, we turn up the heat.

That's the will to power, not lusting for political power over others. We don't like not to know or understand things, so we are driven to create beliefs and meaning to feel more at ease. We are our beliefs, and we are driven to create beliefs that are useful to us. In the same way, Nietzsche saw the slave morality and its idea that morality is based on good and evil as a useful facade. Underneath, it was the slaves' will to power. But now, instead of hiding behind the veneer of Christian European morality, we need to rise up and master ourselves.

What is so radical about Nietzsche's will to power is that he doesn't just think that we *do* create our own truths but that we *should* create our own truths. This requires, as Nietzsche fully understood, the destruction of all dogmas. *All* dogmas. People bigoted against religion love Nietzsche because he was so antireligion. Nietzsche didn't hate religion, as some atheists do; he believed that Jesus really existed. True to Nietzsche's belief in the will to power, he called Jesus the only true Christian and said that everyone who follows Jesus is a sheep. Don't follow anyone, Nietzsche would say. Do what Jesus did and forge your own path. "What have we Sons of God to do with morals?" (*Beyond Good and Evil*, IV.§164) Return to the master morality. Strength, accomplishment, and pride are good; timidity and weakness are bad. The will to power is spontaneous, aggressive, and expansive, giving us new interpretations and directions to our lives.

Nietzsche's view of Christianity is similar to Kierkegaard's conception of Christendom, and he sees the ideas and words of Christianity as no longer useful. They are just so many archaic dogmas and social traditions that need to be discarded, just as the dogmas of science and philosophy must be discarded. Nietzsche wanted to tear down everything, literally everything, and start anew. In this, he was similar to Marx in calling for the radical restructuring of society that he thought humanity desperately needed.

This is where Nietzsche is the most cynical—he believes very few people have the courage to master themselves, much less restructure society and forge a new path. Very few people have the courage to create their own truths. Nietzsche was a person filled with optimism about what people could be but despair at how little people actually achieve. This is Nietzsche's cynicism. He thinks he sees a brilliant, positive future beyond our current humanity when we accept our will to power and express our perspectives. We then can create new beliefs, share them with others, and work together to find life-affirming truths that are useful to us.

Nietzsche calls a person with the courage to participate in this process an "Übermensch," which literally means "overman." Not "superman" as has been widely misinterpreted (even dictionaries get this wrong), but a man who overcomes. (Yes, "man" because Nietzsche was still in the sexism of his time.) What the Übermensch overcomes is not others, but himself and his human tendency lazily to accept the dogmas given to him. The Übermensch accepts his will to power and joyfully creates new beliefs and new truths. Those who lack the courage to accept their will to power Nietzsche derides as "little gray people" and "shallow ponds" of humanity. They remain stuck in being "all too human." But Nietzsche was confident that the time of the Übermensch was coming, because the old European morality was dead and humanity was evolving beyond it.

Transcendentalism

A rather different take on individualism came from a circle of American writers in the mid-1800s. They were also inspired by German idealism and the Romantic movement in literature. They emphasized intuitive understanding of the world through subjectively experiencing it. Like Kierkegaard and Nietzsche, the transcendentalists exalted individualism and feeling over rationality. The transcendentalists' distinctive idea was the possibility for individuals to achieve intellectual and spiritual enlightenment, a possibility they were very optimistic would be achieved.

The definitive start of American transcendentalism was 1836 when a group of intellectuals founded the Transcendental Club in Cambridge, Massachusetts. They took the name "transcendental" from Kant because they also sought to understand what is universal in human intuition that structures our experience. Its most famous members were authors **Ralph Waldo Emerson** (1803–1882) and **Henry David Thoreau** (1817–1862), educators **Elizabeth Palmer Peabody** (1804–1894) and **Amos Bronson Alcott** (1799–1888, father of poet **Louisa May Alcott** (1832–1888)), and feminist **Margaret Fuller** (1810–1850, see Chapter 18).

Similar to the circle in Jena (see Chapter 9), the Transcendental Club published a literary and philosophical journal, *The Dial*. They accepted Kant's Categories, but like the German idealists, they thought that individuals could extend their knowledge beyond those mental structures. Their philosophy focused on the individual transcending the restrictions of social institutions and those institutions' deficient understandings and ethics. Each person can find within himself or herself a piece of the greater whole.

One strong influence on the transcendentalists was **Friedrich Schleiermacher**, a member of the Jena circle of German idealists who sought to reform Christianity by prioritizing individual feeling, similar to Kierkegaard's thought. Schleiermacher accepted Kant's Categories as the foundation of human knowledge but emphasized the need for individuals to extend their consciousness beyond intellect into an active holistic perception and experience of nature, humanity, and the universe.

New English translations of scriptures from the religions of India were another strong influence on the transcendentalists. The approach of Indian philosophers, highly rational but displaying a different set of assumptions and concerns, encouraged the transcendentalists to look at philosophical questions from perspectives beyond the Western tradition.

Perhaps the quintessential transcendentalist philosopher was Thoreau. His worldview was a mixture of Rousseau's antipathy for civilization, a Romantic poet's love of nature, a monastic desire for a life of simplicity, and Kierkegaard's and Nietzsche's passion to overcome social restrictions to create something new and better. His book, *Walden; or Life in the Woods* (1854), inspired environmental philosophy. His 1849 essay, "Resistance to Civil Government" (later republished as "On the Duty of Civil Disobedience"), expressed Lockean sentiments that government is a convenience of expediency and that an ethical person need not surrender his or her conscience to that government. In the essay, Thoreau expressed the conviction that one has a duty to oppose unethical legislation and governmental actions. However, Thoreau's idea of civil disobedience was motivated by concern for the well-being of fellow people, not Locke's concern for property rights. Thoreau called for protest against slavery, the genocidal treatment of indigenous Americans, and the U.S. war against Mexico (1846–1848).

The individualism of the transcendentalists led them to advocate for the abolition of slavery and for women's rights. Their philosophy of feelings over rationality led them to urge a reconnection with nature. Fuller and Thoreau wrote essays against industrialization and its exploitation of the environment. Thoreau and Emerson wrote passionately about the good that comes from finding truth and psychological grounding in the natural world. The strong spiritual component of transcendentalist philosophy inspired new forms of religion and spiritualism in the United Sates, and transcendentalist writings on the importance of nature inspired the environmental movement.

Chapter 12

AMERICAN PROGRESSIVISM AND PRAGMATISM

Western philosophy's long conversation reached the United States fairly early in the nation's history. The European settlers in the United States understandably brought with them European ideas. Any early openness in the 1700s to the ideas of America's indigenous people soon dissipated amid the rush to expel the native populations to expand territory for more European settlers.

It took awhile before the United States developed any of its own movements in philosophy, but in the 1800s, two distinctively American philosophies emerged—progressivism and pragmatism. Both movements were influenced by British epistemology and social philosophies, but both reflected the developing attitudes and culture of the United States. Progressivism was a social philosophy, and pragmatism was mainly a philosophy of science and reasoning. However, **Jane Addams** (1860–1935) and **John Dewey** (1859–1952) combined these two interests.

American Progressive Reform Movements

Progressivism in the United States was inspired by philosophy but powered by working class people. Progressivism has been an openly political movement attempting to improve society by making it fairer and better for working people. It took some inspiration from the British social reform philosophers (see Chapter 10) and French socialist theorists who predated Marx. The movement has been focused on reforming society rather than tearing it down as Marx thought was necessary. That does not mean that progressivism has not been radical in its ideas or its demands for social and political changes. Numerous progressive ideas and causes, once deemed radical, are now widely accepted mainstream ideas, such as universal suffrage, civil rights and liberties, labor laws including the 40-hour work week and banning child labor, free primary education, corporate accountability, environmental protection, and others.

There have been progressive theorists, but one of the crucial elements of progressivism has been the need to engage in concrete actions to improve society. Progressivism is important in the history of philosophy because the ideas and the social changes generated by the movement have inspired and informed much of the philosophy of the late 1900s and our current century.

Social reform theories and movements in the United States developed a distinctive character in response to the new country's distinctive social and economic circumstances. Some key insights into the distinctness of the United States came from French writer **Alexis de Tocqueville** (1805–1859). In his 1835 book, *Democracy in America*, Tocqueville was critical of the United States on several points. Tocqueville was conflicted on the issue of democracy. He was, like John Stuart Mill, a strong believer in personal liberty, but he expressed misgivings about democracy in terms similar to Plato's, that in democracy the majority can be too easily led by a tyrant with enough charisma and guile to secure their loyalty and grab power.

Democracy could work, Tocqueville thought, but was on shaky ground in the United States. He observed that people in the young nation of the United States had views of class and property that were different from those of Europe. Lacking an aristocracy and its hereditary ownership of land, the United States offered the promise of gaining wealth though hard work, a hope unavailable to the lower classes in Europe. Wealth in the United States could be attained through working the land as a farmer—land having been stolen from indigenous populations being made freely available by the government—or through work in the growing industrial sector.

The problem, Tocqueville thought, was that although being a laborer was more respected in the United States than it was in Europe, this situation created a population focused on middling values. By this he meant that working people had the false hope that hard work alone could make anyone wealthy, and they thus ignored the needs for education, talent, and intelligence. His attitude dovetailed with his views on the dangers of democracy, and he saw America's industrialization as a catalyst for the democracy's majority rule of mediocrity. In a passage reminiscent of Nietzsche, Tocqueville decried America's "depraved taste for equality, which impels the weak to want to bring the strong down to their level" (*Democracy in America* 1.I.3). Like Nietzsche, Tocqueville wanted men with superior talent and intelligence to have more social power than the "flock of timid and industrious animals" that America was creating (*Democracy in America* 1.VI.5).

Tocqueville's elitism aside, his observation was sound that the United States was a different society because of its different circumstances in class and property ownership. There were wealthy elites in the United States but not an aristocratic class. That and the belief that the North American continent was free land there for the taking, led to the notion of a "Manifest Destiny" for the country and its (white male) citizens. This land was their God-given land, and they could create on it what they wanted. These circumstances invited many people to change their thinking about what was possible.

Social reformers in Europe had to work in response to the traditional class structure. Reformers in the United States were able to work with a much blanker slate. Reformers seized the opportunities to experiment.

The United States itself was an experiment in a new kind of nation, and idealistic people took advantage of available land to conduct some radical experiments in planned communities.

For example, the Oneida, New York, community was founded in 1848 and the Amana Colonies, Iowa, in 1855 as communal industrious societies based on the principles of equality, democratic governance, communal property, and mutual support and benefits to fulfill the needs of the people, including housing, health care, education, and daily necessities. Oneida and Amana were the most successful of dozens of such communal societies attempted in the 1800s. Most failed within a decade for a variety of reasons. Oneida and Amana eventually transitioned into the corporations that still bear those names today.

What these experimental communities had in common was the ethical conviction that society should serve the interests of all of society, not just the interests of the ruling class, and function for the benefit of all, not a few. Then and now, this ethical position is called "socialism." The word "socialism" has become a negative term because Marx used it to label his theorized intermediate stage between capitalism and communism. The Soviet Union called their country, and the countries they controlled in Easter Europe and Asia, "socialist," and their peculiar style of political dictatorship came to be associated with the word "socialism."

The idea of socialism had existed for some time. **Thomas More** (1478–1535), had imagined a socialist society in his book, *Utopia* (1516), and Francis Bacon's *New Atlantis*, published posthumously in 1626, outlined a scientific socialist utopia. French aristocrat **Henri de Saint-Simon** (1760–1825) was the first to set down the principles for a political socialism in his book, *L'Industrie* (1817). He foresaw that society was about to be transformed into an industrial one, and he wanted to ensure that the working-class people who were essential to society were supported. He therefore urged a restructuring of society that would dismantle aristocratic feudalism (he renounced his title) in favor of a hierarchical meritocracy. Social hierarchy would be based not on heredity but on who were the most talented in scientific decision-making.

Saint-Simon's vision was not unlike Plato's with technocrats, chosen for their skills, running industries for the benefit of society. Saint-Simon did not see a conflict between industry managers/owners and workers, as Marx did. In Saint-Simon's vision, everyone who engages in productive work is a member of the industrial class. The role of government is to ensure what is good for society as a whole by ensuring the productivity of industry. Marx rejected Saint-Simon's vision of socialism because it did not end hierarchical management of industry, which Marx thought was crucial to fully liberate the working class.

Various forms of socialism sprang up over the next century and were based on various assumptions about human nature and society, from scientific reductionism to religious perfectionism to romantic agrarianism.

All these forms shared in common the desire for a society structured to allow all in society, not just an elite class, to participate in society and benefit from it. Many forms had a utopian vision of what society could be, often unrealistically so. Regardless, the ethical passion for a society that works for society as a whole was appealing to many, for obvious reasons.

The progressive movement in the United States in the last half of the 1800s and first half of the 1900s worked to implement socialism's ethical goals in society at local, state, and national levels. Progressivism is the belief that instead of waiting for social change to come from the top down, people need to make change happen through their own activism. Progressives wanted to see society progress to include greater prosperity and freedom for a greater number of people.

Through philosophical writings and political and economic action, progressives organized in favor of workers' rights, women's rights, abolition of slavery and then racial equality, immigrants' rights, environmental protections, electoral reform, and economic justice, including reigning in the excessive power of landlords and corporations. If reading that, you think, "Wow, those are the same issues people argue over today," you are correct. These philosophical and political issues have been fought over for nearly 200 years.

Progressivism developed in a distinct way in the United States for reasons already mentioned, but also because the country had a different political structure than European countries did. In the United States, the Declaration of Independence and the Constitution promised citizens more liberty and justice, something progressive activists could point to and use. Individual states and large cities had more political power than their European counterparts, so social reforms could be won more easily at lower levels of government. For example, some progressives called for direct democracy—meaning people voting for specific laws—and the popular referendum was introduced in South Dakota in 1898 and in Oregon in 1904. On a national level, the push for greater civil rights and political inclusion won legalization of the 40-hour work week, labor organizing and collective bargaining, child labor laws, the breakup of corporate trusts and monopolies, food and drug safety laws, environmental conservation, and women's suffrage, to name just a few.

One of the most important progressive philosophers was **Henry George** (1839–1897) who proposed a radical rethinking of landownership. Writing in *Progress and Poverty* (1879), he argued for the value of land to be taxed while the value added by people's work would be retained by them. Similar to Locke, George believed that land and natural resources in principle belonged to all of humanity. Departing from Locke, George thought that labor entitled a laborer to ownership of the products derived from the land but not to the land itself. George thought a central cause of poverty was that United States law allowed wealthy landowners to monopolize land use and charge economic rent to those who lived and worked on the land. George called this a system of slavery in which workers were taxed heavily on their income from productive labor while the landowners were taxed little on their unearned income from charging rent for use of the land. Worse, landowners were incentivized to speculate on land, holding it and hoping it would appreciate in value. Furthermore, they could buy up land around a natural resource and hold a monopoly on access, enabling them to charge others exorbitant rent to use it.

George's solution was to tax the value of the land itself, not income from labor, leaving the only tax to be levied the tax on economic rent received from ownership of land. In that way, he argued, economic justice would be achieved. George's philosophy of the land tax was an expression of the time. Westward expansion in the United States spurred a rush to control land and natural resources. That, the Industrial Revolution, and a huge wave of immigration fed, on the one hand, a sense of limitless progress, but on the other hand, a sense of despair over economic exploitation and poverty. Land speculators and business monopolies had too much economic and political power. The country's overall wealth was increasing but so was poverty. George eloquently encapsulated the economic inequalities of the 1870s in *Progress and Poverty*, and he correctly pointed the finger at land barons, landlords, and business monopolies and the exorbitant rents that they could charge people.

Unfortunately, like Karl Marx, George was a better diagnostician than prescriber. His land tax solution was never feasible, legally or economically. Nevertheless, George's book was a catalyst for new thinking about the fairness of business practices and the need to rein in corporations and robber barons. George inspired many people, including President Franklin D. Roosevelt, John Dewey, and Albert Einstein. In general, progressive thought in the 1800s inspired numerous threads of social and political philosophy. We will discuss a number of them later in this book.

Charles Sanders Peirce—The Pragmatic Scientist

Influenced by the Kantian ideas of the Categories of Understanding and the active mind (see Chapter 8), as well as the emerging sense of historicism (see Chapter 9), the core ideas of pragmatism are that knowledge is an ongoing activity and that truth emerges from the practical utility of ideas. In other words, we engage with the world to develop useful ideas with which we can do things in the world; successful and useful ideas become true ideas. Pragmatism is aptly named.

Charles Sanders Peirce (1839–1914; note that his name is not the more common "Pierce" and is pronounced like the word "purse"), who invented the philosophy of pragmatism, turned Descartes's use of doubt into a practical and important part of learning for individuals and humanity as a whole. Peirce developed the basic idea of pragmatism as a method for improving the accuracy of science in its search for truth. His father was a mathematician on faculty at Harvard University, which enabled the younger Peirce to get his own education at Harvard and to meet a number of important and interesting people. He did poorly in his university courses and graduated last in his class, but clearly the hierarchical grading system of Harvard at that time did not accurately correspond to intellectual ability. Peirce's innovative philosophical method created a new school of philosophy. He was, first and foremost, a physical scientist, spending more than 30 years studying minute differences in the Earth's gravitational field. The importance of exact measurements and rigorous interpretation of data motivated his philosophy.

Peirce approached in multiple ways the question of what truth is. His first approach is to renew the old idea that words are signs. The first to discuss words as signs was John Duns Scotus (ca. 1266–1308), who inspired William of Ockham's nominalism. Peirce, informed by John, William, and Immanuel Kant, takes the idea of signs further and uses the term "semiotics" to refer to the study of the formal use of signs. Signs were traditionally seen in a formula of signifier (the word) and signified (that to which the word refers) as seen by John, William, and even Augustine before them, and in Peirce's time, by Swiss linguist **Ferdinand de Saussure** (1857–1913).

Peirce added to this the "interpretant"—the social set of meanings that are used to interpret signifiers. Signs succeed as symbols standing for things because interpretants relate them to those things. A sign itself is a brute fact. It is the social system of meanings that makes the symbol meaningful. A flag is just a piece of cloth, but the interpretants of the social habits and feelings that the flag are meant to elicit in people relate the piece of cloth to what it signifies. All signs generate further signs to interpret the use of signs. An example of the interpretant is the dictionary. It uses words to interpret the meanings of words.

Our universe is suffused with signs, Peirce says, and the elaborate system of signs makes up the world and makes up our individual and collective consciousness. A society is a web of signs, words, symbols, meanings, significances, and interpretations that combine and interact in an ongoing process of interpretation of objects and ideas. Our language of signs is not inert but is in constant motion as we reinterpret what is true. This portrayal of how signs work informed Peirce's pragmatist definition of truth.

Another way Peirce explored the concept of truth was to consider what practical effects our conception of an object has because our conception of these effects is the whole of our conception of the object. What Peirce means by this is that we define what we think an object is by what we believe an object does or what we can do with it. In other words, our idea of an object is our idea of its sensible effects. On the one hand, this is a rejection of speculative philosophy of the kind Kant and others had done. On the other hand, it is an affirmation that our words and ideas must be testable. Peirce said that if a quality or idea of an object cannot be tested, then our idea and word for that quality are meaningless. This idea is much of what Peirce means by pragmatism—it is a philosophy of experience. As philosophers and scientists, we need to focus on the practical, testable effects of objects. Anything other than that is meaningless.

Peirce understood that what we call "truths" are really beliefs. A list of what we think is true and a list of our beliefs would be the same. He defined beliefs as something that we are aware of, that mollifies the irritation of doubt, and that produces habits in us. This thinking is reminiscent of Hume's, but Peirce emphasizes that our beliefs, being habits, are tied to physical actions or psychological expectations. Our habits predispose us to respond in certain ways to certain situations, and the essence of belief is the establishment of habits that assist us in our dealing with the external world.

Despite his scientific orientation, Peirce recognized that all we have are beliefs about the world. Peirce was focused on mathematics and hard science, so he did not explore the full social implications of how society produces and depends on habits and the signs that signify beliefs. He did, however, provide an excellent basic start on how we come to develop and maintain certain beliefs.

The Fixation of Belief

In his article, "The Fixation of Belief" (1877), Peirce identifies the ways that we develop habitual beliefs and how they become fixated in our minds. First, however, he explains how beliefs work. Our beliefs, he says, guide our desires and shape our actions; they create in us psychological states from which we act. Believing something or believing in someone instills in us habits that will condition us to behave in certain ways.

Like Hume, Peirce has no problem with our truths being formed by habits; Peirce sees our habits as good for us, as long as they lead to positive practical effects. We believe a leader, so we have the habit or inclination to obey that leader because we believe that obedience will yield us positive effects. Doubt, Peirce says, is very different from belief. Belief is a calm and satisfactory state that we enjoy and want to hold on to. "Doubt is an uneasy and dissatisfied state from which we struggle to free ourselves and pass into the state of belief" ("The Fixation of Belief" III.3).

A way to think about what Peirce is saying is this. If we have a comfortable pair of shoes, then we enjoy walking in them; but if something breaks in our shoe and makes walking uncomfortable, we will stop and repair our shoe or get new shoes. The irritation that doubt causes is an important part of learning. Descartes used doubt as a way toward certain knowledge. Peirce didn't have certain knowledge, but more useful knowledge, as the goal, so he viewed doubt in that context.

Our beliefs are not exact representations of truth, and we would be wrong to think they are. Our beliefs should be continually self-correcting in response to our experiences as we seek beliefs that have practical value. We should be open to doubt. Doubt spurs us to reflect on our beliefs, reject beliefs that are not satisfactory, and struggle to attain new beliefs that ensure better habits and better results.

At least, that's how we should behave, Peirce says. We don't always, though. Peirce identifies four different methods by which we eliminate the irritation of doubt and fix our beliefs. He discusses the four methods from most undesirable to most desirable and begins with a common behavior caused by the nature of belief itself.

> The instinctive dislike of an undecided state of mind, exaggerated into a vague dread of doubt, makes men cling spasmodically to the views they already take. The man feels that, if he only holds to his belief without wavering, it will be entirely satisfactory. . . . [He] hides the danger, and then calmly says there is no danger; and, if [he] feels perfectly sure there is none, why should [he] raise its head to see? A man may go through life, systematically keeping out of view all that might cause a change in his opinions. ("The Fixation of Belief," V.1)

Pierce labels this behavior "the method of tenacity." He says it is unstable because those who use this method to fix their beliefs continually encounter against evidence to the contrary and people who think differently. Nevertheless, we frequently see people using this method. Such people attempt to eliminate doubt by ignoring all evidence and reasoning that could call their beliefs into question.

The method of tenacity is at the level of the individual person. Peirce identifies a second similar doubt suppression method that works at the level of a community or social institution. This is "the method of authority" that Peirce says has been used by all great civilizations in which each established a set of correct doctrines and taught them to its people. Peirce acknowledges the method of authority brings about greater consistency of belief in a community by producing a comfortable, communal belief system with associated habits. The problem with this method is that it effectively raises the method of tenacity to the level of a community or whole society. It also is unsustainable because an institution cannot control every opinion of every person. Similar to Ibn Rushd (see Chapter 3), Peirce says that the method of authority will always govern the mass of people who have no impulse higher than to be intellectual slaves. However, there are also people who possess a wider social feeling and become aware of other beliefs, a situation that causes doubts to emerge.

A third method of eliminating doubt and fixing belief is simply to hold opinions that are agreeable to reason. Peirce calls this "the a priori method," after the common philosophical belief in knowledge separate from experience. These are just opinions, though, Peirce says, opinions that are not based on evidence but on that which we find ourselves inclined to believe. Peirce correctly charges many philosophers with using this method. This method is more intellectual than the methods of tenacity and authority, but it turns inquiry into something similar to a matter of taste. What is agreeable to reason is a subjective issue that reflects one's personal sentiments and experiences. Peirce rejects speculative rationality because, in his opinion, the field is a warring collection of opinions, with philosophers expressing their personal preferences. The a priori method is little more than intellectual prejudices.

The shortcomings of these three common methods show that the proper method of finding belief is important. We will have beliefs—we can't operate without them—and they are all that we have. The question is how to find ones that produce good tangible results. What we need is a method of fixing belief in which our beliefs may be caused by nothing personal but rather by some external permanency—by something beyond our personal thinking. Peirce is not calling for our minds to be passive but to be responsive to the world and to the evidence it shows us. What he calls "the method of science" is when we use our active minds to follow a disciplined method of observing the real things in the world that are independent of our minds. We start with known and observable facts and proceed to the unknown. We let the evidence, not our feelings, show us what to believe. We are using the method correctly when new information throws our beliefs into doubt.

If you are not open to being puzzled or questioning your beliefs, you are not capable of the kind of inquiry that will lead to knowledge. The force of habit and the desire for comfortable conclusions will always tempt us, but reflection on the facts will overcome these temptations. The method of science is an open-ended method that lets the evidence guide our thinking. With this method, our beliefs are a response to the world, not to our personal prejudices. We learn what experience has to teach us.

Science as Public Meaning

Contrary to many philosophers and scientists in his time, Peirce rejected the notion that the universe is stable and perfectly predictable. He held instead that the universe is constantly evolving, and, although it mostly shows indications of order, it also has an element of randomness. We will see a similar idea from **Henri Bergson** (1859–1941) in Chapter 13. In "The Fixation of Belief," Peirce dealt with the difficulties of human subjectivity. In his article, "How to Make Our Ideas Clear" (1878), he addresses the other end of the problem of knowledge—how to deal with a chance-laden universe.

~~Peirce said that~~ the meanings of our beliefs are defined in terms of our interactions with the world. Those interactions are publicly observable, and the actions that people perform give us the meanings of signs and beliefs. Meaning is performative and public. The public aspect of Peirce's definition is important. All we have are our beliefs, but we can't say that whatever we believe is real and true because, as we saw earlier, people can fix their beliefs on reasons contrary to evidence. Our beliefs are meaningful when they can be shown to connect with what is real—what is the case independent of our beliefs.

But how do we determine what is real? What brings meaning, truth, and reality together for Peirce is science. The beliefs of any particular person do not determine what is real, but people collectively can determine what is real. Science, broadly construed, is about collecting information through observations. Peirce is not overly concerned with a particular correct method of conducting science; as a scientist himself, he knew that experimenting with different methods was a good approach. He is confident that different scientists using different methods of observation will initially yield different results but that

> as each perfects his method and his processes, the results will move steadily together toward a destined center. So with all scientific research. Different minds may set out with the most antagonistic views, but the progress of investigation carries them by a force outside of themselves to one and the same conclusion. ("How to Make Our Ideas Clear," 300)

Peirce places his faith in an objective reality that is discernable by a community of dedicated humans. One person, or even a number of people, can be mistaken in their beliefs, but through concerted effort, humanity as a whole will come to understand reality. People collectively determine truth.

> The opinion which is fated to be ultimately agreed to by all who investigate is what we mean by the truth, and the object represented in this opinion is the real. That is the way I would explain reality. ("How to Make Our Ideas Clear," 300)

Peirce's conception is similar to Hegel's in the basic idea that knowledge progresses from incomplete to more complete understandings. Also like Hegel, Peirce is optimistic that humanity will in time solve all questions. Peirce was far more oriented toward science and observation than Hegel was, and he rejected Hegel's notion of *Geist*. Peirce did not have the direct influence on the methods of science he had hoped to achieve, but he did have a strong influence on his friend, William James.

William James—Pragmatic Beliefs

American **William James** (1842–1910), brother of novelist **Henry James** (1843–1916), was a medical doctor turned philosopher. William James literally wrote the book on psychology—*The Principles of Psychology* (1890)—establishing the field as a legitimate science in the United States. Later in philosophy, James built on the work of Peirce to bring the principles of pragmatism into everyday life. The purpose of philosophy, James declared, is to determine what definite difference various beliefs will make to us and our lives; therefore, his search was for beliefs that make practical, positive differences in our lives. His most notable works in philosophy are *The Will to Believe* (1897) and *Pragmatism: A New Name for Some Old Ways of Thinking* (1907).

The Cash Value of Beliefs

For William James, the principle question for us as human beings, and therefore, what the principle question for psychology and philosophy must be, is what practical use beliefs are to us.

"Will you or won't you have it so?" is the most probing question we are ever asked; we are asked it every hour of the day, and about the largest as well as the smallest, the most theoretical as well as the most practical, things. (*The Principles of Psychology* 1182)

James's early work in psychology led him to realize that we each experience the objective world centered on our own subjective experiences as a body in space. He is not denying that there is an objective world that can be measured and charted as points in space. He is acknowledging that our lived experience of that world is indeed *our* experience, a reality that has significant implications. James therefore shifts the focus of philosophy to the perspective of the individual and the implications of experience and action for the individual.

Like Peirce, James says that what is true is an issue of whether a belief is useful to us. Truth *happens* to an idea, he said, when it succeeds in predicting new sense experiences; in other words, extending the ideas of Kant and Hegel, James says that we are active participants in what becomes true. Also like Peirce, he was a staunch empiricist, seeing all of our knowledge coming from sense experience. However, Peirce emphasized the public and collective aspect of empiricism, whereas James argued further that it was the right of the individual to understand the consequences of beliefs in his or her own personal life. Truth is what works pragmatically, and the individual determines the practical and satisfactory consequences of a belief.

It may seem that James is saying that anything goes—if we like a belief, we can say it's true—but this is misunderstanding him. It's up to the individual to decide what is true, but this decision is not arbitrary; this decision should be based on solid empirical evidence. James understood that the notion that truth is a detached objective reality is nonsense. Truth is a tool by which we do things, or, to use James's bold analogy, truth has a practical cash value. Whether a belief is useful or valuable can be determined only by the individual. That's because knowledge comes only from experience, and experience is always subjectively lived by the individual. We share many circumstances in common, but many particular circumstances differ from person to person. A belief is true if it works *for me* in *my* particular circumstances, although it is incumbent on me to be sensible in deciding what works; it's not a matter of whim. I should be able to demonstrate that my beliefs correspond to evidence.

Everything in James's philosophy rests on practical usefulness. Truth *happens* to an idea, not because we want it to, but because we *make* it true through our actions. A scientific hypothesis is true only after we have tested it sufficiently. Our personal goals are true only after we have taken action to accomplish them. James understood that truth is pluralistic, meaning that a particular belief could work in practical terms for one person but not another, meaning it is true for the first person but not the second person. Also, different beliefs work in different situations; there are multiple ways to do any particular task, so there are multiple truths.

What James was doing generated controversy. Critics attacked him as being too subjective and relativistic. It was a seismic shift to measure truth not by it being universal but by it being useful. James's idea went against most of what was held by philosophy and all of the political, scientific, and cultural expressions that stemmed from philosophy. However, as James noted in the title of his book, *Pragmatism: A New Name for Some Old Ways of Thinking*, he was pointing out the way people had always behaved in their everyday lives. Truth is a matter of usefulness, and if an idea is useful, it is true—that's how we act. James's ideas on truth are similar to what Nietzsche had said a few years earlier, but we do not know if he read Nietzsche's writings.

Like Peirce's, James's pragmatism was subjective but grounded in objective human experience. His critics were mistaken in thinking he meant that willful belief alone makes something true. He stressed that when we say a belief works for us, we don't mean that it simply feels good to us. We mean that we have tangible experience that it works: "experience, as we know, has ways of BOILING OVER and making us correct our present formula" (*Pragmatism* VI.44, emphasis his).

There is no absolute truth, James goes on to say, but we are still wise, even obligated, to strive continually to ensure that our beliefs are in harmony with the evidence before us, and we need to adjust our beliefs in accordance with new experiences.

> Meanwhile we have to live to-day by what truth we can get to-day, and be ready to-morrow to call it falsehood. Ptolemaic astronomy, Euclidean space, Aristotelian logic, scholastic metaphysics, were expedient for centuries, but human experience has boiled over those limits, and we now call these things only relatively true, or true within those borders of experience. (*Pragmatism* VI.45)

Truth is only the expedient in the way of our thinking—expedient in the sense of the most direct path to what works, and what works is what becomes true. This is how we learn and grow from childhood on, and this is how science operates. Truth is dynamic in always growing and changing.

A Right to Believe

There is no absolute truth, only our best attempts at it. James applied this realization in *The Will to Believe* (1896), in which he responded to a paper by mathematician **William K. Clifford** (1845–1879). Clifford asserted that it is morally wrong, everywhere and for anyone, to believe something on insufficient evidence. Clifford meant this as an attack on religious belief, and he had written other essays hostile to religion. James rightly called out Clifford's bigotry and also identified the larger issue that if we followed what Clifford demands, we would not be able to believe anything, anywhere.

Having read this far in this book, you realize that absolute, certain knowledge is impossible. Beyond this reality, which is ignored by Clifford and other positivist philosophers (see Chapter 13), James observed that generating beliefs is a process and that we can identify multiple dimensions to that process. We must make choices about what to believe and how we will act, James said, similar to what Kierkegaard had said. Affecting our freewill choices are the dimensions of the options among which we must choose. Options can be living or dead, forced or avoidable, momentous or trivial. A live option is when more than one option has appeal ("which sauce to you want with that?"); a forced option is one for which there is no possibility of not making a choice ("accept this or not"); and a momentous option is one that is unique, irreversible, and/or has significant effects on you ("move to Europe with me").

We can dismiss the other sides of the dichotomies. Dead options are irrelevant, avoidable ones are just that, and trivial options are of no consequence. Therefore, our decisions about dead, irrelevant, and trivial matters are of no great import, so we can concede to Clifford's demand to withhold belief and action without sufficient evidence. For example, the hypothesis that "aliens built the pyramids in Egypt" is a dead option because it is not plausible, it is not a forced option because I have no reason to even consider it a possibility, and it is not a momentous option because how I live my life is not affected by whether I agree with it. I therefore do not need to consider the hypothesis seriously and can justifiably withhold belief and action.

Only options that are of the living, forced, and momentous kind can be called genuine options for us. With these genuine options, we have a right to believe what we think is the practical decision, even when the evidence could be considered insufficient. When options are forced, these are decisions that we have to make, and we have a right, even the duty, to make decisions even though we do not have complete evidence. Plus, James reminds us that some beliefs can become true only when we first place faith in their possibility. He gives as an example the option of cultivating a friendship: "Do you like me or not?" he asks. There is little chance of you coming to like me if I do not act toward you with the faith of believing you are worth trusting and capable of liking me. But, he says, "if I stand aloof, and refuse to budge an inch until I have objective evidence, until you shall have done something apt, as the absolutists say ... ten to one your liking never comes" (*The Will to Believe*, IX.2). On religious beliefs, which Clifford attacked, James says that these are clearly live options. We will live our lives either with or without a religious perspective, so it is a forced option. Undeniably, it is a momentous option because the choice to live with a religious mindset, or not, affects us in profound ways, James says. Therefore, on pragmatic principles, if the hypothesis of God works for us satisfactorily—if it has cash value—it is true.

We Have Free Will

One truly genuine option is whether we believe that we have free will. It's a simple hypothesis: I have the ability to choose freely what actions I will take. Whether that hypothesis is correct—or its opposite is correct, that our choices are determined by external forces—is impossible to prove by logic. It is, undeniably, a living and momentous option to believe we have free will, and James says we are forced to make a choice. Therefore, he said, we have a right to choose the option that works for us. James emphatically chooses to believe that he has free will—and not only to believe it but to act with it and believe in his individual reality and creative power.

Not content with his freewill choice to believe he has free will, James wrote an essay entitled, "The Dilemma of Determinism" (1884), in which he refuted the deterministic hypothesis. We've seen several versions of determinism already in this book, when philosophers assumed that believing in determinism was understanding how the world works. James rebuts that belief with the following argument:

1. Many actions that people perform are later regretted (murder or other cruelties, for example) and we wish things could be different.

2. Determinism professes that it is impossible for anything in the universe to be otherwise than it is.

3. Determinism claims that everything is the inevitable result of previous causes, but that implies that judgments of regret are in error; to regret something is to believe that things could have been different from the way they are.

4. Determinism is the pessimistic position that evil and cruel actions are necessary and unavoidable and therefore should not be regretted but accepted.

5. The only way a determinist can avoid this fatalistic pessimism is to say that acts of cruelty are actually good and rationally necessary and that regret is irrational and bad, so we are left with the dilemma that either regret is good and cruelty is bad or that cruelty is good and regret is bad, but determinism says that both cruelty and regret are necessary and unavoidable events: this is a contradiction.

6. Therefore, James concludes, if determinism is true, then "something must be fatally unreasonable, absurd, and wrong in the world" It instead must be the case that we have free will. ("The Dilemma of Determinism," 164).

Belief in determinism suppresses the reality of our moral and practical lives. It not only is an unreasonable, self-contradictory belief, it also does nothing for us—it has no cash value. If, instead, we believe in indeterminism (free will), then, James says, we open ourselves up to the reality that our choices and actions make a difference. James said that he chose to believe in free will and that that had made all the difference in his life.

The best way to sum up James is to understand that everything in his philosophy is based on his notion of individual psychology. The individual engages in freewill choices according to his or her subjective situation. We are beings who must choose and act; to act, we create beliefs that have value to us. Each one of us maintains our beliefs as long as they work for us. That pragmatic worldview has value for science, philosophy, and our personal lives.

Jane Addams—People-centered Pragmatism

Jane Addams (1860–1935) made significant contributions to sociology and social philosophy, but sexism has reduced her role in history to simply being a radical activist. That's not to suggest that Addams's activism was at all small. In 1889, she founded Hull House in a slum near downtown Chicago. It was a settlement house, a concept she learned about while visiting London, and it was one approach to progressive social reform designed to help poor, marginalized people. Like the British settlement houses, Addams's Hull House provided educational, recreational, and supportive social services to the neighborhood. More importantly, for Addams, activities at the house addressed the social and environmental factors connected with poverty. Hull House became a renowned working laboratory for progressive social reforms, a working class version of a salon (like Madame de Staël's) in which people from all areas and circumstances could come and interact, including at regular meetings of the Hull House philosophy group.

As a scholar, Addams was active in the philosophical school of pragmatism and was a close friend and associate of John Dewey. Although they did not officially publish any philosophical works together, Dewey credited Addams with influencing his philosophy, and he assigned Addams's books in his courses at the University of Chicago. Addams taught at the Extension Division of the University of Chicago for a decade, having refused offers to join the regular faculty. (She consistently refused to align herself officially with any company or organization.) The university faculty supported awarding Addams an honorary doctorate in 1916, but the administration vetoed the decision. A different administration did confer the degree in 1931. Addams also befriended and influenced sociologist **George Herbert Mead** (1863–1931) and influenced his work on the power of symbolism in society. Although sadly largely ignored today, Addams positively affected American philosophy, sociology, and education.

Listening to Experience

In her philosophical work, Addams focused on the interchanges between theory and practice and between activities and perspectives. The idea that we learn from experience goes back to Hobbes and Locke, but Addams took the idea to a deeper level. People from different walks of life will have different experiences and will develop different perspectives on the world. From this, Addams developed an early version of what is now known as "standpoint theory," which we will discuss in more detail in Chapter 18. Different people have different standpoints. Theorizing, no matter how rational, cannot tell us what people perceive and who they are; the practice of asking them about their experiences and activities and listening to their answers will tell us much more.

Up to the late 1800s, a serious blindness in philosophy, and scholarship in general, had been that the perspectives of only wealthy, privileged people (almost all men) were considered. Addams understood that philosophy and sociology, much less progressive social activism, needed to include the perspectives and experiences of underprivileged people. She grew up in a rural area in an upper-middle class family. She understood that although she now worked with and lived among marginalized people in an underprivileged urban neighborhood, she could never understand their lives and perspectives as fully and intimately as they did. She therefore sought not universal ethical theories but firsthand accounts of the lived experiences of marginalized people. For Addams, theory had to follow experience.

Addams demonstrated this methodology in her published articles. For example, her 1896 study of women domestic laborers, "A Belated Industry," took testimonies from women who had lived at or had been involved with projects conducted from Hull House. She attempted, she wrote in the study, to tell the story of the plight of domestic workers "from the point of view of those women who are working in households for wages" (A Belated Industry" 536). This is standard methodology in social sciences today, but Addams was at the genesis of American sociology and was instrumental in instituting the practice of gathering information from personal interviews.

As is consistently the case for Addams, she applies her ideas pragmatically. Listening to the experiences of others is good not only in scholarship but also in life. We have an obligation, she insists, to seek out and take in other people's perspectives. That meant, in particular, bridging the gaps between social classes and between the sexes. Foreshadowing later continental social philosophers such as Axel Honneth and Christine Korsgaard (both of whom we will meet in Chapter 15), Addams sees the individual as developing through intersubjective social actions—lessons she learned in observing the interactions of the residents of Hull House. William James says truth is dynamic in always growing and changing. Addams is saying people are similarly dynamic, and this is why philosophy and social democracy must be pragmatically engaged with people.

Pragmatic Social Democracy

Addams's scholarly work is in keeping with her ethical conviction that society cannot claim progress unless all social classes are benefiting. She calls for "lateral progress," by which she means social gains held in common across society. Her idea was in contradistinction to the prevailing practice, then and now, of focusing on the achievements of the rich and famous and thinking that the large successes of a few at the top prove that society is progressing. A good political leader, Addams says, discovers what people really want and provides for them the channels through which their moral force can flow. In so doing, the leader attains progress not for a few but for the many. It is better, she says, for the multitude to move up a few feet higher than for a few to climb a mountain.

Addams most fully expresses her social philosophy in her book, *Democracy and Social Ethics* (1902). She applies her ethic of lateral progress to numerous aspects of society. We are obliged, she writes, not just to speculate on what is good and ethical but to act on it in concrete ways that care for other people. She advocates for a social democracy in which people are continually looking out for each other and the good of the community. That means lateral progress for the poor in society who are victims of circumstances and bigotry against immigrants and women.

She criticizes the traditional attitude that people are poor because of their vices (such as alcoholism) or their laziness. Society is obligated to understand what the poor are experiencing and develop means to improve their lot. Charity is not the answer, she says, for that is a temporary transfer of goods or money. The social institutions that cause economic inequality need to be changed so that people have equal economic opportunity. That includes a full social democracy. People need not only to be fully represented in government but also to be fully involved and have an active stake in social progress.

Democracy for Addams is based not on theory or principles but on mutual sympathy and regard for the well-being of other people. Unless all people in all classes contribute to the good of a society, then we cannot be sure that that society is worth having. She calls for businesses to move from the "aristocratic management" style of managers thinking they know more than the workers to democratic management in which workers have a voice and a stake in the business. In this, Addams shared Marx's desire for the emancipation of the working class, but she saw a more constructive solution than violent revolution.

John Dewey's Instrumentalism

John Dewey (1859–1952) was the next generation of pragmatist philosopher. He combined the scientific orientation of Peirce, the pragmatic view of belief and truth of James, and the emphasis on individual development and need for social reconstruction of Addams. Dewey's scientific orientation was biology, and he was influenced by the developments in evolutionary biology. His philosophical starting point was the fact that people exist within a biological environment. We create beliefs to adapt to our environment. Dewey created the term "instrumentalism" to describe the human activity of developing and using beliefs as tools or instruments for solving problems and altering our environment to meet our needs and desires. One of Dewey's primary aims, in part inspired by Addams, was to reform education to help children develop problem-solving skills—instruments to solve problems.

Instrumentalism and Truth

We exist in a world, and we must react to it and try to navigate within it to accomplish our goals. Our intellectual abilities, Dewey said, are developed in response to our world. The world places demands on us, and we are beings who must make choices and act. The implication of this for Dewey is that we need to understand human intelligence as the continual activity of developing more profitable relations with the objects we encounter. This view rejects the passive mind of Locke and Hume and adopts James's "cash value" theory of beliefs. Dewey said that our thinking doesn't make mental copies of the objects in our environment but we think about how to interact with and better use objects. Dewey intentionally speaks of "intelligence" rather than "mind" to focus on mental activity rather than on a mental entity.

Dewey sought to promote human inquiry, which he saw as the core of successful instrumentalism. Similar to Peirce, Dewey saw doubt as an unsettled and confused state from which we seek to free ourselves by attaining a unified and resolved situation. Dewey, as he consistently did throughout his philosophy, spoke of doubt as a response to the environment—we are doubtful because the situation is doubtful—rather than an intellectual exercise à la Descartes. In this way, Dewey is not talking about academic doubt but practical and functional doubt. We are thinking about real life rather than conducting thought experiments. Here is one of the examples of inquiry that Dewey gives.

A man traveling in an unfamiliar region comes to a branching of the roads. Having no sure knowledge to fall back upon, he is brought to a standstill of hesitation and suspense. Which road is right? And how shall perplexity be resolved? There are but two alternatives: he must either blindly and arbitrarily take his course, trusting to luck for the outcome, or he must discover grounds for the conclusion that a given road is right. Any attempt to decide the matter by thinking will involve inquiry into other facts, whether brought out by memory or by further observation, or by both. The perplexed wayfarer must carefully scrutinize what is before him and he must cudgel his memory. He looks for evidence that will support belief in favor of either of the roads—for evidence that will weight down one suggestion. He may climb a tree; he may go first in this direction, then in that, looking, in either case, for signs, clues, indications. He wants something in the nature of a signboard or a map, and his reflection is aimed at the discovery of facts that will serve this purpose. (*How We Think* 10–11)

This forked road situation is analogous to how we deal with every problem we face, from deciding what to have for dinner to solving complex scientific or moral problems. We are confronted with a question; we gather information; we try a solution; and if that doesn't work, we seek another, and so on until we come to a satisfactory conclusion.

Dewey's idea of truth is essentially the same as for Peirce and James. His notion of instrumentalism focused the idea of practicality onto specific tasks. The tool analogy is quite apt. Dewey said that the question is not, "Is a hammer adequate?" That's too general to be meaningful. The question is, "Is a hammer adequate for pounding in nails?" The answer is, "Yes." The answer is, "No," to the question, "Is a hammer adequate for dividing a board in two?" We understand that we use different tools for different tasks, and Dewey asks us to think of beliefs in the same way. Which belief or idea is adequate to solve the situation before me? That's what thinking is, what ideas are, and what truth is. Dewey says, "Ideas are not then genuine ideas unless they are tools in a reflective examination which tends to solve a problem" (*How We Think* 109).

Education

Education was Dewey's prime concern because it is through education that we learn how to solve problems, and this is the way we can improve society as a whole for the long term. Students are individual people and should be cultivated as such. Education should not be taught by rote or en masse. Dewey thought that, in schools, students were seen as theoretical spectators who were under the instruction of experts. Dewey criticized education and academia itself as not perceiving the uniqueness of individuals. Individuals have an infinite diversity of active tendencies, and education, and society as a whole, must account for this. Dewey thought that education is best when it includes active involvement, not passive seeing or hearing.

Central to his educational reforms is the need to get away from rote memorization of facts and instead adopt processes of open inquiry. Our experiences in life are a continually developing circuit of activities, and learning needs to be presented similarly. Good education, he thought, teaches individuals how to solve problems and engage better with their society. His forked road situation is an analogy for how he thinks students should be presented with a problem that they need to work through, moving through potential solutions until they find one that works. Students need to be active questioners—hands-on participants in both practices and dialogue. Discussion is an important part of education, and the students need to be able to ask questions of their teachers, discuss among themselves, and discover truths for themselves.

Dewey's ideas called for a complete rethink of curriculum, the role of the teacher, and the teacher–student relationship. The influence of Jane Addams is clearly evident in how Dewey saw education as the means of increasing democracy. Dewey said that democracy is the idea of community life itself, and that democracy should be understood as more than voting in elections—democracy should be understood as how the community deals with the problems it faces. Dewey's idea of instrumentalism also works at the community level. Education teaches individuals not only how to solve problems but also how to be fully participating citizens in the community. Dewey is not, of course, advocating indoctrination of students into being a citizen in a particular way. He wants education to respect students' freedom, recognizing them as unique, contributing individuals who participate in changing the society of which they are a part. Working as he did with Addams and Mead, Dewey understood every child as a self who emerges from and is constructed through that child's social and personal experiences. A school must be a microcommunity that mirrors social life and prepares students for democratic participation in society.

Dewey's proposed reforms along these principles, far lengthier and more detailed than we can hope to discuss here, have inspired many educators since. Not all, though. Dewey's philosophy of education demands more effort of teachers than some are willing to expend. Sadly, some educators, including those with advanced degrees, still insist on requiring "teaching to the test" and treating students as passive vessels to be force-fed facts that they must memorize and regurgitate back to receive a grade. Education still has not achieved Dewey's vision of a learning process of problem-solving and creative thinking.

> There will be almost a revolution in school education when study and learning are treated not as acquisition of what

others know but as development of capital to be invested in eager alertness in observing and judging the conditions under which one lives. Yet until this happens, we shall be ill-prepared to deal with a world whose outstanding trait is change. ("Between Two Worlds" 463)

The Influence of Pragmatism

The philosophical approach of pragmatism is grounded in everyday experience. Pragmatist philosophers insist that all human experience needs to be understood as an interaction between people and their environment. These philosophers take into account individual perspectives but don't discount the effects of environmental factors on beliefs as existentialists sometimes do. Pragmatism's approach to philosophy, truth and meaning, and society is therefore timeless and adaptable to any culture and life situation. As James would say, pragmatism has cash value.

The pragmatist approach has had particular influence on philosophies of language, education, feminism, the hard sciences, and the social sciences. Dewey's thinking on education has been highly influential in educational reform and the development of pedagogy. Some analytic philosophers have drawn from the pragmatists, but by and large, the continental/process realm of philosophy has been more open to pragmatism's recognition that human perception and reason are inherently relative, contingent, and imperfect. The divide between analytic and continental philosophy is the topic of the next chapter.

Chapter 13

PHILOSOPHY'S GREAT DIVIDE— POSITIVISM VERSUS PROCESS

In Chapter 9, I mentioned the divide between continental philosophy and analytic philosophy. The rest of this book deals with these two different major trajectories of philosophy. In this chapter, we will look at the beginning of that divide as the difference between applying a logical positivist paradigm (analytic philosophy) and focusing on ongoing processes (continental philosophy). There are specific schools of philosophy that went by the names "logical positivism" and "process philosophy," but we will see how the terms can be more broadly applied.

Positivism—The Birth of Analytic Philosophy

We have seen several philosophers who sought to find a solid foundation for science in philosophy. Positivism is the attempt to turn that relation around and find a solid foundation for philosophy in science. French philosopher **Auguste Comte** (1798–1857) invented the term "positivism" to describe that to which he thought philosophy should aspire—positive knowledge completely devoid of speculation and superstition. In itself, this wasn't a new idea, but Comte's conception of a positivist philosophy, which he set forth in a series of writings in the 1830s, was colored by his deep hostility toward religion. He viewed human history as a matter of historical progress, but unlike Hegel, Comte saw history as humanity's journey of overcoming religion's pernicious influence. He rejected every idea that could not be reduced to logic or scientific observation as "superstition." This credo was taken up by the later "logical positivists," discussed later in this chapter. Comte rejected all speculation about causes, even within the sciences. He said we should not ask what gravity is but simply account for the phenomenon in the experiences of objects falling. In other words, even scientific theory and modeling, such as what Newton had used, was to be rejected.

Comte suggested that beyond the "hard" sciences of mathematics, physics, chemistry, and so on, there should be a further science that he called "sociology" that analyzed phenomena in human society to uncover the materialist laws that govern human behavior. His idea inspired the field of sociology, and his particular approach inspired a common materialist reductionist method of doing social sciences. Comte also proposed a scientific religion that would set down the ethical laws for human interactions. He condemned the idea of God, but he correctly pointed out that atheism was an equally dogmatic position. Rather than waste time on debates between theism and atheism, a scientific religion would seek to aid human beings, a sentiment he admitted was a positive value found in traditional religions.

Bertrand Russell's Quest for a Logical Language

Positivist philosophy did not follow the strict regimen that Comte had laid out, but it found a new foundation in the work of **Bertrand Russell** (1872–1970). The core of this new foundation was logic and mathematics and the idea that they were one and the same. Russell could justifiably be called the first analytic philosopher from his method of mathematical–logical analysis of philosophical problems.

Russell was a very English philosopher, a member of the aristocracy and House of Lords, and godson of John Stuart Mill. His wealthy family had been one of the leading political families in England for the 350 years prior to his birth, his grandfather even having been prime minister. The family had long been staunchly liberal politically, and Bertie (as he preferred to be known) followed in that tradition, being very active and outspoken in progressive political causes, especially antiwar and anti-imperialist causes. Strangely, he never wrote any social or political philosophy despite his nonacademic advocacy for preserving human life, and his philosophical writings were detached from the concerns of society and human life.

Russell's great love was mathematics; he himself used the word "love" to describe his lifelong fascination with it. His first book (*An Essay on the Foundations of Geometry,* 1897) was on a philosophy of geometry based on Kantian ideas, but he later rejected his own book. Russell wanted to identify the foundation of mathematics, which he came to see as an extension of logic. He abandoned Kant and embraced the mathematical ideas of Italian **Giuseppe Peano** (1858–1932), the founder of set theory, and of German **Gottlob Frege** (1848–1925).

Frege was a then unknown scholar whom Russell, as he became well known, came to champion. Frege had invented a new system of logic that used quantified variables to convert propositions into symbolic logic. He then argued that mathematics was not a separate entity but an extension of logic and, thus, mathematical laws and proofs are understood to be pure logic.

Russell took inspiration from Frege and Peano, and, with his professor, **Alfred North Whitehead** (1861–1947), Russell wrote a formal system of the logical foundations of mathematics. Their *Principia Mathematica* was published in three volumes from 1910 to 1913. It is a contender for the densest book ever written. For example, here is their proof that $1 + 1 = 2$:

$*54\cdot43.\quad \vdash :. \alpha, \beta \in 1 . \supset : \alpha \cap \beta = \Lambda . \equiv . \alpha \cup \beta \in 2$

Dem.

$\vdash . *54\cdot26 . \supset \vdash :. \alpha = \iota'x . \beta = \iota'y . \supset : \alpha \cup \beta \in 2 . \equiv . x \neq y .$

$[*51\cdot231] \qquad\qquad\qquad\qquad\qquad\qquad \equiv . \iota'x \cap \iota'y = \Lambda .$

$[*13\cdot12] \qquad\qquad\qquad\qquad\qquad\qquad\quad \equiv . \alpha \cap \beta = \Lambda \qquad (1)$

$\vdash . (1) . *11\cdot11\cdot35 . \supset$

$\qquad \vdash :. (\exists x, y) . \alpha = \iota'x . \beta = \iota'y . \supset : \alpha \cup \beta \in 2 . \equiv . \alpha \cap \beta = \Lambda \qquad (2)$

$\vdash . (2) . *11\cdot54 . *52\cdot1 . \supset \vdash . \text{Prop}$

From this proposition it will follow, when arithmetical addition has been defined, that $1 + 1 = 2$.

Proof 54–43 in Principia Mathematica, Volume I, 1st edition, p. 379.

It's OK, I don't understand it either. The point of this proof, and of all of *Principia Mathematica*, was to argue that we know mathematical truth from logic because all of mathematics can be reduced to logic.

Russell then turned to the idea that if all of mathematics can be reduced to logic, then all language expressions could also be reduced to logic. There was a growing sense in the late 1800s and early 1900s across philosophy that the role of language in knowledge needed to be addressed. How we express our ideas and how we understand ideas depend on the language we use. Surprisingly, little philosophical work had been done on the nature of language. **William of Ockham** had written a little bit about the need to be clearer on the names we use to construct philosophical arguments. **Kierkegaard** had mentioned that philosophers needed to take heed of the significant role of language in philosophy. He observed that language is partly something given to people but is also something that people develop freely, a realization that foreshadowed the later Wittgenstein, discussed later in this chapter.

Russell's dream became to show that all language can be expressed with a logical syntax that can accurately and with certainty describe the world. Obviously, not all linguistic expressions make logical sense, but that, Russell said, is because the syntax we use in our ordinary language is problematic. Our usual ad hoc, imprecise language too easily leads us to misunderstandings and absurdities. Here is an often-used example of the problem that Russell identified with ordinary language:

Argument 1	Argument 2
a) There is a fire in my kitchen.	a) There is a pain in my foot.
b) My kitchen is in my house.	b) My foot is in my shoe.
c) Therefore, there is a fire in my house.	c) Therefore, there is a pain in my shoe.

Both arguments have the same grammatical structure, but Argument 1 makes sense as written, and Argument 2 does not. The problem is with the word "in," which has a spatial meaning in Argument 1 that it does not have in Argument 2. Our imprecise syntax can disguise and distort the underlying logical forms of arguments, leading us to incorrect conclusions. Russell was confident that the tools he developed in *Principia Mathematica* could be applied to reformulate ordinary language into precise logical language.

Russell's quest for a logical language was inspired by, but ultimately doomed by, his assumption that because language describes the world, there is a necessary link between language and the world. Russell believed that every word has a factual meaning—namely, the basic entity to which it refers. This was his theory of "logical atomism"; by "atom" he means the original Greek sense of irreducible entities, not necessarily literal material atoms. In the theory of logical atomism, all truths ultimately depend on a layer of atomic facts, which consist either of a simple particular exhibiting a quality (that tree is tall) or multiple simple particulars standing in a relation (that tree is taller than that other tree).

Russell assumed that we can attain certain knowledge about the world's logical structure if we can clear up the muddle of our ordinary language. If the world is composed of a finite number of basic entities, our language should be composed of a finite number of basic linguistic units. Match every entity in the world with a corresponding linguistic unit, and we have a logically perfect language that we can use to describe everything.

The methodology of logical atomism is a process of analysis whereby one attempts to define or reconstruct more complex notions or vocabularies in terms of simpler ones. According to Russell, such an analysis would lead to a language containing only words representing simple particulars, the simple qualities and relations thereof, and logical constants. The language resulting from the analysis would, despite its limited vocabulary, adequately capture all truths.

With the tools of a logically perfect language, Russell believed we could construct logical arguments in which every proposition corresponds directly with a fact in the world. For example, we have the atomic proposition "this is taller than that," which corresponds to the atomic fact that one particular object is taller than another particular object. Atomic propositions can be combined to create molecular propositions. Russell claims that our knowledge of objects like a tree is a logical construction—a molecular proposition—formed from atoms of sense data. The atoms of sense data, of course, correspond to the atomic facts of the object.

The tools of the logical language would be the collection of atomic propositions and the logical operators such as "and," "or," "not," and "if/then." This logical process often reveals that what we take to be brute necessities are instead purely logical. Such a logical language would clear up illogical arguments like Argument 2 and, Russell thought, would solve most philosophical problems.

The problem with logical atomism is that although it's a great dream, it doesn't work in real life. In Russell's quest for the simple, fundamental units of the world and our language, he ran into multiple problems. He realized that, on the one hand, we experience hard data that are unreasonable to doubt and that, on the other hand, we have beliefs containing soft data about which we are less certain and we need to infer what we are experiencing. He wanted to be able to be certain about every bit of sense data and never have to resort to inference, so he needed to reinterpret all soft data as logical constructions based on hard data.

This leads him down a difficult path. He considers that example that when you walk toward an object, in your visual field are the shifting sense data of blocks of color of particular sizes and shapes. You can be certain of those bits of sense of data; they are hard data. Russell said that out of habit (like Hume said in Chapter 7), you group together these bits of sense data and treat them as belonging to a class (all tables) you have learned to call "table." But he eventually had to admit that this general idea of the class of objects we call "table" is soft data that cannot be converted to hard data.

Words like "table" refer to an inferred entity of which we cannot be absolutely certain. Russell can be certain only that "table" is a class term that refers to a collection of hard sense data. Our experience of something flat, smooth, and hard are all hard data, but we can only believe that the object we are experiencing is a table through inference. As Kant shows, our mind actively contributes to our knowledge and that knowledge is a limited inference that cannot know the noumenal object itself. Russell is forced to concede that I f many of our words are actually inferences with an uncertain relation to our sense data, then many of our ideas about external objects are uncertain. Therefore, only some of our knowledge is direct, and the rest is indirect. But this defeats the whole project of logical atomism that sought to make certain direct connections between our language and objects in the world.

To make a long story short, Russell's path led him to the very skepticism he wanted to avoid. He had to admit that we can state with certainty only such propositions as "flatness is here." About entities in the world, he can say only that "if I have tablelike sense data at one moment, I can reasonably expect similar tablelike sense data in the next moment," but he can justify those propositions only by appealing to human habit. (Hume would be chuckling at this point.)

It took Russell's famous student Ludwig Wittgenstein (whom we will discuss later in this chapter) to find ways out of these conundrums of language. Wittgenstein, after initially accepting his teacher's project of logical atomism, rejected it in favor of a new theory of language. As a short side note, one has to feel sympathy for Bertie who devoted his life to a project, helped by both his favorite professor, Whitehead, and his favorite student, Wittgenstein, only to see them both reject his project and go in very different directions, as we will soon discuss.

The Logical Positivists

In the 1930s, before Russell reached a dead end with logical atomism, a group of philosophers in Vienna were inspired by Russell's work to develop what they called "logical positivism." Their intent was to create a perfect philosophy based on a method of rigorous logical analysis. They came to be known as the "Vienna Circle." German **Rudolf Carnap** (1891–1970), English **Otto Neurath** (1882–1945), Austrian **Herbert Feigl** (1902–1988), and Austrian **Friedrich Waismann** (1896–1959) were the most active members of the Vienna Circle, and they evangelized their new method across Europe, successfully igniting a philosophical movement.

Foremost in the minds of the logical positivists was a fierce distaste for metaphysics—the philosophy of the nature of reality—which they interpreted as speculation beyond what is observable. Like Russell, they sought to build a logically perfect language. Their method was the "verifiability principle"; they insisted that only propositions that could be verified by logical or scientific observation should be permitted. With that core principle as a machete, they cut away and discarded most of the history of philosophy that had come before them.

The verifiability principle stated that a factual statement is meaningful only if it can be verified in experience. A statement, "There is a tree next to the driveway," is meaningful because it can be verified as being either true or false by going to the driveway and observing. In logic or mathematics, a proposition can be verified through logical proof. In science, a theory is meaningful only if the theory can be tested and verified. In the opinion of the logical positivists, statements such as Hegel's "freedom is the idea of *Geist*" cannot be verified and are therefore meaningless. Also eliminated by the verifiability principle was Kant's synthetic a priori judgments because they cannot be verified by observation; they can only be inferred. All theological statements are rejected. Both the theists' "God exists" and the atheists' "no God exists" are unverifiable and meaningless. Similarly, the logical positivists rejected all ethical theory. Its English convert, **A.J. Ayer** (1910–1989), went so far as to dismiss all moral statements as mere emotional reactions. He claimed that saying that an act was morally wrong was like simply saying "boo!" and saying an act was morally good was like simply rooting "hooray!"

The logical positivists' ideal principles ran into real-life issues similar to Russell's. The verifiability principle immediately ran into a feasibility problem. "There is a mountain on the far side of the moon" was not verifiable in the 1930s. That objection was easily remedied by adjusting the principle to state verifiable in experience *in principle*. Sure enough, technology advanced to where we could observe the far side of the moon. Scientists objected that many important scientific statements, including the laws of physics, were not conclusively *verifiable* through observation but could only be *supported* by observation. This thinking corresponded to Hume's observation that science can only infer probable truths because the next experiment could always yield a different result. The logical positivists had to concede that point, and Carnap replaced "verification" with "confirmation" in the principle.

Then developments in subatomic physics and quantum mechanics forced them to modify their principle again to accept that statements about unobservable subatomic particles are meaningful because other observations suggest their existence is probable. Logical positivism completely melted down in the face of **Werner Heisenberg's** (1901–1976) uncertainty principle and **Erwin Schrödinger's** (1887–1961) cat being both alive and dead (ask your friendly, neighborhood physics professor).

The final blow to logical positivism was the critique that its central principle of verifiability was itself unverifiable by either logic or observation. Hume would be laughing out loud at this point because the verifiability principle is neither a relation of ideas nor a matter of fact; it is simply an assertion. The logical positivists had to admit that their verifiability principle was only a recommendation. The demand of the logical positivists that all human knowledge conform to a specific structure ultimately was an empty demand.

Henri Bergson Explains Process versus Positivism

At the same time that Russell was developing positivist analytic philosophy, French philosopher **Henri Bergson** (1859–1941) was developing a very different philosophy. For several decades, he was probably the most famous philosopher in the world. He is now tragically largely forgotten in English-speaking lands because his work is incorrectly dismissed as mere speculation because it is not reducible to the now-dominant methods of analytic philosophy. Bergson saw knowledge as an ongoing process of development, but he rejected the mechanistic causality of Hegel's historicism. Bergson developed a highly original approach to philosophy that took into account elements of Kant, Hegel, and pragmatism.

Bergson proposes that in the quest for understanding the world, there are two methods of gaining knowledge of an object. There is analysis, which seeks to know an object absolutely, and there is intuition, which seeks to understand an object relatively.

Since Aristotle, philosophy had seen everything in the universe as discrete substances that maintain their identity even while undergoing change. When you look back at the philosophers we've covered so far, you can see how much of their work was dealing with the problems created by that assumption that everything is a substance—how objects are, how they are similar yet different, how they change, and how we can have knowledge about them.

Analysis is the method that comes from this assumption of discrete substances. It is the detached and disinterested method of separating the object from its surroundings, conceptually breaking down an object into parts, interpreting the divided parts, and reconstituting a view of the object after analysis. The method of analysis is how science and positivist philosophy think empirical knowledge of the world is obtained, and it is the habitual way that Western people have learned to think.

But, Bergson says, analysis depends on symbols that represent parts of the objects and then uses these symbols to mentally reconstruct a picture of the object. This is similar to Locke's epistemology in which discrete simple ideas combine into complex ideas, but this is the approach that Bergson wants us to stop using. Symbols, words, and language are, he said, barriers between us and reality.

Bergson says that the true empiricism is intuition. Bergson uses "intuition" differently than we've seen previously. Philosophers from Descartes to Russell used "intuition" to describe an immediate knowing. Bergson used "intuition" as a sympathetic entering into what is observed, rather than going around it from the outside. By "sympathetic," Bergson does not mean an emotion but operating through affinity and interdependence, as in a sympathetic vibration of two strings. Intuition is entering into experience to be a part of what is observed. Intuition is an integral experience, a series of acts within what Bergson calls "duration," (explained soon) and thus a method of experience.

One of the examples Bergson gives of the difference between the method of analysis and the method of intuition is experiencing a city. Looking at photographs of a city, even a collection taken from every viewpoint and perspective, you can't reconstruct what it is to be in the city. Only by entering the city and walking through it can you grasp what it is to be there. His other example is reading a commentary on a poem by Homer. No matter how many commentaries you read, you can never grasp the value of experiencing the poem's original language. Analysis can give us photographs and commentary, but it can't give us the experience of the things themselves. Analysis has its own value and provides us with some understanding, but knowing the things themselves requires the sympathetic entering into of intuition. Bergson says that by using intuition we can seize reality from within.

[margin note: analysis gives understanding. Intuition - experiencing the world]

Duration—Bergson's Philosophy of Time

Intuition begins with entering into the "duration." Duration is Bergson's conception of time and consciousness that he proposed to help correct the problems with the method of analysis. Bergson's philosophy of time is an ingenious and highly innovative exploration of a difficult topic that few philosophers address.

Bergson identifies two ways that we can think about time. One he calls "scientific time" or "clock time." This is time as conceived of by the method of analysis, discussed earlier. Science attempts to measure time with precision, but science's concept of time is actually an abstraction based on the concept of space. Clock time disaggregates the flow of time into arbitrary atomized units—hours, minutes, seconds.

The other time is "duration" or "real time." This is time as we experience and live it and is time as it exists in nature. Bergson realized that reality is not static substances but a continuous flow of activity. The method of analysis approaches our experiences in terms of quantitative multiplicity—separating discrete sense data from each other within a homogeneous space. We saw Hume separate sense impressions in that way, which is why with his billiard ball example he claimed there was no reason to believe in causation. Kant tried to solve this problem with the Categories of Understanding. Bergson views our experiences in terms of *qualitative* multiplicity—we organize conscious states into a whole; within the whole, our experiences permeate each other and become richer.

The concept of qualitative multiplicity attempts to bridge the gap between our experiences and reality, seeing both as fluid, continuous, and contextual activities. Duration is understanding both our experience and the world as qualitative multiplicity. Everything is constantly changing, and fundamental to the flow of reality is time. We experience time, Bergson realized, but not with our senses or by reason, but through an inner sense. Duration is the nature of time both as it is and as it is experienced by people.

Bergson's first book on duration was *Time and Free Will: An Essay on the Immediate Data of Consciousness* (1889). As the subtitle indicates, Bergson is studying the contents of consciousness, similar to Husserl's project of phenomenology (we will meet him in Chapter 14). Bergson accepted the reality of free will and said that other philosophers saw free will as a philosophical problem only because of their detached and disinterested method of analysis. Kant had to locate free will outside of time and space because he confused all time with immobile space that is subject to causality. Bergson differentiated time and space, removing time from mechanistic spatial causality and placing it within duration. Free will is located within duration.

So, what is duration? Our language isn't fully adequate to define it, but Bergson gives some analogies. Bergson visualizes duration as being like two spools. The first spool is constantly unrolling as time flows forward, and the second spool is rolling up, continually collecting memories left by the other spool. The second spool is consciousness, symbolizing how we take up duration and gather experiences in it. Each moment in consciousness is different from all previous moments because the present is added onto the memories of the past. Over the first spool we have no control—time unwinds inexorably before us. The second spool, the past, we can control, to an extent, within our memory. Bergson was the first philosopher since Augustine who truly appreciated the wonder of our memory. We can rewind our spool of memory, playing it back in various ways and, most importantly for Bergson, not in the sequential order in which current time unwinds but in the order of meaning. We recollect and order our past not in clock time but in duration—arraying and living through our memories according to the qualitative importance we place on them. Our subjective and intentional experience and reexperience show that our consciousness is not a process of the material world.

Bergson's next analogy is how we experience time like we experience the color orange, which also illustrates how duration is connected with intuition. If we make the effort to enter into the experience of orange, we would sense ourselves between red and yellow. We would perceive a variety of shades of orange between red and yellow. Further effort opens us up to perceiving lighter and darker shades of each color and the whole spectrum of colors and saturation. Similarly, we can be introspective and enter into our own duration. When we do, we can sense ourselves among many other durations. Making an effort, we can expand our intuition to come into contact with a community of durations of different shades and saturations. We can follow durations upwardly toward spirit and downwardly toward inert matter—indeed, in a manner similar to that of Plotinus.

Reality is fluid, not a sequence of discrete units, so, for Bergson, duration is not a perception of images as an empiricist would understand it but is instead the entering into a flow. We can, to use a contemporary analogy, "dial up or down" our experience of time. We do this unconsciously, as indicated in the old saying, "Time flies when you're having fun." Also, you know how time can drag when you have to wait for an unpleasant experience to finish, like listening to a dull professor lecture. Not a philosophy lecture, of course; philosophy is riveting fun! (Just seeing if you're still paying attention.) Time is a flowing, indivisible continuum. Clock time is an artificial abstraction created by humans. We can and do divide time into distinct, measurable units—hours, minutes, seconds—and these divisions are useful, but an hour does not in itself exist. We have to stuff ourselves into these artificial units of clock time, and Bergson adds that these units of clock time become harmful to us when we mistake them for reality.

Experiencing Process

When we don't treat objects as substances and don't treat time as a sequence of discrete units, we open ourselves to experience how reality truly is. When we understand that process, spontaneity, and creativity are fundamental to reality, we can understand order and stability in objects as patterns within the flux of the dynamic flow of reality.

> This reality is mobility. Not things made, but things in the making, not self-maintaining states but only changing states, exist. Rest is never more than apparent, or, rather, relative. The consciousness we have of our own self in its continual flux introduces us to the interior of a reality, on the model of which we must represent other realities. All reality, therefore, is tendency. (*An Introduction to Metaphysics* 65)

Bergson's idea that reality is mobility and tendency, a process, is incredibly influential in continental philosophy and all of the sciences and humanities that take inspiration from it. Bergson's process philosophy finds resonance in quantum physics and chaos theory, among other branches of the hard sciences.

Through intuition and duration, we see that we aren't dealing with substances. The question, "What will the weather be tomorrow?" is not inquiring about a substance. A friendship, a vacation, a university, an ecosystem, and public opinion are all concepts we can think about and use meaningfully in sentences, but they aren't substances. Such concepts are expressions of collections of more primary activities and events. Rain is not a quality of a substance called weather; rain happens in the course of weather as a result of the interplay of various forces and objects. Weather is a dynamic process, ever changing as one set of events gives way to a new set of events. There are recurring patterns (it rains more in the autumn than in the summer, perhaps) but not permanent qualities.

The core of Bergson's philosophy is that we will better understand objects when we consider them as dynamic processes, like weather, rather than as static substances. You might think that a university has a static geographical location, but is a university a set of GPS coordinates? Would it cease to be if it moved location? Or if it changed its name? What universities are, and most of what we experience and think about, are entities not reducible to substances. A friendship does not have a static character, no matter how strong it is; it has its ups and downs, its ebbs and flows. Public opinion is ever changing within shifting demographics. An ecosystem is a community of living organisms interacting and flowing as a system with no exact boundaries. Even inanimate objects have identity within a set of relations and events.

With reality being a dynamic process of change, we do well to make the effort to put aside the habitual method of analysis and enter into the process of reality, allowing our mind's categories to be shaped by reality. Entering into the duration, we can expand our awareness to experience the reality that each duration that comes into existence must be related to others.

Self, Life, and Élan Vital

Bergson applied his concepts of intuition and duration to the consideration of who we are and the living world around us. We've seen that Hume dismissed the idea of a self and that Kant accepted Hume's idea that we don't experience a self in-itself but argued that we can rationally assume that there's a noumenal self underneath our experiences. Bergson believes that we do have a self—a creative, spontaneous beingness—that can be observed and known in the same way we observe and understand other things.

We can encounter our real self through the method of intuition, which, remember, is a sympathetic entering into what is observed. Bergson criticized the then-growing fields of psychology and psychiatry as seeing the human self as nothing but a sequence of separate psychological states—what Bergson called the method of analysis. According to Bergson, this thinking led practitioners of psychology and psychiatry to believe that each distinct psychological state was caused by the previous state and, therefore, that human behavior is determined. Belief in determinism follows from a false assumption about the human self. The self is not a sequence of separate psychological states. We experience our self as a seamless totality—a qualitative multiplicity. Our actions flow from our whole self as free actions. Bergson is slightly overstating his case here because we are aware that we can be "of two minds" and that we occasionally act from compulsions, but his argument that determinism is a belief that comes from a faulty psychology is valid. Bergson's sympathetic intuition reveals that we have free will. We saw William James make a not-too-dissimilar argument for free will. James, late in his life, read the younger Bergson's books and hailed Bergson as a genius.

Somewhat like the existentialist philosophers, whom we will meet in Chapter 14, Bergson said that people can choose to live on a superficial level, passively reacting to the world, or they can choose to live authentically. It's easy to see how Bergson's theory that there are two methods of approaching the world—analysis and intuition—apply to living our lives. Bergson is consistent throughout his philosophy in claiming that reality *is* a seamless continuous flow of activity, and that intuition is the way to experience reality clearly.

In terms of who we are, he says we discover our freedom in our own experience. Psychologists, when using the method of analysis, view *other* people as objects whose behavior is determined. However, and this is Bergson's crucial observation, no one can view his or her *own* self as determined because we all experience ourselves as a creative, spontaneous agent capable of responding with free will to the external world. Sure, you can *choose* to think of yourself as an object by denying your own deep, authentic self, but that is denying the reality of who and what you are.

Interestingly, Bergson does not reserve the idea of a creative, spontaneous agent to human beings. He saw this power as existing to an extent in all life. He called it "élan vital," literally "vital force" in French, and saw it as the creative principle immanent in all living organisms. We can see the élan vital in our continuous experience of duration, in our ability and desire to experience, express, and grow. "Our personality shoots, grows, and ripens without ceasing. Each of its moments is something new added to what was before" (*Creative Evolution* 8). This vital life force is present in all of nature. Life's surging, expressing, growing force will strain against inert matter to overcome or get around resistance. We can see this in how plant roots and stems will find any cracks in rocks or walls to break through and grow. In this way, life is ceaselessly changing into something new and adding to what was before.

Bergson extends this idea to the whole biosphere, seeing élan vital as the engine of evolution. Bergson accepted biological evolution, which had been theorized independently by Englishmen **Herbert Spencer** (1820–1903) and **Charles Darwin** (1809–1882) in the mid-1800s. Bergson rejected Spencer's positivist "survival of the fittest" model of evolution. He also disagreed with Darwin's theory that evolution was driven by random variations, some working, some not, in helping an organism survive. Bergson responded that if mere survival were the force in evolution, it would have stopped at single-celled organisms.

The appearance of complex "higher" organisms must have had some other force at work. That force, Bergson said, was the élan vital. It is a force that comes from life itself, not from an outside realm—Bergson also rejected Hegel's idea that *Geist* drives development. Evolution isn't driven by power, randomness, or reason but rather grows organically from the free will of life. Evolution is an unceasing gushing out of life, continually rising, falling, and rising again into new forms. In the vital activity of evolution, we see "a reality which is making itself in a reality which is unmaking itself" (*Creative Evolution* 248).

Bergson's Legacy

Few remember Henri Bergson's name today, but the influence of his philosophy has rippled throughout society. In a number of ways, he was ahead of his time, and we can see many of his themes echoed in current continental philosophy and popular culture. Those who practice the method of analysis—scientists and, of course, analytic philosophers—have dismissed Bergson as an irrational anti-science mystic. But Bergson was not against science. He cautioned against the reductionist method of doing science that reduced reality to static discrete entities. He pointed out that infinitesimal calculus, now central to physics, is based on the realization of continuity and change rather than the earlier static conception of the world. Part of the accusation that Bergson is anti-science came from his opposition to **Albert Einstein's** (1879–1955) theory of space-time. Bergson agreed with most of Einstein's theories but observed some inconsistencies in Einstein's static model of space-time, although the nature of his objections is too complex to address here. A number of theories in physics, increasingly being accepted now, consider the universe to be dynamic in the way Bergson described. It remains to be seen, but a revival of interest in Bergson may soon happen, just as some other past philosophers have found renewed fame and discussion long after they formed their ideas.

Alfred North Whitehead's Natural Theology

Yes, you saw Whitehead's name earlier as the coauthor with Bertrand Russell of *Principia Mathematica*. That was during Whitehead's first life as a professor of mathematics. His second life, as a professor of philosophy, was, he said, inspired by his wife's vivid appreciation of beauty and capacity for love. From her vital force, he realized that there was more to appreciate beyond the confines of logic and science. Whitehead's dramatic transformation from analytic mathematician to process philosopher, from a professor teaching mathematics and logic to a professor sharply critical of logical and scientific reductionism, is unparalleled in academia. The themes and direction of Whitehead's philosophy are similar to those of Bergson, but there's no evidence of any interactions between the two.

The Quest to Understand the Ultimate Categories

Immanuel Kant's Copernican revolution had reset the foundation of philosophical inquiry. That the mind is active in structuring experience was now accepted by all except for some within analytic philosophy. Whitehead accepted the basic idea of Kant's Categories, but he did not like that Kant had left open the possibility that the human mind's structures might not mirror the structure of reality. Whitehead thought that the successes of science in discovering truths about the world must indicate that the structures imposed by the human mind on experience must emulate structures found in reality. Evolutionary theory backed up Whitehead's idea: wouldn't the human species develop mental abilities in concord with how reality is? This gave Whitehead the hope that it was possible to attain an understanding of the structure of reality itself.

In a series of books, beginning with *The Concept of Nature* (1920), Whitehead developed the method of process philosophy. Central to his philosophy is that reality needs to be understood as a series of states within constant processes.

Whitehead's method for gaining knowledge was to start with our understanding of a particular region of experience and then take the concepts discovered in that region and use reason and "free imagination" to see if those concepts could be generalized to describe other regions of experience. Whitehead described the method by using the analogy of an airplane flight (a new technology at that time). The flight starts from the ground of experience, elevates into the air of imaginative generalization, and lands again for new observations now enhanced by rational interpretation. It's important to realize that Whitehead is not talking about flights of fancy beyond reason. His point is that good explorers of reality need to be imaginative, or creative, in their thinking.

The region of experience from which Whitehead preferred to start was biology. Similar to Bergson, he saw life and its dynamic, vital processes as a key to understanding all of reality. Whitehead referred to his method as the "philosophy of organism." Being organisms, we human beings can use our own flow of dynamic experiences as a great place to begin our flight of discovery.

To the positivists who dismissed metaphysics (the philosophy of the nature of reality and being), Whitehead countered that everyone has metaphysical beliefs; such beliefs are unavoidable. Every scientific man (sic), Whitehead said, feels that he has to say he dislikes metaphysics to preserve his reputation but that what he means is he dislikes having *his* metaphysics criticized. Indeed, the positivists, analytics, and scientists all operate based on a system of metaphysical beliefs that guide their thinking. The fashion to deny that truth, rampant in Whitehead's time and still present today, is sheer conceit. Whitehead said that as long as metaphysics is grounded in logical principles of coherence and consistency, rather than undisciplined speculation, it was healthy and necessary.

Against the Metaphysical Assumption of Reductionist Materialism

Whitehead pointed out that it is a common metaphysical belief that reality is constituted by fundamental units of matter independent of one another. Whitehead rejected that positivist assumption in favor of a process view of reality that looked at events, not objects, as primary, all events being interrelated and interdependent. He proposed his event-based or process metaphysics as a replacement for the reductionist, materialist metaphysics of classical Newtonian physics. He identified four metaphysical assumptions in reductionist materialism—(1) that particles of matter retain their essential identity through time, (2) that each particle's essential identity is self-contained and independent of relations with other particles, (3) that each particle has a definite location in time and space, and (4) that the state of each particle at a specific time is completely determined by prior causes.

Anyone familiar with advances in physics over the last century will recognize that most in the field now agree with Whitehead that these four reductionist metaphysical assumptions are false. Writing in the 1920s, Whitehead was aware that quantum physics was beginning to question these assumptions. He was ahead of the curve and still is. Being consistent with his idea that concepts discovered in one region of experience can be applied to other regions, Whitehead was keenly interested in applying the concepts in nonclassical quantum physics to other areas of reality. He saw a correspondence between the reductionist tendency in classical physics to consider particles in isolation from each other and people's growing sense of alienation from the natural world.

Whitehead traced people's alienation back to the rise of the modern mechanistic view of the world in 1600s philosophy. That tendency, from Hobbes and Descartes on down, led to what Whitehead called "the bifurcation of nature," separating the world of experience from the world of objects. He called the reductionist, mechanistic view strained and paradoxical. He questioned whether the standardized concepts of science are too limiting and narrow for science itself. They certainly are too limiting and narrow for our lives. His process philosophy overcomes this false separation, denying neither the world of experience nor the world of objects.

> For us the red glow of the sunset should be as much part of nature as are the molecules and electric waves by which men (sic) of science would explain the phenomenon. It is for natural philosophy to analyze how these various elements of nature are connected. (*The Concept of Nature* 29)

Process and Reality

In Whitehead's view, reality is always in process, always changing in an indivisible flow of time. The fundamental units of reality are not material particles but rather events or momentary actions. Whitehead calls events the "actual entities" of reality. Actual entities range from the single vibration of an electron to a single thought within your stream of consciousness and everything in between and beyond. The temporal extension of an event is as much a part of any entity's identity as is its spatial extension, but science had only considered spatial extension. The only actual entity that could be atemporal, or without extension in time, would be God. Everything else would be extended temporal occasions of experience. When we perceive an object in the world, what Whitehead's event-based philosophy tells us we are perceiving is a composite of many occasions of experience that have occurred over time. What an object is, then, is how it became what it is. For each actual entity, its being is constituted by its becoming.

Seeing reality as temporal process allows us to see how actual entities are interrelated, not separate, things. Every entity in the universe has its particular character that comes from its relationship with everything else. Other philosophers discuss the importance of understanding objects within their context, but Whitehead takes the idea to the level of existence itself. Actual entities *are* all affected by each other. Every entity is everywhere at all times, and every location involves an aspect of itself in every other location. Therefore, every spatiotemporal standpoint mirrors the world, and reality is a web of interconnected events. Whitehead's conception was met with astonishment at the time, yet at the same time, theoretical physics was beginning to confirm his conception, and it is now widely accepted within physics that it is at least a possibility (for example, the theories of quantum entanglement and the wave function).

Whitehead's interest wasn't in physics per se but in a mix of biology and philosophy. For him, the interconnectedness of actual entities manifests in subjective feeling. This is where Whitehead's philosophy loses some people because he states that every entity in reality has subjective experience and can be said to have some level of awareness and feeling. Not only humans but also all organisms, even single-celled organisms, have feelings. One way to understand what Whitehead is saying is to avoid overly anthropomorphizing this awareness and feeling as conscious self-awareness but instead see such awareness as every organism responding to its environment and seeking out conditions more conducive to its health and survival. This concept fits with Whitehead's statements that electrons are not passive entities but are active entities that react to their environment. Here, too, multiple theories in physics describe electrons and other subatomic particles in ways that Whitehead would find familiar.

Ultimately, for Whitehead, the web of interconnected events and the actual entities in it are all characterized by creativity. Similar to Bergson, Whitehead saw everything as lively and continually evolving. Entities come into existence, their becoming being a process of self-creation reacting to their immediate past in synthesis with their environment. The universe is dynamic, constantly creating and changing. Entities are aware and interconnected. Nothing can be considered in isolation because particular entities form societies of larger entities. This last idea of Whitehead's is the same as the current scientific idea of ecosystems— communities of organisms interacting and living as a system.

Ludwig Wittgenstein—From Positivism to Process

Straddling both sides of the analytic/continental divide is the Austrian-born **Ludwig Wittgenstein** (1889–1951) who did most of his philosophical work in England. He was a student of Bertrand Russell's, trying to understand the foundations of logic, and his early work galvanized analytic philosophy and remains an influence. He then stepped away from philosophy for a decade; when he returned, he rejected his own early work and adopted a kind of pragmatism, centered on a new view of how we use language, the meaning of which philosophers still debate. How best to consider Wittgenstein's philosophical career is a matter of debate, but I'll opt for the view that we can see Wittgenstein as having three stages: the early period of the *Tractatus Logico-Philosophicus*, a middle period in the 1930s, and a later period during and after World War II.

The Early Wittgenstein: The *Tractatus*

In 1911, Wittgenstein, then an engineering student, learned about Russell's work on the foundations of mathematics. Ever the strong-willed and impetuous person, Wittgenstein traveled to the University of Cambridge where Russell taught and requested to be his student. Russell saw Wittgenstein's potential and took him on, mentoring him in philosophy and his theories on mathematics.

Wittgenstein was inspired to write a book that combined Russell's logical atomism with Frege's philosophy of logic. He wrote much of the book, *Tractatus Logico-Philosophicus* (1921), while serving in the Austrian army in World War I. It is a bizarre book, and Wittgenstein knew it. In the preface to the book, Wittgenstein wrote the odd comments that its value consists of two things—that thoughts are expressed in it and that it shows how little is achieved when these problems are solved. The problems he refers to are the problems of philosophy defined by the work of Frege and Russell. The second comment is the first hint that Wittgenstein thought the *Tractatus* was a failure.

The short book consists of numbered propositions in seven sets. That format is similar to Russell's *Principia Mathematica*, which was a list of numbered mathematical proofs. In the *Tractatus*, there are seven main propositions, with sets of numerous sub- and sub-sub-propositions.

Proposition 1.2 belongs to the first set and is a comment on proposition 1. Proposition 1.21 expands on proposition 1.2, and so on. I'll start with some important and representative propositions from the first part of the book, and this is leaving out many propositions:

1	The world is everything that is the case.
1.1	The world is the totality of facts, not of things.
2	What is the case, the fact, is the existence of atomic facts.
2.1	We make to ourselves pictures of facts.
3	The logical picture of the facts is the thought.
3.4	The proposition determines a place in logical space.
4.001	The totality of propositions is the language.
4.01	The proposition is a picture of reality. The proposition is a model of the reality as we think it is.
4.0311	One name stands for one thing, and another for another thing, and they are connected together. And so the whole, like a living picture, presents the atomic fact.
4.04	In the proposition there must be exactly as many things distinguishable as there are in the state of affairs, which it represents.
4.121	. . . Propositions show the logical form of reality. They exhibit it.
4.2	The sense of a proposition is its agreement and disagreement with the possibilities of the existence and non-existence of the atomic facts. (*Tractatus*)

I'll pause there for now. Make sense? No? Well, philosophers still argue about what it all means, and I just gave you some of the easier bits.

Let's look at what Wittgenstein was trying to accomplish in the early part of *Tractatus*. In its first part, the book is a description of logical atomism and the basic elements of a logically perfect language. That was Wittgenstein's, and Russell's, goal. He was essentially laying out the idea that the world is a logical world (the totality of facts) and that what we do is represent the facts in the world with our own logical pictures so that each picture, each word, corresponds to a fact. That is what thinking is. When we learn the proper methods of constructing and using logical propositions, we cannot fail. There can never be surprises in logic, he said (*Tractatus* 6.1251). Except . . . well, we'll get to that in a bit.

Philosophers are guilty of taking from the *Tractatus* what they like and leaving the rest. The logical positivists loved the complex rules for constructing logical propositions that Wittgenstein gave in the middle of the book and just ignored the statements Wittgenstein made about the limits of logic in the last part of the book. Here are some of those important and representative propositions from the last part of the book, again leaving out many of the more complicated propositions:

5.43	. . . All propositions of logic say the same thing. That is, nothing.

5.6   The limits of my language mean the limits of my world.

5.621 The world and life are one.

5.63   I am my world.

5.641 There is therefore really a sense in which in philosophy we can talk of a non-psychological I. The I occurs in philosophy through the fact that the "world is my world." The philosophical I is not the [hu]man, not the human body or the human soul of which psychology treats, but the metaphysical subject, the limit—not a part of the world.

6.1   The propositions of logic are tautologies.

6.11   The propositions of logic therefore say nothing. (They are the analytic propositions.)

6.41   The sense of the world must lie outside the world.

6.432 How the world is, is completely indifferent for what is higher. God does not reveal himself in the world.

6.522 There is indeed the inexpressible. This shows itself; it is the mystical.

6.54   My propositions are elucidatory in this way: he (sic) who understands me finally recognizes them as senseless, when he has climbed out through them, on them, over them. (He must so to speak throw away the ladder, after he has climbed up on it.) He must surmount these propositions; then he sees the world rightly.

7   Whereof one cannot speak, thereof one must be silent. (*Tractatus*)

The logical positivists, and many analytic philosophers to this day, avoid these passages. Wittgenstein is acknowledging the very things they are most against accepting: logic tells us nothing about the world, perception is subjective, there is a real nonpsychological "I," and there is a mystical realm beyond logic and philosophy that cannot be reduced to words. Not that Wittgenstein gave us any help in understanding what he was getting at with these concepts or what to do with them. Are we to accept what he says, climb this "ladder" over them (to what? the mystical?), and then be silent?

Wittgenstein seemed to adopt silence after finishing his book in 1919 (although it took two years to find a publisher). He went back to Austria, apparently walking away from philosophy.

The Middle Wittgenstein: The Blue and Brown Book Lectures

About eight years later, Wittgenstein came to one of the meetings of the Vienna Circle, invited to talk with them about the *Tractatus*. They greeted him like a hero because to them, Wittgenstein's book (except for that last icky bit they avoided) could form the basis of a logical language. Rudolf Carnap, a member of the Vienna Circle, later wrote that it soon became apparent that they weren't thinking the same as Wittgenstein anymore, if they ever had. Wittgenstein told them he no longer agreed with much of the *Tractatus*. His later work showed that he agreed only with the statements toward the end of that book that I listed. His later thought focused on the meaning of language and the word outside of logical atomism and pure propositional logic.

Wittgenstein was persuaded by contacts at the University of Cambridge to return. He was now famous, and not only in philosophy circles, because of the *Tractatus*. He returned in 1929. Cambridge University wanted to hire him as a professor, but he did not have a PhD. At Russell's urging, Wittgenstein submitted the *Tractatus* for his PhD in philosophy at Cambridge. Bertrand Russell was one of the examiners. Russell loved parts of the book but confessed he didn't understand all of it. The story is told that in the middle of the viva (where a candidate defends his or her thesis to be confirmed for the PhD), in response to Russell again expressing confusion over a passage in the book, Wittgenstein stood up, said, "It's OK, you'll never understand it," and walked out. He was awarded the PhD and offered a teaching position.

For the next twelve years, Wittgenstein was a lecturer at Cambridge. He published nothing, but his lectures began to show a bold new style of philosophy. His students reported that his lectures were highly unconventional. He did not have a set topic but instead talked about whatever was on his mind, with long pauses as he thought deeply about a philosophical problem. What was usually on his mind were the philosophical problems of language. He had come to realize that he had not solved all the philosophical problems of language in the *Tractatus*. In two academic years, several of his students took lecture notes and made copies of them with a mimeograph machine, bound them in cloth, and shared them with other students and faculty. The lecture notes are known by the color of their cloth covers—1933–1934 in the blue book, and 1934–1935 in the brown book.

In these books were the roots of a new philosophy. Wittgenstein had abandoned logical atomism and developed a different view of language's relation with the world. He now realized that we don't learn language through strict rules, and we don't use language according to strict rules. Yes, most of us were taught the rules of grammar, but the many ways that we *use* language are ways that we acquired through a plethora of life experiences. We learn how to use language by using language. We learn by doing, by applying ways of doing things with language.

Wittgenstein's insightful analogy is to call what we do with language a "language-game" ("*Sprachspiel*" in German). In any game—from checkers to baseball—we learn the basic rules, but it is only through practice that we *really* learn how to play. We learn how to play a game well by playing the game. Language is the same. There are rules, but the rules are not all-encompassing, and we can know the rules but still not know how to speak the language effectively in life. Anyone who has taken a foreign language course and then traveled to a country where that language is spoken will experience firsthand what Wittgenstein means.

By playing the language-game we learn the language. That's because words do not have the logical one-to-one correspondence with objects that Wittgenstein had written about in the *Tractatus*. Words are inexact. An example he gives of how this works is learning the word "pencil." One could try to teach the word by pointing at a pencil and saying "pencil." But the listener could associate the word with a number of things: the pencil as a whole, the wood it is made of, the shape of it, and so on. Only through context and use of the object do we come to understand the words for it. Then, when we use language, we are playing a language-game. In this middle period, he was still working out the implications of this new theory of language.

The Later Wittgenstein: The *Philosophical Investigations*

Wittgenstein continued to develop his new philosophy through the 1930s. He largely stopped during World War II, volunteering instead for the British war effort for several years. By 1946, he had written a new book, part one of what he planned to be a two-part book. It was accepted for publication, but Wittgenstein, being a perfectionist, withdrew it before publication, worried that it wasn't finished. Only after his death did several of his former students gather his first part and, along with some of his notes that would have been components of the second part, publish the book as *Philosophical Investigations* in 1953.

Philosophical Investigations expands on the themes of his Cambridge lectures in the 1930s. It is less bizarre than the *Tractatus* but similarly is a collection of thoughts rather than a systematic narrative. What becomes obvious from the contents is that Wittgenstein is doing philosophy as an activity of open imagination and thinking. Often, he is telling stories of real-life situations that demonstrate how language works. His style is like using Whitehead's method of imagination taking flight to go from one region of certainty to a new one.

Wittgenstein's stories demonstrate his new theory of language and what it means for philosophy. He begins by, at length, indirectly criticizing his theory of language in the *Tractatus*. Words do not get their meaning from a logical one-to-one correspondence with objects but from their use. That shift in definition leads to a further shift from the *Tractatus*. Instead of seeing philosophical problems as problems of logic, he now sees them as the lack of a clear view of the use of our words.

To get a clear view of the meaning of words, we need to examine their use in the language. He uses the example of the word "game" itself. What is a game? How would we define it? We can't, as he says, just point to various games and define the word by examples. A short clarification: Wittgenstein wrote in German, and the German word he uses for "game" is "*Spiel*." The German word has a broader sense than the English word "game." *Spiel* extends in its use to the act of "play" and "playing," so this German sense of the word is more suggestive of an action or activity, which helps us understand Wittgenstein's meaning in his discussion of games.

Wittgenstein discusses several possible meanings for "game," "*Spiel*"— competition, enjoyment, having a set of rules, and so on—but he shows how each is inadequate to describe games. What we see when we think about the meaning of the word "game" is that all of the many objects and activities that we call "games" share family resemblances. When you look at a biological family, they don't all look exactly the same, but they share enough common features of appearance that you recognize them as members of the same family. They may all have "the same nose," but they don't need to all share one particular feature to resemble each other. They have enough similar features that we see the family resemblance. The same is true for the word "game," Wittgenstein says. Solitaire, checkers, water polo, slot machines, and mind games all share enough similar features that we can see the family resemblance that they are all games. What he takes from this exercise is that an exact definition is neither possible nor required for the word to have meaning. If someone says, "Let's play a game," we understand what is meant despite the lack of specificity.

Similar to the pragmatists, Wittgenstein said that we use words as tools to do things in the world. Language is part of our activities in the world, and our uses of language are as varied as our activities are. Wittgenstein describes the many activities in which we use words to do things as various language-games. He mentions giving orders, describing an object's appearance, speculating about what may happen, making a joke, translating from one language to another, requesting something, thanking someone, cursing, praying. Within each type of activity, the various ways of expressing ideas and actions have internal family resemblances that show they are related and can be called "language-games," despite how much they vary.

Our many ways of speaking do not all conform to a single model, but their commonalities include that they are all activities, they all have purposes and goals, and they all are used by people who have a shared understanding about the rules of the language-game. This last resemblance is crucial. Words and sentences do not have meanings in themselves; they have the meanings that we give them through how we use them. If I say "table," I have not communicated anything to you unless we are both playing the same language-game. If you are asking me where to set something, you'd know I mean to put it on the table. If I'm teaching you English, you know to point to the table. If I am quizzing you on

German, you could respond with "Tisch." As Wittgenstein says, we don't simply speak; we do things by speaking.

Language-games, then, are human activities in which words help us accomplish our goals. Words are tools, and just like we would use a hammer to pound nails, but not to cut a board in two (we'd use a saw for that) we use different words for different purposes in different situations. Plus, we often will use the same word in multiple different situations or different language-games. Take the word "lose." We can lose our keys, lose sleep, lose a game, lose our train of thought, lose confidence in someone. If we are playing the language-game of talking about going for a drive, and you say you lost your keys, I can help you find them. But "can I help you find it" is without sense if we are talking about how you are losing sleep because you are worried about something.

The point to all of this, according to Wittgenstein, is that the demand of the logical positivists that we have one set of logical language rules to which all language must conform is wrong. There are as many sets of rules as there are language-games. Wittgenstein now realized that the mistake he made in the *Tractatus* was to try to force language to conform to the crystalline purity of logic. But language isn't calculus. Language is living. Logic does not tell us how to live. The logical positivists were mixing language-games by trying to force the rules of logic language-games onto other language-games. Speculative philosophy, such as Leibniz's, can make the same mistake by trying to impose the language-game of talking about worldly things onto higher, deeper ideas. This is one area where Wittgenstein still agreed with his *Tractatus*—there is indeed the inexpressible, the mystical that is beyond words.

The role of philosophy, Wittgenstein says in the *Philosophical Investigations*, is not to try to impose structure on language or life but to learn from them. He states that when philosophers use a word like "knowledge," and try to grasp the essence of it, they need to ask how the word is used in the language-game that is its original home. The philosopher needs to bring the word back to its everyday use. Wittgenstein seems to suggest that philosophy needs to stop trying to find perfect forms and perfect knowledge and step aside to let everyday normal life show us what is the case. Philosophy simply puts things before us and need not explain things. Philosophy should not question or interfere with how language is used but can only describe it. That is the proper role of philosophy.

People use language within language-games, and language-games are played within an activity. Wittgenstein further describes our activities as occurring within a "form of life." Our actions, and thus our language, are interlaced with our practices, interests, goals, and understandings. All of these are shaped by our culture and our place within it. On a social level, the interlaced practices and understandings of a culture are its form of life. The point is that it is the cultural forms of life that provide people with the meanings of words, and it is this social backdrop of meanings that renders language intelligible. This is a similar idea to Peirce's interpretant—that which gives signs their meaning. Human culture is organic—it grew and continues to evolve on its own; it did not and does not ask philosophers to justify what it does. For that reason, forms of life are the justification for definitions of words and the rules of language. No further justification is needed, and there is no further logic to it. Language simply works. It enables us to communicate and do things. It lives and grows with us.

Two Different Approaches to the World

The analytic/continental divide in philosophy is between two different approaches. **Thomas Flynn** (1936–) describes it in these terms: "[the turn] away from experience, ideas, and systems of thought to the analysis of concepts and ordinary language is often seen as the move that separated so-called 'analytic' philosophers from their 'continental' colleagues" (*Existentialism* 107). **Allison Stone** (1972–) defines continental philosophy as "describing the world as it really is—not as an aggregate of static items but as an ever-shifting web of relations" ("The Politics of Clarity" 614).

One could also look at the difference as the analytic approach studies the parts and the continental approach studies the whole. Both approaches are valid if they then use the one to move to the other: using the whole to explain the parts or the parts to explain the whole. Philosophers on both sides aren't always successful at this move.

Interestingly, both sides claim science is on their side, but continental philosophy is based more on the social and life sciences and analytic more on physics, logic, and mathematics. Philosophy of language, on the analytic side, has given us some important insights into social behavior, but it also tends to reduce social issues to problems of language and reduce language to logic. Despite all protests to the contrary, we cannot prove that mathematics and logic exist outside the mind. So how do we think of logic when we try to apply it to the world? Continental philosophy doesn't deny the value of logic but instead looks at the world as a system more akin to an organism than a set of mathematical equations. The continentals tend to base their work on Hegel and Marx and tend to reduce social issues to problems of socioeconomic systems like Marx did. But, of course, you can take what I write in this paragraph to four different philosophers and get four different opinions on how wrong what I just wrote is. Such is the nature of our profession.

Chapter 14

PHENOMENOLOGY AND EXISTENTIALISM

Phenomenology is exactly what it sounds like—the study of phenomena appearing within consciousness. We've seen philosophers discussing mental phenomena before. What the philosophical movement of phenomenology does differently is establish a method of analyzing mental phenomena and making those observations the foundation of philosophy. There are multiple flavors of phenomenology, as we shall see, depending on what a phenomenologist is seeking. What they all have in common is the phenomenological method. Instead of trying to understand the essence of an object like the medieval philosophers did or look only at the facts about an object like the philosophers of a scientific bent did, we observe what is present in consciousness during experience.

Existentialism is, almost exactly as it sounds, about the issue of our existence. The name comes from the French writer, **Jean-Paul Sartre** (1905–1980), to describe his idiosyncratic take on philosophy. "Existence precedes essence," he declared as the fundamental issue facing not only philosophy but also every person. Because there are similarities between Sartre's approach and those of Kierkegaard and Nietzsche, those two earlier philosophers have also been called "existentialists," although they would not have recognized the term.

The philosophical approaches of phenomenology and existentialism have similarities and overlap. You will see why as we go through this chapter.

Edmund Husserl's Phenomenology

Moravian philosopher **Edmund Husserl** (1859–1938) was trained in mathematics, and his early writings were on the philosophy of mathematics. The teachings of German psychologist **Franz Brentano** (1838–1917) changed Husserl's thinking.

Brentano said that we should look more carefully at our mental processes. He was rejecting the then-dominant Hegelianism and its study of the universal *Geist*. Focusing on *Geist* to which humans are only peripherally related, the Hegelians were not learning what actually transpires in human consciousness. Brentano said that psychology, like all other sciences, must begin from observations of individual cases. For human consciousness, that means beginning with what is immediately present to perception. He therefore proposed that we try to eliminate all assumptions about causes and consequences of consciousness, to bracket out those assumptions. By "bracketing out," he means placing the content of our inquiry in the center and temporarily ignoring everything outside of it (like this).

Bracketing Perception

Bracketing at first sounds simple enough, but thinking about how best to do it so that it yields us useful information took up the rest of Husserl's life. In a long and prolific career of writings and lectures (1894–1936), Husserl developed and redeveloped his methodology of phenomenology. Husserl was blazing a new trail, and he acted as the pragmatists said we should, building knowledge step-by-step by testing hypotheses and altering our beliefs on the basis of the evidence. Husserl was a perfectionist to a fault, constantly tinkering with his methodology and trying to identify the best method and understanding of consciousness. Trying to condense Husserl's highly complex and technical phenomenology into something easily digestible and understandable is extraordinarily difficult, but I will try to give you the most important elements.

Husserl's initial priority was to understand how to bracket our perceptions off from preconceptions so that we can directly observe the workings of our consciousness. In simplest terms, bracketing is our "suspension of judgment," for which Husserl adopted the Greek word for that idea—"*epoché*." It's an idea similar to Descartes's rule of avoiding precipitancy, and Husserl, following Brentano's idea of bracketing, called for the *epoché* to be the first act of our analysis. We suspend all of our judgments. We do not assume that what we are experiencing is caused by external objects, much less an accurate representation of them. We do not assume that any external objects exist. Here, too, this is similar to what Descartes was doing, and both Descartes and Husserl were seeking certainty of knowledge. The difference between their approaches is that Descartes's method focused on what we can know about external objects, whereas Husserl's method focuses on what mental phenomena reveal about the structures of consciousness.

The first purpose of the *epoché* was to free us from what Husserl called the "natural standpoint." This is the assumption that we all make that there is a world that exists independently of us and that our consciousness is caused by objects in that world. Husserl is not denying the existence of the external world, and he is not suggesting that the natural standpoint is an illusion or foolish to hold. It is a natural assumption that we accept without question, and it serves us well when we are immersed in everyday concerns. The problem with the natural standpoint is that when we stand in it, we cannot see our own experience. Bracketing it off is necessary to get to the pure experience that can enable us to understand consciousness. An example of applying the *epoché* is to look at the experience of fear. Rather than assume that our feeling of fear is caused by an external object, we bracket off the world and examine the nature of fear itself.

Immersion in Experience

The object of Husserl's study is the pure experiences in the phenomenal world of consciousness. Kant had identified the noumena, that which is outside of our experience and thus unknowable by us. The German idealists had rejected the idea of the noumena, but Husserl cautioned that philosophy had gone astray in debating the noumenal world and was neglecting the important study of consciousness. Some philosophers, such as Locke and Hume, had tried to understand consciousness. Husserl's study was both more intensive and without as many presuppositions.

Husserl wanted to focus on the first-person experience. What is it that *I* experience? What is experience, and what does it mean to have an experience? Husserl is using "experience" in its broadest sense of anything that is mental awareness or consciousness. Applying the *epoché*, he, and we, can focus on the contents of consciousness and identify what is intrinsic to all of our mental processes. We can then understand what features of consciousness transcend any particular phenomenon and are present in all experience. We accept only what is directly evident in consciousness, and what is left is the essence of the experience. The essence is in the experience itself, not in the external object.

Applying the *epoché*, Husserl identifies that what immediately comes to our awareness is our consciousness itself. In the natural standpoint, we are having experiences of a world, but we are unaware of our own consciousness and how our consciousness contributes to our experiences. When we bracket off the world, we can discover our consciousness at work. Husserl does not see consciousness as a thing; it does not have qualities like an object or a substance. On the one hand, Descartes was mistaken in thinking of the "I" as a substance. On the other hand, Hume was mistaken in thinking there is nothing to consciousness but a collection of different perceptions. We can see in our consciousness a structure that is independent of the contents of consciousness.

One key feature of the structure of consciousness is "intentionality," an idea Husserl adopted from Brentano. All consciousness, every thought and feeling that we have, is directed at something—it has an intention. If you are consciously perceiving or thinking of a tree, your perception of the tree is the "*noema*" of your consciousness. "*Noema*" (plural "*noemata*") is the word Husserl developed (from the Greek "*noesis*," meaning "thought") to describe the object of our conscious intention. Husserl's concept of intentionality reflects the reality that consciousness is a relation between a knower and something that is known. You know that you have a perception of a tree, and that perception is the *noema* at which your consciousness is directed.

Intentionality is integral to consciousness. Even when we are "mindlessly" doing something like watching television or typing, we are actively using our mind and there is a mental intention. This situation raises some interesting quandaries. Not all intentions are at the surface of our consciousness, which is an interesting reality to dive into. How deep and broad is our consciousness? So much of what we are is beneath that surface layer of our direct attention. Our consciousness works similarly to how our eyes can see a wide field of vision but can only focus on one narrow point. Most of what we see or think is peripheral.

The *noema* that is the intention of our consciousness need not actually exist externally to us. When we are imagining something, we are still intending our consciousness toward a mental object. If you are walking in the woods and hear a rustling in the bushes, you may fear it is a bear. The intentional object of your consciousness is a bear, even if there is no bear there. Even a hallucination is a perception with a conscious intention—our consciousness is directed at the hallucination. If you believe in trees or believe in unicorns, your intentionality is the same. The basic structure of consciousness is the intentional act of experience and the object that is experienced. Husserl agreed with Brentano that intentionality is unique to mental phenomena and is a distinguishing feature of human consciousness.

Of course, that there exists a relation between a knower and something that is known requires that there is a knower. The knower, the human self, must necessarily exist by virtue of the existence of intentional mental acts. However, Husserl agrees with Kant that the self is transcendental to consciousness but never the object of consciousness; in other words, we cannot perceive the "I"—we are always a knower but never known. What, then, is the self? Husserl has no answer to this. In his conception, I have experiences, I conduct intentional acts, the entity conducting these intentions must be me, but I am not identical to any of these intentional acts. Husserl spent a great deal of time trying to find the "I" within consciousness, but never succeeded to his satisfaction.

Having established this most fundamental structure of our experience, Husserl then applies a process of phenomenological reduction to uncover the essential features of the phenomena of the objects we experience. One important feature is our "time-consciousness." If we are looking at the tree, the *noema* is the visual phenomenon of the tree. When we close our eyes, the *noema* is our memory of the tree. These are two different perceptions, but we understand that they are both of the same tree separated by extent in time—the memory of a past visual experience.

The parts and qualities of the *noemata* in our consciousness are separate from the parts and qualities of the object perceived.

That separation of our consciousness from the object is important because our consciousness is continually processing the contents of consciousness. Hegel had demarcated sense certainty from perception, the latter being the mind's active interpretation of sense experience. Husserl similarly saw sense impressions as nonintentional, the raw materials presented to consciousness on which consciousness acts. What we are capable of doing, Husserl says, is taking the *noemata* in our consciousness of the object and using our imaginative capabilities to consider the object behind the *noemata*. As mentioned earlier, many of our thoughts, *noemata*, are on the periphery, but we can will a *noema* into our direct intention. We can consider the various phenomena we have sensed, separated by time. We can hold in our thoughts our past experiences and can imaginatively experiment with the *noemata*: "what if the object was this other color, what would it look like upside down," and so on. Through comparisons and imagination, we develop an objective understanding of the object.

Husserl points out that this objective understanding belongs only to our experience, not to the external object. The object is unaffected by our contemplation of it. We can imagine the tree as being blue, but that does not change the actual tree into being blue. This situation leads to the problem of the connection between our perceptual consciousness and the world of objects, a problem with which philosophers since Locke had struggled. Husserl, like Kant, understood that our mind is active in experience, but like the German idealists, Husserl understood that, because we are involved in our experiences, we can make conscious connections to objects. We develop interpretations of our perceptions, and our conscious thoughts place us in touch with the perceived objects themselves. Our perceptions are not mere passive representations of the objects as Locke believed. This means for Husserl that we have knowledge of objects in the world through a continual process of perceptual experience and thinking about our experiences that can transform perceptions into knowledge.

Layers of Consciousness

Husserl discovered a vitally important insight into how our perceiving and thinking consciousness works. In short, our current experiences are shaped and colored by our past experiences. How we interact with the objective world is a deeply subjective individual experience.

It's not wholly wrong to say we experience objects in the world, but it is far more correct to say that we experience objects in consciousness. Objects exist for us, Husserl said, as objects of actual and possible consciousness. There's a hint of Berkeley in this, and another indication that Berkeley wasn't so daft. A rock on a planet light-years away from you is not an object that you can actually or even possibly perceive. Weirdly, however, it kind of is because now you are thinking about such a possible object. That proves Husserl's point. Nothing is meaningful for us unless our consciousness makes it so by our consciousness intending toward the object. Intending toward (thinking about) something gives it meaning, at least temporarily.

If objective understanding is within our consciousness and it is our intentional consciousness that makes things meaningful, then how can we have certain knowledge of objects independent of our mind? Are we left with nothing but completely subjective judgments about objects? Husserl's intriguing and insightful answer is to embrace the subjectivity and include that in our consideration of the world.

There are two levels of subjective consciousness, one within you and one outside of you, and both of which affect our consciousness. The first level is within you, the individual. The *epoché* shows that phenomena are constituted by our consciousness, as Kant and the German idealists all agreed. What Husserl adds to this is that our past experiences contribute to how our consciousness constitutes phenomena. Every act of consciousness, both sense experiences and thinking, affects our consciousness, which affects our future experiences. Husserl calls it the "sedimentation of meanings" that builds up, layer by layer, within our consciousness. Our experiences, our reactions to those experiences, our thoughts and feelings about those experiences and reactions, all create sediments of meaning in our consciousness. Those meanings literally change how we perceive and think about things.

Consider experiencing a person. You meet the individual, you develop a first impression, and that first impression, as we all know, affects how you experience that individual. As you interact more with that person, you learn more about the individual and you develop a fuller conception of who that person is. Let's say that over time you become friends with this person, and of course that friendship affects your perception of the person; the more time you share with this person, the more those experiences and feelings about the person shape your perception of your friend. But now suppose this friend betrays you in a serious way that hurts you badly. Can you ever look at this person the same way again? That's the influence of sedimentation. Using your time-consciousness, you can look back through your memories and think about past good times and warm feelings you had, but now things are different. Your perceptions are altered by your past experience.

The second level of subjective consciousness exists beyond you as an individual but is connected to your individual life. Husserl introduces an idea that becomes very important in continental philosophy—the "*Lebenswelt*" in German or "lifeworld" in English. The lifeworld is the world in which we live; it is the world that we experience, and it is another layer that affects you perceive things. Just as we don't experience objects apart from our own sedimentations in consciousness, we can't experience objects apart from the context of a world. For example, you don't experience a computer; you experience it as being on a desk, in a room, in a building, in a society. We never experience anything isolated from its surroundings. Moreover, we never experience any object apart from the collection of meanings that social life places on them. You experience objects and events within a social context—your culture—that imbues those objects with meaning, and those meanings affect your experiences of objects. Other individuals in other lifeworlds will experience objects and events differently.

Taking these layers of consciousness into account, Husserl calls scientists "self-forgetful theorizers." The central assumption in science is that it can reveal the true reality to us. This was the optimistic hope since science's beginning in the late 1500s (see Bacon in Chapter 4), and it continued in Husserl's time. The truth, Husserl stresses, is that we do not experience pure objects; we experience objects through the filters of our own sedimented consciousness and the lifeworld in which we live. Scientists are not exempt from that truth. Science gives us an idealized and naively objectivized nature, Husserl said. Scientists forget that they are doing science as people within a lifeworld. Science is a social activity within a social context, a lifeworld, that instills activities with social meanings. Scientists also forget that they are individual people who experience everything, including their experiments, through their personal sedimented consciousness.

Husserl is not saying that science is too biased to be of use, but he is saying that we need to be aware of the layers of meaning and consciousness within which and through which science is conducted. Science is an attitude that sees the world through its particular understanding of it. Because our knowledge structures how we perceive the world, the scientific approach structures perceptions to see the world in a certain way. Forgetting the effects of our biases makes us blind to them and the way they distort our perceptions.

Husserl's critique that people are self-forgetful is not limited to scientists. We all suffer that implicit bias of seeing the world through our own sedimented consciousness and limited lifeworld. Husserl in 1930 bemoaned the lack of dialogue among philosophers. He thought that philosophers with differing views needed to discuss their conflicting theories seriously to find a basis for common ground and together grow their knowledge. This idea is similar to what the pragmatists were suggesting. Instead, Husserl said, philosophers remain in their own subjective views and narrow fields of study and don't consider other views.

This criticism can apply not only to philosophy but also to all academic fields and subfields. Academics are only human, of course, and the criticism that people remain within their subjective biases and don't listen to others applies universally. The antidote to this is found in the philosophy of Husserl and other phenomenologists and existentialists. We need to acknowledge that every one of us experiences the objectively real world as individuals and that that understanding is a process that includes listening to each other.

Max Scheler's Philosophy of Life

Philosophers are notorious for discounting human emotion. The strong preference for rationality goes back to the ancient Greeks, particularly Plato and Aristotle. Rationalism has overwhelmed philosophical conversation ever since, its strongest expression being positivism. The problem with rationalism is that it falsely reduces all human experience to a tiny realm of logic, and it too easily denies the reality of the human person as an individual with thoughts and feelings beyond the strictly logical. **Max Scheler** provides a healthy corrective to that rationalist reductionism by emphasizing the supreme value of the individual person.

German philosopher Max Scheler (1874–1928) is tragically still virtually unknown in English-speaking countries, but his influence on philosophers in Europe is immense. Scheler studied Husserl's published writings and developed his own version of the phenomenological study of consciousness. Scheler's exploration of consciousness led him to a rich philosophy of the individual person within social life and the awareness of the importance of emotions in human life, especially love and joy.

Husserl's phenomenology was based on logic. Scheler instead emphasizes a focus on our original experiences that we have before we apply logic and other interpretive criteria to them. In other words, we have experiences before we think rationally about our experiences. Our sense experiences of objects are given to us only in the experiencing act itself. By extension, the philosopher needs to engage with the phenomenological facts of experience without first applying a logical or scientific method to them.

The Meaning of Life

What does it *mean* to be a person? That's a different question from what *is* a person? Scheler's motivation was to steer philosophy away from the reductionism of positivism and toward the question of the meaning of human life. He saw people as more than rational beings (as positivism depicted) or practical tool makers (as pragmatism depicted). We are those things, Scheler said, but we are also beings who can seek into and understand the world in its essences and being.

In other words, we are capable of more than dealing with practical concerns; we are also capable of wondering about the deeper meaning of life. Partially influenced by Husserl's work on sedimentation in consciousness, Scheler recognized the importance of our attitude. How we approach the world structures how we perceive it, which is why Scheler separated practical knowledge from other types of knowledge. Practical knowledge is motivated by the desire to avoid error, like Descartes's method. The practical approach of science and modernity is an attempt to understand the world in terms of the utility of objects. Scheler says this approach is motivated by a desire to control and dominate the world. The practical approach yields useful knowledge, but it does not give us a full picture of the world.

Scheler's second form of knowledge is erudition ("*Bildungswissen*" in German), which is motivated by a sense of wonder. Philosophy begins in wonder, an idea that goes back to Aristotle, and Scheler sees wonder as a participation in the world. The quest for practical knowledge is motivated by a sense of lack. The quest for erudition is motivated by a reverence for the abundance of meaning in the world. Scheler called philosophy a loving act of participation in the essence of all things. This appearance of the concept of love in philosophy may seem surprising, and it is something we haven't seen since Augustine. But Scheler brought back to philosophy something significant and influential—a sense of wonder about the world and a willingness to engage with it and have feelings about it rather than hold the world at arm's length.

Love, for Scheler, is not sentiment or yearning. Love, Scheler said, is a movement of opening oneself up to the world of values—that which we find valuable. In contrast, hatred is closing oneself off from the world of values. Love involves acts that extend into the world, and hatred involves acts that narrow one's reach into the world. Phenomenology is an attitude of openness. It does not negate the practical or scientific attitude, but it suspends judgment on them. Scheler saw phenomenology as a trusting attitude toward the world much preferable to the skeptical attitude of the modern positivist era.

A Person Is One Who Values

Scheler realizes that all of our perceptions are also experiences of values. For example, a tree has green leaves and is tall, but it is also beautiful and gives cooling shade, and often these values of beauty and pleasure are what are important to us. Scheler is thinking of value as emotional worth, not a logical meaning. Valuing is not a rational act but an act of the heart. All objects of experience carry values, and all of our experiences are value laden. Values are objectively real, Scheler said, although we experience and act on them subjectively. Values do not exist in objects but in the act of perception. Scheler said that when we perceive a painting, we are seeing its beauty like we are seeing its shapes and colors.

Our awareness of value is our most primordial relation to the world. Scheler says we relate to the world through two basic acts—the act of love and the act of hate. Scheler calls these emotional acts movements toward or away from objects and people. Our acts of love are movements that value an object or person and deepen our relationship with that object or person. Our acts of hate are movements that devalue an object or person and degrade or even destroy our relationship with that object or person. This kind of thinking may sound similar to Hobbes's theory of the endeavors of desire and aversion. The difference is that Hobbes saw endeavors as forces that happen *to* a person, determining actions. Scheler sees the movements of love and hate as coming *from* a person as expressions of valuing.

The specific type of being who can experience values is a person, Scheler said, and other people are values in and of themselves. For Scheler, the person is a moral actor, present in every act; however, the person is not reducible to any particular act but is the unity of all acts the person performs. That means every person is unique because each person is a unique center of acts, and every person has his or her own unique style of acting, loving, and assigning meaning. Therefore, the person should not be objectified—or subsumed under stereotypes or categories. A person's meaning is determined by the unique way in which that person brings meaning to the world.

Scheler describes his moral philosophy as "personalist" and makes personal values supreme. Because every person is a unique center of acts with unique meaning, Scheler said we ought to value each and every person as an individual. As young children we come to know that other people exist before we come to know that the world as a whole exists. Philosophy must take that into account, and morality must center on the person.

A Philosophy of Community

The value of the person is the foundation of Scheler's political philosophy, or truer to his wording, a philosophy of community. Community is about shared values and love. We understand each other through valuing others, and through valuing others we form community. In turn, the sharing of values and responsibilities within a community is the context (or "lifeworld" to use Husserl's term) in which people form and realize themselves. As a human community, we build our community to be what we value, what we believe ought to be. Differing from most philosophers going back to Aristotle, Scheler said that what ought to be is not derived through logic. We intuitively feel what ought to be and what ought not to be, and we intuitively feel that some values are higher than others.

Scheler values the individual and the perceptions, emotions, and acts of each individual, but he understands that every person perceives, feels, and acts in the context of experiencing with other people. Permeating all of Scheler's lengthy and detailed discussion about building a community of love and solidarity is the "attitude of valuing." Sharing, empathy, and respect are some of the ways that we value other people. An attitude of valuing other people is an act of giving meaning or cocreating meaning. Through genuine open expressions of co-feeling and co-living, we form a life-community in which we share with others both a sense of self and a sense of belonging. A life-community is formed through intentional acts, not of intellect, but of love.

Scheler distinguishes between a *life-community* that is formed through genuine movements of loving co-feeling and *society* that is formed consciously but artificially. Individuals form society for mutual benefit, but their connections are no deeper than the level of utilitarian coexistence. In perhaps a rebuke of Hobbes's social contract, Scheler negatively views society as motivated by mistrust of others, grudgingly getting along for the sake of security and convenience, characterized by an attitude of indifference. The bottom line for Scheler's thought is that our salvation as persons lies not in the attitude of indifference toward suffering but in acknowledging pain in ourselves and in others and sympathizing with it. Sympathy and empathy for others are positive values that bring us together as a community. Scheler says that the deepest and most profound level of community is when each one of us takes responsibility for our own actions and responsibility for others. We feel a sense of solidarity with other people and with our collective community, and we seek to build each other up.

Scheler was also able to see the negative possibilities of human interaction. In 1914, when the outbreak of World War I looked inevitable, Scheler wrote the short book *Ressentiment*. Scheler defined ressentiment (which is a different concept than resentment) as an incurable, persistent feeling of hating and despising accompanied by equally incurable feelings of impotencies or weaknesses. Ressentiment manifests as grievances against a perceived other. Scheler makes the crucial distinction between legitimate grievances and imagined ones and between true moral judgments and false ones. Ressentiment is not a justified anger about being mistreated but a particular form of hatred that arises from beliefs that one is socially impotent. Struggles against injustice are movements toward higher values such as justice, truth, and love. Ressentiment is a movement toward lower values such as vengeance, spite, and malice. Ressentiment can permeate a whole culture or era and even an entire moral system.

Unlike feelings of love for oneself or others that inspires people to positive actions, ressentiment is a state in which one has lost a relation to values. This state triggers feelings of hopelessness and frustration that predispose one to regress to self-destructive indulgences or outward hostility to try to resolve the sense of impotence. The frustration and impotence characteristic of ressentiment is less a reaction to an actual external oppressor and has more to do with a self-inflicted sense of inadequacy over one's own real or imagined limitations.

The feelings of ressentiment lead to false moral judgments on others that Scheler calls "value delusions." These delusions are a form of moral blindness that results in "a tendency to belittle, degrade, dismiss or to 'reduce' genuine values as well as their bearers." Individuals and groups in the psychological state of ressentiment are hampered in their ability to make sound moral judgments and tend to see values and other people through a filter of negative prejudice. Other people are made into surrogates to compensate for a sense of impotency and then are turned into targets for hostile judgments. Ressentiment and the feelings it triggers become self-perpetuating. Even more, they become part of one's identity. The individual self-defines as cynical, aloof, and a judge of others, value delusions leading to arrogance and double standards.

Scheler warned that when people "join ranks" in ressentiment, united by angry unhappiness, they only spread their unhappiness. This makes it a political, not simply a personal moral issue. Writing about that in Germany in 1914, Scheler was eerily prescient of the coming horror of the Nazis who knew how to exploit anger and unhappiness as a political force. Scheler said that we need to reject the false strength of hardening against suffering or of glorifying such suffering. Instead, we need to acknowledge that pain is pain but that joy is joy and goodness comes from joy. There is pain, but there is also love.

Edith Stein's Phenomenology

Husserl, as a philosophy professor at the University of Freiburg, had two particularly notable students. One was **Edith Stein** (1891–1942). Born into a practicing Jewish family, she converted to Catholicism and eventually became a nun. Her conversion was after, but not incompatible with, her philosophical career, in which she studied the philosophy of emotions, especially empathy.

She studied under Max Scheler and earned her PhD in 1916. Her PhD thesis adviser was Edmund Husserl, for whom she later worked as his teaching assistant. Despite fulfilling all of the professional qualifications, Stein was refused habilitation (a postdoctoral certification required to be a full professor in the German system) in 1919 because she was a woman. Despite the support of Martin Heidegger (we meet him later in this chapter), she was again denied habilitation in 1931 by the University of Göttingen, again, because she was a woman. She did land a teaching position at the German Institute for Scientific Pedagogy, where she taught for several years and worked on her philosophy. Stein is still unfairly ignored, no doubt because she is a woman and because she was spiritually minded.

Stein's Philosophy

Stein applied Husserl's phenomenological method of the *epoché* (bracketing off of assumptions) to understand consciousness and human empathy. Her philosophy of the person centers on the distinction between the internal psychological/spiritual world and the external natural world. Her conception of this distinction is very different from Descartes's complete separation of mental and material substances. Stein saw that the psychological and natural worlds are intertwined, each with their own sets of causality. Experiences of the natural world affect the psychological world, but the latter world, the human psyche, has its own sets of causality.

When we observe our psychological world, we see a stream of consciousness that flows along in an undivided and indivisible continuum. Within consciousness, we see not only mechanical causation (for example, light hitting the eye) but also experiential or psychic causality. Unlike mechanical causality, which has a mediating event connecting a cause to an effect in a one-way relation (Aristotle's efficient cause), experiential causality interconnects two events that change both and affects the course of consciousness.

This different operation of causality within our psychological world means several things. A mechanistic view of determinism does not sum up the mind and the flow of consciousness because experiences of the external, natural world do not wholly cause consciousness. Experiential causality also is present and affects the flow of consciousness. An individual's psyche is affected by, but not determined by, external events. The psyche is also affected by internal events in consciousness. The psychological world is a multidimensional one of incessant occurring and incessant effecting, subject to laws of psychic causality, but the effects of these causes cannot be exactly predicted. We can, knowing the psychic facts of a person, infer how that individual will act in the future, but such inferences can be nullified by the individual's own choices. People are, after all, autonomous beings with their own will, motivations, and powers. We can only observe the occurrences and effects of the psychological world by using the phenomenological method.

Stein's application of the phenomenological *epoché* led her to discover "life-feelings" ("*Lebensgefühle*" in German), which are experiential states in a person's consciousness. Life-feelings affect what a person perceives, thinks, feels, and wills and strongly affect how the person experiences conscious states and bodily awareness. Stein's examples of life-feelings include weariness, freshness, vigor, and irritability, which affect one's feelings toward the world and influence the whole course of one's experiences. In her example of weariness, she points out what we have all experienced, that when we feel weary, it affects all of our sensations, deadening colors and sounds, and so on. → *things influence others*

She said that life-feelings are experiential causality, and she compares them to mechanical causality. That weariness would enliven our stream of consciousness is as inconceivable as it is that throwing a ball downward would cause it to rise upward. Mechanical causality has external effects on us, but experiential causality has internal effects not wholly determined by the external world. Stein defends human free will and personal agency by observing that we can control life-feelings, at least to a degree. By engaging with and controlling our life-feelings, we affect our self and our experiences of the world. When we feel weariness, we can choose how much attention we pay to it and, to a degree, how much we let it affect us.

Scheler had said that we intuitively feel that some values are higher than others, and Stein builds on this idea. Stein identifies five levels of feelings. The first four are (1) sensory, (2) common (bodily life-feelings that affect us), (3) moods (spiritual life-feelings that affect us but objectively connect with the external world), and (4) emotions that are intentional states (feelings directed at an object). For example, I can be looking at a tree in the sunshine, have the sensory feelings of the light reflecting off shimmering leaves, and a cheerful mood starts to take hold of me, but my (common) feeling of bodily weariness deadens my cheerful mood, and about that I feel disappointed.

We can't make *moral* judgments about the first four types of feelings, but Stein says that we can and should make *rational* judgments about emotions because emotions are intentional states anchored in the "I." We can consider whether someone is keeping his or her emotions within an appropriate hierarchy of values. Stein's idea is that some pleasures are higher than others because they have greater long-term benefit for someone. Therefore, we can say that certain emotions are rationally appropriate if the emotion fits with the emoter's moral, practical, and prudential values. Becoming very upset over something that has no bearing on a person is an unfitting emotion and could be considered inappropriate.

Stein's fifth type of feeling is sentiments, the attitudes we direct toward other people. In sentiments, she includes love and hatred (like Scheler) and other feelings like gratitude and vindictiveness. Sentiments are emotions that have conscious intention toward another person and always are correlated to personal values. Sentiments, because they are outwardly directed at other people, are subject to moral judgments.

Stein's Unfair Fate

After reading the autobiography of Theresa of Ávila, Stein converted to Catholicism in 1922. She wanted at that point to became a Carmelite nun, but the order encouraged her to continue writing philosophy. They also encouraged her to teach instead of joining a convent, which she did at several institutions until 1933, when the Nazis banned people of Jewish heritage from all teaching positions.

After the Nazis banned her from teaching, Stein moved to a Carmelite convent. As social conditions in Germany worsened under the Nazi regime, in 1938 her order moved her to a convent in the Netherlands. This kept her safe only for a few years, however. Because Stein was born Jewish, the Nazi occupiers tracked her down, arrested her at her convent in 1942, and shipped her to Auschwitz concentration camp where they murdered her.

Pope John Paul II beatified Stein in 1987 and canonized her as a saint in 1998. Years earlier, in 1954, Pope John Paul II, then known as Karol Wojtyła, earned a PhD with his thesis on the moral philosophy of Max Scheler.

Martin Heidegger—Being and Time

Understanding **Martin Heidegger** (1889–1976) is extraordinarily and maddeningly difficult. That statement is not only about his philosophy but about him as a person. He was Husserl's other most notable student, working as Husserl's assistant after Edith Stein had moved on. When Husserl retired in 1929, he recommended Heidegger be his successor to the chair of philosophy in Freiburg, Germany, a recommendation the university accepted. When the Nazis came to power and seized control of all universities, Heidegger joined the Nazi Party. He was then appointed rector of the University of Freiburg, but he resigned a few months later for reasons he never made clear. Scholars have ever since debated how much Heidegger agreed with Nazi ideology. The position that he did is buttressed by statements in his written papers and the fact that even though he lived and lectured for more than 30 years after the war, he never formally condemned the Nazis. We will talk about Heidegger's ideas, just as, for example, we talked about Aristotle's ideas, even though Aristotle supported the abhorrent idea of slavery. Being involved in the quest for understanding means being able to consider ideas and take what is valuable and leave behind what is not.

A Phenomenology of Being

Heidegger is described as either a phenomenologist or an existentialist. Each description is true, to an extent, but it is more accurate to say Heidegger presents a unique hybrid of the two. His philosophy captures the spirit of Husserl's study of phenomena by focusing on the phenomena in experience, but his application of the *epoché* led him to focus on the science of Being. That's "Being" with a capital "B"—existence itself. All objects are beings (small "b"), and all objects have Being (capital "B"). Particular beings pass in and out of existence, but Being remains. One can try to study Being in and of itself. Some ancient and medieval philosophers did, some associating Being with God. Heidegger rejects this idea, pointing out that God is simply the highest being among all others.

When Heidegger brackets off the world and all assumptions about it, what he finds remaining is Being—the fundamental phenomenon in which all experience is grounded and from which all experiences derive meaning. Every object that we encounter in the world is a manifestation of Being. Heidegger fixates on one particular manifestation—*our* existence.

We exist. But that is a qualitatively different statement for us than "that tree exists." To describe the distinctive character of our existence, Heidegger used the concept that we are *Dasein*. The term "*Dasein*" could be literally translated as "being there," but typical of Heidegger's thought, it means "being there" and other concepts indicated by it. That we are *Dasein*, in essence, means that we are beings *in* the world, not separate from it, and we are beings for whom our Being is a central concern for us. The biggest misunderstanding that one can have about this concept of being concerned about our existence is that it is simply a concern about whether we are alive. That's only a small part of it. We are also concerned about the quality and meaning of our life. For Heidegger, it's not enough for us merely to live—we also want to live meaningfully. But that's getting ahead of ourselves.

So far, so good. Quickly after that, Heidegger's study of *Dasein* and Being becomes very complex. He invents multiple terms to describe deep and sophisticated concepts that philosophers have spent thousands of pages trying to define and explain. We don't have that much space, so let's try to break it down as simply as possible.

Being-in-the-World

"*Dasein*" means "being there," and the "there" is the world. One of Heidegger's most significant ideas is that we are not detached from the world. We are not a consciousness trying to understand a world that is separate from us. Instead, Heidegger said we are Being-in-the-World ("*In-der-Welt-sein*" in German). The hyphenation in this word expresses that our Being and the world cannot be separated. The best way to think about Being-in-the-World is that you are a consciousness *embedded* in the world. "Embedded" means that we are inextricably in the world. Heidegger says we *dwell* in the world; we fully exist within it, are absorbed in it, and are taken up with it. All of our thinking and acting is not *about* the world, or *at* the world, but is an inextricable part of the world in which we are embedded. Heidegger uses only "*Dasein*." That's because he is trying to capture in *Dasein* the uniqueness of the type of beings we are beyond the fact that we are embedded in the world.

Dasein is not one object among the many objects in the world. *Dasein is* not just one more tree in the woods. Heidegger describes *Dasein* as a clearing in the midst of a dense forest of Being. It is a clearing in the sense that *Dasein* is a region where Being is fully revealed to itself—and Heidegger refers to *Dasein* as an "it," though if it helps you to grasp these concepts, substitute "we" for *Dasein*. It's from the vantage point of this clearing that *Dasein* (we) can analyze the meaning of Being. *Dasein* is aware, first and foremost, of its existence and that it exists within a world. From that perspective, from its clearing, *Dasein* can relate to the world. This is not an objective understanding, but such an understanding is not possible.

Heidegger's most famous book is *Being and Time* (1927). He used that title because *Dasein* has two unique characteristics that make it distinct from all other beings (animals, plants, rocks, and so on)—awareness of its own existence and awareness of time. *Dasein* exists, and it is aware that it exists. *Dasein* can question why it exists in ways that all other worldly objects cannot. *Dasein* can also question why it is situated in the world the way that it is and what its possibilities are in the world. Considering possibilities entails an awareness of time. *Dasein* is oriented not only to the present; *Dasein* can also remember its past and project itself into the future. Heidegger saw this as a crucial element of *Dasein*. It is always living-ahead; its here and now is always oriented toward future possibilities. That *Dasein* is aware of time means it is Being-ahead-of-itself, oriented toward the future, which affects *Dasein's* everyday actions and its anxiety.

Regions, Involvements, and the Everyday

Ultimately, *Dasein's* situatedness is not the world itself but is its set of relations to the world. Because *Dasein* is Being-in-the-world, it necessarily has an understanding of its place and possibilities in the world, even if that understanding is without reflective intellectual content. Most individuals think of themselves in terms of their social acceptance or their material comforts while they are immersed in the everydayness of life. Being Dasein, we are beings who can ask—not so much in an intellectual way as in a practical, worldly way—what we can do in the world. We can take a detached view of our life, considering the world and ourselves as a philosopher or scientist might, but that is not how we live. We live in our everyday Being-in-the-world.

The "everyday" is an often neglected key aspect of Heidegger's philosophy. To understand it, we also need to understand two other important concepts for Heidegger—regions and involvements. We are embedded in the world, but, more accurately, we are embedded in particular regions of that world. Where you live, where you work, who you interact with, what information you take in—these are small regions of the wider world. You, as *Dasein*, are embedded in a number of regions—home, work, school, friends, and so on.

Regions are important because they are modes of *Dasein's* existence where *Dasein* works out its involvements. Husserl said that every new experience is structured by our past experiences. Heidegger accepts that and adds the idea of involvements—which is a concept similar to goals, but because they are related to *Dasein* and Being-in-the-world, involvements have meaning for us beyond simple goals. The concept of involvements steams from the reality that what happens to us matters more than what happens to other things, and all that we experience we relate to ourselves in one way or another. All of our actions and relations are tempered by and structured by our involvements with the world. We care about what happens, and we are concerned that our actions work for us. Each of us has our own projects that we care about—for example, passing a university course. We each want objects to work for us, like our computers, cars, and phones. We act on projects and use objects because we want to fulfill our involvements.

An important insight that is revealed in the phenomenological analysis of *Dasein* is that, contrary to most previous philosophy, we do not experience a world of objects. Instead, we engage with *equipment* that we use to fulfill our involvements. When all is going well—the equipment works and people behave as we expect them to—all is fine, and these objects become invisible to us; they recede into the everyday.

For example, we never think about what our computer mouse (or touchpad) does until it doesn't work. It's transparent to us. You don't think, "I am moving the mouse and the mouse is helping me do my work."

No, you think about the tasks you are performing. The intentionality of your consciousness is on the work that you are doing. The mouse is invisible equipment. This is the case as long as everything is going according to plan and your intentions and your concerns are lined up and you are getting the results that you want. As soon as something interrupts that flow, that's when you start to think of equipment in a different way. Only then do you consider the mouse as an object of inspection. Your intention then shifts to how to get the object to work to fulfill your involvements. You are constantly thinking or not thinking about things, but you're always involved in the world in which you are embedded through your concerns. You are Being-in-the-world, and you are involved in the regions in which you are embedded.

Heidegger's concept of involvements also includes the question of who we are. *Dasein's* identity exists as *Dasein's* own first-person evaluation of its place in the world that reflects its involvements. Heidegger said that it is not enough for us simply to survive; we wish to have a meaningful set of relations with our regions and the people and equipment in our regions, and even in relation with our life itself. It is not enough simply to live; one must live meaningfully. If this reminds you of Kierkegaard, good! You're paying attention, because that's who Heidegger got the idea from. However, although Kierkegaard was passionately emotional about the meaning of our life, Heidegger was eerily dispassionate about the meaning of a person's life. There is nothing warm and personal about Heidegger (*Dasein* is an "it," remember), even though his philosophy is perhaps the most personal of them all.

Thrownness, Authenticity, and Anxiety

The coldness of Heidegger's thought is found most vividly in what he calls the "thrownness" of our existence. We are beings who are thrown into the world. We were born. We didn't choose where, we didn't choose when, we didn't choose our parents, we didn't choose our siblings. We were thrown into a region of the world, and because we are thrown into these choiceless realities of our life, our life is a matter of constant tension.

Heidegger says we should have an authentic existence. Now this is where Heidegger probably goes a little off the deep end because when he tries to talk about authentic versus inauthentic existence he gets into difficulties. What being authentic means for Heidegger he never quite makes clear, but his discussion centers on being aware. We need to be aware that we are *Dasein*, that we are embedded in a world as Being-in-the-world, and that we are continually in time as *Dasein* Being-ahead-of-itself (involvements with our own future). Above and beyond our everyday involvements, we constantly have to think about our place in the world and who we are now, have been in the past, and could be in the future. If you're not thinking of these things, that seems to be what Heidegger means by an inauthentic existence. If we are lost in the everydayness of life, we are fallen. When we don't deal with the fact that we are thrown into a world that we did not choose, we have nothing but anxiety. Not that we never do not have anxiety, according to Heidegger, just that we have more if we are avoiding our thrownness.

Influenced by Nietzsche, Heidegger thought that part of our thrownness is that we realize that our system of social meanings has no ultimate ground, including ethical values; those meanings are simply what have developed over time. Influenced by Kierkegaard, Heidegger accepts that we are beings who must choose and act; therefore, Being-in-the-world means being forced to act despite having no absolute values or directions on which to base our actions. To be *Dasein* is to be finite and full of anxiety. We simply exist in the world into which we've been thrown.

What any of this has to do with Heidegger's enigmatic relationship with Nazism no one can explain. Maybe Heidegger saw himself as being thrown into that world and convinced himself that he didn't choose to be a German in the 1930s and shouldn't concern himself with the everydayness of politics. Plus, he thought that there is no ultimate ground for ethical values. That would certainly be a grotesque denial of moral responsibility, especially since Heidegger writes about the importance of a moral conscience, but it's a possible explanation because, again, there's no sense in Heidegger of a warm and personal relationship with the world or people. His discussion of "care" is not related to love, family, or community but is about resolving one's own anxiety—care is simply understanding that one is *Dasein* thrown into the world. He says some things about obedience to your society and following the law as part of being authentic, but his discussion of conscience is about *Dasein* being called to make itself aware of its potential.

That's the big, big paradox and irony of Heidegger. His philosophy deals with the most fundamental questions of who we are and what we want from life, but the closest he comes to an answer is letting-be—being open to *Dasein* returning to its potentiality-for-Being-its-Self. After reading Heidegger's philosophy, one comes away feeling he raises so many excellent questions and issues that he fails to pursue beyond his sense of general anxiety.

Karl Jaspers's Existentialism

German **Karl Jaspers** (1883–1969) applied the phenomenological method to clinical psychiatry. In his 1913 book, *General Psychopathology*, he described diagnosing mental illnesses by using a patient's symptoms and personal history rather than by using preconceived notions about psychological delusions. The role of the psychopathologist, he said, is to learn how to observe, ask questions, and analyze phenomena. Jaspers is better known for his later work in existentialism. He was, in the 1930s, the first to identify the common theme of personal freedom in Kierkegaard and Nietzsche. With his blend of psychology and existentialist philosophy, Jaspers uses expert empirical knowledge but goes beyond it.

Like the other existentialists, Jaspers saw that our existence and our freedom are challenges, but he was more optimistic than the others about facing those challenges. He also acknowledged that most people retreat from the challenge. Most people, when they encounter the frighteningly limitless possibilities of human existence, retreat into false certainties. People construct psychological worldviews that interpret the world in inflexible antinomies of subject and object. They incorporate strategies of defensiveness, suppression, and deception against the world, forming an objectivized cage of false certainty. We can see how these inflexible worldviews work in attitudes of prejudices that limit a person's ability to take in information. Jaspers saw the role of psychology as helping people past restrictive antinomies.

Jaspers's philosophical project, expressed most fully in his three-volume book, *Philosophy* (1932), was to retain Kierkegaard's decisive and passionate commitment to authenticity, while overcoming what he saw as the limitation of Kierkegaard's interiority and inability to speak to that in the world that prevents individual authenticity. Jaspers stated that an individual's authenticity can come only from shared dialogue with others. To accomplish an existentialist view of communicative dialogue, Jaspers combined elements of Kant's doctrine of transcendental ideas with Hegel's idea that consciousness forms through our actively cocreating our understanding—we learn through experience and by applying reason to our perceptions. From these elements, Jaspers crafts a view of human existence and perception in some ways similar to Heidegger's but without Heidegger's cold vagueness and anxiety-ridden isolation. Jaspers says that our knowledge frames our orientation toward the world and our existence is formed by our active self-reflection informed by continual dialogue with those around us.

Self-reflection is at the core of Jaspers's existentialism because he says we do not confront Being itself but only as it is *for* us. Similar to Heidegger, Jaspers understands being and time to be intertwined, and Jaspers identifies four modes within which we exist in time. He refers to the modes as encompassing horizons in that they surround us, and, because we are within them, they recede no matter how far we progress in realizing them. The modes resemble Kierkegaard's spheres of life with elements of Husserl's phenomenological insights.

The most basic mode is *Dasein*, meaning existence in its most minimal sense. Jaspers does not portray *Dasein* in the almost mystical terms in which Heidegger does. For Jaspers, *Dasein* is the mode of living within the environment of space and time. We are embedded in a physical world, and in this mode we relate to that world in the dichotomy of subject–object. The approaches of science and the everydayness of life are within the realm of *Dasein*.

The second mode is "consciousness-as-such" ("*Bewußtsein überhaupt*" in German), which is Jaspers's term for our conscious awareness. We are, as Descartes had said, thinking beings. We do more than act; we can think about our actions. In this mode, we are consciously interacting with the world and self-conscious of what we are or can be. It is the mode beyond the everydayness of *Dasein* and perhaps is equivalent to whatever Heidegger was meaning about authentic awareness. In consciousness-as-such, we are contemplating objects, as Husserl had discussed in using our imaginative capabilities to consider the object behind the *noemata*.

The third mode is spirit, not to be confused with Hegel's use of the term, or anyone else's for that matter. Jaspers means it more in the sense of Kant's transcendental method applied to our being in time. In this mode, we develop ideas about what something is. We act in time and space (*Dasein*), and we can act consciously aware of what we are doing (consciousness-as-such), but we can also act with transcendent ideas (spirit). "Transcendent" here means ideas that transcend any particular experience and are more widely present in our thoughts, expressions, and actions. In an example similar to Bergson's discussion of the idea of a university, Jaspers discusses how the idea of university has a core meaning that differs in various contexts and applications. We have a concept of what a university is or can be, and we have in mind that idea when we think about or act in relation to a particular university. We see what Jaspers means when people create something tangible from their ideas, from a work of art to a university. We see it when people invest their life or their surroundings with meaning. Ideas are transcendent when they are present beyond any particular person. The mode of spirit is not individualistic but is intersubjective. We develop our ideas through communicating with others and learning about their ideas. Spirit, as shared community, is a mode of Being beyond consciousness-as-such.

Finally, there is the mode of *Existenz*, by which Jaspers means the realm of self-being or authentic being. Here, Jaspers speaks of our never-ending task of becoming through our choices. As Kierkegaard says, we are beings who must choose and act. In the mode of *Existenz*, one takes full responsibility for one's actions as an individual, consciously applying one's transcendent ideas to one's existence. Jaspers says, "I am not merely *Dasein*, not merely the subject of consciousness-as-such, . . . but in all of them I can [either] be myself or be lost in them" (*Basic Philosophical Writings* 154). When I am myself, fully present in the world but not subsumed by it or avoiding it, I am in the mode of *Existenz*, and I am authentic. Beyond that very basic description of *Existenz*, Jaspers's discussion about this mode is too complex and opaque to discuss here. Suffice to say that for Jaspers, *Existenz* is the expression of Being that comes from questioning our place in the world and manifesting our conscious choices in the world.

Jaspers's conclusion seems to be that our authentic existence is not as an isolated rational consciousness but as a beingness of shared humanity found in the resources of social life and cultural tradition. In other words, we become authentic through communication with other people.

Jean-Paul Sartre's Existentialism

Then there is the Frenchman **Jean-Paul Sartre** (pronounced SART, 1905–1980). If Heidegger is cold, Sartre is frozen solid. Some people find some things to like in Sartre, but others hate his philosophy of nihilistic existentialism. The saying "life's a bitch and then you die" is a flippant but not entirely inaccurate summary of Sartre's philosophy. He was also influenced by Kierkegaard but with even more fear and trembling.

Heidegger's principal book was *Being and Time*, but Sartre's principal book was *Being and Nothingness* (1943, written after he read Heidegger's book), and this gives a hint as to what separates their philosophies. Sartre agreed with Heidegger that we are finite beings thrown into the world without absolute values on which to base our actions. However, whereas Heidegger writes about our involvements and our concerns, Sartre writes that we simply exist and are full of anxiety. Sartre does not agree with Heidegger's notion of *Dasein*, or that we are Being-in-the-world.

Sartre thought that knowledge of facts has no meaning in an objective sense, but he also oddly decided that subjective consciousness has no meaning in a subjective sense. Consciousness is nothingness, Sartre claimed. The root of this concept comes from Husserl's realization that consciousness is not a thing like a tree is a thing. Sartre takes that concept to the extreme conclusion that consciousness is separate from the world of things. At first that may sound like Descartes, but Sartre means something very different. Sartre labels objects "in-itself," signifying that they are self-contained, static entities. He labels human consciousness "for-itself," signifying that it is a self-aware and self-projecting entity. Objects in-itself have static identities determined by external sources. Consciousness, as for-itself, is spontaneously free and lives in terms of possibilities.

After deciding that we are conscious beings separate from the world, Sartre embraces a stark conclusion. We are not so much thrown into a world of objects as we are thrown into freedom. That we have complete and total freedom is a logical consequence of Sartre's belief that there are no values, no structure, and no meaning to life. We can do whatever we want. Sartre also said that, because there are no objective values, structure, or God, our existence precedes our essence, meaning that we are not defined by the essence of humanness as so many previous philosophers had believed. We are, Sartre wrote, nothing but what we make of ourselves. Similar to the pragmatists, Sartre believed that bare facts have no meaning until we assign a meaning to them.

We might ask, "well, that's all good, yes?" Sartre said, no, freedom is a horrible thing. It's a horrible feeling of discomfort to know that you are free and that the type of entity you are is incompatible with the type of entities that are the objects all around you. You exist, and Sartre says that you have nothing behind you or before you. You have no objective values, no means to justify or excuse your actions. We are left alone, he says, with the overwhelming burden of freedom. Humans are condemned to be free, and our existence is absurd and meaningless.

Even worse (yes, even worse) according to Sartre, he knows that other people are free, totally free to think about him whatever they want. His most famous play, "No Exit" (1944), ends with the line "hell is other people," an appropriate conclusion to a play that explores how helpless we are in the company of others. His semi-autobiographical novel, *Nausea* (1938), details the rest of his ideas about the absurdity of existence. He describes objects in the world as grotesque, bloated existence. Other people he describes as empty beings practicing "bad faith" in that they live in the everyday, denying their freedom. However, when the central character of *Nausea* acknowledges his freedom, all this acceptance does is make him nauseated, hence the title. The realization of freedom and taking responsibility for one's actions are the only authentic acts of which we capable, but Sartre asks, if our very existence is absurd, and there are no values, what good is freedom? We are condemned to be free, condemned to absurdity.

Perhaps Sartre was so pessimistic because he lived through the Great Depression, Nazi occupation of France during World War II (he was imprisoned by the Nazis), and the end of France's empire. Other French intellectuals of that period were also gloomy about life and the future, but few, if any, as much as Sartre.

Maurice Merleau-Ponty's Phenomenology

Frenchman **Maurice Merleau-Ponty** (pronounced mer-LO-pon-TEE, 1908–1961) was influenced by Husserl and Heidegger but created a radical phenomenological approach to analyzing human perception. He proposed, most notably in *Phenomenology of Perception* (1945), that the material body, not consciousness, is the only source of human knowledge. All perception, he argued, was of the body, so philosophy should center on the body-subject not the Cartesian self. Therefore, Merleau-Ponty's phenomenology focused on the body's sensorimotor functions, and his version of the *epoché* was to bracket off all propositions about the world beyond the body's involvement with the world.

What Merleau-Ponty arrives at through his *epoché* is that perception is primary to thought. Merleau-Ponty claimed that there are bodily perceptions that do not fit Husserl's idea that consciousness is always a relation between a knower and something that is known. Merleau-Ponty claims that there are phenomena of the body that can be considered to be immediately known, not separable between knower and known. Merleau-Ponty adopts Heidegger's concept of Being-in-the-world and recasts it as bodily perception, not mental perception, and states that the body's involvements in the world is the condition of experience. We understand ourselves as a body in space, and all that we perceive comes from bodily perception not mental perception.

On the one hand, Merleau-Ponty's phenomenology offers some valuable insights into how the human body exists in and perceives objects in space. He correctly observes that one's own body is never experienced as one objective thing among others; one's own body is the distinctive source of perception. In this, he is properly fleshing out human experience. On the other hand, Merleau-Ponty's fixation on the human body swings the pendulum too far and he ends up downplaying the contributions of human cognitive judgment and free will. In denying Husserl's insight of conscious intentionality, Merleau-Ponty reduces the individual to a material body, reacting to the world at an animal level. Merleau-Ponty's phenomenology thus looks at the human being as a somewhat conscious animal that can transcend its corporality only in limited linguistic and artistic expressions.

Merleau-Ponty's reconception of phenomenology inspired an exploration in epistemology known as "bodily cognition." This emerging field of phenomenological exploration of what it means to be a body in space has influenced a number of current philosophers.

Chapter 15

CONTINENTAL SOCIAL AND POLITICAL PHILOSOPHY

All of the philosophers in this chapter adopted the approach of process rather than positivism in social and political philosophy. We earlier saw the rise of modern political philosophy in the 1600s and 1700s, but by the early 1900s, human society had changed significantly, as had ways to think about it.

Multiple factors influenced social and political philosophy in the 1900s. One influence was the new focus on how individual people live within society. This included the Hegelian-inspired understanding that people live within a social milieu that influences how they perceive and think. Also, phenomenology and existentialism had brought to the fore the importance of how individuals perceive and live their lives within their social lifeworld. The growing awareness of these social realities ushered in a shift from political philosophy—about the macrostructures of governments and nations—to social philosophy—about the structures of life as lived by groups and individuals.

A second influence was the social changes brought by the Second Industrial Revolution of the late 1800s in Europe and the United States, sparked by technical advances in steel, chemicals, petroleum products, and electricity. Society was transformed to an even greater degree than it had been during the First Industrial Revolution of the late 1700s. The transformation was most keenly felt in capitalism, which expanded and strengthened, instead of collapsing as Marx had predicted.

The political philosophy of Karl Marx was also a major influence in Europe, as was the Bolshevik Revolution in Russia, eventually leading to the creation of the Soviet Union, which described its ideology as Marxism-Leninism but which became a totalitarian state more akin to a fascist dictatorship than a pro-workers state. Some philosophers criticized the Soviets for not following Marxism, as we shall see. By the 1920s, the fact that capitalism was now stronger than ever forced those who agreed with Marx's critique of capitalism to figure out why it had not collapsed as Marx had said it would.

Philosophers also had to deal with the rise of fascism in the 1920s and 1930s. For various reasons, Europeans had been optimistic that science, technology, and increased communication and social freedoms would lead society into more reasonable and peaceful forms. Instead, an unimaginable darkness descended over Europe. The Nazis and their regime of terror directly affected several of the philosophers in this chapter. Everyone had to deal with fascism in one way or another. These events inspired some philosophers to attempt to describe oppressive power structures and provide alternatives to them.

Wilhelm Dilthey—Lived Experience

A major influence on continental social philosophy was German psychologist and philosopher **Wilhelm Dilthey** (1833–1911). He wrote on topics we now call "sociology," but he refused that label because of its then association with Auguste Comte's positivism. Dilthey, along with German sociologists **Max Weber** (1864–1920) and **Georg Simmel** (1858–1918), insisted that the positivist methodologies of the hard sciences cannot work for studying the social realm. What we need so that we can understand society is to analyze the interactions between individual initiative and communal tradition. Dilthey's social philosophy laid the groundwork for many subsequent philosophers.

In works Dilthey wrote between 1894 and 1911, he disagreed with the Hegelians' assertions that social institutions define all of human life for people and that individuals are subordinate to social institutions. Dilthey said that to understand human life we need to look at cultural systems—associations that individuals voluntarily join to accomplish goals in cooperation with other people. Cultural systems are complex networks that exert influence on individuals, but that's only one side of the social dynamic. It is also the case that individuals contribute to cultural systems and that social institutions operate through the participation and cooperation of individuals.

Similar to Husserl's conceptualization of the sedimentations of consciousness, Dilthey sees an individual's psychic life (as in psyche/psychology, not extra sensory perception) as a structural nexus developed from purposeful interaction with the external world. Individuals are in a continual process of interacting with the world. They face external pressures that they feel as resistance to their will. In response, Dilthey says, individuals are continually striving to adapt mentally to events, a conception similar to that of the pragmatists. In other words, we all develop a psychic or mental structure of how to respond to the world *while* we respond to the world, and that structure then affects further how we interact with the world.

Where Dilthey goes beyond Husserl and the pragmatists is in discussing how our psychic content relates to the objects in the world through attitudinal stances. These are our indefinite judgmental attitudes toward the world. He lists these as attitudinal stances: "asking, believing, presuming, claiming, taking pleasure in, approving, liking and its opposite, wishing, desiring, and willing." (*The Formation of the Historical World in the Human Sciences* 43) Dilthey's list of stances is similar to Descartes's list of abilities of a thinking thing, but unlike Descartes, Dilthey does not see a person as a detached observer making rational judgments about objects in the world. Dilthey sees our attitudinal stances as more than rational cognition; we are striving to fill each moment with value, fulfill our purposes, and establish rules for the future, even if just for ourselves. A person also has feelings, and feelings are more than subjective pleasures and displeasures. Feelings are, Dilthey says, attitudinal stances by which we evaluate the world.

Interestingly, in several of Dilthey's books, he seeks to understand texts, history, and other people by using the same approach for all of them, as though their meanings are essentially the same. It is a view adopted from the German idealists and Romanticism—history as expression. Understanding people as expressions within history means that, although we are all individuals, we are, again, responding to the world in which we find ourselves.

To become conscious of my own individual self requires me to approach myself as others do—that is, from the outside to the inside. Dilthey does not use Hegel's recognition theory, but subsequent philosophers have seen the parallel. We are who we are in large part because of how other people think about us. Our interactions with other people and society at large are what develop the structural nexus of the many elements of our psyche. Dilthey shows that our psychic life is always a continuum of our purposeful interactions with our world.

In emphasizing the need to examine individuals' lived experiences within society, Dilthey, like Jane Addams, helped influence a nonpositivist approach to the social sciences. We learn about people not through intellectual, abstract understanding but through how people experience their social world. Dilthey's ideas about the individual within society greatly contributed to the development of social philosophy.

W.E.B. Du Bois—Accepting Paradox

William Edward Burghardt Du Bois (pronounced du-BOYCE, 1868–1963) is best known for his philosophy of race, which we will discuss in Chapter 19, but he was also a sociologist and social philosopher. He was the first Black person to earn a PhD from a U.S. university—a doctorate in sociology from Harvard. His academic work was always related to his concern for social justice for individuals who subjectively feel experiences of injustice. Du Bois was, as a Black person, most keenly concerned with the injustices caused by racial prejudice.

In his social philosophy, Du Bois sought a methodology of sociology that would gather knowledge that can contribute to social reform. To this end, he rejected the positivist approach of Auguste Comte, which he forcibly critiqued in his paper, "Sociology Hesitant" (ca. 1905). Du Bois argued that instead of Comte's view of society as a concrete whole in which people are discrete units, we need to see society as composed of the deeds of people. Instead of Comte's science of society as a whole, Du Bois saw sociology as a science of human action.

What that means in practice for Du Bois is that we accept what he called the paradox that on the one hand there is the evident rhythm of human action, and on the other hand there is the evident incalculability of human action. (Comte had strangely wavered in the face of this paradox, but Du Bois said we must face it directly. There are primary rhythms of human behavior caused by physical laws and secondary rhythms of social regularities that can cease or change. Laws of physics cannot be changed, but social regularities can and are changed by human will.

Sociology, and all human sciences, must include not only the determinate forces of physics on human society, as Comte had, but also include, as Comte had not, indeterminate choices of human free will. We must attempt to measure the degree to which physical laws and social regularities constrain the range of choice and action that is undetermined by and independent of actions that had occurred before. Du Bois said this approach to sociology was the application of William James's pragmatism to all of human action, revealing the life of people beyond the distinct limits of physical laws.

Du Bois called this "the assumption of chance" principle. By "chance" he means the reality that people act in ways that not the mere result of physical laws—that not all individual actions are determined. He is not implying that human action is entirely random but rather that it is free and not determined, as James had said. This issue for Du Bois is not restricted to a methodology of study; it also applies to the efforts of social reform. By establishing space to accept "chance" in human action, we open up possibilities that the structures of society can be changed. Society is not completely determined by physical laws and social regularities—it can also be changed by personal actions. Therefore, racial injustice, a matter of great concern to Du Bois, is not unalterable—people can choose to change society and work toward justice.

Society is a paradox of partly determined and partly undetermined human actions. We can measure the determinate forces on human behavior, and we can also, Du Bois insists, observe the tangible reality of people's freewill actions. As we shall see in Chapter 19 when we talk specifically about race, Du Bois applied this methodology to the question of the lived experience of being Black in a society dominated by notions of white supremacy.

José Ortega y Gasset's Philosophy of Life

Spanish phenomenologist and existentialist **José Ortega y Gasset** (1883–1955) crafted a philosophy of life from elements taken from **John Stuart Mill**, **William James**, **Edmund Husserl**, and **Immanuel Kant**. He believed that the purpose of philosophy is to challenge our beliefs and prejudices to open up new ideas that better explain reality. He stated that "reflection on the phenomenon 'human life' is the basis of all my thought" (*Obras*, VIII: 273, n.2). Ortega defended the importance of the lived experience and perspectives of individuals living in the world.

Like other philosophers we have seen, Ortega was not anti-science, but he did see the limits of science's ability to describe the world, especially human life. He took inspiration from Albert Einstein, who had demonstrated that there is no single frame of reference, only the relative space-time perspective of the observer. From this new physics, and from the phenomenology of Husserl, Ortega concluded that "one and the same reality may split into many diverse realities when it is beheld from different points of view" (*Obras*, III: 360–64)

I Am I and My Circumstances

Ortega saw human life is a dynamic dialogue between the individual and the world. Each one of us is an individual human who lives in a reality of situations, people, and things. He said that every individual human life is a point of view directed upon the universe. Each person's perspective is a component of reality, and all knowledge is knowledge from a definite point of view. Every truth thus connects to a person's perspective placed in space and time. Ortega saw his philosophy as perspectivism—the principle that all perception and knowledge is bound up with the interpretations of the individual person. He saw perspectivism as expressing Einstein's theory of relativity—replacing in philosophy the classical Newtonian mechanics from which physics had now stepped away and accepting the relative perspectives of individuals.

The individual person attempts to order his or her world from the point of view of life. "Living," Ortega says, "is to reach outside of oneself, devoted ontologically, to what is other, be it called world or circumstances" (*Obras*, V: 545). It is I who lives and knows the world. Who am I? Ortega says, "I am I and my circumstances" (*Obras*, VI: 347–48). Each of us is an individual human person, living in a particular time and space with a particular perspective on the world and on our life within the world.

Our life, Ortega says, is a question of what to do with it. He poetically says that we find ourselves shipwrecked in a sea of circumstances, and we save ourselves by holding onto our consciousness and the essence of our lives as an "I" who must face the problem that I am lost but capable of solving this problem that is life itself. His is a philosophical approach that focuses on the vitality of life, like Dilthey and **Henri Bergson** did. Human experience and being cannot be reduced to a mechanistic or logical determinism. Human life is dynamic and active, reflective of the individual in his or her time and space. Each of us is an "I," but not an "I" imprisoned in subjectivism as some have interpreted Descartes as describing. Ortega's "I" is a conscious self that always finds itself in the world. Our lived experience is our being in the world.

From his approach that centers on lived experience, Ortega sees time in a way similar to Bergson's concept of time as duration. Ortega's term is "historical time," by which he means how we experience reality in terms of narrative reason. In the physical world, change happens to objects, but in the social world, events happen. To comprehend social events, it is necessary to tell the event's narrative history in terms of human motive, actions, and reactions. All historical events are unique, in contrast to physical laws that enact the same forces on similar circumstances.

Therefore, the history of the individual means more than mere change within time—what Bergson called "scientific time." Human actions occur in historical time—events created by human individuals. My history is important to me because, although humans are future oriented, all we have to go on is the past. Who I am as an individual is the result of my history, my choices within my circumstances. These realities are why Ortega sees history as the supreme science. Like Kierkegaard had said, life can only be understood backwards, but it must be lived forwards.

Ortega's philosophy of life understands individuals as active beings with free will living within a social world. We humans have been placed by circumstances in a unique situation. Physical objects—rocks, plants, and animals—are predetermined in what they are. We humans are not determined by an essential nature, and our choices are not determined by rational necessity. Similar to the pragmatists, Ortega says, "We do not live to think, on the contrary: we think in order that we may succeed in surviving" (*Obras*, VI: 34; 5: 304).

The individual did not choose his or her circumstances, which are defined by history. We are nevertheless free beings. Physical or social forces do not determine our actions or deny us freedom, but they do create our circumstances that constitute the conditions of our freedom. We are free to act within our circumstances. That is why Ortega defines himself (and us) as "I am I and my circumstances." Each individual faces a unique set of circumstances, and each individual makes a unique set of choices.

Our life occupation is to respond to the always present variety of possibilities for action from which we are obligated to choose. Like Kierkegaard, Ortega says we are beings who must choose and act, continually in a confrontation with the world. Similar to the pragmatists, Ortega saw that our knowledge of the world consists of interpretations we make within human life. Similar to **Martin Heidegger**, Ortega says that everything we experience is found within our individual lives and that the meanings of physical objects depend on what they mean to us and for us. We humans are entities that make ourselves and our lives by applying reason to historical time, objects, and ourselves.

We need to accept the radical reality that I am an "I"—a self—and that everything radiates from our unique self, our unique life. We construct our world and our orientation to it within our circumstances, freely choosing our actions from the possibilities before us. Like Sartre, Ortega says that we are coerced to be free, but Ortega provides a more balanced view than does Sartre, who saw freedom as a condemnation. Life is anguish, Ortega says, but it is also enthusiasm and delight.

The Individual within Society

Pursuing the phenomenology of human social life, Ortega realizes that he (and each of us) is an "I" who is in a human world and society. We find our authenticity in our individuality, as other existentialists say, but I do not exist in solitude, even though my being and my thoughts are mine and mine alone. I share the world with others. I have my life, for being an "I" means for me *my life*. You have your life, and your thoughts and convictions do not exist for me, but you are another "I" like me, and that means for you your life. We share this world.

In the social world, an individual is being-for-and-with-others. One cannot and should not view possibilities as exclusively one's own but understand that social life is an interactive process relating to a common world of possibilities. I am I and my circumstances—my circumstances being extended to include other "I's."—because in the context of social life, I measure who I am by my interactions with others. Life is a continual dialogue with our environment, in particular with our fellow humans.

Society is not entirely natural in Ortega's opinion because we find our authenticity in being unique individuals, yet we live in a world composed of a multitude of unique individuals. Society is therefore filled with tension and requires structures that integrate and include individuals. Ortega criticized capitalism as having demoralized humanity, but he was equally critical of Marxism. He favored a sociopolitical structure that would protect from abuses of power individuality, freedoms of speech and thought, and minority rights.

Similar to **John Stuart Mill**, Ortega was concerned about the possible tyranny of the majority in mass society. In his book, *The Revolt of the*

Masses (1930), he sets out an almost elitist qualitative division of society into two types of people. He is not making a distinction of economic class but of mindset. A minority of people, Ortega claims, strive to improve themselves, whereas the majority of people are content with their lot in life. Ortega would say this is not an elitist division because the minority does not see itself as superior, which is why it seeks continual improvement.

He argues without being entirely accurate that in the past, the minority who strove for self-betterment directed political states, preserving society by means of their greater knowledge, and the masses accepted that higher authority. In the 1800s, he says, advances in technology and liberal democracy empowered the majority. The rise of mass culture created the "mass-man," ignorant of history but seeking its own superiority and self-fulfillment rather than self-improvement. In the early 1900s, the mass-man is revolting against history, the supreme science, blindly herding forward, mistakenly thinking that civilization is self-supporting and without the need of the qualified minority's guidance.

Ortega's *The Revolt of the Masses* is a complaint reminiscent of **Rousseau's** and **Nietzsche's** in decrying how the masses threaten to eliminate anyone who is not like everybody, the mass brutally crushing beneath it everything that is excellent, individual, and qualified. Nietzsche in the 1880s had predicted that Europe was headed for a social cataclysm. Ortega's prediction in 1930 was more specific. Because the masses believe themselves to be the state, everyone will end up enslaved by the state; society will be militarized and bureaucratized, with individuality crushed in favor of mass mediocrity. Consciously or not, Ortega predicted the rise of fascism—Benito Mussolini in Italy, Francisco Franco in Spain, Adolph Hitler in Germany.

Neo-Marxism—Why Hasn't Capitalism Failed?

A large number of philosophers can be called neo-Marxists. What they had in common was the desire to separate Marxism from the distorted version practiced by the Soviet Union and later China. Beyond that common ground, there has been a bewildering array of different theories, emphasizing different aspects or outgrowths of Marx's ideas. Neo-Marxist philosophies include historicist, scientific, analytic, and sociological Marxism, all competing for the label of the "real" Marxist theory and often with antagonism for each other. All but lost in the ideological jostling were a few democratic socialists, like **Rosa Luxemburg** (1871–1919). She placed the honor and voice of the workers in the center of neo-Marxist thought, calling for a revolutionary socialist democracy in which workers had a direct voice in government, instead of the Leninist one-party totalitarianism under the guise of socialist revolution. Luxemburg was killed by a paramilitary unit amid a failed workers' uprising in Germany in 1919.

György Lukács

Among those taking a historicist interpretation of Marxism was Hungarian **György Lukács** (1885–1971). He wanted to return Marxism to its totalizing vision of historical determinism. He agreed with most of Marx's economic analysis but said that, ultimately, it is not economic motives that drive history and class consciousness but the all-pervasive supremacy of the totality over all its parts. He saw capitalism as an objective totality of social relations determining history, but he said that the bourgeoisie is not conscious of the transitory character of capitalism. Only the proletariat, who receive no benefit from capitalism and no interest in its continuance, are able to see the reality that capitalism is doomed for what it is. This idea that each class has its own consciousness is Lukács's most significant idea. Our class consciousness is our subjective awareness of the objective reality of society and history. It is subjective by economic class, not by individual.

In 1918 and 1919, amid the anarchy after the end of World War I, a wave of revolutions swept the territories of the former Austro-Hungarian Empire, and several communist states were established, including Hungary. Lukács was involved in the short-lived Marxist-styled Hungarian Republic of 1919 as Commissar for Education and Culture. He survived the bloody purges that followed the collapse of that government and escaped to the Soviet Union. There, Lukács uncovered and translated Marx's early writings on alienation and, in 1932, published them as "Economic and Philosophic Manuscripts of 1844." Those manuscripts included Marx's theories on human alienation, which, thanks to Lukács, changed how we interpret Marx. Nevertheless, Lukács did little to incorporate alienation into his theories. Ever the Soviet-style Communist, he became involved again in government when the Soviets took over Hungary in the late 1940s.

Antonio Gramsci

A sociological approach to Marxist came from Italian Antonio Gramsci (GRAM-shee, 1891–1937) who introduced perhaps the most important concept in neo-Marxism—cultural hegemony (dominance). Marx and most Marxist theorists had seen the bourgeoisie as maintaining control through political and economic coercion. Gramsci extended this idea of coercion to all of culture. Capitalism was maintained by the hegemony of bourgeois ideology in cultural institutions. Marx had mentioned this idea, but Gramsci moved it to the forefront of social critique. Gramsci observed that the bourgeoisie propagate their values through their control of the press, the education system, and the arts. Their values become "common sense," part of the common background of culture. The proletariat learns to associate their good with the good of the bourgeoisie. Bourgeois culture and values have hegemony throughout society.

Gramsci and others could now explain why the proletariat had not revolted: more than economic factors were at work. This concept allowed Gramsci to develop a view of emancipation from capitalism not dependent on the fatalism of economic determinism. Influenced by Henri Bergson, Gramsci accepted what Marx had not—that there were social forces beyond the material. This informed his idea of cultural hegemony and his division of society into the political (police, military, legislative, and judicial systems) and the civil (family, trade unions, and other forms of social activism), both divisions part of the bourgeoisie's cultural hegemony. 4 middle class

He proposed that the working class develop a counterhegemony, a working-class culture that would develop values alternative to those of bourgeois ideology. Working-class people were not stupid, he stressed; they can organically grow their own intellectuals. Organic intellectuals will not be separate from the people, as the intelligentsia too often are, and won't reduce society to scientific rules, but will, in dialogue with the working class, help them develop ways to articulate their feelings. Gramsci saw it as a duty of intellectuals to speak for those who are excluded from the cultural hegemony. He introduced the term "subaltern" to describe the segment of society that is denied agency and a voice in society. Gramsci died in prison, a victim of **Benito Mussolini's** (1883–1945) brutal fascist suppression of intellectual freedom.

The Frankfurt School

Gramsci wasn't exactly an optimist, but he seems one compared to the pessimism of the Frankfurt School. The most prominent members of the Frankfurt School were Germans **Max Horkheimer** (left in picture, 1895–1973), **Theodor Adorno** (right, 1903–1969), and **Herbert Marcuse** (1898–1979). They were consternated about why capitalism had not collapsed and why the workers' revolutions of 1919 had failed. Like other neo-Marxists, they opposed Soviet totalitarianism and sought a new theoretical basis for emancipating the working class from capitalism.

They called their approach "critical theory" because they saw their project as a theoretical critique of society. Their use of the term "critical theory," a term still used in philosophy, should not be confused with the use of the term in other disciplines, such as literary theory and analysis. In the late 1920s, the Frankfurt School developed a system of philosophical critique founded on the social sciences. The plan was to use sociology's empirical research methods developed by Max Weber and Georg Simmel (they rejected Wilhelm Dilthey's approach to human sciences as too general). Their interpretive method was deliberately antipositivist in not reducing social science to logical, deterministic categories but instead trying to understand cultural groups on their own terms and from their own points of view. They did, however, bring to their social science the assumptions of Hegel's historicism, Marx's economic theory, and the psychoanalytical theory of Austrian neurologist **Sigmund Freud** (1856–1939).

The Frankfurt School's program was deeply affected by the rise of the Nazis. Horkheimer, Adorno, and Marcuse were all Jewish, and they were fortunate enough to be able to flee Germany shortly after the Nazis gained power. Horkheimer and Adorno found academic refuge at Columbia University in New York City. While there, they wrote *Dialectic of Enlightenment* (1944), a Hegelian take on Marxism. In their view, historical determinism had led not to the collapse of capitalism but rather to its strengthening in new forms of domination—fascism and state capitalism—that amounted to a one-party police state, as in Germany and Italy.

Like Gramsci, Horkheimer and Adorno saw society as being dominated by bourgeois culture, but unlike Gramsci, they were fatalistic about the prospects of overcoming the cultural hegemony. Horkheimer and Adorno certainly condemned fascism, but they said that its state capitalism had abolished the competitive tensions in market capitalism.

Marx had said that those tensions among capitalist producers and the demands that capitalist production place on labor and raw materials were contradictions that would bring capitalism down. This prediction had obviously failed, and from Horkheimer's and Adorno's perspective as German Jews, who had lived through the failed workers' revolutions of 1919, fascism had "won." Their sought to explain why.

Dialectic of Enlightenment was their attempt to answer the "why?" question, an attempt more scattershot than precise. They prudently rejected totalizing theories, such as those in positivism. They instead drew on a variety of sources, but primarily they combined Marx's historicism and Freud's theory of repression of human drives. What they came up with was that historical determinism had produced the modern culture industry, the method authoritarianism used to manipulate and dominate the masses, repressing the proletariat's independence and agency. They pointed to the rise of technological methods of culture dissemination, most notably radio, that assimilated people into a mass consciousness dominated by the bourgeoisie. This is basically Gramsci's idea of cultural hegemony, but Horkheimer and Adorno saw no way out, alluding only to a vague notion of gradual cultural awareness.

Adorno doubled down on this pessimism in his solo book, *Minima Moralia: Reflections from a Damaged Life* (1951). Adorno saw historical determinism as an overwhelming objectivity that has ended the subject (his word for "person"). The subject still thinks of itself as autonomous, but it has been historically condemned and nullified by the concentration camp. Adorno saw the Nazi concentration camps as emblematic of the despair of the time. There is no poetry after Auschwitz, he declared, and the possibility of social progress is now in doubt. Adorno no longer believed in Marx's promise of the working class's emancipation, declaring that the reality or unreality of redemption or human emancipation hardly matters.

All was despair for Adorno, even music, which, in *Philosophy of New Music* (1949), he declared was a tool of the culture industry that saw absolute oblivion as its goal. His only answer was a negation of existing cultural forms among small groups of men (his gender-exclusive language). He also saw these small groups as determined by history, which fates certain individuals and certain arts to hold out the faint possibility of future truth.

Adorno's cynical condemnation of nearly everything, and his notion that only a select few chosen by history can fully discern what's happening, has appealed to some, but Adorno has been widely criticized. **Jean-François Lyotard** (who we meet in Chapter 17) rejected Adorno's negative dialectic as an arbitrary religion of history. Lukács accused Adorno of inhabiting the Grand Hotel Abyss, equipped with comfort, perched on the edge of the abyss of absurdity, and contemplating that abyss. **Axel Honneth** (see later in this chapter) said Adorno's historical-philosophical negativism was a failure of critical theory. Honneth and **Jürgen Habermas** (see later in this chapter) are considered later generations of critical theory philosophers related to but separate from the Horkheimer and Adorno generation.

Hannah Arendt—Against Totalitarianism

German **Hannah Arendt** (1906–1975) is most famous for her book, *Eichmann in Jerusalem: A Report on the Banality of Evil* (1963), her report of the trial of Nazi war criminal **Adolf Eichmann**. However, the philosophical views that she expressed in that book were formed much earlier. At the University of Marburg, Germany, when only 17, Arendt began a long romantic relationship with Martin Heidegger, 18 years her senior. They kept their relationship completely secret, and it wasn't discovered until 1982 when Arendt's biographer discovered their hidden correspondence. Heidegger's philosophy was a major influence on hers, as was the philosophy of Karl Jaspers, who was the adviser on her doctoral dissertation, entitled, "On the Concept of Love in the Thought of Saint Augustine" (1929), and she remained friends with Jaspers for the rest of his life. She was also influenced by Romanticism, although more by its literary side than its philosophical side.

A German Jew, Arendt had believed in Jewish assimilation into mainstream culture, but the rise of the Nazis forced her to radical action. She used her home as way station to help those persecuted by the Nazis (socialists, Jews, Marxists, and others) to escape the country—like the American Underground Railroad that helped people escape enslavement in the 1800s. She wrote essays opposing the Nazis and became involved in Jewish political resistance until she was arrested at a state library in 1933 for conducting "illegal" research—namely, the extent of Nazi anti-Semitism. She was released to await trial, but realizing she had little hope for a future in Germany, she and her mother fled using the underground escape route she had helped others to use. She later only narrowly escaped the Nazi occupation of France and was one of the fortunate few helped to emigrate to the United States.

Against Totalitarianism

The Nazi tyranny deeply affected her personally and philosophically. Her book, *The Origins of Totalitarianism* (1951), took aim at what she called this "novel form of government." She argued that totalitarianism differs from despotism, tyranny, and dictatorship in its use of terror to subjugate mass populations instead of subjugating only political adversaries. Totalitarianism also seeks to control all aspects of society as a prelude to world domination, whereas autocratic regimes seek only regional political power.

Arendt's definition of totalitarianism led her to the claim that the essential target of Nazi terror was not the Jewish populations—they were merely a convenient excuse for the general Nazi practice of mass subjugation. Arendt's controversial claim is supported by the fact that the Nazi concentration camps were initially built not for Jewish people but for leftist political activists. Arendt in no way diminishes the anti-Semitism of the Nazis but places it into the wider historical context of the marginalization of minority populations, including colonialism.

Arendt claimed that totalitarianism seeks to eliminate the intellectual, spiritual, and artistic initiative of all individuals. She considered the persecution of intellectuals, religious leaders, and artists by both Nazi Germany and Stalinist Russia as springing from their resentment of everything they could not understand. Total domination of society cannot allow people to have free creative initiative because creative energies are not predictable. Totalitarianism, Arendt says, preferring predictable mediocrity, persecutes all who show talent and initiative and replaces them with crackpots and fools because those with a lack of intelligence and ingenuity are the most likely to stay loyal to the regime.

No doubt, it was Arendt's conception of the uncreative, unintelligent functionary within the totalitarian state apparatus that led her to see Adolf Eichmann in that way. In *Eichmann in Jerusalem*, she wrote that he was an unthinking dutiful functionary who was "terribly and terrifyingly normal." She concluded that evil isn't always radical; it can also be simply a function of thoughtlessness. Totalitarianism exploits the tendency of ordinary people to conform willingly to mass opinion and obey orders. **Stanley Milgram's** (1933–1984) psychological experiments in the 1960s, inspired by the case of Eichmann, although ethically questionable, shone some light on people's willingness to obey orders when they are told it is for the greater good. This allows evil to become banal—something normalized as acceptable behavior. Arendt described Eichmann as a human example of the banality of evil—a bureaucrat who facilitated horrific crimes because he found personal meaning and importance within the Nazi movement.

The Human Condition

In her book, *The Human Condition* (1958), Arendt argued that people develop within the social realm more than within the political realm. Showing Karl Jaspers's influence, she outlines a view of the human condition as one of existential and aesthetic action. Central to her discussion is her concept of "natality," which she first used in her doctoral dissertation on Augustine that Jaspers oversaw. Natality is in sharp contrast to the pessimism and the obsession with mortality found in later existentialist philosophers like Heidegger and Sartre). Arendt says that people are not born in order to die but in order to begin. Natality is the root of the human capacity for action, by which people can continually find new beginnings. It is a more existential version of Bergson's élan vital that generates not only life but also choices in how to live. Arendt identifies two essential human actions—forgiving past wrongs that unfix the fixed past and promising future benefits that fix the unfixed future.

Looking at how people respond to their condition, Arendt distinguishes among labor, work, and action. "Labor" is action directed at biological survival—procuring food and shelter—and is therefore a repetitive, cyclical process conducted with an air of futility. "Work" is different from labor in that it has clearly defined beginnings and ends because work produces durable objects. The concept of work includes both making instrumental tools (like hammers) and creating works of art. "Action" is the ways in which people disclose themselves to each other. In this sense, our actions distinguish us as unique people. What we do and what we say establish and communicate our individuality. Unlike labor and work, which are directed at material objects, action is always directed at other people. Action generates human relationships. Action, because it is an expression of an individual, leads to human plurality of individual expression.

Arendt notes that philosophers since Plato have disliked and dismissed human plurality, but she considers it a basic human condition that has the twofold character of equality and distinction. Acknowledging the diversity of people allows us to see what is possible in action and to see how action generates a kind of objectivity in the understanding of the ways in which action can be witnessed from different perspectives. Human plurality creates tensions, to be sure, but Arendt's answers to those problems are the two essential human actions of forgiving the past and promising the future.

Isaiah Berlin's Political Philosophy

Isaiah Berlin (1909–1997) was born in Russian-occupied Latvia, but his family emigrated to England after the Russian Revolution. At Oxford University, he became acquainted with ordinary language philosophy (a form of analytic philosophy we will discuss in Chapter 16) and developed an interest in social and political philosophy. He had a strong intellectual interest in, but not agreement with, Marx's philosophy.

Against Reductionism

Berlin accepted Kant's Categories of Understanding, but, like the German idealists, he thought our minds were malleable rather than fixed and the same for all people. The Categories in terms of which we make sense of the world are shaped by our experiences and in turn shape our experiences. Philosophy, Berlin says, is the study of the "thought spectacles" (as in eyeglasses) through which we perceive and understand the world. Those spectacles change over time; therefore, philosophy is a study of human history. Philosophy is a critical study of society and its presuppositions, identifying errors and misunderstandings. Therefore, philosophy is inherently subversive and troubling, although this is what makes philosophy valuable as it assists us in better understanding ourselves and our world.

One of Berlin's subversive acts was directed at philosophers who misused logic. He insisted that it is a fallacy to believe that there is a single criterion for meaningfulness and certainty. The quest for certainty is actually self-defeating. Reality is a web of interconnected and overlapping elements, varied and complex, and it is not reducible to formal deductive or inductive logic. Our sense impressions are

> too many, too minute, too fleeting, too blurred at the edges. They crisscross and penetrate each other at many levels simultaneously, and the attempt to prise them apart, as it were and pin them down, and classify them, and fit them into their specific compartments, turns out to be impracticable. (*Concepts and Categories* 119)

He gives as an example trying to prove rationally the proposition "I am not on Mars." There is no one simple reason for believing that I am on Earth, no direct test that can on its own prove it with absolute certainty. We instead accept the total texture of the countless strands of our experience to believe what we believe. He rejects the reductionism of positivism, saying that both deductive and inductive logic rest upon the general texture of experience. Our rudimentary awareness of the patterns and textures of experience constitute the foundations of our knowledge.

Like multiple other continental philosophers, Berlin refused to reduce human beings to mere matter in space. We are active beings with free will pursuing our chosen ends and shaping our own and other people's lives. Our thoughts and ideas are not determined by external forces or history. Belief in determinism is actually self-defeating, Berlin says, because denying that we have free will would lead to the complete collapse of all meaningful rational activity. Our free will is a precondition of our human experience.

Two Concepts of Liberty

Berlin is most famous for his contribution of the distinction between two kinds of political liberty. By definition, a human has free will, but political theorists have thought about human freedom, or liberties, in two different ways. In his lecture, "Two Concepts of Liberty" (1958), he identifies these as negative and positive liberties. Negative liberties include what we are free from—restrictions and coercive forces like bullying and intimidation. Positive liberties include what we are free to do—having the ability to act on our free will.

Another way to think about these two types is to consider negative liberties as the absence of forces that restrict the options available to you and positive liberties as the abilities to act on available options and effect changes that you want in the world. Berlin showed that negative and positive freedoms can be rival, incompatible interpretations of a political ideal, both interpretations claiming the words "liberty" and "liberal."

For the most part, Berlin preferred that our political thinking emphasize negative liberties, pointing out the dangers of excessive emphasis of positive liberties. He criticizes Rousseau's concept of the general will as a dangerous perversion of positive freedom. Consistent with his rejection of positivism and the idea of singular truth, Berlin rejected Rousseau's notion that there is a single "true" public interest. Rousseau's theory denied the reality of individuality and the need, Berlin says, to respect social pluralism. Individuals have varied interests, Berlin argues, and must be free to express and pursue genuine human values. The human self is individual to each particular citizen, and Rousseau was wrong to try to transfer the self and will to the larger community.

Berlin traced this transfer of the self from the individual to the whole through the ideas of Fichte and Hegel, the latter insisting that the individual achieves freedom only in obedience to the rational dictates of the state. Berlin argues that this attitude is a social monism that denies the reality of human pluralism and suppresses personal expression. Berlin asserts that Hegel's monism paved the way for totalitarianism—the political ideology that claims to liberate the people by subjecting them to the greater good.

Berlin is not saying that positive liberties are to be avoided—only their perversions. What Berlin opposed were ideologies that abused the ideas of positive freedom to justify the abandonment of negative liberties. Positive and negative liberties must be balanced against each other. Our human autonomy is essential to our well-being. People should be free from coercion and oppression, and individualism and pluralism should not be precluded. Berlin did, however, also point out that evils have been committed in the name of defending negative liberties, such as exploitation under laissez-faire capitalism (but we will meet some philosophers who defend laissez-faire capitalism in Chapter 16). People must be free to make choices as to their values and actions, but people must not violate other people's freedom of choice.

Jürgen Habermas—Communication and Culture

Jürgen Habermas (1929–) is a German sociologist and philosopher who originally associated with the Frankfurt School but branched out into other areas of social philosophy and drew on Husserl's phenomenology. Habermas was influenced by fellow German **Hans-Georg Gadamer** (1900–2002) who had argued similarly to Heidegger that people are embedded in a particular culture and from that culture have a historically effected consciousness. Gadamer saw the role of philosophy as the interpretation of culture to understand what happens to us over and above what we want and do. Habermas took on that project by seeking to understand communication in culture and how everyday communication affects consciousness. Habermas disputes Gadamer's contention that language determines the material practices of life, claiming instead that it is ideology and the material conditions of labor and domination that determine culture and communication. Habermas was not a Marxist, but he did take up Marx's ideas of historical materialism and the illusionary consciousness created by the ideology of the superstructure.

The Public Sphere

Habermas's two key concepts are the "public sphere" and "intersubjective communication." In *The Structural Transformation of the Public Sphere* (1962), he departed from a strict Marxist interpretation of history by considering the rise of the public sphere. Habermas saw the public sphere as a bourgeois sphere, but not one completely controlled by the ruling powers. Historically, the public sphere grew from the noncapitalist merchant class in the late 1600s (John Locke's time) as society shifted away from feudalism into a liberal constitutional order. Before then, Habermas said, European culture was dominated by the ruling powers who imposed their views and values on people.

The growth in the 1600s and 1700s of printed materials like newspapers and broadsheets and the rise of coffeehouses created the public sphere. This change gave the emerging middle class opportunities to learn about and discuss each other's ideas. This social sphere was still dominated by men of some economic means and was, therefore, not an ideal form, but it was a significant historical development. Habermas credits the public sphere for innovations in political philosophy like those of Locke and Rousseau and for the development of liberal constitutional governments. He argues that the public sphere began to decline with the rise of commercial mass media, consumer capitalism, and the post–World War II social welfare state. Habermas said the latter development started with good intentions but eventually collapsed the bourgeois public sphere. The historical triumph of consumer culture and mass media serving capitalist interests has stifled rational and critical dialogue. This shift leads to Habermas's second key concept.

Communicative Action

In his book, *The Theory of Communicative Action* (1981), Habermas analyzes how our everyday lives are affected by formal social systems and how we can revive the public sphere. Habermas had become pessimistic about the state of society, and this book was his ambitious program to set things right. The book is more a work of sociology than philosophy, but it makes several important philosophical observations.

The first is his rejection of the assumption of the primacy of purposive rationality in people's actions. This common positivist, objectivist assumption in philosophy and the social sciences obscures the subjective intentions of human actions. Habermas pushed for a practical, pluralist approach to understanding human behavior that examines intersubjective communication shared among people. It is important to realize that in talking about subjective intentions and pluralism, Habermas is not embracing any conception that the individual's concerns or a political pluralism should be the focus of society's concern. He instead advocates for a collective rational engagement with institutional norms. Rational communication will bridge individual differences, form a single consensus, and lead to social integration under a unifying communicative structure.

Habermas's second observation is the division of social life between the systems of modern capitalist society and the lifeworld of personal everyday life. This two-level concept of society is perhaps his most important concept. As we've seen discussed by a number of philosophers, society is composed of systems that shape human life. Habermas agrees with the general Marxist conception that social systems are dominated by the capitalists and that the political, legal, and media systems serve the capitalists' interests. Habermas adds to that the lifeworld, using the concept in a manner similar to Husserl's usage, but with greater emphasis on the objective community.

Habermas sees the lifeworld as formed by communicative action—the cooperative acts people take within a continual process of deliberation. Communicative actions transmit cultural knowledge, mold new mutual cultural understandings, coordinate people in moving toward social integration and solidarity, and continually enable people to form their identities. Communicative action forms the lifeworld in which people live and coordinate their behaviors on the basis of consensual social norms.

That's Habermas's descriptive definition of communicative action, but he also adds a prescriptive definition in distinguishing communicative action from "strategic action." In strategic action, individual actors are primarily interested in achieving their individual goals rather than in cooperation and mutual benefit, which potentially leads to manipulation and coercion instead of cooperation. The systems of capitalism encourage strategic action—acting for one's own benefit. Habermas advocates for communicative action, in which people discuss and coordinate their desires and goals, seeking a shared understanding that their goals are inherently reasonable or worthy. Habermas gives a lengthy discourse on appropriate speech acts that lead toward successful communicative action.

The bottom line is that Habermas stresses the importance of the rationality of discourse, in which people provide reasons for their speech acts that are open for discussion—both criticism and justification. In this view, communication is judged not by claims of empirical facts—as found in positivism and analytic philosophy—but by where the speech act falls on the spectrum of validity claims, which are claims that include appeals to moral rightness, authenticity, sincerity, and so on. The person making a speech act still must provide justification for his or her claims, but the validity claim is not an appeal to transcendent logic or science. Instead, it is an appeal to validity within a social context.

Habermas is being prescriptive in calling for an intersubjective dialogue that is both consensual and reasonable—a process that leads to justified cooperation. Habermas opposes legal systems that are controlled by political parties or corporate interests that impose laws on the public sphere. These systems in capitalist democracies do not legitimately represent the political will of a public sphere practicing deliberative communicative action. In plainer language, he is calling illegitimate a government that represents special interests rather than the voice of the people. When intersubjective dialogue is practiced in the public sphere and communicative action is strong, the lifeworld is healthy, and individuals can better resist the coercive forces of the capitalist systems that attempt to colonize the lifeworld and stifle communication and cooperation.

Communicative action is therefore a means toward advancing democratic public life and the revival of the public sphere. Habermas's goal is for the current social systems to be replaced by political organisms of deliberative democracy in which people are actively involved in dialogue about issues and decision-making. He is on the one hand rejecting totalizing narratives such as found in Hegel, Marx, and others but on the other hand is also rejecting individualism and pluralism, insisting that the rationality of discourse will lead to consensus, with a hint of Rousseauean conformity to a general will.

Axel Honneth's Recognition Theory

German philosopher **Axel Honneth** (1949–) is considered part of the third generation of the critical theory trajectory established by the Frankfurt School. He studied under Habermas who is considered the second generation. Honneth takes on critical theory's mission of critiquing society to bring about human emancipation from injustice. His distinctive approach to critical theory is to replace Marxism as the center of the critical theory project with Hegel's theory of recognition (see Chapter 9). This approach enables Honneth to talk about how social institutions affect people positively and negatively and what causes people to demand justice.

Honneth sees himself as continuing the critical theory project but rejects the historicism and pessimism of Horkheimer and Adorno and the neglect of the individual's experiences of Habermas. Honneth's view of injustice extends beyond capitalist exploitation, oppressive laws, or unequal distribution of resources. Injustice also occurs when recognition is lacking or an individual is actively misrecognized.

Honneth's hypothesis is that all integration of a person into society depends on reliable forms of mutual recognition. Human integrity owes its existence at a deep level, he says, to the patterns of approval and recognition. There are two keys to Honneth's conception of recognition.

The first is that individuals are socialized into a lifeworld of recognition norms that prescribe how we should respond to people's behaviors. Social norms inform us about what behaviors are worthy of praise or censure in ourselves and in others. They tell us what is expected of us, from moral behavior to social niceties, creating shared communal bonds. Furthermore, people learn what justice is through these processes of socialization.

The second is that receiving recognition on the basis of these norms enables an individual to develop a positive "relation-to-self"—one's sense of place within the various social spheres in which one lives—and, most importantly, one's autonomy to be able to determine and realize one's own desires and intentions freely. Thus, to achieve their goals in society, individuals desire and need to both receive and give recognition. When we receive recognition and enter into relations of mutual recognition with others, we develop an identity.

Placing recognition at the center of social critique allows Honneth to expand the usual definitions of injustice beyond violations of laws or rights. In his book, *Disrespect: The Normative Foundations of Critical Theory* (2007), he says that misrecognition is an active withholding of recognition, such as denying rights or refusing social inclusion. Exclusion, insult, and degradation violate and damage one's self-confidence, self-respect, and self-esteem. People experience misrecognition as moral injuries. These injuries to one's integrity, honor, or dignity, Honneth argues, are the core of how people experience injustice.

Honneth extends Habermas's idea of communicative action into everyday intersubjective relations in which people can form rational responses to their suffering of moral injustices. Through socialization, people learn society's moral values, and they come to expect that society will recognize them in accordance with social recognition norms of just treatment. When instead they receive misrecognition, people experience the resulting disappointment as violence to their sense of identity. This, Honneth says, motivates people to struggle for recognition.

Struggles for Recognition

In *The Struggle for Recognition: The Moral Grammar of Social Conflicts* (1996), Honneth states that most social movements for justice are, in fact, struggles for recognition. Even social conflicts over resources or political power are at their heart struggles based on the concern that moral values are not being reflected in actual recognition relations. Groups denied rights or integrity seek to reestablish relations of mutual recognition. We can see a recent example of Honneth's idea in the Black Lives Matter movement. Yes, this group is struggling for legal rights, but at the heart of their movement is the struggle for recognition—that they are human beings who deserve to be treated according to the moral values that society claims it believes in but is not fully extending to Black people. That denial of recognition of Black people is what Honneth calls a "pathology of reason." It should be obvious that Blacks are people with the same rights as other people. However, capitalism has distorted people's ability to reason about moral relations and norms, leading to a failure to identify misrecognition.

When people experience misrecognition, Honneth says, their suffering motivates them to take action. Their damaged self-esteem and relation-to-self can be repaired only by recognition. They therefore join an existing political movement that is struggling for recognition. Honneth also sees large-scale political movements as necessary to motivate an individual to take on a struggle for recognition. This position leaves him unable to explain how such movements get started. His theory also can't explain how a person damaged by misrecognition could manage to resolve to struggle for recognition or why many people who suffer from misrecognition don't enter into a struggle for recognition.

The reality that individuals deal with different recognition norms in multiple social spheres—family, friends, workplace, civil society, and so on—means that individuals have to navigate multiple lifeworlds or forms of life, which helps explain the complexities and anxieties of our lives.

Honneth improves on earlier critical theory accounts of the individual by opening a door to a fine-grained analysis of the struggles individuals face to live in these multiple overlapping forms of life. However, Honneth's reliance on a Hegelian view of society as formal, distinct, institutional spheres of family, civil society, and state leaves him unable to recognize the myriad ways that individuals respond to experiences of misrecognition outside of institutional paths. Despite the shortcomings of Honneth's version of recognition theory, he has established recognition as a social reality that political philosophers need to address.

Freedom and Socialism

More recently, Honneth has turned his attention to the ideal of social freedom. In *Freedom's Right: The Social Foundations of Democratic Life* (2014), he moves the discussion of justice away from abstract principles and toward normative claims anchored in real-world situations and institutionally established practices. Influenced by his own theory of recognition, and Habermas's view of the public sphere, Honneth establishes the paradigm of the "democratic ethical life." He argues that a grounded theory and practice of justice requires concrete social institutions that generate the standards of what is just. Ideally, particular social spheres define a particular aspect of individual freedom and bring about its realization. Here, too, however, Honneth focuses on social institutions, neglecting possibilities for individual social actions.

In *The Idea of Socialism: Towards a Renewal* (2017), Honneth seeks to reclaim the idea of socialism from the damage caused by many decades of capitalist defamation of socialism. Socialism, he says, is the realization of personal freedom in social solidarity. He reclaims socialism by renewing its basic tenets that were originally formed in the industrial era of the 1800s. To respond to the realities of our postindustrial society, Honneth replaces archaic Marxist assumptions with Dewey's instrumentalism to expand social freedom through mutual dependence, cooperation, and shared social experimentation with new forms of mutual recognition and participatory democracy. His thinking is in keeping with his career-long avoidance of totalizing theories.

Honneth is still advancing his philosophy. He has responded to constructive critiques of his philosophy from a number of philosophers including Judith Butler (who we will meet in Chapter 20). In his most recent book, *Recognition: A Chapter in the History of European Ideas* (2020), he gives a historical grounding for how recognition theory can apply to political philosophy. He now admits that mutual recognition relations extend beyond social and legal institutions into the personal habits of social life. He now sees that conflicts over how recognition norms are interpreted and put into practice occur not only within social institutions but also among people in various social circles. He admits that he has opened the door to a discussion of the full implications of interpersonal recognition relations, but he has yet to walk through it, leaving that, perhaps, to a fourth generation of critical theorists.

Christine Korsgaard—Self-Constitution

Christine Korsgaard (1952–) is an American philosopher who works in ethical theory but who has also offered a view of the individual human in society that is important to social philosophy. In her book, *Self-Constitution: Agency, Identity, and Integrity* (2009), she states that we are all guided by different practical identities. In a previous book she had defined a practical identity as "a description under which you value yourself, a description under which you find your life to be worth living and your actions to be worth undertaking" (*Sources of Normativity* 101). In life, we develop multiple practical identities that orient our reflections on values and our own commitments to others. We engage in rational thinking about social norms but we also consider the subjective elements of our personal lives.

Korsgaard understands individuals as being the authors of and responsible for their actions. Korsgaard's view is that

it is as the possessor of personal or practical identity that you are the author of your actions, and responsible for them. And yet at the same time it is in choosing your actions that you create that identity. What this means is that you constitute yourself as the author of your actions in the very act of choosing them. (*Self-Constitution* 375)

She acknowledges that this may sound paradoxical but says that "the picture here is not of a craftsman who is, mysteriously, his own product. The picture here is of the self-constitutive process that is the essence of life" (*Self-Constitution* 703). Life, Korsgaard says, does not create itself but in its biological processes is continually maintaining itself through its actions.

For human beings, this means that, in addition to the animal activity of continually making ourselves through processes like taking in nutrition, we also must continually maintain our social practical identities. Our self-constitution is not a state that we achieve and then act from; like breathing, it is continual motion, not a static condition. There is no *you* prior to your choices and actions because your practical identities are constituted by your choices and actions in response to your environment. We also are capable of considering whether to do one thing or another, yet to say we are capable is the wrong emphasis. Like Kierkegaard, Korsgaard acknowledges that we are *compelled* to respond to our world—

it is our plight—and we use our human rationality to respond. It is the plight of being human that we must continually choose and act and make ourselves the authors of our actions by the way that we act.

Each one of us possesses a set of practical, socialized identities under which we, as individuals, value ourselves and find our actions worth undertaking. One's practical identities are composed of one's roles and relationships, membership in social groups, associations with causes, professions and positions held, and so on. We value our roles and relationships; therefore, our conceptions of our practical identities within those roles and relationships govern our choice of actions. This is the case because to value ourselves in a certain role is at the same time to find it worthwhile to undertake certain actions for the sake of fulfilling that role.

An individual, as possessor of practical identities, is the author of his or her actions, and in choosing those actions, creates his or her identity by drawing on the normative resources in society. Our deliberate practical choosing and acting is what makes us human. Korsgaard is not suggesting that humans make up their practical identities out of whole cloth or on their own. Our practical identities are contingent on experiences and the environment from which we learn and acquire them. Some practical identities we are born into environmentally, and others we adopt, but our practical identities are made by our active experiences of them. If you continue to endorse the reasons the identity presents to you, and observe the obligations it imposes on you, then it is you.

Korsgaard's view of self-constitution means that individuals are not entirely formed by social forces but contribute to who they are and how they act. This insight goes beyond simply accepting the reality of human free will. The idea of self-constitution shows why our practical identities within our various social roles and relationships are such a vital concern to us. We are occupied not merely with instrumental concerns of physical survival and comfort nor only with social recognition and acceptance—we are also deeply concerned with our identity, with who we are. That question of who I am splits into a multitude of subquestions of who I am within particular roles and relationships. Being human means being constantly engaged in making who we are, which affects how we perceive situations and other people and, thus, how we act. The implications for social and political philosophy are obvious.

Chapter 16

ANALYTIC PHILOSOPHY

Despite its inherent difficulties and weaknesses, as discussed in Chapter 13, analytic philosophy has been the dominant approach to philosophy in the United States for decades. Its appeal lies in the ease with which it can connect with logic and mathematics and to a lesser degree with the "hard" sciences. Logic and mathematics have always held out the promise of certain knowledge, and there is a strong allure to a method that can break down problems into small discrete chunks.

Analytic philosophy was founded by Bertrand Russell. He described his philosophy as "logical atomism," which had a metaphysical meaning and was his method for doing philosophy. Russell's metaphysical view was that the universe consists of many independently existing things exhibiting qualities and standing in relations with each other. Although few subscribe to a strict logical atomism today, analytic philosophy has the basic metaphysical assumption that the world is composed of logical entities and that the correct use of logical language can tell us about the world. In its essence, analytic philosophy is the faith in logical analysis to solve all problems. It focuses on logical problems and says that anything that is worth discussing is worth discussing in terms of getting at the underlying logic of the problem.

Analytic Philosophy of Language

Perhaps analytic philosophy's greatest contribution has been in establishing the importance of the consideration of language. It's surprising how little attention was paid to language in philosophy before the 1900s. One exception was the German philosopher **Johann Gottfried von Herder** (1744–1803), who was perhaps the first to insist that language shapes the framework by which a linguistic culture thinks. Most influential to subsequent philosophy of language has been Herder's further idea that thinking and language are synchronistic. The source of all language is thinking and all thinking is thinking in language. Thus, words reflect the experiences and interests of a human culture, and the particulars of words and their uses define and shape that culture.

Charles Sanders Peirce, **Gottlob Frege**, and **Ferdinand de Saussure** independently but around the same time put forward theories about the connections between words and their objects. They shared the same idea that a word (a "signifier") has a meaning (the "signified"), although Frege used the terms "sense" and "reference," respectively. The study of signs—semiology or semiotics—looks at how language shapes society and human behavior. Saussure said that signs are arbitrary. For example, the signifier "dog" has no actual connection to the particular animal that it signifies in the English language. In other words, the word that is used is a matter of social convention. Take the signifier "Gift." It means a present in English but a poison in German. Differences are crucial.

Structuralism

The study of semiotics gave rise to the philosophical field of structuralism, which was led by French anthropologist **Claude Lévi-Strauss** (1908–2009). Beginning in the 1950s, he applied the semiology of Saussure to anthropology and the structure of language, and he believed that human culture is a system of symbolic communication. From that viewpoint, he reasoned that the structure of language is the prototype of familial and social relations. All human cultures, he claimed, share the same structure, which is a set of rules that are communicated by mythology—"myth" refers to all stories underpinning a culture and does not imply that they are false stories. The linguistic structures of the myths express the basic unconscious structures of the mind, which are universal to all human beings. Lévi-Strauss claimed that structure is dominant. The structures of the mind determine how people live and make sense of the world—that is, through language. Culture is a signifying system. It *is* language. For Lévi-Strauss and other structuralists, this idea means two things. One is that in trying to understand anything about humanity, we need to analyze the system of signs that structure society. The other is that humans do not create language. Instead, language structures humans at social and individual levels. We do not use language to describe and create reality. Instead, language constitutes reality for us. The structure fixes the system of culture, all human culture being fundamentally the same, and the structure positions all individuals within the system of culture. Consequently, structuralism denies free will.

Some analytic philosophers reject structuralism because it assumes a metaphysical basis of the structure, which cannot be verified. Others have adopted the basic idea that human thought and society are governed by essential structures. French literary critic and theorist **Roland Barthes** (pronounced BART, 1915–1980) agreed with Lévi-Strauss on the importance of understanding how myth structures human society, but he emphasized myth as a narrative. He was much more open than Lévi-Strauss was about different cultures interpreting the narrative of myth in different ways. He also was willing to use structural analysis to critique the myths of bourgeois society. French psychoanalyst **Jacques Lacan** (1901–1981) applied structuralism to the field of psychoanalysis that had been invented by Sigmund Freud. Lacan argued that the structure of language also determined the structure of the human unconscious. Lacan's structuralist psychoanalysis interpreted Freud's concepts in terms of the all-encompassing hegemony of language. He developed an elaborate and hopelessly complex symbology mapping how the unconscious and conscious parts of the mind are structured, determining human behavior.

Ordinary Language Philosophy

Ludwig Wittgenstein's philosophy has spawned its admirers; detractors; and, more than all else, people struggling to understand what it all means. His ideas are deceptively straightforward; we get what he seems to mean, but then when we consider the deeper implications of his ideas, we see we are only just beginning a journey toward understanding language. One important offshoot of Wittgenstein's later philosophy is "ordinary language philosophy."

Ordinary language philosophy is so called because it operates from the idea that philosophy should look at how language is used in everyday life. It shares concepts with Wittgenstein's language-games and forms of life, but it has its roots in the philosophy of Englishman **Gilbert Ryle** (1900–1976), who, in 1949, independent of Wittgenstein, published *The Concept of Mind*, which had many ideas similar to Wittgenstein's in *Philosophical Investigations*. Ryle laid out a map of human thinking as consisting of categories to which concepts belong. Within a category, there are concepts and associated words that logically fit together, and it is the language category that gives words meaning. His famous example is a visitor being shown around a university campus. After the full tour, the visitor asks, "I have seen all the classroom buildings, research centers, and dormitories, but when are you going to show me the university?" This, Ryle called a "category mistake." The visitor has placed the concept "university" in the wrong category, thinking it is an entity separate from the buildings, people, and activities. In ordinary language usage, the university is the way in which all of its parts come together to form an organized whole.

Ryle uses his concept of a category mistake to attack Descartes's division of the human into two substances, mind and body. Descartes assumed that the mental and the physical were different substances, but Ryle counters instead that the words "mind" and "body" belong to different categories. Ryle argues that when we encounter a noun, we assume that the word refers to a distinct thing. Descartes assumed the noun "mind" referred to a substance.

Ryle's provocative idea is that "mind" is a misleading concept, similar to the university example. Mind is not separate from the acts of learning, remembering, imagining, knowing, or willing. "Mind" is a term we use to describe the abilities and dispositions that explain a person's public actions. Thus, he argues, Descartes was wrong to assume there are mental acts separate from physical acts. In *The Concept of Mind*, Ryle derides that idea as "the dogma of the ghost in the machine." It is a category mistake, according to Ryle, to talk about mental acts causing physical acts. For example, "I will to raise my arm" and "I raise my arm" are not separate concepts. For Ryle, they are correctly seen as one and the same act. All issues of intelligence, he claimed, are not clues to the inner workings of minds; they *are* those workings. He is not claiming that there are no mental processes (though a few later analytic philosophers have), only that there are no hidden chambers from which these processes are directed. Ryle's work is categorized as ordinary language philosophy because of his efforts to get us to clarify our use of words to describe the world. However, his philosophy is more influential in the field of philosophy of mind (discussed later in this chapter).

Englishman **John L. Austin** (1911–1960) was another major proponent of ordinary language philosophy. In his most important book, *How to Do Things with Words* (1962), he takes the position that philosophy can contribute to an understanding of our language and concepts. Austin proposed that we classify uses of language similar to the way in which science classifies species of organisms. Instead of Wittgenstein's claim that philosophy can only clarify language, Austin's position is that the analysis of ordinary language is the first step in improving our knowledge.

Similar to the pragmatists and Wittgenstein, Austin views words as tools. That being the case, he says, we should know what we mean and what we do not mean when we use language tools. Austin also sides with Wittgenstein's position that the meanings of words lie in their use. As Austin frames it, we have a common stock of words that embodies meanings and distinctions that people have found worth making and have found to be successful. Because our words have stood the test of time, he says that we should be looking at how those words are used rather than trying to create a better language ourselves. This idea is a rejection of the agenda of the logical positivists, which Wittgenstein had also rejected. Instead, Austin says an analysis of ordinary language will give us an understanding of human experience. There is, he says, no exact definition of any particular word—only a family of other words related to it, a concept similar to Wittgenstein's family resemblances.

Austin develops the idea of "speech acts," his version of Wittgenstein's language-games. Remember that Wittgenstein's German word *"Spiel"* includes the idea of action, and that is the sense that Austin wants to express in his term, "speech acts." He identifies three components in speech acts. The locutionary act is the act of saying or writing words, the illocutionary act is what the person is doing by speaking or writing (informing, ordering, warning, and so on), and the perlocutionary act is the response of the listener or reader that the speaker or writer hopes to elicit. For example, in my speech act of writing this sentence to you, my locutionary act is these actual words, my illocutionary act is to inform you, and my perlocutionary act is for you to learn something. Another way to think of it is to ask what is said, why the speaker is saying it, and what the speaker hopes will happen as a result.

We can, Austin says, learn a great deal about human behavior by examining speech acts in this way. As you can quickly imagine, there are many, many possibilities for what lies behind any speech act. Is the speaker reporting a fact, expressing an opinion, trying to inform me, trying to distract me? Analysis of speech acts quickly becomes very complicated and subject to differing interpretations and debate. Still, interest in what Austin proposes is high in analytic philosophy.

Analytic Political Philosophy

A nonstructuralist but still analytic approach to human society can be found in two diametrically opposed traditions—liberalism and analytic Marxism. In the context of analytic philosophy, "liberalism" does not mean liberal politics as most people think of it now and certainly does not mean what continental philosophers think of as liberal. Liberal continental political philosophers focus on the ideas of greater distribution of civil liberties, fair application of the rule of law, and freedom from oppression. Liberal analytic political philosophers focus on the ideas of laissez-faire government, meaning minimal regulatory intervention and oversight of business and low or even no taxation. The different approaches include different definitions of what liberty and equality mean.

Liberalism

Again, "liberalism" is not liberal or progressive politics but political theory based on the rational ideal of liberty or freedom and may or may not include the idea of human rights. American **John Rawls** (1921–2002) is a highly influential analytic political philosopher. In his classic book, *A Theory of Justice* (1971), Rawls tries to answer the question of what justice is (a question as old as Plato). Rawls's answer is that justice is fairness. He believed that the common view that freedom and equality are in conflict is an illusion. His answer was that freedom and equality can be integrated into a unity when we see that justice is a matter of fairness. He demonstrated his answer through a thought experiment similar to Hobbes's and Locke's thought experiments about the state of nature.

Rawls's thought experiment is to imagine all of us in what he called the "original position." Like Hobbes and Locke, Rawls asks us to imagine a world without social institutions and ranking of social status. Unlike Locke, Rawls offers a hypothetical scenario that is grounded in logic, not the natural world. He asks us to imagine that, prior to the creation of the world, we are deliberating on how we want society to be structured politically and economically. Society doesn't exist in this scenario, so anything is possible. What kind of society would we agree to want to live in? The catch is that we are in an original position, before reality. We are behind what Rawls called the "veil of ignorance"; we do not know, once society is created, what gender, race, age, intelligence, wealth, skills, education, religion, and so on we will have in this society. All we would know, Rawls says, is an internal sense of justice and the knowledge that in the society we create we would be able to pursue our conception of the good life. So now what kind of society would we agree to want to live in?

The idea behind this thought experiment is that if we are not guaranteed any kind of social status in this to-be-created society, we logically would not choose any political and economic structure that would deny justice and the pursuit of the good life to anyone. Rawls says it would be irrational for us to propose a society in which certain people are denied justice because, behind the veil of ignorance, we would not know if we would end up being one of those people denied justice. In other words, it would be illogical for anyone to agree to a society that discriminates against women or Black people if there was a chance you would be a woman or Black person in that society. We would instead choose a society that guarantees equal justice for everyone. That is the only logical choice for us, Rawls says.

Rawls's purpose in giving us this thought experiment is to clarify our thinking and get us to the correct standpoint in thinking about justice. The thought experiment of the original position removes all presuppositions and focuses our attention on what is truly just. He thinks that we would agree to general principles of equal freedoms for all, including freedoms of conscience, association, expression, and democratic rights, and that we can establish a just society. We would agree that the ideal society would have adequate structures to ensure basic rights and freedoms for all. We would never agree to a society in which one gender, race, age, or any other property that a person could possess would entitle that person to more rights than people without that property would have. A just society, for Rawls, would be one that is based solely on a rational implementation of the good without regard to hierarchical divisions.

Rawls's theory has been much discussed, and he has both defenders and critics. Not surprisingly, much of the division is along the lines of the analytic/continental divide. Rawls called his thought experiment an engagement in "ideal theory," meaning that it allows us to reason from idealized assumptions about rational norms to discover the best possible social structure. Ideal theory, by design, does not attempt to address real-world problems but seeks instead to establish rational general principles, an approach similar to Plato's and Hobbes's. Rawls's ideal theory of a just society is for this reason best categorized as analytic philosophy.

Philosophers such as the Indian British **Amartya Sen** (1933–) and the Jamaican American **Charles W. Mills** (1951–2021) have criticized ideal theory as too idealized. Directly addressing Rawls, Sen published a book,

The Idea of Justice (2009), arguing that a thought experiment about justice should not be like Rawls's transcendental and institutional approach but instead should be a comparative approach that is focused on people's capabilities concerning what they are and can realize in their real-world society. Mills similarly argues that ideal theory is overly idealized and is, in fact, an ideological denial of the real-world realities of racism and sexism, among other forms of oppression. Sen and Mills both agree with Rawls that equality and justice are important norms. Mills thinks that Rawls provides us with some good ways to think about these norms, but he thinks Rawls's theory is utterly unfit to deal with racial justice.

An analytic response to Rawls, and a highly political one, came from American **Robert Nozick** (1938–2002). In his book, *Anarchy, State, and Utopia* (1974), Nozick applied his own version of ideal theory but had sharp disagreements with Rawls. He agreed with the norm of justice but not equality. Nozick objected to Rawls's idea that justice should consider the well-being of those who are worse off, Rawls having argued that lifting up those who are worse off benefits everyone in society. Nozick counters that those who are well-off have no obligation to assist others for the sake of bettering society. Nozick based his argument on the idea of inviolable natural rights for individuals, an idea that can be traced back to the time of Locke. From this idea, Nozick states that an individual can do whatever he or she wants as long as he or she respects the rights of others. But what "respect" means for Nozick is the respect for the right to "positive freedom"—to do whatever they want. He makes the extraordinary claim that any behavior is allowed as long as compensation is paid for any damage caused to others. Critics have pointed out that such a view favors those with greater financial resources.

Nozick offers a modified version of Locke's social contract in which people agree to the convenience of a state, but the only role for the state in Nozick's vision of utopia is to defend the rights of individuals. Nozick also adopts a strict version of Locke's labor theory of property; Nozick claims that acquisition of property creates an inviolable right of the individual to do whatever he or she wants with that property. He offers no means to correct abuses of property acquisition, only a suggestion that such abuses are wrong but wouldn't happen in an ideal society.

Nozick arrives at a tamer version of Hobbes's state of nature, but Nozick's is made less nasty and brutish by a minarchist state—a government with only minimal powers to enforce the law. A state is preferable to anarchy (the absence of all government and normative order) in that it can protect individuals' rights, mainly property and financial rights. Throughout his philosophy, Nozick favors the assumption that those who are well-off acquired their property justly and are thus justified in their wealth. Nozick thus rejects all ideas of social welfare, equates taxation with theft, and even frowns on nongovernmental efforts to promote greater social equality.

Nozick's book has been cemented into the foundation of the political ideology of libertarianism, an extremist view that there should be no government at all. Libertarianism has a social component and an economic component. In social theory, libertarianism states that individuals should have complete freedom to do whatever they want as long as they are not aggressive or coercive toward others. This view is similar to the views of John Stuart Mill, who was a nonanalytic liberal. Most libertarians reject the idea of positive human rights ("I have a right to . . . "), believing instead in negative rights ("no one has the right to coerce me"). In economic theory, libertarianism rejects governmental regulation of business. One branch of this theory, anarcho-capitalism, states that corporations should be allowed to create their own private enforcement agencies to defend their property rights. Nozick had said that the minarchist state was preferable to anarchy, but libertarianism generally prefers anarchy to the state.

Many analytic political philosophers, including libertarians, accept the view of economic liberalism—the theory that economic activity is governed by laws similar to the way in which the motion of bodies is governed by physical laws of motion. That view has its roots in Adam Smith, a friend of David Hume and the "father of capitalism." Recent versions of economic liberalism include the idea that human society, especially government, should not interfere with the natural processes of financial transactions. A milder form of libertarianism is known as "neoliberalism" or "corporatism," which sees the role for government as protecting the interests of business corporations with only minimal oversight and regulation, but not the complete absence of government.

Analytic Marxism

Similar to liberalism in its analytic approach but leading to very different conclusions is analytic Marxism. Karl Marx could be considered an analytic philosopher if you look at his theory of economic determinism as an exercise of logical analysis. Certainly, that was the view of French Marxist **Louis Althusser** (1918–1990). He divided Marx's philosophy into two time periods—the earlier humanist Marx who wrote about human alienation and the later scientific Marx who wrote about the logical structures of capital. Althusser dismissed Marx's early writings as consisting of bourgeois delusions and instead insisted on a structuralist interpretation of Marx. He saw capitalist society in terms of a totality, with the structure of the social totality dominating all social life. However, he rejected being associated with the structuralists because he didn't agree that signs determine the structure. He thought that the complex social totality formulates all social practice, including a person's characteristics, desires, intentions, and choices. Althusser thought Marx's economic determinism was just one level of the totality, and Althusser placed greater importance on the role of ideology as forming people into concrete subjects filling concrete roles within the totality. He saw the structure of ideology as unchanging throughout history, or, as he said, ideology has no history, and history is a process without a subject. For Althusser, there is no individual to feel alienated from life; there is only the totalizing theory of the ideological structure.

Another enthusiastic analytic Marxist, but highly critical of Althusser's structuralist reductionism, was Canadian philosopher **Gerald Allan Cohen** (1941–2009). In his book, *Karl Marx's Theory of History: A Defence* (1978), Cohen updated Marx's theory to include subsequent technological advancements but otherwise gave a version of economic determinism faithful to Marx's original theory. A key addition by Cohen is the idea of rational choice theory—an analytic theory in economics that states that people make rational cost-benefit calculations to determine what option is best for them. Cohen's application of this theory to Marxism is to explain the changes in economic epochs, with new modes of production being adopted when it is rational for people to do so. Human history is thus explained as a series of rational steps to increase economic productivity.

In reaction to Rawls's ideal theory, a number of analytic Marxists have taken on the challenge of what justice is. They see the challenge as developing a concept of justice liberated from bourgeois ideology. Cohen argued that a theory of justice must be built from the idea that all people are fundamentally equal in worth and moral status, a position not far off from Rawls's. Cohen restates the Marxist idea of the unjust exploitation of workers. Instead of Marx's contention that the capitalist steals the workers' labor, Cohen says it is the system that denies workers their autonomy. This exploitation will be overcome when there is a society in which no class is able to control the means of production and workers not only own the products of their labor but also have sovereignty over their own person. Cohen stresses that his concept of self-ownership is egalitarian, distinguishing it from Nozick's notion that an individual's right to himself or herself extends to a right to acquire and control external resources.

Analytic Epistemology

The most opaque area of analytic philosophy (save for formal logic itself, which we will prudently leave to courses devoted to advanced logic) is epistemology. We have seen, so far, a great deal of epistemology based on sense perception. Analytic epistemology is based on logical analysis of propositions.

 The analytic take on epistemology largely rests on the three-page paper, "Is Justified True Belief Knowledge?" (1963), by American **Edmund Gettier** (1927–2021). Perhaps no paper in the history of philosophy has caused more discussion and uproar than Gettier's simple little paper. It has spawned a cottage industry in creating examples that prove Gettier's point. They have come to be known as "Gettier problems."

Gettier takes on the ancient idea, going back to Plato, that we can define knowledge as justified true belief. In short, if you believe something, have a good justification for holding that belief, and that belief is in fact true, then you can be said to have knowledge of that truth. The point is that it's not knowledge if your belief just happens to be true; you need to have a good, justified reason for believing it. This idea was so well accepted as common sense that few philosophers ever discussed the topic, which is why we haven't addressed it in this book up to now. What Gettier pointed out is that one can believe something; that one can have very, very good justification for that belief; and that the belief is true, however, that one being correct in all this could be a matter of epistemic luck, so it cannot count as knowledge.

A simpler version (dozens have been offered over the years) of Gettier's convoluted original examples was given by **Alvin Goldman** (1938–). It is a classic example of a Gettier problem that justified true belief is not knowledge. Henry is driving through Barn County and sees numerous structures that look like barns. Unknown to Henry is that Barn County is littered with barn facades—structures that aren't barns but from the road look exactly like barns. Henry therefore has a justified belief that he is seeing barns, but it is a false belief. When he next looks at one particular structure, he is looking at the one real barn in Barn County. In this instance, Goldman says, Henry's belief is justified and true, but it is a result of luck, so it cannot count as knowledge ("Discrimination and Perceptual Knowledge"). Other examples of Gettier problems include a farmer who believes there is a sheep in the field because he sees what looks like a sheep, but he does not know that what he sees is a dog disguised as a sheep; the actual sheep is hidden behind the dog. So the famer's belief that there's a sheep in the field is correct but cannot count as knowledge. Other Gettier problems offered are even more fanciful.

Analytic philosophers have offered many solutions to the quandary Gettier created. Some add additional conditions to the argument; others substitute "adequate evidence" for "justified"; and some others add causal conditions, defeasibility (canceling) conditions, and so on. You may have noticed that some subterfuge is involved in the barn and sheep examples. Henry and the farmer believe for incorrect reasons because they were deceived. This is true for Gettier's original examples in which the believer holds a belief because of deliberate deception or ignorance caused by bad luck. This has led some to propose the "no false premises" solution, which, exactly as the name suggests, says that a belief can count as knowledge if its justification does not rely on false premises. This does clear up Gettier's original examples, the barns and sheep examples, and most if not all other Gettier problems.

However, the no false premises solution requires the believer to check for the possibilities of deception and even self-deception. This is the simple solution offered by the pragmatists long before Gettier—in particular Peirce, who said that what is true is determined by the opinion that is ultimately agreed to by all who investigate. As you have probably thought, Henry can get out of the car and look more closely at the barn facades, and the farmer needs simply to walk into the field to see the dog is disguised as a sheep. William James would say that all of this arguing about the Gettier problems is an exercise in pedantry; there is no absolute truth or knowledge, so what is true, and by extension what is justified knowledge, is tangible experience that works for us.

The no false premises solution requires us to accept that we have fewer justified beliefs than we think we have. Pragmatism says that's what we have to live with, so we do our best to be sensible and verify our beliefs and carry on. These conclusions are not acceptable to most analytic epistemologists. They carry on with ever more detailed and elaborate logical analysis of propositions. Ignoring Wittgenstein, they have returned to the logical positivist dream of a logically perfect language. This effort was led by Polish American logician **Alfred Tarski** (1901–1983) who proposed the "correspondence theory of truth," which says that statement "p" is true if and only if p, where p is the proposition expressed by "p." A real-world analogy is as follows: "snow is white" is true if and only if snow is white. However, Tarski stresses that any ordinary language examples are not illustrations of his theory of truth because his theory works only in logical language. In many ways, Tarski's program is a revival of Russell's program of reducing language to logic.

American **Donald Davidson** (1917–2003) was sympathetic to Tarski's correspondence theory of truth but argued that no account of truth can be given. Truth, he maintained, is a central concept that cannot be reduced to other notions; it can be applied only to sentences understood within a particular language. Words can be true and meaningful only within a holistic understanding of the structure of language. Thus, Davidson advocated for a holistic conception of truth and meaning that has been interpreted by some as a connection between analytic and continental philosophy. His ideas also are compatible with pragmatism's views of truth and meaning.

If you took a course in advanced epistemology at a U.S. university today, you would probably spend most of the course hearing in great detail about Gettier and Tarski. Trust me, I know this firsthand. The analytic epistemology course *may* mention analytic philosopher **Willard Van Orman Quine** (1908–2000), who in his paper, "Two Dogmas of Empiricism" (1953), demonstrated that all analytic statements are actually synthetic statements (see Chapter 8) that appeal to the way in which people normally define terms in social discourse, people including analytic logicians. The classic example of an analytic statement, "all unmarried men are bachelors," is actually a synthetic statement because it is defined by the meaning of the terms as people use them, as Wittgenstein had concluded. Logical notation of "if p then q" doesn't escape this problem because the meanings of those terms—"p" and "q"— are as people use them, even if logicians are the only ones using them. Quine also conclusively showed that the entire analytic project was based on reductionism, the belief that particular statements can be verified or falsified in isolation from other statements. This dogma is false, Quine says, because no statement, even ones of formal logic, can be verified outside of a broader belief system and all of its assumptions about the world. As **William of Ockham** said, logic cannot tell us about the world. Quine says that all of our knowledge, from observations to laws of logic, is part of a human-made fabric of beliefs that impinges on experience only along the edges. He adopts the approach of pragmatism that the efficacy of a belief, not logic, is what makes the belief true. He also adopts the continental approach that terms are defined by the broader social environment. Quine essentially guts the entire analytic project. And yet it continues because some people choose to believe in it for their own reasons.

Analytic Philosophy of Mind

Philosophizing about the nature and workings of the human mind has been around since **Augustine** (see Chapter 3), but the development of computer technology, particularly artificial intelligence research, has raised new questions and suggested new methods and directions within the philosophy of mind. A relatively new field has emerged called "cognitive science," which reduces the human mind to a biological computer and uses artificial intelligence, analytic philosophy, psychology, neuroscience, and linguistics to build a deterministic model of human mental functioning. The computational model of the mind—the human mind as a computer—is the basis for cognitive science. Nevertheless, although computers are new, cognitive science's assumption of a deterministic mind equivalent to a programmed computer picks up the deterministic, man-is-a-machine visions of **Hobbes**; **Leibniz**; and, in particular, **Julien Offroy de La Mettrie** (1709–1751) in his 1747 work, *L'homme Machine (Man a Machine)*. Many cognitive scientists work in the field of artificial intelligence in the attempt to make computers duplicate the deterministic model of human intelligence.

Analytic philosophers of mind, such as Canadians **Patricia Churchland** (1943–)and **Paul Churchland** (1942–), adopt the computational model and believe that an adequate scientific understanding of the material brain will expose terms such as "mind," "self," "beliefs," "desires," and "intentions" as "folk psychology." They believe that all future talk about human cognition will be in terms of neurological brain states or functional statuses dependent on material brain structures. The Chruchlands' neurological approach is a strong movement within philosophy of mind, leading to either a denial of human consciousness or a reduction of consciousness to the firing of neurons in the brain.

The problem with cognitive neuroscience and related analytic philosophy of mind is the methodology of assuming the conclusion of biological determinism. As Husserl had pointed out, science, as a social activity, gives us an idealized and naively objectivized nature. The lifeworld of cognitive neuroscience assumes biological determinism and the computational model that the human is a machine, assumptions that structure the design of scientific experiments, and this bias of assumption leads to confirmation bias in the results. The assumption that an image on a monitor has captured a brain state and thus explains a person's conscious activity may be no more than the logical fallacy of conflating cause and effect.

One of the leading critics of the computational model of the mind and the possibility of artificial intelligence duplicating the human mind is American **John Searle** (1932–). His now famous 1980 "Chinese room" thought experiment ("Minds, Brains and Programs") goes like this: Imagine that you are in a room with a large and detailed rule book giving you directions in English on how to respond to Chinese phrases with appropriate Chinese replies. You have no knowledge of the Chinese language, but the manual contains formal rules for analyzing one set of Chinese symbols and constructing another set of Chinese symbols that a native Chinese speaker would recognize as an appropriate response. However, the manual does not explain what any of the symbols mean. While you are in the room, Chinese speakers slip paper messages written in Chinese under the door. These slips of paper contain various marks made up of straight and curved lines, none of which you understand. You look up the symbols in the rule book, and, following the instructions, you write out appropriate sets of symbols on new slips of paper and pass these messages back under the door. The Chinese speakers outside read the slips you gave them, and they read them as articulate Chinese responses.

You have fooled the people outside into believing that you are fluent in Chinese. However, you still don't understand any Chinese. Searle argues that something different clearly is going on when you copy the Chinese symbols from the rule book than would be the case if you were receiving and responding to messages in a language that you do understand. Searle claims that this formal manipulation of symbols is comparable to what goes on in a computer's artificial intelligence program. His point is that no matter how effective a computer program may be in simulating human conversation, it will never produce actual understanding or knowledge of language. A computer program can only simulate intelligence; it can't duplicate it. Searle claims that a computer program is nothing like a human mind and that artificial intelligence does not duplicate human cognitive states.

Searle adopts the idea of brain states, but he does not deny consciousness. He argued in his books, *Intentionality: An Essay in the Philosophy of Mind* (1983) and *The Rediscovery of the Mind* (1992), that we consciously have intentionality, in Husserl's sense, that our thoughts are directed toward objects in ways that cannot be explained by the computational model. He also rejects other analytic theories that deny consciousness, saying that consciousness is a subjective experience, even if it is the product of the physical processes of a biological brain. All conscious experiences are subjective intentional states guided by a cultural background that structures the brain.

Another critic of the attempt to explain away consciousness is Australian **David Chalmers** (1966–). In his highly influential book, *The Conscious Mind: In Search of a Fundamental Theory* (1996), he divides the neuroscience approach to human consciousness into the easy problems and the hard problem. Easy problems are problems on which neuroscience has made some progress, including the mind's ability to discriminate, categorize, and react to environmental stimuli; the integration of information; the ability of a cognitive system to access its own internal states; and so on. However, Chalmers says that even if all of these sorts of problems have been solved by the neuroscientist, there still remains the hard problem of consciousness.

The hard problem for neuroscience, as defined by Chalmers, is to explain the subjective experiences of awareness that characterize human consciousness. To be conscious means that one is a self with an inner life. Consciousness is the subjective quality of experience. When you view a tree, your eyes and brain are physically affected by the light reflecting off the tree. Obviously, though, there is more going on in your mind than what happens when a manufactured photoelectric cell is affected by the light reflecting off the tree. You have a subjective experience of the qualities of the tree, experiences the machine does not and cannot have. From this, Chalmers argues that all of the progress claimed by the brain sciences has been on the easy problems. They have not and, Chalmers claims, will not be able to solve the hard problem of explaining consciousness.

Chalmers is open to alternative theories, but his suspicion is that consciousness is a fundamental and irreducible feature in reality that operates according to its own set of laws. He points to how scientists in the 1800s had to introduce the new entity of the electromagnetic charge because the existing physics of the day could not explain certain observed phenomena. Similarly, Chalmers thinks that there is an explanatory gap in existing scientific models of our mental life. Eventually, we will need to introduce a new, nonreductive theory of consciousness. Or, perhaps, accept one of the nonreductive theories that have long existed.

Chapter 17

TEARING DOWN PHILOSOPHY— POSTMODERNISM

The word "modern" basically means "new," with the implication that a "modern" something is better than the old version. Different areas of human culture use the term "modern" to denote different eras, and the term is relative to that cultural area. For example, "modern art" and "modern philosophy" occur in different centuries. "Modern philosophy" is considered to have begun around 1600. Philosophers active from the time of Descartes to the time of Kant are often referred to as "early modern philosophers," and philosophers in the immediate post-Kant period as "modern philosophers."

In general, the concept of "modernity" is associated with the Enlightenment worldview. Loosely defined, that worldview is that there is one true picture of reality that humans can know through reason and science. We saw this worldview with Bacon and especially with Descartes's concept of the rational, knowing mind as the source and ultimate judge of all ideas. Modernity is the strong faith that rational thinkers, collectively, are continually discovering theories that are increasingly better at describing reality. From this faith in the triumph of reason, modernity has an optimistic view of human progress driven by human rationality. Analytic philosophy is an example of modernism.

"Postmodernist" is the name given to a loosely connected group of thinkers united in their opposition to modernity in all of its manifestations and its assumptions of the supremacy of reason and continual human progress. Now, this does not mean that these philosophers are opposed to progress or do not want to improve the human condition. What they oppose is what they see as modernity's simplistic categorization of reality and its empty faith in social and intellectual structures. Postmodern philosophers engage in a critique of modernist assumptions about truth, reality, and human knowledge. They are doing what philosophers should do—seeking the fundamental principles that lie beneath the surface of cultural conventions.

There is a bewildering array of postmodernist intellectuals and artists, and we will have to restrict our discussion to a few significant philosophers. Their postmodern tradition—though they would likely object to being called part of a tradition—is based on the observations and arguments of philosophers like **Nietzsche**, **Scheler**, **Heidegger**, and the later **Wittgenstein**. Those previous philosophers were inspired by the tradition that had long percolated within philosophy of unmasking the pretensions of rationalism and the illusions of dogmatic speculation.

Postmodernists forcefully believe that the modernist dream of discovering the central set of rational categories for understanding reality is dead. Nietzsche's metaphor that "God is dead" applies to the death of modernity. We now must face our uncharted lives with no universal essences to which we can appeal or certitudes on which we can base our lives. We are the products of history, as Hegel had said, but opposite of Hegel, postmodernists declare that history is a purposeless, nonrational interplay of shifting material and social forces. What we can do, perhaps the only thing that we can do, they say, is critically analyze or "deconstruct" the modernist dream of rationally knowable objective truth to expose how modernity's illusions arose and why they seemed so real. We cannot remain trapped within the false worldview of the Enlightenment.

Postmodernists call for philosophy, as it has traditionally been understood, to be torn down. That includes modern philosophy's conceptions of epistemology, metaphysics, logic, and science. Postmodernism obviously rejects the approach of analytic philosophy. The postmodernist thinkers, by and large, also reject Marx's grand theory as inadequate for understanding the complexities of human society. Postmodernism could be categorized as continental philosophy, with which it has significant cross-pollination, but it is probably more honest to consider postmodernism as detached from, if not opposed to, much of continental philosophy.

It may seem that postmodern philosophers are rejecting everything; however, it is more accurate to say that they are rejecting totalizing theories—that is, theories that offer a singular explanation for everything. That rejection of grand theories and narratives explaining reality does mean a rejection of most worldviews. This situation leaves the postmodernists with few to no fundamental values on which to base their ideas, but with the potential promise that by, so to speak, clearing the field of false metanarratives (narratives about narratives), we can begin to understand ourselves and our condition better.

The Precursors of Postmodernism

Kant's Copernican revolution (see Chapter 8) influenced almost all subsequent philosophy. His influence on postmodernism is not immediately evident, but his central revolution placing the active human mind at the center of experience initiated trains of philosophical thought that contributed to postmodernist thinking. Kant said that our experience of objects conforms to the structure of our mental faculties, meaning that we cannot know things in themselves but only perceive representations of those objects produced by our mind.

The German idealists had accepted the former but not the latter of Kant's concepts. They tried to show how we can change our approach to the world so that we can experience reality more fully. Inspired by German idealism, Romanticism emphasized the free expression of what we think and feel. Then the first existentialists, Kierkegaard and Nietzsche, defended the subjective experiences of the individual. We've seen how philosophers such as **Scheler**, **Stein**, **Jaspers**, **Dilthey**, and **Ortega y Gasset** further explored how individuals perceive and make choices within their social environments. Heidegger drew attention to the reality of humans being thrown into the world, a clearing of being within a forest of society. Circling back to Kierkegaard and Nietzsche, we see that they warned how each one of us faces the danger of being subsumed under modern society's pressures to conform to its abstract notions of how people should think and feel. Marx and the various philosophers he inspired also criticized how society and capitalist ideology harmed people. A common theme among these and other philosophers was the growing awareness that there is a gap between our perceptions and whatever reality there is and that what we call "truth" and "reality" are social constructions.

Postmodernist thinkers reacted to this mix of philosophical ideas and the events of mid-1900s, most significantly World War II and the acceleration of technology. Postmodern thought reflects the tension between the rising awareness of the importance of the individual and the social, political, and technological factors that suppressed individuality and caused other forms of human suffering. Whether or not you agree with postmodernism, you should be able to see how these thinkers are responding to the modern human condition. Some of their responses are so radical they are difficult to accept, but their ideas have significantly affected our society and our perceptions.

The Hazy Dawn of Postmodernism

We cannot reduce the breadth and complexities of postmodernism to a single source, but it's helpful to consider a significant spark—French artist **Claude Monet** (1840–1926) and his painting of boats in the morning haze, *Impression, Sunrise* (1872). Not that it occurred in isolation, of course. Nothing does. Here is some context to understand the social and philosophical significance of Monet's painting.

In the 1860s, the French art scene was dominated by the institution of the French Academy of Fine Arts. In particular, they controlled what artworks were exhibited at the Paris Salon, the largest and most influential juried art exhibition in France. The jury of the Academy tended to accept only paintings that displayed the stolid, traditional realist style of painting. That style included that the painter's brushstrokes were blended to invisibility so as to portray realistic portraiture and historical, religious, or mythological scenes.

Four painters—**Frédéric Bazille** (1841–1870), Claude Monet, **Pierre-Auguste Renoir** (1841–1919), and **Alfred Sisley** (1839–1899)—partially inspired by Romanticism, broke from the staid tradition defended by the Academy For inspiration, they gathered to paint in the open air rather than in a closed studio the better to capture the sunlight and the senses of nature and social life. Importantly, they wanted to capture the *feeling* of what they saw. They did not limit their artistic expression to lifelike realism. They also did not hide their brushstrokes. The artists inserted themselves and their personal feelings and styles into the paintings, and they weren't afraid to use bold colors and new techniques. The Academy rejected their submissions to the Paris Salon as too radical.

After this de facto censorship by the Academy, in 1873 Monet, Renoir, and Sisley, along with fellow painters **Paul Cézanne** (1839–1906), **Edgar Degas** (1834–1917), **Berthe Morisot** (1841–1895), and **Camille Pissarro** (1830–1903), formed the Cooperative and Anonymous Association of Painters, Sculptors, and Engravers and exhibited their artistic creations independently of the Académie. Their rogue exhibitions, held eight times over the next 12 years, were ridiculed by the cultural establishment, and the artists were even harassed by the authorities. One art critic disparaged Monet's painting as being only an "impression" and not a finished work of art. Owning the mockery, the embryonic movement embraced "impressionism" as the label for their movement, a movement that changed art forever.

Artists ever since have tried to recapture that aura of the rebel artist defying convention and snobbery. But that unique era, the same decade of the 1870s in which Nietzsche exploded into prominence, can never be replicated. The impressionist art movement had little immediate effect on philosophy, but it served as a backdrop for a general skepticism about cultural conventions, a skepticism that fully blossomed in the artistic and intellectual counterculture of the 1960s, as we will see in postmodern philosophy.

Michel Foucault—Disciplinary Society

French philosopher and historian **Michel Foucault** (pronounced me-SHELL foo-KOH, 1926–1984) is a central figure in postmodernism. His most influential books, all published in the 1960s, are *Madness and Civilization: A History of Insanity in the Age of Reason* (1961) *The Birth of the Clinic: An Archaeology of Medical Perception* (1963), *The Order of Things: An Archaeology of the Human Sciences* (1966), and *The Archaeology of Knowledge and the Discourse on Language* (1969).

Archaeology of Knowledge

An   He saw his postmodernist task as that of an archaeologist digging beneath the surface of our social-intellectual traditions to expose the strata—which he called "*épistémès*," the Greek word for "knowledges"—of historical eras that led to our current "knowledge." Each *épistémè* is the dominant conceptual framework of a given historical era, that era's definition of "truth"—"a system of ordered procedures for the production, regulation, distribution, circulation and operation of statements" ("Truth and Power"). Throughout history, each era's truth is the product of that particular historical era. Foucault insists that the modernist notion of one, universal truth belongs to the *épistémè* of an earlier era and is no longer workable for our postmodern era.

Foucault considered an *épistémè* to consist of structured linguistic or discursive patterns. Foucault was interested in are those patterns that society had awarded the status of truth—patterns that were used to control that society. His archaeological approach looks at the normative discourses of medicine, psychiatry, law, and morality to expose the dominant discursive patterns—rules of language use—and the practices of an era—rules that go beyond grammar and reason. Discursive patterns define what is permissible and impermissible for people to say, what questions are meaningful, and how human behaviors are to be described. These patterns define social reality and indicate how the world should be divided into categories such as true/false, moral/immoral, rational/irrational, mad/sane, and normal/perverse.

Foucault applies this idea of discursive patterns to the meanings of words themselves. The meaning of a word is not the object to which it refers because words don't really refer to objects as much as they constitute them. Similar to Wittgenstein in his later philosophy, Foucault said that words receive their meaning from their role within the network of social discourse and practices. To understand the meaning of a word, you can't point to a certain object or action. Instead, you have to understand the complex network of words and practices of the *épistémès* in which the word occurs.

True to the emerging postmodernist tradition, Foucault says there is no universal, objective meaning of words. Their meaning is part of the world of social institutions and ideals within a historical era. Words don't literally create a tree, but we know a tree as the sort of thing that it is in terms of a network of social meanings. Similar to Derrida, Foucault asserts that there is no transcendent truth or meaning to words or statements, only the multitudinous relations that statements have with each other.

Reversing the modernist assumption that philosophers' ideas create society, Foucault claimed that the system of social structures (*épistémès*) determines our ideas. The Enlightenment *épistémè* created the Enlightenment intellectuals; the intellectuals did not create their age. Foucault says that the discursive practices of a society are governed by "rules of production." These rules were never consciously invented and are never explicitly stated but are part of an unconscious play of forces within each historical era. We can understand these rules, Foucault said, by "decoding" their patterns. Through this decoding, we can expose as an illusion the notion that human institutions and history exhibit rationality and continuity. Instead, he claimed, we see that history is an aimless sequence of ruptures, displacements, transformations, and gaps as socially created institutions and *épistémès* rise and fall without order or reason.

A Genealogy of Power

After the violent May 1968 general strike in France protesting against capitalism and imperialism, Foucault turned his attention to the role of power structures in society. His thinking shifted from placing discourse as primary in the constitution of social reality to seeing discourse as merely one product of the ever-expanding institutionalized social power structures. His focus also shifts from "archaeology" to "genealogy." Nietzsche used the word "genealogy" to describe how the will to power expressed itself in covert ways, and Foucault had a similar idea.

Foucault invents the term "power-knowledge" to indicate that power and knowledge directly imply one another. He claimed that there is no power relation without the correlative constitution of a field of knowledge, nor is there any knowledge that does not presuppose and constitute power relations. From this, Foucault concludes, similar to the way Marx does, that intellectual history is nothing more than a demonstration of the ways in which the conception of truth has been used by power structures to mask the knowledge and power that always operates just beneath the surface. Each society, and each *épistémè*, Foucault said, has its own regime of truth, its "general politics" of discourse that it accepts and makes function as truth.

Foucault's later political philosophy has inspired a number of philosophers. His emphasis on power structures seems to duplicate much of the structuralist program, but Foucault is correctly seen as a fierce critic of those structures, one who is unearthing how those structures are used to oppress people. He goes beyond descriptions of structure to an analysis of the power inherent in the structure. His analysis weighs very heavily on how social institutions and the prevailing *épistémè* use power to control and discipline people's minds and bodies. Similar to, if not inspired by, analytic Marxism's theory of power relations, Foucault's theory saw power as an all-encompassing set of social relations used by the ruling class to maintain inequality.

In his 1975 study, *Discipline and Punish: The Birth of the Prison*, he used the evolution of the architecture, policies, and practices of prisons in the 1800s to illustrate how the mechanisms of power and control evolved. Foucault referenced historical documents to show how the same "technologies of control" used in prison systems were mirrored in the organization of armies, schools, hospitals, and factories. Foucault showed how all of these institutions exercised new mechanisms of power and control under the guise of scientific, enlightened, humanitarian social reforms. Through its regimes of truth, society's power structures impose their historically relative truths on people, inventing labels such as "criminals," "students," "patients," and "workers" to divide them into categories such as moral/immoral, sane/mad, and normal/perverse. One of Foucault's examples of how power relations use these labels is from his own life as a homosexual person—all his life he was told he was immoral, mad, and perverse for being who he was.

Foucault translates his observations into a model of society as being entirely controlled by the power structure. His model is a paranoid vision of all norms, institutions, and practices existing to control and discipline people. The power structure observes, orders, and examines all of us and enacts punishment against deviant behavior. Within Foucault's model of the disciplinary society, every aspect of cultural expression is interpreted as an enactment of observation, ordering, examination, and discipline. And I do mean *every* aspect—school attendance records, medical records, and every other documentation of our lives is used, Foucault says, to label us as normal or abnormal, leading to discipline that controls our behavior. We are completely controlled by the power structure. Foucault's model of society has influenced many dystopian books, movies, and video games you may have seen.

Jacques Derrida—Deconstruction

Jacques Derrida (1930–2004) was born of Jewish ancestry in French-occupied Algeria. He originally studied phenomenology, and he came to prominence in 1967 by using Husserl's philosophy to critique structuralism. He coined the term "deconstruction" as the answer to the problems he saw in structuralism in three books all published in 1967: *Writing and Difference*, *Voice and Phenomenon*, and *Of Grammatology*. Derrida emphasized the thread of Husserl's thought that sought to understand phenomena by identifying the processes and events that led to them. Derrida's simple question was this: if there is an all-encompassing structure as structuralists supposed, what led to it? Any structure has to have a genesis, and that genesis had to have its own structure in order to be the genesis of something else. Change had to come from a complex structure, what Derrida called an "original complexity" capable of generating change. He saw as the central flaw of structuralism its assumption of a transcendental constant signifying system. In simpler words, within the structuralist approach, the answer to all questions about everything is "the structure." Structuralists didn't see this as a problem, but Derrida did.

Derrida's conclusion was that despite its positive contributions to understanding cultural myths, structuralism suffered from the same pretension of reason that had plagued the whole history of Western philosophy. Derrida called it the "metaphysics of presence." His concept is best understood as pointing to the idea that there is a central presence that is given or fixed and that anchors the rest of the structure. The center was whatever the philosopher or school of thought assumed was the foundation of certainty on which the rest of the philosophical inquiry or system was built. Examples include Plato's Forms, Aristotle's substance, Descartes's thinking self, Newton's material particles, and so on.

The center serves the useful function of orienting, balancing, and organizing the structure, but, Derrida claims, it mostly serves to anchor thought and language in a dualism of presence and absence of what the center signifies. The metaphysical presence sets up binary oppositions defined in terms of good/bad, right/wrong. These oppositions are used to repress and marginalize that which differs from the center or foundation that is considered good and right. People, especially women, people of color, the poor, and so on, are deemed bad and wrong. Derrida thus favors an abandonment of the reassuring foundation of the center and an affirmation of play or openness to unexplored possibilities and new approaches. This decentering he calls "deconstruction," a deliberate play on the pretensions of structuralism.

For Derrida, deconstruction means rejecting the myth of the center or foundation and exposing and dismantling any philosophical constructs that depend on foundationalism or binary oppositions. This deconstruction of philosophy, he hoped, would reveal that which has been repressed and marginalized. In turn, that means accepting that there is no certainty and no possibility of finding any. Derrida took this line of thought to a set of radical conclusions about texts. There are no meanings to the language we invent, he declared, and everything is interpretation He means this in terms of understanding texts, not ethical or scientific truths, asserting that there is nothing that is out of context. A text must be understood within its context, but because there are no transcendental meanings of language (no metaphysics of presence), language cannot refer to anything beyond itself. All words receive their meaning from distinctions within the language. This is not as weird as it may at first sound because if you look up the meaning of a word in a dictionary, you find that the word is defined by other words.

This being the case, Derrida says that there are no limits to the play of meanings and interpretations that a reader can bring to a text, which implies that the author is less important, an implication that Derrida accepts, even in his own books. He endorsed the thesis in Roland Barthes's essay, "The Death of the Author" (1967). Barthes rejected the traditional idea of incorporating the author's intentions when interpreting a text, an idea that assigned a single interpretation to the text—the author's. Bathes contended that the text's meaning actually lies with the reader. The creator and the creation must be considered separate, Barthes said, and Derrida agreed. Some interpret Derrida to be suggesting that we entirely disregard the author.

The problem for Derrida and all deconstructionists is that believing the assertions that there are no author, no rational subject, and no fixed meaning to anything leaves the believer with no basis or justification for a critique of philosophy and society at large. Derrida expresses concern for those subordinated by hierarchies, but if one wants to stand up for subaltern people who are repressed and marginalized by the "myth of presence," one must be able to appeal to some source of validity for the claims that repression is wrong and rectification of justice is good. Deconstruction offers the tools to tear down pretensions but not the tools to build up the good.

Jean Baudrillard—Signs and Simulacra

France was a hotbed of postmodernism from the 1960s through the 1980s, and one prominent postmodernist was **Jean Baudrillard** (pronounced bo-dree-AR, 1929–2007). He could be classified more as a social critic than as a philosopher, but despite writing more than 50 years ago, his social critique is eerily accurate to us today and has profound philosophical implications. Baudrillard based his philosophy on the life of signs and how technology affects people and society.

Signs

In three books, *The System of Objects* (1968), *The Consumer Society: Myths and Structures* (1970), and *For a Critique of the Political Economy of the Sign* (1972), Baudrillard combined the philosophy of semiology (signs) with the critique of everyday life offered by his PhD adviser, French sociologist **Henri Lefebvre** (pronounced le-FEV, 1901–1991). Lefebvre, a Marxist, argued that capitalism had colonized everyday life and had turned it into a zone of consumption, pushing people to believe that they needed to relieve the boredom of everydayness through purchasing products or experiences. Lefebvre had also shown how space is a complex social construction based on social values, and he considered capitalism to be the dominant social value that produces social space.

Baudrillard thought that Lefebvre's Marxist critique of life as everydayness had some merit but was insufficient and needed to be enhanced by a theory of signs—how words and symbols signify and represent meaning. Baudrillard accepted that signs are an integral part of society because they articulate social meanings and are organized into systems of meaning.

He argued that commodities should be characterized not strictly through their use and exchange value, as Marx had said, but by their "sign-value"—what those objects signify and represent. For example, the value of a luxury watch lies more in its sign-value as an expression of prestige, wealth, and style than in its "use-value" as a timekeeping device or its monetary exchange value. In everyday life, people purchase and display their commodities as much for their sign-value as for their use-value.

Baudrillard's insight is even more true now, decades later, as consumerism is increasingly dominated by the sign-values of brand loyalty and the need to be "on trend." Look around you to see how many people are wearing clothing emblazoned with a brand name, having paid for it many times the actual use-value of the clothing.

Baudrillard argued that identities and meanings are constructed by the appropriation of cultural signs—images, codes, and models—that determine how we view ourselves; how others view us; and, therefore, how we relate to each other. Baudrillard broke with the Marxist grand narrative that social class differentiated boundaries between people. That was true in modernity, but in the postmodern world, differentiation by class, gender, politics, economics, culture, and sexuality are imploding under the force of simulation. Baudrillard claimed that people have so much access to signs, which are exchanged so freely, that differences between groups collapse amid the dissolving social boundaries and structures on which society is built and on which social theory is focused. What he means is that groups that were divided by class, culture, and so on can now unite around signs—the signs now being their common connection.

Simulacra

Presaging developments in electronic media in the early 2000s are Baudrillard's notions of the "simulacra" and the "real." He laid out in his 1981 book, *Simulacra and Simulation*, that we are now ruled by simulation. Understand that he was not thinking about computer simulation but the social reproduction of signs. Baudrillard defines simulacra (singular, "simulacrum") as the truth that conceals that there is no truth; the simulacrum, the simulated image, is true. He sees as fundamental to the rupture between modernity and postmodernity the idea that modern societies are organized around commodities but that postmodern societies are organized around simulation and play.

Electronic media and digital technologies propel this transformation. They deliver users a constant stream of signs and references without any consequences to them. For example, the top-grossing film in 1980, the year Baudrillard was developing his theory of the simulacra, was *The Empire Strikes Back*. Millions watched the film, but none of it was real.

The on-screen death and destruction had no consequences for the viewers, yet the images and signs of the film excited people into a state of what Baudrillard called "hyperreality," in which entertainment provides experiences more intense and involving than the realities of everyday life.

We see how common it is for people to identify themselves by their fandoms of television shows or music artists. From amusement parks, to shopping malls, to television shows, to video games, to social media, to cosplay, the images, codes, and models of hyperreality are more real to people than real life is. Real life is a desert compared to the fantasylands offered by simulation.

The postmodern person is awash in simulacra. Human society has always had signs that mediated reality for us—that's what words have always been. Now, in the postmodern world, society has replaced reality with signs, and our human experience is a simulation composed of simulacra. "From now on," Baudrillard wrote, "signs are exchanged against each other rather than against the real" (*Symbolic Exchange and Death* 7). Our life now is a procession of simulacra—all of culture's images, codes, and models that construct our perceived reality—and our society is so saturated with simulacra that meaning is infinitely mutable to the point that meaning is now meaningless.

Pause to understand something important here. As I write this in 2022, people debate the effects of virtual reality, computer simulations, the so-called metaverse, and deepfake videos. These are *not* what Baudrillard was talking about 40 years ago. He's talking about the broader cultural forces of which these new simulation technologies are simply expressions. The technology of virtual reality is an extension of television and films, which immerse viewers in simulacra.

Television, even live television, at best shows us copies of reality. Watching television, we don't see the U.S. president giving a speech; we see an image of that person. That's not in itself problematic, but when the on-screen copy is unfaithful to the underlying reality, it obscures what's real. The image before us is what's real for us because the image is what we experience. If the image is fictional, maybe a television drama about a real U.S. president that has an actor pretending to be that person, it is a copy divergent from an original, even though it pretends to be a faithful copy.

Then there's the pure simulacrum—perhaps a television show about an entirely fictional president. In these images, signs reflect other signs without any claim to reality. The simulacra of the president are what is real and become more familiar and real to viewers than the actual president. Sounds far-fetched? Well, a 2015 opinion poll found that the fictional presidents of several television shows had a higher favorability rating than the actual U.S. president, Barack Obama (Rampton "Fictional TV presidents more popular than Obama: Reuters-Ipsos poll.").

Baudrillard's notion of the simulacra isn't just limited to the realm of entertainment. Their more pernicious appearances are in advertising and political propaganda. We are besieged by advertisements, and Baudrillard is dead on in describing them as simulacra that, at best, pretend to be real but more often present a completely manufactured set of signs that is connected only to other signs. Advertising sells a fake world, a hyperreality in which everything is better than in everyday life; all you have to do is purchase what the simulacra are selling, and you will be as happy as the simulacra people in the commercial.

Political propaganda similarly provides signs that are conjured up to seem to be connected with reality but are engineered to deceive. Today, some people talk about us living in a "posttruth" society, but back in the 1980s, Baudrillard observed that simulacra have always existed. What differs now, he claims, is that there is only the simulation, only copies of copies, and originality is a meaningless concept in our society. Just look at the music, television, and movie industries today, plus the social media world where people endlessly copy what they see others doing—copies of copies, endless simulacra.

On the one hand, it is almost eerie how Baudrillard's ideas seem much more true now than when he proposed them. In his 1988 book, *America*, Baudrillard describes the "ecstasy of communication," a state in which a person has close instantaneous access to a plethora of information and images. In this state of ecstasy, a person becomes a pure screen. The person is pure absorption, a surface on which is shown an overexposed, transparent world of simulacra. Baudrillard expressed these thoughts before the Internet, before smartphones, and before advanced video games.

On the other hand, it is easy to criticize two of Baudrillard's claims. The first is the idea that postmodernity would result in differentiation among groups imploding, which is partly I. He was correct that electronic media and digital technologies have brought about much easier sharing of cultural and intellectual ideas. Concepts of cultural identity and gender are more fluid than ever, but differentiation of categories of class and race are still sharply drawn. True, technology has changed the nature of society and communication, but has it changed human nature and tendencies?

Baudrillard's second questionable claim is that he seemed not to foresee how hyperreality could affect real life. In Ukraine, a television show about a fictional president was so popular that when the actor playing that president ran for election, he won, becoming President Volodymyr Zelenskyy. No one could say, though, that he is not a real president conducting real actions.

Jean-François Lyotard—Against Metanarratives

French philosopher and sociologist **Jean-François Lyotard** (pronounced leo-TAR, 1924–1998) was a fierce critic of universalizing theories and "metanarratives." In his book, *The Postmodern Condition: A Report on Knowledge* (1979), he proclaimed that we have outgrown our need for metanarratives or grand narratives. Metanarratives are grand totalizing theories and explanations about what reality is and why reality is the way it is. Hegel, Marx, and structuralists (and perhaps even Foucault) all offered metanarratives. Such ideas are also found more subtly in widespread assumptions like the idea that science will provide us with all knowledge. Lyotard claimed that people have lost faith in these grand narratives and are forced to find new, smaller narratives to address social issues. His idea is similar to Nietzsche's idea that "God is dead." The old stories are no longer believed, and society is now fractured as people search for knowledge and meaning.

Metanarratives and the Differend

Lyotard took the "post" in "postmodern" seriously. We are moving out of modernism. What we are moving into, Lyotard said, is the postmodern awareness that we are not all the same and that the grand narratives don't describe most of us. We have become aware of our differences and are beginning to accept the reality of human diversity. The shift from modernity to postmodernity is a shift from metanarratives to micronarratives. To explain micronarratives, Lyotard uses Wittgenstein's concept of language-games, although Lyotard prefers the term "phrase regimen" because "language-game" implies that one can opt out as a player, which is not possible. He uses phrase regimens to map society's diversity. Human society is not the monoculture that is portrayed by the grand narratives. Society is a multiplicity of communities, and each community has its own phrase regimen of the meanings and rules it has developed.

Modernity's grand narrative of human progress and increased liberty favors the wealthy and powerful but does not offer progress and emancipation to all communities. Those other communities have to develop their own understandings—their own phrase regimens. Language has traditionally been understood as words (signs) that refer to tangible things in reality (referents). Lyotard observes that in the postmodern age, we have come to realize that reality is not so cut-and-dried, and that instead, reality is a complex set of senses attached to referents through signs. The correct sense of a phrase cannot be a simple direct reference to reality because it is the phrase regimen and its complex set of senses that creates "reality." In other words, signs have meaning within a set of meanings that are created by the signs in an ever shifting set of social relations.

Lyotard does not see diversity as negative in itself, but he acknowledges one negative side effect of different communities having different phrase regimens. He calls it the "differend," a term he coined in his 1983 book, *The Differend: Phrases in Dispute*. He defines the differend as

> the unstable state and instant of language wherein something which must be able to be put into phrases cannot yet be. . . . The human beings who thought they could use language as an instrument of communication, learn through the feeling of pain which accompanies silence. (*The Differend* 13)

The plurality of phrase regimens among different communities is real, creating instances of differend.

The differend has clear political dimensions. One is when two communities that seem to be at a political impasse have different phrase regimens within which they have different interpretations of situations. Their "realities" are different, and the differend between their uses of language makes communication difficult.

Another differend occurs when the phrase regimen of the dominant power structure denies other communities the language to express the injustices they experience. These people from other communities think they can use language to communicate their experiences, but their expressions are not valued equally by the dominant mode of "reality," creating a differend. People who express their experiences of injustice are met with silence.

We can and should then understand that there are oppressive "realities" that define meanings within the dominant phrase regimen. A community in power can use the phrase regimen of a grand narrative to silence other communities. Colonialism is the perfect example, as are the many ways that the rich dictate meaning to the poor. In so doing, the community in power can silence discourse by using the ambiguity of meaning (remember that meanings are not absolute), thereby forcing its interpretation on others, denying diversity, and causing injustice.

It's possible for people in different communities and phrase regimens to find links between their diverse language rules and meanings, but this possibility requires the willingness of all sides to do so. It is our obligation in the postmodern age, Lyotard says, to deny the phrase regimens of oppressive "realities" and accept and honor the many ways that communities are and how they view and express themselves.

The Postmodern Computer Age

Lyotard was one of the first philosophers to consider the social implications of computer technology. The postmodern computer age has displaced the thinking individual in favor of the technological mechanism. Computers have transformed knowledge into information, a new phrase regimen in which new kinds of judges have emerged who can analyze computer data. Science's increasing reliance on computer and data technologies has shifted the emphasis from the goal of human knowledge to the means of acquiring data. Knowledge is now externalized from the knower; data are now a form of exchange value.

> Knowledge in the form of an informational commodity indispensable to productive power is already, and will continue to be, a major—perhaps the major—stake in the worldwide competition for power. (*Postmodern Condition* 5)

Knowledge is power, as Francis Bacon had said, but not quite in the way he had in mind.

Science, which had been the centerpiece of modernity, now contributes to postmodernity's loss of narrative. Science had long been compartmentalized, as Francis Bacon had foreseen, and the separate phrase regimens of scientific disciplines developed independently. Each scientific and technological field is using its own phrase regimen and cannot legitimize anything outside of its narrow discipline. Science cannot even legitimize itself. Lyotard claims that science believes, without substantiation, that empirical evidence cannot lead to multiple contradictory proofs. Science's tendency to exclude other domains of knowledge has cut itself off, leaving it unconnected to broader society and without philosophical grounding.

Science is not the only genre of discourse that suffers a problem of legitimacy. Any genre of discourse cannot appeal to metanarratives from outside itself for validation because any genre of discourse can be validated only through the internal consistency of its phrases. Genres of discourse (science, politics, sports, and so on) have internal rules for linking together mixed phrases, Lyotard says, rules that are proper for attaining certain goals within the genre. We communicate through phrases, linking them using the rules of a phrase regimen, and the phrases are understood in the context of other phrases. In other words, as Wittgenstein had discussed, statements (phrases) are validated by how they are used within the context of language-games (regimens).

Knowledge is no longer narrative, Lyotard says, because society is a plurality of phrase regimens. We have to move between different phrase regimens and combinations of data in our daily lives, and this movement hinders the individual's ability to form a coherent identity.

The Creative Event

In *The Inhuman: Reflections on Time* (1991), Lyotard focuses on how postmodern capitalism is harming the individual. Computerized, technocratic capitalism has reduced the human to modes of efficiency in the name of development—a dehumanizing inhumanism. Lyotard would see this trend toward inhumanism strengthening further in the 2020s digital corporatism, in which computers are constantly collecting data on humans and commoditizing personal information. Our existence is devalued, and our humanity is threatened.

But Lyotard's version of postmodernism is neither nihilistic nor defeatist. His postmodernism is not an era that follows modernity but exists within the modern. In the midst of the dehumanizing inhumanism of contemporary society is the "creative event," which can bring us beyond the oppressive "realities" of metanarratives. Creative events are the artistic, literary, and philosophical inventiveness of individuals. A youthful child, Lyotard says, is open to possibilities for the future, ever present in possibilities that the youth cannot yet speak. There are events to come that cannot be preprogrammed, and the way we can resist dominant modes of "reality" is to be prepared to receive what thought is not yet prepared to think.

In avant-garde thinking and expression, we can resist the social, economic, and technological forces that devalue our existence. Lyotard speaks of the painter, the musician, and the thinker who asks the question, "is it happening?" This cryptic question precedes creative events in the face of the fear and misery that "nothing might happen." That feeling of combined fear and pleasure is, for Lyotard, at the heart of all creation, and creation is the act, the event, that gets us beyond inhumanism. If you can't entirely make sense of what Lyotard means, don't feel bad. With the artistic creative event, he is referring to something mystical, beyond the descriptions of phrase regimens, but in this mystical happening is redemption.

Lyotard does not restrict artistic redemption to a select few as had Adorno. It is open to anyone who can stand against being assimilated and reduced by dominant narratives and who instead creates new phrases and phrase regimens. The creative event is not reducible to a definition, and this is the meaning of postmodern art, Lyotard says. For him, the postmodern condition bears witness to the fact that those who claim the "reality" of metanarratives are merely trying to assert one phrase regimen over all others.

Chapter 18

RETHINKING PHILOSOPHY— FEMINIST PHILOSOPHY

Because society has historically silenced women's voices, the history of philosophy is dominated by male voices. Too many philosophy textbooks either entirely leave out women who are philosophers or they tack on a brief mention of them almost as an afterthought. Previously in this book, I included several influential women who were philosophers, Mary Wollstonecraft (see Chapter 6), Madame de Staël (see Chapter 9), Jane Addams (see Chapter 12), Edith Stein (see Chapter 14), and Hannah Arendt (see Chapter 15). Because this book is ordered chronologically, it is appropriate to bring up feminist philosophy at this point, not as an afterthought, but because society has taken this long before philosophy began to take seriously the issue of the rights of women and society's systemic sexism.

I would like to state at this point that this chapter is in no way a comprehensive exploration of feminist philosophy. It is only an introduction. Feminism is an approach to the world and everything within it. Therefore, feminism has been applied to all aspects of philosophy and to an analysis of most past philosophers. Everything up to now that this book has discussed has also been analyzed using the feminist philosophical approach.

Feminist philosophy could be said to be part of postmodernism in that it also seeks to tear down the modernist view that there is one superior form of universal, objective knowledge. What feminism adds to, when it does not diverge from, postmodernism is a focus on the role of beliefs about gender in shaping the historical patterns of thought and society. It is very wrong to consider feminism a hatred of men. Feminism is an acknowledgment of the ways in which our male-dominated social traditions have historically excluded women, and it is an attempt to decode and change those traditions. Feminist philosophy calls for women to be given full intellectual and political participation in society. Advocates seek to open up social institutions, correct traditional distortions about gender roles, and modify intellectual disciplines to bring about the emancipation of women from patriarchy—the system of male domination.

There are multiple ways to describe feminism because it is not a monolithic entity; it is as diverse as society itself. Feminism is essentially a philosophical movement because it is a quest to understand the nature of society, the nature of people, and how traditional assumptions about men and women have affected society. Most feminist philosophers are women, but, as we shall see, there are male philosophers who understand

and agree with the feminist critique of society. However, all feminist philosophy shares two main themes—positively affirming that women are full human beings and negatively critiquing the social attitudes and structures that denigrate women. The history of feminist philosophy can be described as three waves of thinking and social activism. Connecting ideas and activism is an integral part of feminist philosophy.

The First Wave—Human Rights

Most women's voices were censored, and even those who managed to publish their philosophical arguments found their writings relegated to obscurity, an unfairness that persists to this day. Two women whose arguments for women's equality survive are **Marie de Gournay** (1565–1645), who wrote, "On the Equality of Men and Women" (1622), and **Mary Astell** (1666–1731), who wrote, *A Serious Proposal to the Ladies for the Advancement of Their True and Greatest Interest* (1694). But it's not that no men agreed that women are equals; Catholic priest **François Poulain de la Barre** (1648–1723) wrote, *On the Equality of the Two Sexes* in 1673. Their arguments were sadly mostly ignored.

Englishwoman **Mary Wollstonecraft** was an early feminist who decried the exclusion of women from full freedom and social equality in her book, *A Vindication of the Rights of Woman* (1792). At about the same time in France, **Olympe de Gouges** (1748—1793) wrote *The Rights of Woman* (1791), her direct response to *The Declaration of the Rights of Man and of the Citizen*, the foundational document of the French Revolution.

Gouges pointed out that the supposedly universal *Declaration* did not include women. She also stridently argued that the revolution and the Enlightenment was contradictory in extolling the natural rights of the citizen while at the same time insisting that there are natural differences between the sexes that justify denying those natural rights to women.

Nowhere was this contradiction more evident, Gouges said, than in marriage, which she described as a perpetual tyranny of institutionalized inequality. That men hold all the power and property within a legal marriage creates weakness and social deficiency in women, violating her natural rights as a human being. Drawing on Jean-Jacques Rousseau's concept of a social contract, though removing his belief in the inferiority of women, Gouges proposes that marriage be a contract between equal rights-bearing partners. A marriage contract between equal persons agreeing to share all legal rights and responsibilities within the marriage creates the condition for both partners to flourish.

In 1792, Gouges published *The Philosopher Prince*, a utopian novel in which she explores the benefits of changing the definition of "universal rights" from pertaining to men to pertaining to all human beings, including women. In the world of the novel, the principle of the marriage contract between equals is extended to all aspects of social life, including government. Women are educated the same as men are to prepare them for full participation in public life. Gouges seeks to demonstrate that other than the obvious biological differences that women can become pregnant, give birth, and nurse newborns, there are no natural differences between men and women. What differences there are should in no way preclude women from full participation in society and government.

Gouges's writings were not widely read in her time, but enough to raise the ire of the French revolutionary state, which executed her in 1793 for her political writings, in particular, her insistent demand that women be given full free speech rights in the new republic. Nevertheless, Gouges wrote on themes that became common subjects for later first-wave feminist philosophers.

First-wave feminism focused on arguing that women should have human rights equal to those of men. The first wave is exemplified by American **Margaret Fuller** (1810–1850), a member of the Transcendental Club (see Chapter 11). Her book, *Woman in the Nineteenth Century* (1845), directed the philosophy of transcendentalism to the question of the place of women in society. People were burdened with selfish desires, Fuller said, but are now on the verge of an awakening to a new era when men and women will be equals. She argued that people in the United States were not achieving equality because they had inherited the depravity of Europe, as evidenced by its horrific treatment of the indigenous people of the Americas and Blacks, who were still enslaved when Fuller wrote her book. She criticized the hypocrisy of people who claimed to believe in divine love but did not practice it. She finds this hypocrisy in slavery and in marriage, although she doesn't equate marriage with slavery. She does condemn the legal reality of her time that women were considered equal to children but not to men.

Similar to Wollstonecraft, Fuller called for women to receive the same intellectual and religious freedom as men. The highest marriage, she said, is a union of equals on a pilgrimage toward a common shrine. Fuller suggests that an "old maid" (the colloquial term in her time for an unmarried woman), because she was free from the restrictions of marriage, would have the best opportunity for close communion with the divine. Fuller also discussed the subject of gender, saying that the souls of men and women are the same but that individuals vary in their levels of masculine and feminine energies. There is, she said, no wholly masculine man and no purely feminine woman.

John Stuart Mill, in *The Subjection of Women* (1869), made arguments similar to Wollstonecraft's and Fuller's that women of sufficient intellect and abilities should be given equal place with men in education, opportunities, and intellectual and political leadership. He and his wife, Harriet Taylor, campaigned for legal reforms that would guarantee equal rights for women.

These three philosophers—Wollstonecraft, Fuller, and Mill—are part of what has been called "equity" or "first-wave" feminism. Fuller especially touched on some of the primary issues for which first-wave feminists fought—the right to vote (women's suffrage), the right to employment, the right to inherit, and the right to divorce. In the last part of the 1800s and the early 1900s, many brave women in many countries struggled for recognition of their human rights. This era of activism, by both philosophers and nonphilosophers, won a number of key reforms. Women could vote in most countries by the 1920s, but they still were denied equal opportunities in many areas of society and still were seen as second-class citizens.

The Second Wave—Liberation

In the 1960s, the second wave of feminists claimed that the fundamental structures, assumptions, and discourse of human society reflect male domination. The second wave was fundamentally different from the first wave in its motivations and scope. It was also separated by several generations and major social and political changes. The first and second waves existed in quite different social realities. It's arguable whether the second wave continues today or that it ended in the 1980s as some claim, replaced by a third wave; indeed, feminists still argue over that question. Another way to look at feminism since the 1960s is the difference between "mainstream feminism" and "radical feminism," which have, as the names denote, a difference in philosophical approach and positions. In some respects, the second wave can be seen as more mainstream and the third wave as more radical, although some feminist philosophers would not fit into that characterization. I'll stick with a chronological order of second- and third-wave feminism.

Simone de Beauvoir—The Second Sex

The second wave was informed by two important books. The first was **Simone de Beauvoir's** (1908–1986) book, *The Second Sex* (1949), which became one of the foundational texts for feminist philosophy. Her title evokes the central issue of all waves of feminism—that human society has always treated women as an "other" secondary to men. The first volume of the two-volume The Second Sex is a brilliant, detailed history of the subordination of women in all aspects of society. Beauvoir sets forth the theory that women's second-class status can be explained largely by motherhood. Being pregnant, giving birth, and nursing the baby left a woman "riveted to her body" and made it possible for men, who are free from "reproductive slavery," to dominate her. Social institutions, science, and writers—from philosophers to poets—have contributed to myths about women being an "everlasting disappointment." Beauvoir gives numerous examples of how revered men in history have perpetuated the great collective myths about women as unclean, inferior, and insignificant beings.

Like Wollstonecraft, Beauvoir said that in those few circumstances when women are not denied opportunity, they prove that the insignificance to which men have historically relegated women is unfounded. The reason women are considered inferior is not because of any inferiority within women but because men have forced that judgment on them. One is not born a woman, de Beauvoir declared, but is made a woman by society. (We will see an identical claim made about society making one Black in Chapter 19.)

Beauvoir is the first to make the distinction between sex, which is biological, and gender, which is a social construction. She observes that society oppresses women from birth, through childhood, adolescence, and into adulthood, forcing the social construction of gender onto them. She especially decries marriage as an absurd and perverted social institution that oppresses both men and women. She says that women historically got the worse end of marriage. Because women were historically denied legal rights, marriages imposed on women a servitude that almost always destroyed them, denying them their sexual and life desires, and turning them into passive instruments.

She also has a negative view of traditional motherhood, describing it as endless sadomasochistic living through one's children that forces a woman to give up her identity and self. She suggests instead communal child-rearing. In like manner, Beauvoir analyzes many aspects of women's lives, from how society expects women to dress to how society expects women to behave. The common denominator is that society continually places women in situations in which they can be nothing more than useful servants to men and children. She says that only a very few women in history have achieved any real independence but that these women have had little significant effect on challenging the human condition. She concludes by calling for women to be free to take their own chances in life, and she is hopeful for a future when women and men are equals.

Taking on the same issues of motherhood, Italian-born **Silvia Federici** (1942–) provides a Marxist feminism. She argues that because capitalism needs a constant supply of capital to perpetuate itself, it extends this need to the expropriation of women's unpaid labor. She sees the labor that women perform in child-rearing and keeping house as a condition for a capitalist economy that also depends on the exploitation of wage labor. Feminists have frequently debated how to think about housework, tasks overwhelmingly performed by women. Feminists have widespread agreement that women should not be restricted to a life of housework with no other options, but they have not arrived at a consensus on how exploitative of women housework is. Other feminists have used Marxism or neo-Marxism to explain the subordination of women in economic terms—as the exploitation of women's labor.

Betty Friedan—The Feminine Mystique

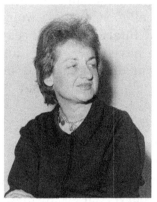

The second influential book was American **Betty Friedan's** *The Feminine Mystique* (1963). Friedan (1921–2006) consciously set out to craft a new form of feminism. Women in the first wave had won women the right to own property and to vote, and they had destroyed the old image of what a woman is. Still, according to Friedan, they were not able to "paint the new image of what woman might become." The obstacle to that new image, Friedan claimed, was the powerful force of society's distorted view of women.

Friedan continued the critique made by Wollstonecraft and de Beauvoir that women were treated as second-class humans and denied the opportunities and rights that are allowed to men. Friedan updated the feminist critique to the post–World War II period and took a more psychological perspective on how women were personally faring in that society. Women were being denied their basic human need to grow, Friedan said.

> The core of the problem for women is a problem of identity—a stunting or evasion of growth that is perpetuated by the feminine mystique. (*The Feminine Mystique* 77)

That mystique. she claimed, is the twofold assumption that truly feminine women had no desire for an advanced education, a career, or a political voice because women are predisposed to find personal fulfillment in marriage, child-rearing, and keeping house.

Friedan argued that the mystique had strengthened after World War II, when men had returned from war, and women, who had capably filled many traditionally male occupations, were expected to return home and return to being more "feminine." This expectation was strengthened by the cultural propaganda of the Cold War that portrayed the idealized American nuclear family as a bulwark against the Soviets. American media and popular culture fortified the feminine mystique, but when Friedan interviewed women, she found that women felt pressured to live up to the mystique, which was leaving them unhappy, unfulfilled, and even neurotic, all of which was affecting families and the broader society.

Friedan called the symptoms these women were suffering the "problem that has no name."

To overcome the feminine mystique, Friedan called for a revolution of social attitudes deeper than winning legal equality, although political and legal reforms were absolutely necessary. She didn't engage with political remedies for the feminine mystique, opting instead to encourage women to believe they could have a successful career along with a family. Women could be both wife and mother if they found genuine fulfillment in doing so, but they could, at the same time, act in ways to form a personal identity beyond wife and mother. She urged women to find the work, cause, or purpose that evoked creativity in their lives. That encouragement spoke to many women who wanted more for their lives than what society dictated as a woman's place.

Political Activism

In the United States, women who had been active in the 1960s in the civil rights movement and the protests against the Vietnam War saw that a struggle for recognition was needed for women. The political successes of the civil rights movement for Black people encouraged second-wave feminists to push for political action on women's issues. In 1966, the National Organization for Women (NOW) was established, with Friedan as its first president. NOW's founding manifesto called for women to have "full participation in the mainstream of American society" and "develop their fullest human potential" (The National Organization for Women's 1966 Statement of Purpose). Friedan and NOW quickly became a significant force in U.S. politics.

Feminist activism brought about several legislative victories for women's equality in the 1970s, including greater equality in the workplace, equal education funding in schools (Title IX), equal access to credit and financial services (such as women being able to have their own bank accounts and credit cards), no-fault divorce that made it easier for women to leave an exploitative or abusive husband, and the outlawing of marital rape. However, their efforts to pass the Equal Rights Amendment failed, leaving the unfathomable reality that in the United States, the equal rights of women are not constitutionally guaranteed. The 1973 Roe v. Wade Supreme Court ruling striking down laws against abortion was not a result of legislative action but fit in with the growing awareness of women's equality and rights.

Second-wave feminism also produced changes in the broader society. In 1970, San Diego State University was the first to offer women's studies courses, which remain an important part of higher education to this day. In 1972, **Gloria Steinem** (1934–) led a group of women in founding Ms. magazine, devoted to women's liberation, which was an immediate success. Institutions that had traditionally excluded women, from golf clubs and business associations to the U.S. military, now integrated women into their membership. Women were increasingly visible in mass media, in television in particular. In 1966, That Girl, played by **Marlo Thomas** (1937–), was the first TV show centered on a woman who was not married or living with her parents. It wasn't until 1976 that the first woman was named a national TV news anchor, but **Barbara Walters** (1929–) still had to share the role with a man.

Women working as philosophers became more common in the 1970s as barriers to women earning advanced degrees eroded and women's interest in philosophy increased. In her book, *Sexual Politics* (1970), **Kate Millet** (1934–2017) analyzed how the portrayal of sex in art and literature is infused with politics and dominated by patriarchy. She looked at fiction and nonfiction writing and showed how they propagate patriarchal myths that subjugate women. Uncovering and deconstructing the underlying patriarchy in texts became, and still is, a major thread in feminist philosophy. A feminist critique of science began with a 1978 special issue of *Signs: Journal of Women in Culture and Society*. Thirteen papers in the issue critiqued the gender bias in science that had for centuries prevented women from being leading scientists. Women had been allowed to work only as assistants to men who did the "real" science. In the second wave of feminism, the focus in science was on the lack of equal opportunity for women within it. As we shall see, the feminist critique of science later developed into a critique of the way science was conducted.

One thread in second-wave feminism was to use the then-current faith in technology to solve all human problems. Emblematic of this was Canadian **Shulamith Firestone** (1945–2012), who wrote *The Dialectic of Sex: The Case for Feminist Revolution* (1970). Firestone claimed that gender equality could not be achieved until women's identity is separated from their biological traits. Firestone drew on Marx's philosophy of class struggle to develop the idea that biological sex was a class in itself. Firestone argued that the distinctions between the male class sex and the female class sex were caused by the traditional division of labor and roles in childbirth and child-rearing. The biological division of labor in reproduction is the root cause not only of male–female inequality but also of economic class exploitation, racism, imperialism, and even men's reckless exploitation of the environment. She acknowledged there were real biological differences between men and women, but she said these should not be a basis for discrimination of one class of sex over the other. Firestone said the goal of feminist revolution must be not just the elimination of male privilege but, through technological advances, the elimination of the sex distinction itself. The centerpiece of Firestone's vision of a future utopian society was replacing what she called the barbarity of pregnancy and natural childbirth with artificial means of gestation and birth.

Mary Daly's Feminist Theology

American **Mary Daly** (1928–2010) offered a more radical version of feminism in the 1970s. She said that feminism's issue shouldn't be the push for equality with men but the abolition of patriarchy. Almost all societies in history have been male dominated. Men hold political and economic power and therefore enjoy social privilege and first access to natural and social resources. Patriarchal society subordinates women under men. Daly's mission was to overcome patriarchal oppression through an analysis of language and ethics. Daly's method was not like the analytic philosophy of language methods we saw in Chapters 13 and 16. She looked at how words are used, especially how words are used to assert patriarchal power and disempower women.

Her first two books, *The Church and the Second Sex* (1968) and *Beyond God the Father: Toward a Philosophy of Women's Liberation* (1973), dealt with the use of patriarchal language in religion. Daly applied the approach of existential theologian **Paul Tillich** (1886–1965) who had been influenced by Kierkegaard and Heidegger. Tillich had written about replacing theology's abstract and impersonal language with the language of the personal encounter with the divine. Tillich's personalism allows us to move away from the language of God as the invincible tyrant that characterizes both the "theological theism" of traditional religion and the atheist revolt against it and empowers us to reclaim religious language and signs for ourselves.

Daly expanded Tillich's personalism to replace theology's patriarchal language, observing that the impersonal language of traditional religion expressed the impersonal hierarchy of male domination. She set out a way to rehabilitate "God-talk" in religion and spirituality for the women's liberation movement, creating a woman-centered theological anthropology. Her approach has inspired others, women and men, pro-religion and anti-religion, to take on a deconstruction of patriarchal language in religion and make it more gender-neutral or woman-centric.

Daly then turned her approach to the wider society in her book, *Gyn/Ecology: The Metaethics of Radical Feminism* (1978). Her central premise is that men have always sought to oppress and use women. Patriarchal language and behavior are far larger than religion, and all of society can and should be rehabilitated. Religion didn't create patriarchy; patriarchy is itself a religion. Daly was not anti-religion—she maintained an affinity for Christianity—she was only against organized religion because, like all social institutions, it was structured on the basis of patriarchal interests. In her highly influential Gyn/Ecology, Daly showed how women had historically been portrayed as emotional creatures subversive to rationality, objectivity, and morality. Women's contributions were thus dismissed and women oppressed as unhelpful, if not dangerous and evil.

Daly called for women to embrace the traits that patriarchy ascribed to them—emotionality, nurturing, and so on—and reclaim them as good moral traits rather than as harmful and wicked traits. She called for women to embrace their femininity, not as men defined it, but as women find in their own female energy—an energy that includes the ability to create and nurture life. This female energy lay dormant, suppressed by patriarchy, and needed to be revived. She associated male energy with death-dealing and even evil and female energy with birth and goodness.

Daly's philosophy articulated two crucial questions that have since become major topics within feminist philosophy. One is the question of whether men and women have essentially different natures, which we'll discuss in the next section. The other is whether we should try to reform the current system and win equality for women or acknowledge that the system is too corrupt so that the answer is to smash the system of patriarchy. Daly thought that reforming patriarchy was impossible and that women needed to separate wholly from men in order to express themselves freely and bond with each other. Only clear of oppressive male energy can female energy thrive.

Contributing to the revolutionary camp was Australian **Germaine Greer** (1939–) and her book, *The Female Eunuch* (1970), in which she analyzed how patriarchy has shaped women's views of themselves. As her title suggests, Greer argues that women's sexuality has been lost, a result of the limitations imposed on them by society. Women need to come to know and accept their own bodies and liberate themselves. Men hate women, Greer contended, and women need to realize this. Change can come only through radical revolution.

The Third Wave—Intersectional Feminism

Some have characterized the third wave of feminism that began in the early 1990s as a more radical version than the second wave. There is some validity to that, but radical versions of feminism had already been around for a long time. The birth of third-wave feminism was openly declared in a *Ms.* magazine article, "Becoming the Third Wave," (1992) by **Rebecca Walker** (1969–), daughter of novelist Alice Walker (1944–). Only 22 years old, Rebecca Walker was responding to the confirmation to the U.S. Supreme Court of Clarence Thomas. A predominantly male group of senators voted in favor of Thomas despite the testimony of Professor **Anita Hill** (1956–), who gave credible testimony that Thomas had sexually harassed her. Walker pointed to Hill's testimony being disregarded as an example of the oppression of the female voice. Her call for a new wave of feminism was a call to integrate equality and female empowerment into the very fiber of life. Women needed to search for personal clarity and join together in sisterhood to understand power structures with the intention of challenging them; Walker defined this as the third wave.

Third-wave feminists address multiple issues, but we can focus on three. First is the issue of complacency over past feminist gains, second is intersectionality—the idea that feminists also need to include considerations of race and class—and third is the need to expand feminism to confront more issues. We will look at each in turn.

Complacency and Backlash

By the late 1990s, anyone under the age of 30 had lived his or her whole life in the presence of feminist social and political gains. Feminism had retreated into the background as just part of the landscape. Women were in Congress, women were TV and movie stars, and women were topping the pop music charts. Many felt that gender equality had been achieved. Young women, who benefited from the advances won by the second-wave feminists but had no awareness of the prior reality, couldn't relate to that older generation of feminists.

The emergence in the mid-1990s of a strongly reactionary strain of right-wing politics in the United States stoked a backlash against feminism, both politically and culturally. Radio personality Rush Limbaugh (1951–2021), mouthpiece of the political movement, invented the myth of the "feminazi," dismissing all feminists as un-American man haters who wanted female supremacy. As had happened so often in history, women who spoke out were being vilified.

Women, too, were starting to waver about feminism. Friedan's idea that women can have a career outside of the home was now being accused of pressuring women into believing they needed to "have it all"—career, marriage, and motherhood. Helped along by the propaganda that feminism had gone too far, some women were turning against the word and concept of feminism.

Aware of the problem, some third-wave feminists turned to personal narratives as a form of feminist theory. The first and second waves had focused on specific legal issues—the right to vote and the end of workplace, educational, and financial discrimination. Those legal rights were under threat from the right wing, but in an age dominated by mass media consumer culture, third-wave feminists needed new ways to raise the consciousness of younger women. That meant shifting feminism from a focus on mass political agendas to a focus on the experiences of individual women and from universal definitions of "woman" to personalist definitions of what it means to be a woman. In *Manifesta: Young Women, Feminism, and the Future* (2000), Jennifer Baumgardner (1970–) and Amy Richards (1970–) wrote about not doing feminism in the same way that the second wave had done; instead, women needed to find their own way for their own generation. That sentiment fit nicely with the growing awareness of intersectionality.

Intersectionality—Audre Lorde and bell hooks

Fundamentally, intersectionality is philosophical and sociological analysis informed by the social reality that real human beings cannot be categorized in just one way. Every individual fits into multiple categories of social definitions of race, gender, class, age, and so on. Every individual thus has multiple identities, not simply a race identity or a gender identity.

Intersectionality was born out of the feminist struggle for recognition and the realization that it was not the only struggle to overcome injustice. **Kimberlé Williams Crenshaw** (1959–) introduced the term "intersectionality" in her paper, "Demarginalizing the Intersection of Race and Sex: A Black Feminist Critique of Antidiscrimination Doctrine, Feminist Theory, and Antiracist Politics" (1989), although Crenshaw says the idea of intersectionality is as old as Black feminist experience. One way to look at intersectionality is to see that society marginalizes and excludes multiple groups of people and that, though those groups have tangible differences, they all share the common experience of being marginalized. Uniting around common ground and common cause to emancipate all marginalized groups, while not forcing those groups to minimize their differences, is the basic idea of intersectionality.

Perhaps no one epitomizes intersectionality better than American **Audre Lorde** (1934–1992). She described herself as "Black, lesbian, mother, warrior, poet." She is best known for her poetry, but she also wrote several interesting works of philosophy. Her book, *Sister Outsider: Essays and Speeches* (1984), lays out Lorde's intersectional strategy. Different groups of people need to come together in common cause, emphasizing their shared lived experiences. She focuses most on the need for white women and Black women to find common ground. They need to face their differences directly and use that diversity as a source of strength rather than as an excuse for alienation. The patriarchal divide and conquer, she wrote, must become define and empower.

Lorde's overarching philosophy of intersectionality is best expressed in her essay, "Age, Race, Class, and Sex: Women Redefining Difference," within *Sister Outsider*. There, she speaks from the perspective of being a Black lesbian from a poor family experiencing social structures of dominance. Lorde's ability to think of herself beyond single components—Black, lesbian, woman—and as a whole person empowered her to see the qualities of each aspect of herself. She then turned this self-awareness to people in general and society at large to see how people are conditioned to respond to difference with fear and loathing. They are further conditioned to ignore difference, reassert dominance, or destroy what they are told is subordinate.

From this, Lorde concluded that people need to recognize all forms of oppression, not just one. The structure of all forms of oppression is composed of similar beliefs in the inherent superiority of one group over another and the right and privilege of dominance of one over the other. Racism, sexism, ageism, heterosexism, elitism, classism—these forms of dominance all share the same belief structure of dominance and oppression. Women in the feminist movement, Lorde wrote, felt pressure from patriarchy to conform to their oneness as women and thus didn't recognize their "manyness"—the different aspects of their identities. That behavior, she claimed, explains the feminist movement's inability to form the alliances needed to create a better world.

She underscored the need for people to educate themselves about oppression. It is not up to the marginalized groups to educate the oppressors, as though the marginalized are still servants of the oppressors. When people do educate themselves, they will see that a major tool used by the masters is to keep the oppressed busy dealing with the master's interests. That pattern must be broken, Lorde said, because real change will never come from working with the racist, patriarchal system, because any changes brought about within the system will be diverted and not last.

Lorde stresses the importance of speaking. "Your silence will not protect you," she famously wrote. People understandably are afraid to speak the truth because of potential retaliation, but silence will never protect the marginalized from being oppressed. Silence will choke us anyway, she wrote. Lorde calls for the transformation of silence into language and for all marginalized people to speak up and take action despite the danger of others' reactions.

Another important intersectional feminist is Gloria Jean Watkins (1952–2021), who chose to write under the name "**bell hooks**" after her maternal great-grandmother. As a Black woman, she experienced the effects of both racism and sexism, which she wrote about in her book, *Ain't I a Woman? Black Women and Feminism* (1981). The book is a historical view arguing that Black women have suffered the lowest status and living conditions of any group. She claims that white female abolitionists and suffragettes were more comfortable with Black male abolitionists than they were with Black women. hooks says that white reformers were concerned with white morality and ignored the effects on Black people. She also says that Black nationalism, led by men, was a patriarchal movement. Even feminism itself is a mostly white middle-class movement that does not speak up for the needs of women who are not white and those who are poor.

hooks advocates for a broad social movement that challenges sexism, racism, and classism, overcoming them all to create loving communities. Her version of feminism is more inclusive but still is radical in its fight against oppression. In her book, *Feminist Theory: From Margin to Center* (1984), she points out that women's equality with men is not enough because it doesn't address economic inequality. She calls for women to acknowledge their differences as they build a sisterhood. Feminism should not be led by only bourgeois white women. The feminist movement should also include men, she says, because for real restructuring of the power structure to occur, men must do their part. In all relations, she calls for camaraderie rather than separation so that there is no need for hierarchy or oppression.

hooks's vision for a restructured feminist movement shifts the focus from victimization to mutual understanding and appreciation among all who wish to control their own destinies uncontrolled by patriarchal, capitalist tyrants. That movement requires what she calls "transgressive education," meaning that educators teach students to transgress the racial, sexual, and class boundaries that oppress people. Teachers need to stop using control and power, confining students to an assembly-line approach to learning. Instead, educators should offer students the space to be inventive and make spontaneous shifts. Through acts of transgression, people can achieve freedom.

Expanding Feminist Issues

Beyond opening up to a new generation and being more inclusive of class and race, third-wave feminism also opened up to new issues, many of which reflected more personal issues for women. Anita Hill's testimony had brought into the public eye the concept of sexual harassment in the United States. Women began to share their experiences of being harassed and molested by men. Years of concerted activism by women brought the problem to public consciousness, and now nearly everyone in business and education is trained in the prevention of sexual harassment. However, that the #MeToo movement began in 2017 shows that it is still a large problem.

A related issue is the problem of rape. Everyone would agree in the abstract that rape is wrong, but the deeper questions are what constitutes rape and what the wrongness of it is. Feminist philosophers began to confront this issue diligently in the late 1990s. They faced two main challenges. The first challenge was overcoming the perception that rape was rare, which required discrediting the stereotype that rape was committed by a stranger choosing a random victim. Feminist researchers showed that rape was most commonly committed by men who knew their victims.

The second challenge was the recognition of rape as a crime against the victim herself. Patriarchal culture had always seen women as the property of men—of the father until she was married and then of the husband. In patriarchal societies, the wrongness of rape was construed as a property crime against the woman's father or husband. A raped woman was less valuable, so if the rapist was caught, he was forced to pay compensation to the man who "owned" the victim. Worse, one possible punishment was that the rapist was forced to marry his victim and take ownership of the property he had damaged. Shifting awareness to the reality that the woman was the true victim of rape was helped along by philosopher of law **Keith Burgess-Jackson** (1957–) in his history, *Rape: A Philosophical Investigation* (1996). Yes, men can be feminists, too.

Third-wave feminists remind us that rape is not about sex; it is about power. In recent years, feminists increasingly have talked about the proliferation of "rape culture"—namely, that women are seen as objects to be used by men, implying that forcing sex on a woman is a normal use of her. Feminists also observe that society may no longer see rape as a crime against a woman's male owner but still assume that the woman "did something" to bring on the rape. This is another expression of patriarchy in the implicit assumption that women are wicked and tempt men to do wrong.

Violence against women is a clear aspect of patriarchy. The pervasive ideology of male dominance that says that women are the property of men condones violence against women. Rape is an act of violence. Domestic violence is, of course, acts of violence. **Iris Marion Young** (1949–2006) said violence was one of the "five faces of oppression" (the others being exploitation, marginalization, powerlessness, and cultural domination), which she said were methods of social dominance of groups. Women as a group were dominated by men using these five faces of oppression. Some feminists have extended the concept of violence from the physical to the psychological. One does not need to hit someone to dominate that person but could use mental and emotional violence. The word "violence" is related to "violation," and any act that violates a person's integrity or autonomy is an act of violence. Young gives examples of such violence in her article, "Throwing Like a Girl: A Phenomenology of Feminine Body Comportment Motility and Spatiality: (1980). She argues that young girls are socialized to restrict their bodily movements and are conditioned to think of their bodies as fragile. They will "throw like a girl" not because their bodies are different from boys' bodies but because they are conditioned to think they do have—or ought to have—less physical capability. Many feminists would argue that restriction of free bodily movement is a violation of a person.

There is currently some talk of a fourth wave of feminism on the basis of the use of social media and an increased focus on violence against women, although the claim that this is a "wave" distinct from the third wave is not yet widely accepted.

Gender and the Feminist Critique of Science

Central to feminist philosophy is the critique of the notion of "gender." Feminism makes a distinction between the biological category of sex and the social category of gender. Sex has traditionally been scientifically defined as a biological difference between male and female cells, organs, and reproductive capacities. Traditionally, sex and gender were all but synonymous in Western cultures, but that view began to be challenged in the mid-1900s. Gender is a matter of social definitions of masculine and feminine and the many accompanying assumptions about social roles, sexuality, and psychological and mental differences between men and women.

Some feminists are "essentialists" who claim that there is an essential female nature distinct from a male nature. (Ironically, some male misogynists agree with this idea.) Essentialists include biological determinists who see female nature as rooted in women's unique biology and social determinists who see the female nature as created through the unique and common features of female social experience. Both kinds of essentialists assume that the female gender is composed of stable qualities that cannot be changed without great effort, if at all.

Other feminists are nonessentialists who reject the idea that gender characteristics are fixed, viewing gender as socially constructed concepts that are open to change and redefinition. As we have seen, Simone de Beauvoir stated in her book, *The Second Sex*, that "one is not born, but rather becomes, a woman." She argued that gender characteristics are not biologically or even culturally determined but are arbitrary—either imposed by society or subjectively chosen.

Regardless of how feminists view the genealogy of gender, they tend to agree that women and men experience the world from different standpoints—different perspectives. Because experience and knowledge are situated within a person's social environment, individuals who are socially situated differently will have different experiences; therefore, they will have different views of what is true. This notion, called "standpoint theory," applies to gender, race, economic class, sexuality, and any other socially situated circumstance. There are current efforts in philosophy that attempt to address the social situatedness of marginalized groups by analyzing gender, race, and sexuality.

Feminism rejects modern and analytic epistemology. Feminist philosophers critique traditional theories of knowledge as having been based on the assumption that there is one universal human nature and therefore the gender, race, class, and other sociohistorical circumstances particular to the knower are irrelevant to how that person perceives and understands anything. In Chapter 19, we will see a similar critique from philosophers of race. Feminists reject the traditional assumption that it is possible to obtain purely objective, value-free, and politically neutral knowledge.

Third-wave feminists claim that human perception is always relative to the standpoint of a particular knower; therefore, claims to knowledge reflect the dominant values and political structures of a society. Feminists claim that the philosophical assumption of a universal human nature has actually enshrined men's experiences and interests as the paradigm for all knowledge. The majority position in the Western philosophical tradition has defined rationality as male and emotionality as female and has devalued the emotions. Points of view, particularly those of women, that deviate from the standard picture of universal rationality have been marginalized and excluded as being too subjective and unconventional.

Traditional epistemologists assume a universal standard of rationality, but feminists ask, "standard and rational for whom?" Most feminist philosophers contend that women's experiences and ways of thinking differ from those that have been the basis of traditional (male) epistemologies. Philosophy must make room for other nontraditional ways of experiencing the world and gaining knowledge.

Standpoint theory has also been significant in the feminist critique of science. The feminist critique is centered on science's assumption of objective rationality as the only means of understanding the world. These assumptions have been cast by many feminists as male attitudes. Some suggest that what is called "objectivity" is actually the subjective male viewpoint that is an expression of patriarchy. Whether or not objectivity and rationality are specifically male, what obscures our understanding of the world is the scientific reductionism of all things to hierarchical structures that can be understood only through applications of logic and mathematics. It isn't a purely feminist critique because it was also made by Bergson and Whitehead. Feminist standpoint theory observes that men and women may frame questions differently, leading to different experimental approaches, leading to different data being collected, leading to different conclusions.

An issue raised by feminists interested in science is that women may be more likely to ask questions and notice phenomena that men deem irrelevant. Empirical research has partially verified that more medical research studies are conducted on diseases that affect men than on diseases that affect women. **Judith Stacey** (1943) and **Barrie Thorne** (1942–) in "The Missing Feminist Revolution in Sociology" (1985) observe that in the social sciences, male-dominated scientific paradigms systematically ignore and erase women's experiences. This means that science is not value-free and objective as is widely assumed. It instead reflects the values assumed by patriarchy. Some feminists believe that the notion of objectivity itself is a false assumption and should be dispensed with. Others believe that objectivity is possible and desirable but that to achieve a sufficient level of objective perspective requires first deconstructing patriarchal bias.

One major area of contention about patriarchal bias is in biology, which has long characterized male organisms as active and female organisms as passive. In "Making a Difference: Feminist Movement and Feminist Critique of Science" (2001), **Evelyn Fox Keller** (1936–) argued that this assumption is so fundamental that it extends to the portrayal of the sperm as masculine and the ovum as feminine. This may seem self-evident at first, but Keller points out that it is a projection of gender norms onto cells resulting in false assumptions. We were all taught in high school biology that the male sperm actively compete to get to the passive female ovum and win the race to fertilize the ovum. This oft-repeated story hides the reality that the ovum is in fact just as active in the process. As Keller observes, this illustrates the ways that the language we use molds the thinking and acting of working scientists. The patriarchal paradigm frames the scientists' attention and shapes their perceptions. It also structures and limits the fields of inquiry that scientists are willing to explore. Biology sees the males of species as active and females as passive, projecting onto animals the patriarchal misconception of the strongest male exerting dominance to win the right to pass on his genes.

Feminists also see strong gender bias in psychology. **Sigmund Freud** is a common target of feminists criticizing how patriarchy dominated psychology and psychiatry. Early psychiatry was indeed rife with patriarchal gender bias. For example, the term "hysteria," used to describe a psychological disorder, came from the Greek word hystera, meaning "womb." (Some male physicians thought the womb literally wandered around the woman's body and made the woman crazy—hence the name.) The idea that women were unable to control their emotions and thus were easily excitable and out of control was common in psychology.

American feminist psychologist **Carol Gilligan** (1936–) sees the Freudian tradition and the psychology of child development as fields dominated by men who deemed women deficient in development. In her book, *In a Different Voice: Psychological Theory and Women's Development* (1982), Gilligan observed that psychologists had always assumed that men were the measure of humanity. Their gender bias led them to assume that the "masculine" qualities of autonomy and rationality were the signs of maturity and the "feminine" qualities of emotion were the signs of immaturity. Gilligan found in her own experiences working in psychology that it was a culture that counted on women not speaking for themselves. When she worked in child psychology, she found that the established gauges of child development were predisposed to measure boys as being more mature than girls.

Standpoint theory also reveals a predominant bias in the social sciences that neglects to consider people's lived experiences. The male objectivist paradigm ignores individual experiences in favor of reductionist paradigms that consider particular people to be examples of general types. This view, of course, goes back to Plato. Social science, therefore, has been conducted as a gathering of collective quantitative data because it is considered more objective. Feminist scientists have pushed back on this assumption, saying that if the purpose of social science is to understand people, then social scientists need to listen to people and collect qualitative data about individuals' lived experiences. Jane Addams was an inspiration in this push back against reductionist social sciences (see Chapter 12).

Sociologist **Joey Sprague** (1947–), in *Feminist Methodologies for Critical Researchers* (2005), calls for awareness that the concepts of gender, race, and class are key organizers of social life. Therefore, social science needs to engage in qualitative ethnographic research through conducting interviews and direct participant observations. Sprague also argues that for feminist researchers, understanding how things work is not enough; they need to take action to make the world more equitable.

Feminist Political Philosophy

The feminist philosophical approach has also been applied to political philosophy. The same critiques made in other areas apply here—that political philosophy has been shaped by the patriarchal assumptions that knowledge is purely objective, value-free, and politically neutral. Similarly, there have been assumptions that rationality is the only means of understanding human behavior and political systems and that people predominantly act rationally and out of self-interest. Feminist political philosophy aims, among other things, to overcome these assumptions to gain a clearer picture of how people and institutions act politically.

The exclusion of women from political life and from political philosophy has been a major subject for feminists. Related to that topic is feminist philosophers' interest in the use and misuse of power in society. Central to, and inextricably a part of, feminist political philosophy is the recognition that human societies are structured by patriarchal and similar forms of power dominance.

A prominent aspect of patriarchal power, feminist philosophers of the second wave said, is that biological differences between men and women have been used to structure society in ways that enforce the division of social and household labor according to gender roles. We earlier saw a critique of this by Shulamith Firestone. It is not difficult to see how much of human society revolves around the division of labor according to gender, nor is it difficult to understand that social divisions based on gender overwhelmingly favor the social status of men. Politically, this most obviously manifests in how, traditionally, women were excluded from voting and from serving in government. Feminist political philosophers have debated if it is possible to secure the rights of women by reforming the existing political system or if it is necessary to create a radically new nonpatriarchal political system.

Identity Politics

Feminist political philosophers do not deny that there are biological differences between the sexes but are quick to point out that sex is not gender and that gender is a social construction. A common claim by second-wave feminists is that biological sex is fixed but that gender, being a social construction, is used to divide the sexes and privilege men.

Third-wave feminists emphatically agree that sex and gender are different but tend to take aim at how the second wave defined women. There are two aspects to this. One is the debate between essentialists and nonessentialists mentioned earlier. The other is that the talk of women— sex or gender—as a single group falsely generalizes the interests, characteristics, and concerns of specific women. Third-wave feminists argue that the singular definition of women contains mainly those who are middle-class, white, and heterosexual and makes those people the norm for all. Kimberlé Crenshaw observes that in second-wave feminism, African American men are the norm for civil rights advocates and white women are the norm for women's rights advocates. Women of color simply disappear from view.

Third-wave feminism embraces intersectionality, as described earlier, and this is a profound political shift. In the consideration of political power structures, and in women's struggles for recognition and justice, there is a move away from a binary sexual struggle of men and women toward a broader, pluralistic struggle against subordination and oppression. bell hooks probably has made the most full-throated advocacy for the need to include women's multiple and complex identities and experiences.

The complex question of identity has been a matter of considerable discussion among feminists, and the question of identity includes the questions of the legitimacy and efficacy of identity politics. How should identities of "woman," "Black, "Latinx," "homosexual," and others be understood and used? The question is related to standpoint theory. Human perception is always relative to the standpoint of a particular knower, and this applies to all of life, not just scientific observations. Women face social and political decisions from a different standpoint than do men, and women of color have a different standpoint from white women.

Questions of Power

Recognition of social identities is bound up into questions of power and the binary relation of domination and subordination. That women are treated as second-class people is undeniable; the questions are how to think about that subordination and how to counter it.

Some drew on Marxist thought to explain how society is structured to subordinate women similar to how it subordinates the working class. They pointed to how women are cast in the roles of unpaid domestic and reproductive laborers (or "reproductive slaves" according to Beauvoir) and argued that the economic exploitation of women was essential to capitalism.

Decolonial feminist philosophers, so called because they seek to dismantle the power structures left by colonialism (more on decolonial philosophy in Chapter 20), usually see colonialism as being a global capitalist system of power that classifies and dehumanizes people along racial and gender lines. Not surprisingly, decolonial feminists predominantly come from cultures that have historically been the subjects of colonialism. One example is Argentine **María Lugones** (1944–2020) who argued that colonialism imposes a hierarchy of gender on all people. In her view, European colonization enforces a hierarchical categorization of peoples that dehumanizes all but male Europeans. Lugones calls for a decolonizing of gender as part of a wider project of decolonial resistance.

Some feminist philosophers have pointed out that political liberalism expanded rights only to more men, not to women. Such a criticism certainly applies to John Locke. It also applies to the forms of liberalism discussed in Chapter 16. Several other feminist philosophers, such as New Zealander **Susan Moller Okin** (1946–2004), have attempted to expand John Rawls's version of liberalism to women's political concerns. Those who criticize the liberal tradition claim that it focuses on individual participation in politics and that it assumes that politics is inherently antagonistic—a struggle for power and dominance. This latter criticism is in line with the general feminist tendency to reject the traditional assumption that there are universal, objective political structures.

Finally, another criticism made by feminist philosophers is that the traditional view of politics disregards emotions and personal relationships, not just of women but of all people. People genuinely care about other people, and personal sentiments and relationships affect their social and political choices. Not all political action is seeking domination. There are people who genuinely seek compromise and reconciliation.

Acknowledging the common human desire for cooperation, some feminist philosophers advocate for a politics of more communal participation rather than an agonistic struggle for dominance. This approach is associational—emphasizing reaching political agreements through relations of solidarity and communal action. Turkish American

Seyla Benhabib (1950–) calls for a form of democracy in which political decisions are agreed to by all those affected by their consequences and decided by open debate in which all parties have equal access to participate. Even such political agreements remain open to question, revision, and ongoing discussion as to how they are best applied and carried out. One emphasis in the associational approach is to think of personal agency and freedom in more collective ways. In other words, the associational approach involves looking at how individuals perceive and act within a pluralistic society and how an individual's agency and freedom is strengthened not by conflict but by relationships and solidarity.

Perhaps a good summation of the feminist philosophy that we've discussed so far is *The Gender Knot: Unraveling Our Patriarchal Legacy* (2005) by **Allan G. Johnson** (1946–2017) In his book, Johnson takes the view that patriarchal gender constructions harms both men and women. He argues that the core quality of patriarchy is male-identified control—a dynamic that promotes competition, oppression, violence, and fear across areas of life for all people. Patriarchy's influence on society manifests in a range of oppressive systems, from sexual violence against women, to slavery, warfare, and destruction of the environment. We didn't create these systems, Johnson says, but each of us through our individual choices can contribute towards patriarchy's dissolution. Men can have an active involvement in unraveling the gender knot through taking responsibility, being honest about how patriarchy works, and by having feminist conversations about dissolving the patriarchal system. Johnson says that there is a path to something better than patriarchy and that our individual choices matter more than we realize.

Chapter 19

PHILOSOPHY OF RACE

Feminist philosophy deals with the problem of sexism, and philosophy of race deals with the problem of racism. Both areas of philosophical thought attempt to understand, deconstruct, and counter traditional patterns of dominance and subordination. Feminist philosophy critiques patriarchy, and philosophy of race critiques racial hierarchy.

We discuss philosophy of race late in this book not as an afterthought but because, as with feminism, society has taken this long before philosophy began to take the issue of racism seriously. It's a statement of historical fact, not of politics, that Europeans did not see as their equals many non-European people, in particular the indigenous peoples of the Americas and Africa. The enslavement of non-European people was legally abolished in France in 1794 (but not until 1848 in its colonies), in Spain in 1811 (but also later in some of its colonies), in the Netherlands in 1814, in Portugal in 1819 (but not until 1858 in its colonies), in the United Kingdom in 1833, and finally in the United States in 1865. However, the end of enslavement did not mean equal rights for non-Europeans in any of these countries.

It was not until the early 1900s that the idea emerged of a philosophy dealing specifically with issues of race. Unsurprisingly, the philosophy of race was begun by people of color. Philosophy considers race in terms of its social construction, and it analyzes the cultural and moral effects of attitudes toward race. The philosophy of race deals with how ideas and attitudes about race developed and seeks to understand race relations in the context of social and moral philosophy. The *critical* philosophy of race analyzes and critiques racism, systemic racial hierarchies, and the ways that the racialization of society effects ideas, values, practices, and social institutions.

Similar to feminist philosophy and its focus on gender constructs, critical philosophy of race has a focus on the role of racism and racial hierarchies in shaping the historical patterns of thought and society. Critical philosophers of race acknowledge the ways in which white-dominated social traditions have excluded people of color, and critical philosophy of race is an attempt to decode often veiled words and ideas that power racial hierarchies and attitudes with an eye toward changing those traditions and decreasing racial injustices. It is also critical in calling for an end to the denial of society's past and ongoing racism, including an end to racial segregation, exploitation, and genocide. Being philosophers, critical philosophers of race are especially critical of philosophy's denial of its own racial past.

Philosophy of race is a rapidly widening field of inquiry. It has its roots in the writings of Black Americans in the 1800s protesting against racial prejudice and discrimination against the descendants of enslaved Black Africans.

The Idea of Race

Race is a manufactured concept. Biologically, there is only one human "race," the species *Homo sapiens*, to which all people belong. The idea of race as a biological distinction emerged in the 1700s, most notably with Carl Linnaeus who established much of the taxonomy of organisms in use today. He divided *Homo sapiens* into four varieties—*Europeanus*, *Americanus*, *Asiaticus*, and *Africanus*. Some people took the taxonomy one step further, claiming that there were multiple *species* of human beings, with Europeans a species that had a different origin than other species that originated on other continents. By the late 1700s, it became a common "intellectual" argument that the supposed cultural and moral superiority of whites over non-whites was proof of inherent biological differences between them.

The prejudicial conceit of biological race seeped into the thought of otherwise intelligent philosophers. **David Hume** stated that all non-white species were "naturally inferior to the whites" and that "there never was a civilized nation of any other complexion than white." **Immanuel Kant** wrote that "the Negroes of Africa have by nature no feeling that rises above the trifling." **G.W.F. Hegel** thought that Africa "has no historical interest of its own, for we find its inhabitants living in barbarism and slavery in a land which has not furnished them with any integral ingredient of culture." Even **John Stuart Mill** in *On Liberty* did not extend liberty and the right not to be harmed to the immature "barbarians" of other races.

The idea of biological race gained significant momentum with the development of theories of biological evolution, most notably those of **Herbert Spencer** (1820–1903) in 1857 and **Charles Darwin** (1809–1882) in 1859. The bogus field of scientific racism attempted to demonstrate that Europeans were a superior race through comparative anatomy, dividing humanity into three to five separate races, roughly parallel with the continents. Because Europeans and Americans of European ancestry were the people creating these classifications, the European race was seen as superior to all other races.

Dividing humanity into races is to try to make objective what is fundamentally subjective—to justify personal prejudice. Modern conceptions of racial differences adopt a very old assumption that people are born with inherent characteristics. Way back in Chapter 2 we saw Aristotle's idea that some people are natural slaves—some people have inherent characteristics that mean they are suitable only for the menial labor of a slave. Aristotle was hardly alone in the assumption that some people are of noble birth possessing characteristics superior to those of others. Most people engage in some form of thinking that certain groups of people are born with inferior traits. Race is one common expression of such prejudice.

The assumption that one group is superior and the others inferior can be attached to any difference among people—economic status, profession, religion, ethnicity, and the idea of race. "Racialism" is the assumption that people are born possessing particular characteristics common to all members of that race. Although racialism does not necessarily assume that some races have inherent characteristics inferior to those of other races, it provides the intellectual justification for racist attitudes.

In the mid-1800s, some philosophers began to critique the idea of race that was being used as a justification for slavery. The law in the United States stated that Black people had no civil rights under the law—not even a right of self-defense if attacked by a white person. The most

notable thinker on these issues in the mid-1800s was Black American **Alexander Crummell** (1819–1898). He began arguing in 1840 that civil rights should not be based on skin color as decided by governments but that civil rights are natural rights that exist before any rights granted by law. Crummell's appeal to natural rights was similar to the natural law theory proposed by a number of philosophers, most notably John Locke. Crummell said that the truth that all people, regardless of skin color, have natural rights can be inferred from the primary sentiments of our human nature. Civil rights are not abstract principles that can be arbitrarily decided but are derived from our human nature—sentiment for our fellow humans is part of what it means to be human. David Hume had similarly called for recognizing that our human sentiments are the basis for our moral judgments about what is right and wrong. Crummell added that we use our light of reason to understand the principles of natural rights and our primary sentiments. Using reason, we can see that Black people have natural rights, human sentiment, and human reason to understand moral wrong; therefore, we can understand that slavery and other indignities and wrongs inflicted on Black people are wrong.

The bottom line of Crummell's reasoning is that Black people are fully human and are thus entitled to have their civil rights protected. This would seem to address the fundamental question of race—are non-white people full human beings? Philosophers of race, like Crummell, say that yes, of course, non-whites are fully human. From that fact, philosophers of race reject racialism and racism, ask how those prejudices have affected society and can be eliminated, and ask how the damage caused can be rectified.

Early 1900s Philosophy of Race

The sordid history of white supremacy in the United States is elsewhere better discussed than I can do here and likewise for the history of heroic efforts by people of all races to overcome racism and the damage it causes to people. In the rest of this chapter, we will look at how some philosophers attempted to understand racism and its effects on people. In the late 1800s and early 1900s, philosophers of race generally adopted the idea, popular even in the scientific community, that whites and Negroes were different races, even though they rejected the idea that race is biological, and they certainly denied the fiction of white supremacy.

W.E.B. Du Bois

W.E.B. Du Bois was a sociologist, philosopher, and activist for the civil rights of people of African ancestry in the United States. He was educated at the University of Berlin and Harvard University, and his early work in the sociology of Black communities led him to the position that Negroes (as Blacks were widely referred to at that time) should not assimilate into white society but should accept their African heritage as members of a vast historic race. Race for Du Bois was defined by a common history and shared traditions. Therefore, the difference between descendants of Europeans and descendants of Africans is that they are spiritually distinct races of peoples. The descendants of slaves in the Americas had been cut off from their history and needed to restore their own traditions. Du Bois's sentiment was not antiwhite or Black nationalist but a rejection of the idea that Negroes would overcome discrimination by acting like whites, which would entail adopting a set of social traditions different from their own.

Du Bois's philosophy was influenced by William James, whose courses Du Bois had taken while at Harvard, as well as by the ideas of Alexander Crummell. His primary philosophical work consisted of several essays in his book, *The Souls of Black Folk: Essays and Sketches* (1903). He stated that the problem of that time was the problem of the "color line."

> The problem of the twentieth century is the problem of the color line—the relation of the darker to the lighter races of men in Asia and Africa, in America and in the islands of the sea. (*The Souls of Black Folk* xx)

The color line manifests in society as the segregation of whites away from Blacks that establishes a social hierarchy of white supremacy.

Du Bois analyzed the color line through his sociological methodology (discussed in Chapter 15). We need, he said, to accept the paradox that human behavior has both determinate and indeterminate aspects. In American society, the racial hierarchy determines the objective lives of Black people. Du Bois wrote about not only the objective social problems that afflicted Black Americans but also the subjective lived experiences of Black people. Looking at how Black people responded to white supremacy, Du Bois developed the concept of "double consciousness," a phenomenon he thought was unique to Black people. By "double consciousness," Du Bois meant the awareness that Black people developed within the peculiar social conditions in which they found themselves.

Du Bois describes the phenomenon of double consciousness in the first pages of his book

> Being a problem is a strange experience,—peculiar even for one who has never been anything else, save perhaps in babyhood and in Europe. . . . After the Egyptian and Indian, the Greek and Roman, the Teuton and Mongolian, the Negro is a sort of seventh son, born with a veil, and gifted with second-sight in this American world,—a world which yields him no true self-consciousness, but only lets him see himself through the revelation of the other world. It is a peculiar sensation, this double-consciousness, this sense of always looking at one's self through the eyes of others, of measuring one's soul by the tape of a world that looks on in amused contempt and pity. One ever feels his two-ness,—an American, a Negro; two souls, two thoughts, two unreconciled strivings; two warring ideals in one dark body, whose dogged strength alone keeps it from being torn asunder. (*The Souls of Black Folk*, 1–2)

A Black American develops the consciousness of self but also the consciousness of seeing that self through the misrecognizing eyes of the whites. Negroes in the United States were both Black and American and thus moved in two worlds—their own world and the white world. The Black American is forced by circumstances to try to assimilate to the white world. White Americans, on the other side of the veil of segregation, didn't see the existence of Black Americans. Instead, whites saw only Blacks intruding in the white world.

Black experiences of segregation and discrimination that denied their identities inflicted moral injuries on Black people, yet as Du Bois wrote, Blacks possessed a dogged strength to resist the strife of prejudice and to attain self-consciousness. This strength was anchored in their double consciousness. Despite the realities of white domination, a Black person retains a sense of the dichotomy between the discrimination expressed by the oppressors and a love for self that is not defined by white domination. Blacks have knowledge about their lives in their own world, about life in the white world, and about the functioning of the veil that separates those worlds. Blacks' double consciousness enables them to have deeper insights into society and systems of domination, insights they can use to develop tools and actions against those systems.

The Black person, Du Bois says, simply wishes to make it possible for a man (sic) to be both Black and an American without being cursed and spit on by his fellows and without having the doors of opportunity closed roughly in his face. Du Bois's portrayal of the double consciousness of oppressed people has been broadly influential in critical philosophy of race and postcolonial theory.

Alain LeRoy Locke

The first Black American Rhodes scholar, **Alain LeRoy Locke** (1885–1954), studied at the University of Oxford. In 1918, he earned his PhD in philosophy from Harvard University. He was chair of the philosophy department of Howard University (one of the historically Black colleges) for 32 years, until 1953. Like Du Bois, Locke had American pragmatism as his main philosophical influence.

Locke rejected biological race as an ethnic fiction and instead saw race as a social and cultural reality. Race and culture are synonymous, an inherited phenomenon constituted by social transactions, what Locke calls "culture-heredity." Race operates as tradition, as preferred traits and values, Locke said, preferring to substitute the term "culture group" for "race." There are, then, not the commonly described three to five biological races but as many races as there are distinctive cultural traditions.

Locke saw his cultural view of race as nullifying the idea that a culture is intrinsic to one ethnic group. This view allows us to see that a culture group differs from other groups in terms of social practices, not intrinsic biology, and that social practices are often shared and appropriated between culture groups. A group has a self-consciousness of itself as distinctive from other groups, and that distinction can be based on a domination and suppression of other groups. It does not have to be that way, though. A group can have a sense of itself as distinct and feel pride in its culture.

Dispensing with the fallacy that race is biological helps us to view differences among groups as the result of human choices. Therefore, Locke concludes that racial prejudice is an aberrant psychological assumption with no basis in scientific fact.

Locke is most famous as the leading literary light of the Harlem Renaissance of Black novelists, poets, historians, and artists that began in the 1920s. Locke celebrated art and literature as a way for Black people to express themselves and develop a new mentality within a racist society. Creative self-expression, he said, can help to repair damaged group psychology and reshape social perspectives warped by anti-Black racism.

Black people can develop a new group psychology of more positive self-respect and self-reliance, casting off social dependency and society's double standard of judgment based on race. In creative self-expression, Black people can rise from "social disillusionment to race pride, from the sense of social debt to the responsibilities of social contribution" (*The New Negro* 11). Locke held up the Negro spirituals as the quintessential Black artistic expression because they express the uniqueness of Black experience and the emotions of the singer. He said that the music has universal appeal and demonstrates how folk art becomes classical art.

These sentiments of the value of developing self-esteem and group identity are familiar to us today, and Locke was advocating for them in the face of those within America, both white and Black, who were saying that Black people should accommodate themselves within their secondary social status. Du Bois similarly rejected accommodation with white supremacy and also advocated art as a response. However, Locke saw the benefit of art in personal expression itself, whereas Du Bois insisted that art should express political and moral messages—propaganda (his word) against white supremacy. Locke thought that Black people positively changing how they view themselves would be more effective in making progress in race relations. This disagreement as to whether "propaganda" or self-expression is more effective in making positive social change is ongoing within art and philosophy.

The Lived Experience of Blackness

That biological race is a fallacy does not negate the reality of racial prejudice, discrimination, and oppression. Du Bois and Locke, among others, were vividly aware of the damaging effects of racism on racial minorities. In the mid- to late 1900s, Black philosophers analyzed what it means to be Black in a white supremacist world.

Frantz Fanon

Frantz Fanon (1925–1961) was born in the French Caribbean colony of Martinique. He left the island in 1943 to fight with the Free French Forces in World War II. After the war, he studied in France to become a psychiatrist. His experiences in the colony of Martinique and in France influenced his important book on racism, *Black Skin, White Masks* (1952). Fanon uses a phenomenological approach to explore the lived experience of Black people. He is also an existentialist in that he focuses on questions of subjectivity and the individual's existence, and he was particularly influenced by Jean-Paul Sartre's idea that French identity was in part defined by anti-Semitism. Sartre said in *Anti-Semite and Jew* (1946) that anti-Semites need the oversimplified fantasy of the inferior Jew to escape responsibility for their own actions. Fanon found in Sartre's concept of anti-Semitism a clear parallel with French attitudes toward the people of color in its colonies.

Fanon's central philosophical idea in *Black Skin, White Masks* is that Black people are condemned by their skin color to be a lesser creature in the white world in which they live. The inferiority of Black people is determined by the "white gaze" that sees only the skin of a Black person. Fanon observed that anti-Black racism reduces Black people to nothing more than skin, a skin to which they are chained and by which they are determined. The prejudiced views of the dominant culture are imposed on the oppressed who are represented as mere animal bodies less able to think, reason, or speak properly. Within white supremacy, Black people experience the image of their own body as alien to them, an image of a third person because it is a body defined by the white gaze.

Black people have to learn how to navigate the world in two dimensions. They are one person with their fellow Black people but have to behave differently with white people. Black people are at home in their own bodies only when the white gaze is absent. In the presence of white people, Black people have to move, act, and speak differently, according to the norms of the white world. This self-division is the direct result of colonial oppression (we will discuss philosophical views of colonialism in

Chapter 20). In the white world, the Black person has to be Black in relation to the white, while still being Black. It is similar to Du Bois's description of double consciousness, although there is no indication Fanon knew Du Bois's work.

Fanon criticized philosophy (mostly Sartre, with whom he disagreed aside from the concept of anti-Semitism) for not permitting us to understand the Black person's Beingness because it ignores the lived experience of being Black. Blackness was created in the white world and continues to exist in negation to whiteness. But rational categories can't be used to understand the lived experience of Black people. Sartre talked a lot about suffering, but Fanon said that white philosophers like Sartre forget that Black people suffer quite differently from white people, again, because of colonialism. Black people are trapped in Blackness. Only the Black person who questions the racial entrapment can break out of it.

James Baldwin

James Baldwin (1924–1987) was a novelist and playwright, but his writings had a definite philosophical tone and dealt with topics significant to the philosophy of race. Born in New York City, he emigrated to Paris to escape American racism and to develop his voice as a writer outside of being a Black man in America. His one major work of nonfiction, *The Fire Next Time* (1963), was influential in the U.S. civil rights movement of the 1960s and as a testament to Black experience within racist society. Baldwin set out to reach a white readership to help white people understand the Black experience and their motivations to struggle for civil rights. He was telling whites his story, educating them on his own lived experience. His approach influenced a number of later philosophers and activists.

Baldwin's book contains two essays. The first, "My Dungeon Shook: Letter to My Nephew on the One Hundredth Anniversary of Emancipation," is styled as a letter to his then 14-year-old nephew in which he cautions the young man about racism and how he should react to racial oppression. America has the ability to destroy Black men, Baldwin wrote, but he challenged his nephew to convert his anger over his mistreatment into having a passionate desire to understand the experiences of other Black people.

His second essay, "Down at the Cross: Letter from a Region in My Mind," describes his journey away from organized Christianity, which he felt had repressed his full experience of humanity. His feelings of being repressed came from the combination of his experience as a Black man but perhaps more from his experience as a homosexual. Baldwin also describes the attempt by Nation of Islam founder Elijah Muhammad (1897–1975) to convert him. Baldwin wrote that the Black Muslim movement had replaced Christianity's "white God" with a "Black God." In response to both sides, Baldwin asserted that such binary orientations of white versus Black and an insatiable quest for power underpinned American society's predicament. The attempts to make God one color or another were attempts to legitimize discrimination on the false pretext of safeguarding the truth.

Baldwin rejected hatred and affirmed the dignity of all people regardless of color. The upheaval of that time in America, he wrote, was not caused by a Black revolution. The social strife in the 1960s reflected white America losing its sense of exclusive power to define Black identity. America was seeing the rewriting of history, not only for the liberation of Black people, but for white people who did not really know their own history.

The American civil rights movement was a long and complicated struggle for recognition. It peaked in intensity in Baldwin's lifetime but had roots going back a further century. I cannot hope to cover it adequately in this book, and I hope your other courses will give the long historical struggle for civil rights the thorough treatment that it deserves. Similar to the first and second waves of feminism, the American civil rights movement was originally focused on achieving human rights related to employment, housing, education, and so on. Like feminist philosophers, philosophers of race have views across a spectrum of more moderate to more radical. We also saw in Chapter 18 how Black women developed intersectionality as a method of being open to diverse experiences of gender, race, class, and sexuality. Many of the same themes about cultural hegemony and oppression discussed in Chapters 15 and 18 definitely also apply to the topic of race. In the rest of this chapter, we look at philosophers of race who wrote after the 1960s, who considered what had and had not been accomplished by the American civil rights movement and what still needs to be accomplished for the full emancipation of Black people.

Cornel West

Cornel West (1953–) is arguably the most widely known philosopher in the United States at the time of this writing and is certainly the only philosopher ever named MTV's Artist of the Week (2016). West's first book was *Prophesy Deliverance! An Afro-American Revolutionary Christianity* (1982). In it he advocated for a radical Christianity that worked for the emancipation of all people. He chose "Afro-

American" rather than the common "African American" to denote the Black experience as being not that of immigrants but that of descendants of people who were enslaved and were still experiencing the legacy of slavery.

Like Fanon, West focuses on the lived experiences of Black people, but unlike Fanon, who was hostile toward religion, West highlights the revolutionary experience of Black American churches. West adopts the interpretation of Jesus as a liberator of the poor and downtrodden, a common theme in Black American church communities. In his writings, he frequently references the men and women in the Black churches who struggled for justice—for abolition of slavery, for the end of segregation and violence against Black people, for civil rights, and for social and economic justice for all people. Prophesy deliverance, for West, comes from passionate truth telling and witness bearing to help oppressed people help themselves.

West urges Afro-Americans to understand their dual status as being oppressed by both white supremacy and capitalism. He accepts Marx's critique of capitalism and Marx's contribution to the growth of self-consciousness in the proletariat, but he rejects Marx's materialism, moral relativism, and strangulating totalitarianism.

His version of a revolutionary Christianity is one that replaces the class structure and class antagonisms of bourgeois society with a new association in which the free development of each person is the condition for the free development of all. West embraces a Christian spirituality in which loving concern for others is central. Justice, he says, is what love looks like in public.

West has been compared to Du Bois, about whom West has written a large amount, mostly in solidarity. Published 90 years after Du Bois's *The Souls of Black Folk*, West's *Race Matters* (1993) assesses the position of Black people in the United States and finds that Black people still suffer greatly from white supremacy. West says that the U.S. history of white supremacist beliefs and images has permeated society and culture and has inflicted on Black people emotional scars and existential angst. The lived experience of Black people is to feel unsafe and unprotected, subject to random violence and hatred for who they are. West stresses that experiencing this trauma doesn't excuse immoral acts by Black people, but it does mean that we must be cognizant of the circumstances into which people are born and under which they live.

The circumstances for Black people are a combination of historical white supremacy built into social structures, the continued resistance on the part of white people to accept the humanity of Black people fully, and neoliberal economic structures (see Chapter 16). West opposes what he calls the "free-market fundamentalism" of neoliberalism. This ideology that puts corporate interests first trivializes concern for the common good and puts fear and insecurity into the hearts of workers. West says this ideology is also at the heart of American imperialism and militarism abroad. Despite his opposition to capitalism, West says he is a non-Marxist socialist. He says he is a democratic socialist because he is suspicious of authority and believes in people having a voice in government.

Lewis Gordon

American **Lewis Gordon** (1962–) has applied phenomenology and existentialism to the lived experiences of Black people, developing a distinctly "Africana existentialism." His perspective is that although existentialism is a historically European movement preoccupied with freedom, anguish, responsibility, embodied agency, sociality, and liberation, an Africana existentialism examines the question of what it means for Black people to exist and live as a problem to the white world and to understand the suffering of Black people. Gordon further elaborates on the observations of Du Bois and West that Black people are treated as problems instead of as people, saying that Black people suffer from demands to justify their existence. From those demands of anti-Black racism, Black people suffer dread, a sense of absurdity, and loss of freedom—common themes in European existentialism.

In his first book, *Bad Faith and Antiblack Racism* (1995), Gordon considers the status of Blackness because, historically, the question of race has been directed at "the Blacks." Gordon's concept of "bad faith" includes a variety of phenomena that in one way or another are a choice against choice and an effort to avoid freedom and responsibility. Anti-Black racism includes white people's bad faith efforts of a flight from and war against social reality. This reflects a common theme in philosophy of race that criticizes white people's denial of the humanity of Black people and the history of anti-Black racism. But Gordon also labels as "bad faith" a spirit of sincerity, calling instead for "critical good faith" that respects evidence and accountability, building a world of intersubjective relations.

Gordon emphasizes anti-Black racism rather than white supremacy, arguing that the former can exist without the latter—that people can reject white supremacy and still think that Blacks are inferior. In his phenomenology of racism, Gordon observes that racism requires the rejection of other people's humanity, which is a denial of reality. Because communication remains possible between the racist and the people at whom racist hatred is directed, the social reality that those people are indeed human will inevitably appear, creating a problem for the racist.

In anti-Black racism, the existence of the Black person is the problem. The racist must therefore avoid and deny the social reality of the Black person's existence. In particular, the racist must avoid the embodied reality of the people whom the racist hates—the racist must make invisible the bodies of Black people who are visible. This avoidance of reality, Gordon says, tries to make embodied Black people be entities without points of view or make Black people's points of view as existing without bodies. In other words, racists dismiss Black people as having no point of view or dismiss their point of view as having no tangible embodied reality. This form of misrecognition of Black people denies their humanity, their lived experiences, and their agency in the world.

Agreeing with an argument made by Fanon, Gordon says that racists aren't irrational; they are expressing a hyperrationality of justification for their bad faith of racist thinking. That racist hyperrationality is what causes the highly emotional passions of racists. Feeding that hyperrationalization is the notion that moral obligations are founded on similarity among people and therefore do not extend to people who are different. White people within white supremacy only recognize people who are similar to them and do not feel the need to extend moral consideration to Black people. This is the anti-Black misrecognition that lies at the core of racism.

In *Existence in Black: An Anthology of Black Existential Philosophy* (1997) and *Existentia Africana: Understanding Africana Existential Thought* (2000), Gordon frames Black existentialism as a discipline that studies the problems of Black existence, such as Black social invisibility. Therefore, anyone can contribute to Black existentialism; one does not have to be Black. For this reason, Gordon applies an intersectionality to his philosophy, looking at and welcoming the contributions of people of all genders, races, and religions. He compares racism with sexism and, because he sees society as fundamentally anti-Black, claims that the logic of gender converges with the logic of race. He sees society as a hierarchy of white men who are powerful in their whiteness, then white women as possessing a "Black" helplessness, then Black men who are "female" in being Black, with Black women at the bottom who are doubly Black in being female and Black.

Unlike European existentialism, Gordon says, Black existentialism has to argue that not all Black people are the same; they are not all reducible to anti-Black stereotypes. Gordon combines existentialism with religious thought because, in his opinion, similar to West's, religion offers unique paths that can be taken in the struggles for recognition and liberation.

Critiques of Structural Racism

A *critical* philosophy of race unabashedly condemns racism as a systemic social construction that permeates all aspects of society. **Charles W. Mills** (1951–2021) emphasizes the explicit methodology of this relatively new philosophical approach.

> Critical philosophy of race is distinguished from traditional—
> uncritical—philosophy of race in being multiply 'critical.' It is

critical of racism, as ideas, beliefs, and values, as well as social institutions and practices; it is generally, at least in recent decades, critical also of the traditional naturalistic understanding of race; and it is critical of the denial of the past and ongoing significance of race to the making of modernity and the contemporary world. ("Critical Philosophy of Race" 709)

The new critical approach is not simply a more strident or activist approach to the issues of race and racism. The critical philosophy of race shifts the target of critique from individuals' racist feelings and thoughts to the system of social structures that sustain racial hierarchies of white dominance over people of color. As you probably have recognized, there is a strong similarity between the critical philosophy of race and third-wave feminism in their focus on confronting social structures of dominance and oppression. The aim of both critical philosophy of race and third-wave feminism is to dismantle structures that harm people, making space for people to build a better life for all.

Derrick Bell

We saw in Chapter 15 that critical theory is a philosophical project that critiques society as a whole. Critical theory in the context of legal studies analyzes how laws and sentences are applied to citizens. It is critical in that it questions whether legal institutions discharge their duties equally and accurately. The law is supposedly blind to all differences—class, race, gender, religion, and so on—among people, but critical legal theory critiques this blind assumption within legal scholarship of judicial neutrality and objective truth.

 American **Derrick Bell** (1930–2011) was a professor of law and legal theory who developed critical race theory. His 1973 book, *Race, Racism, and American Law*, has been the seminal textbook on the subject and is now in its sixth edition. Unlike other approaches to critical philosophy of race, Bell's critical race theory looks at racism within legal theory and scholarship. Bell's research in legal aspects of civil rights convinced him that racism is an ordinary presence at the center of society and, thus, that traditions of racial subordination are stronger than legal standards, which affects legal proceedings. He agrees that race is a social construction and that the domination of whites over people of color served important psychological and material purposes for whites. Racism is not a binary white–Black relation but is a pattern of dominance that has shifted to different minority groups at different times, usually in response to economic considerations.

Bell therefore adopted intersectionality—that each race has its own ever-evolving history. From that, he said that people of color need to communicate their histories and experiences to white people, who are unlikely to know the circumstances faced by racialized minorities. The history of race relations in the United States shows that, from the framing of the Constitution, whites have chosen property over justice and that whites will promote civil rights advances only when they also serve white self-interest.

Critical race theory speaks to the heart of the structures of U.S. society and its political and legal institutions. Therefore, its very existence has felt threatening to some people, and some have tried to ban even the mention of it. Critical race theory is not antiwhite or seeking racial conflict, as evidenced by the fact that two of its leading proponents, **Richard Delgado** (1939–) and **Jean Stefancic** (?–), are white. What the philosophy does oppose is systemic racism and the reluctance if not outright refusal of American society to have a conversation about race relations past and present. Philosophy needs to take personal emotion and perspective into account, but philosophy suffers when personal feelings and biases cloud out discernment and open dialogue. Emotion and biases on both sides have hampered an open and reasonable dialogue about critical race theory and its findings.

Charles W. Mills

Jamaican American Charles W. Mills was a political philosopher of race and one of its most strident and contentious voices. He was a critic of and commentator on John Rawls (see Chapter 16). Mills accepts the Rawlsian goals of the flourishing of the individual and justice as fairness. Mills observes, however, that Rawls's ideal theory considers justice in the abstract. Mills therefore rejects the notion of ideal theory because it ignores the concrete reality of structural racism. He therefore also prefers "nonideal theory" as responding to the reality of racism, thus providing a way to explain and expose racist structures. Nonideal theory begins from the standpoint that structural inequalities exist and moves from that to the question of how to reverse those inequalities. Mills's starting point is the idea that white supremacy is a political system in which white political philosophers are so embedded that in their ideal theories of justice and morality that they never consider actual practice. Mills then uses "contract theory" to try to rectify racial injustices.

Mills sees liberalism, the analytic political philosophy defined in Chapter 16, as a political ideology steeped in racism. In his book, *The Racial Contract* (1997), Mills deconstructs the history of liberalism through an analysis of "social contract theory," used variously by Thomas Hobbes, John Locke, and Jean-Jacques Rousseau, as a form of ideal theory. Mills argues that the social contract is not, as assumed, neutral with respect to racial and ethnic differences. Instead, it was intended as a contract only among white people and thus establishes obligations and regulates interactions only among white people.

Racism is at the core of the social contract, Mills says. Racism is not an unintended side effect; racism has really been the rule—an agreement among the tribes of Europe to spread and maintain white supremacy against all non-white tribes the world over. When white people say, "justice," they mean, "just us." Therefore, Mills contends that it is more reflective of the nonideal reality to think of the racial contract as the real character of the world in which we live. The racial contract of white supremacy is the actual social contract. Mills's conception of a racial contract fits well with postcolonial theory (see Chapter 20).

It is not only analytic political theory that Mills says is steeped in white supremacy. He also targets Marxism as not taking racism into account. In *From Class to Race: Essays in White Marxism and Black Radicalism* (2003), Mills, consistent with his views in *The Racial Contract*, says that white supremacy was central to the creation of the capitalist modern world. He calls on "white Marxism" to learn from the radical critique by Black philosophy and activism. He gives the example of his own journey from a self-described orthodox Marxist to a radical Black theorist. He outlines how the Marxist critique of class strongly parallels a critique of structural racism, with white supremacy essentially acting in the same role in which Marx saw the bourgeoisie. Mills's critique parallels that of American **Cedric Robinson** (1940–2016) who rejected the Eurocentrism of Marxism and attempted to recast Marxist thought to inform a radical Black nationalism that would fight against racial capitalism.

Mills defines the central foundational categories of oppression in both internal structural racism and white "settler colonialism," and he refers to white supremacy as a worldwide "domination contract." He also claims that race, not gender, is the primal contradiction, with race being the stable reference point for identifying "them" and "us." This contention understandably raises the ire of radical feminists. Mills in recent years wrote on the need for whites who see themselves as progressives—those wanting to expand recognition, rights, and opportunities—to learn from and unite with Black radicals to generate a new social contract that will rectify injustices.

Tommie Shelby

American **Tommie Shelby** (1967–) characterizes racism as an ideology, which he defines as "widely accepted illusory systems of belief that function to establish or reinforce structures of social oppression" ("Is Racism in the 'Heart'?" 415). Because ideologies are effective tools of domination, racial ideologies emerged to legitimize the subordination and economic exploitation of the African slave trade and the colonization of the non-white world. In this case, the ideological system of racism instills in white people false beliefs about the racial characteristics of non-white people. Ideology reduces non-white people to the subordinate Other by imputing to them an inherent and unchangeable "essential nature." This supposed essence is based on superficial physical characteristics, like Fanon's concept of the Black skin. False and superficial though it is, the set of racial characteristics explains why it is appropriate for white people to exploit and dominate non-white people.

Shelby states that the ideology of racism exerts an influence on the culture, politics, and economic conditions of the United States, enabling and sustaining oppression. This ideology also enables and sustains racist beliefs and feelings in people, influencing their actions toward others.

Shelby constructs a new pragmatic theory of Black political theory in *We Who Are Dark: The Philosophical Foundations of Black Solidarity* (2005). Shelby is more friendly to liberalism than is Charles W. Mills and brings in some of its values of individual liberty and social equality to help form what he calls a "pragmatic Black nationalism." He sees the principles of equality and justice as being important to form an organic Black identity that can generate Black solidarity across cultural or class lines. This concept empowers Black people to ground their solidarity not on a sense of shared identity but on a principled response to the oppression they all face. Also unlike Charles Mills, Shelby is open to connecting his theory of Black solidarity with Rawls's ideal theory of justice. Shelby argues that a concept of justice that seeks to rectify racial injustices presupposes an ideal theory of justice that can be the standard by which we make judgments about when injustices have occurred and when they have been rectified.

George Yancy

American **George Yancy** (1961–) followed in Frantz Fanon's line of thinking with his book, *Black Bodies, White Gazes: The Continuing Significance of Race* (2008). Yancy continues the approach of telling stories from lived experience of being Black in a white world. He speaks of experiences he has endured of being reduced by white gazes to an impersonal Black body—experiences every Black person can relate to.

He tells the powerful story of being a Black body entering an elevator that has a white woman in it. Because of anti-Black racism training that a Black man, even a friendly well-dressed Black man, is essentially dangerous, a white person, especially if she is a white woman, is immediately put on guard. She reacted to Yancy's presence as a perceived threat, moving away from him and clutching her purse. As a Black person with a Black body, Yancy was immediately dehumanized by the white gaze. He was not an individual; he was a Black male body, a different, deviant, dangerous criminal and aggressor.

In multiple philosophical papers, Yancy shares similar stories of how the white gaze, informed by structural racism's poisonous assumptions, had perceived him. In a 2013 article for the *New York Times*, Yancy spoke of an incident when he was a teenager and a white police officer almost shot him because he was carrying a telescope down the street.

> [The police officer] failed to conceive, or perhaps could not conceive, that a black teenage boy living in the Richard Allen Project Homes for very low income families would own a telescope and enjoyed looking at the moons of Jupiter and the rings of Saturn. A black boy carrying a telescope wasn't conceivable—unless he had stolen it—given the white racist horizons within which my black body was policed as dangerous. To the officer, I was something (not someone) patently foolish, perhaps monstrous or even fictional. My telescope, for him, was a weapon. ("Walking While Black in the 'White Gaze'")

Of course, the white gaze has power far beyond such interpersonal encounters. Yancy says that the white gaze in its active form is the site of white power, hegemony, and privilege. Using **Edmund Husserl's** concept of sedimentation, Yancy says that the white gaze, sedimented with experiences of white power and privilege, sees the Black body with disgust and perpetuates violence against it.

Writing amid the spate of police killings of Black people, Yancy establishes the difficult concepts of "suturing" and "unsuturing"—difficult to understand and even more difficult to accept. He says that white people "suture" (close) over the festering reality of lies about their violence against Black people. Sutured, they believe themselves closed off to the reality of Black people as people and closed off to Black people as suffering. White people, he says, must strive to be unsutured—the powerful step of openness to the ways in which their whiteness is a problem. Being unsutured is an openness to the loss and great discomfort of challenging their own identities. Yancy links this to Baldwin's call for a dialogue between Black and white people, a dialogue that necessarily involves an accusation that will require white courageous listening.

Feminist Philosophies of Race

We also need to discuss feminist philosophies of race. Black women have been oppressed both for their race and their gender, and intersectionality addresses this feminist aspect of race. We met two intersectional feminists in Chapter 18, **Audre Lorde** and **bell hooks**, who also wrote about philosophy of race. **Kimberlé Williams Crenshaw**, who introduced the term "intersectionality," has argued within legal theory that the law looks at gender and race discrimination separately but that Black women suffer not simply from a sum of those two discriminations but also from an intersection of them that overlaps the two forms of discrimination.

Arguably the first book on intersectionality (though she did not use the term) was **Angela Davis's** (1944–) *Women, Race and Class* (1981). Davis conducted an orthodox Marxist analysis of the three topics in the title. She covered the problems of second-wave feminism being run by and for white middle-class women, and she discussed the economic role of enslaved Black women in the 1800s. Davis's answer to the problems of race and gender was Marxist revolution.

Non-white feminists have pointed to the social reality that standards of femininity and feminine beauty are skewed toward white characteristics. We have seen other philosophers of race analyze how racism is based primarily on physical characteristics. This prejudice based on physical stereotypes is even more severe for non-white women. The traditional standard of beauty in Western society is a woman with fair skin, delicate features, and blond hair. These are, of course, characteristics that non-white, and in particular Black women, do not naturally possess. Even within the Black community, there is peer pressure for Black women to lighten their skin and straighten their hair. Recently in the United States, Black people, women especially, have been discriminated against for having their natural hair. Feminists of all ethnicities have called for women of all ethnicities to embrace their own beauty rather than be oppressed and shamed by arbitrary standards of white feminine beauty.

In a different vein, American **Kathryn Sophia Belle** (1978–), formerly known as Kathryn T. Gines, has written critiques of Simone de Beauvoir, Jean-Paul Sartre, W.E.B. Du Bois, Charles W. Mills, and in general analytic philosophy and continental philosophy, pointing out the absence of the perspective of Black women in those philosophies. Belle wrote a book, *Hannah Arendt and the Negro Question* (2014), in which she argued that Arendt's discussion of the "Negro problem" failed to recognize that it was actually a "white problem." Belle holds up Arendt as an example of how a rigid distinction between the social and the political stops philosophers from recognizing that racism is both a political and a social problem.

The Future of Race

Philosophy of race is a vibrant and growing field and, regrettably, this chapter can be only a brief introduction. Even a few years from now, this chapter will need to be expanded substantially, and that is a good thing. The Black Lives Matter movement will surely inspire more people to explore the causes of and remedies for structural racism, not only in the United States but also throughout the world.

This chapter is certainly guilty of focusing on anti-Black racism. The majority of research in the philosophy of race has come from Black American philosophers, and they understandably write from their perspectives. It would be an egregious mistake to think that all racism is directed at Black people. The fiction of biological race also identified supposed races of Asians and indigenous peoples of the Americas and Oceania. Colonialism relegated all non-white people to an inferior status.

Can we simply get rid of the fiction of race? American **Lawrence Blum** (1943–) and British Ghanaian **Kwame Anthony Appiah** (1954–) argue that yes, we should dispense with the concept of race. Their basic argument is that because race is a social construction with no biological basis, we should talk about "racialized groups" or "racial identities." Making this shift in language, they believe, will make it easier for us to eliminate discrimination based on racialization. Appiah argues that group identities are socially defined based on race, religion, class, and gender and that they are often used to limit individual freedom. He therefore attempts to deconstruct group identities and replace them with the notion of cosmopolitanism—the realization that we have obligations to each other and need to learn about each other's practices and beliefs.

However, there is no sign that racism is going away anytime soon. The issue of race, therefore, must continue to be a concern for philosophers. Even if we could somehow magically end all racist ideologies and the personal feelings and thoughts they cause, we would still have to address the enduring damages caused by the legacy of racism.

Chapter 20

TOWARD PHILOSOPHY'S FUTURE

I write this book at the beginning of the third decade of the 2000s. Philosophy is accelerating and diversifying. I could easily have written much more about the philosophy of the late 1900s and early 2000s. As you have probably gathered, the field of philosophy has become increasingly fragmented, diverging from the fairly linear development of the first fourteen or so chapters. That's because philosophy is becoming increasingly dynamic and involved in the world, despite those people who want to dismiss philosophy because it challenges their assumptions. The quest to understand fundamental principles and the desire to better our lives are alive, bigger than ever, and never more needed than now. Too many introductory philosophy courses treat philosophy as a collection of "dead white guys," but the reality is that philosophy's conversation is ongoing. This book is about to end, but philosophy will not. Social and political philosophy, feminist philosophy, and philosophy of race will remain vibrant areas of inquiry as these philosophers explore how we are and how we will be. I could write a great deal about the challenges facing us in the future and how philosophy can respond to them. For this last chapter, I want to talk about several areas of philosophy that will be much discussed in the near future.

Philosophy of Science

Our society is increasingly dominated by science and technology. What effects that has on us goes far beyond simply having new tools that make our lives easier. We've seen a number of philosophers who were critical of science, and that critique continues. Some speak of a crisis of science in that science's pervasive reach into our lives is largely unquestioned, despite the real possibility that our science can harm, if not destroy, us. We can't afford to pretend that science is value neutral   science reflects our values. The question then becomes what values do we want science to reflect?

Simply put, philosophy of science is the philosophical exploration of the roots and methods of scientific inquiry. Every discipline of science has its own corresponding "philosophy of ___" that examines the underlying foundations of that scientific discipline and the implications of the questions and results generated by that discipline. For example, philosophy of biology would analyze how biological organisms should be studied, how theories and taxonomies should be constructed, and what the ethical implications are of biological studies and paradigms.

Madison *Emily*

Like most philosophy, though, a serious exploration of science is not simple. Like all good philosophy, philosophy of science tries to improve our understanding and quality of life, and also like all good philosophy, it does not simply accept the dominant paradigm.

The dominant paradigms of science have been "positivism" and "coherentism." We explored positivism before; it is the assumption that all knowledge must conform to scientific statements that are verified through observation and reason. Coherentism is the idea that scientific statements are justified by being part of a coherent system of theory and observations. Unlike positivism, coherentism understands that no scientific theory or observation exists in isolation, nor can those theories or observations be validated on their own. All theories, predictions, and observations are cognitive acts that rely on a broad set of social beliefs. Therefore, it is impossible to test a theory in isolation; we can only justify the overall system, but even then, only in an ad hoc way. Despite their differences, both positivism and coherentism assume that science is a gradual, methodical process of discovery of facts about the world. Some still hold to one of these views, despite the work of Thomas Kuhn.

Thomas Kuhn—Scientific Revolutions

American **Thomas Kuhn** (1922–1996) in his book, *The Structure of Scientific Revolutions* (1962), radically changed our understanding of how science progresses. Kuhn's ideas about epistemology were influenced by philosophers such as Wittgenstein and his own studies of the history of science. He rejected the traditional view that science advances through the gradual accumulation of new discoveries. He argued that science is "a series of peaceful interludes punctuated by intellectually violent revolutions" in which "one conceptual world view is replaced by another."

Kuhn said that scientific work in the longer-lasting, more tranquil periods of "normal science" is guided by a dominant paradigm. By "paradigm," Kuhn means an attitude similar to what Peirce had defined as truth—a consensus within the community of scientists. Science is an approach to reality and questions about the universe that operates from a set of assumptions and preconceptions. Formally or habitually, scientists establish the paradigm of how the universe should be conceptualized, including what fundamental laws and theoretical assumptions we must accept, what problems need to be solved, and what phenomena are relevant to their solution. In normal science, tasks attempt to answer questions raised by the paradigm and then to fit all new data into the prevailing paradigm.

Eventually, however, phenomena will emerge that don't conform to the paradigm. Kuhn describes the process science then goes through. Initially, it dismisses such maverick data as "anomalies" or minor difficulties that science will eventually solve and fit into the paradigm. Science resists the idea that the prevailing theory and paradigm are false, and it resists alternative theories to explain the anomalies. As anomalous data increase, normal science enters a crisis. Eventually, a new paradigm that better explains the data will emerge and gain a following of scientists who will overthrow the established theory, and a scientific revolution has come about. Kuhn points to the scientific revolutions of Galileo's rules of motion replacing Aristotelian science and Einstein's theory of relativity replacing Newtonian mechanics.

Kuhn claims, as **Edmund Husserl** had, that all scientific observation is "theory laden." This means that we don't see objects simply as they are; we see objects in terms of our theoretical, interpretive framework. Because we operate within our paradigm, our belief system, we observe objects according to what our "knowledge" tells us we see, and we consider this to be "normal" and our interpretations "true." Despite our best intentions, we make the phenomena we observe fit the preconceptions of our paradigm. This is not wholly negative because we need conceptual paradigms to process and understand our experiences (Kant's Categories are just the most basic concepts of our paradigms).

We need to be aware, however, that our paradigms shape our perceptions and expectations. An Aristotelian scientist had the paradigm that rest was the "natural" condition for an object; therefore, motion was abnormal and needed to be explained. Galileo, and later Newton, operated under a different paradigm, which said an object in motion "naturally" stayed in motion; therefore, motion didn't need to be explained, but any change in its motion did. An Aristotelian, seeing a weight swinging on a string, would seek to answer what was preventing the weight from coming to rest. A post-Galilean, seeing the same swinging weight would seek to answer what was preventing the weight from continuing to move in a straight line. This difference may seem subtle on the surface, but because the two paradigms organize and view phenomena according to different assumptions, they ask different questions and look at different data—and come to different conclusions.

If all observations are theory laden, Kuhn argues, then there are no theory-neutral observations. That means there is no privileged viewpoint that can decide which of the competing scientific theories is the winner. Numerous philosophers had been making this point since the early 1800s, but science still saw itself as being above this discussion. Nevertheless, no pure observation could decide between Aristotle's or Galileo's physics of motion. What's more, scientists operating under their own theory will interpret the empirical data to make them consistent with their preferred theory's claims.

What counts as scientific inquiry, acceptable standards of scientific evidence, and even rationality itself are defined in terms of the particular preferred paradigm. Remember feminism's critique of science in Chapter 18. Accordingly, Kuhn concludes that we have no purely objective, rational path from an old paradigm to a new one, and, therefore, a scientific revolution (like a political one) is more the result of sociological factors than objective, impartial evidence.

Critics charge that Kuhn has denied the objectivity of science and its goal of producing a true account of reality. But isn't that Kuhn's point? And isn't Kuhn following a trajectory of philosophical thought that goes back to **Immanuel Kant** if not **William of Ockham** or even earlier? Philosophers have long debated how much our so-called knowledge is based on a "true" encounter with objective reality and how much is our own mental construction.

In the current philosophy of science, the debate is between the various versions of scientific realism and anti-realism. Scientific realism is the standard scientific view that the objects and phenomena that scientists talk about exist independent of human theories and that, therefore, science can give us objective knowledge about the world. Scientific anti-realism is the contrary claim that scientific theories are products of humans and do not give us a purely objective account of the world.

The realists correctly point out that it is undeniable that scientific theories can be useful guides to explain the phenomena we observe. The anti-realists reply that past theories continually made successful predictions before they were abandoned because of a paradigm shift. For example, **Ptolemy's** (c. 367 BCE–282 BCE) Earth-centered cosmology reliably predicted the planets' motions for centuries until the heliocentric cosmology was adopted. Truth is not essential for a theory to be accepted and successful. Scientific theories are tools that provide us with fruitful models—"useful fictions," as Nietzsche would say—and ways to systematize and make sense of our experiences.

Furthermore, inspired by pragmatism, anti-realists argue that theoretical models are helpful because they are abstractions, not because they are real. The "average American family" is a useful fiction for economists and social planners, but the average American family does not exist as an entity in the world. Similarly, entities like subatomic particles, genes, and DNA molecules are theoretical constructs that serve a scientific purpose whether or not they are real. Is light a particle or a wave? Both paradigms are useful, and no amount of experimentation can prove one theory or the other the winner. The pragmatic usefulness of a scientific model does not prove that it is providing us with the one and only true depiction of the world. Realists offer a number of responses, mostly centered on the argument that the realist account best fits the success of science.

Michael Polanyi—Personal Knowledge

Another critique of science was given by Hungarian British **Michael Polanyi** (1891–1976). He was originally a chemist who questioned the assumptions of scientific methodology and became interested in the philosophy of science. He rejected the positivist approach to science in his books *Science, Faith and Society* (1946) and *Personal Knowledge: Toward a Post-Critical Philosophy* (1958). The scientific method cannot mechanically produce truth, he claimed. Truth comes instead from personal commitments and judgments. We believe more than we can ever prove, Polanyi said.

Similar to **Henri Bergson**, **Alfred North Whitehead**, and **Max Scheler**, Polanyi thought that a knower does not stand separate from the world but is an active participant in it. Similar to existentialist philosophers, Polanyi thought it is our personal, subjective commitments that motivate and drive our intellectual endeavors. We make scientific discoveries not be being dispassionate, objective observers but by passionately engaging with the subject of inquiry. He uses as an example **Mikołaj Kopernik**, (Copernicus) who he says came to his heliocentric theory not by using a method but by "the greater intellectual satisfaction he derived from the celestial panorama as seen from the Sun instead of the Earth."

Polanyi was a scientist in the process, not positivist, tradition. He rejected positivist reductionism, both that human experience can be reduced to mere sense data and that the human being can be reduced to laws of physics and chemistry. Polanyi contributed to the philosophy of "emergence"—the idea that reality and causation have multiple layers. We are not fully determined by the world, and we have degrees of freedom within the boundary conditions of our circumstances. Our material body acts boundary conditions for us, but our minds are higher realities that depend on the body but are distinct from it. Our will—our commitments—transform our understanding of the world, which is why he rejects positivist science and materialist reductionism. Polanyi condemns all forms of reductionism as moral inversions that attempt to reduce higher-level realities to lower-level realities. Science, and indeed all inquiry, requires free exploration and debate. Only then can science flourish.

Inspired by Polanyi, Austrian philosopher **Paul Feyerabend** (1924–1994) said that science had lost its original purpose and needed to be saved from itself. Feyerabend contends that science had begun as a movement to liberate human thinking and inquiry but had devolved instead into an increasingly dogmatic and rigidly oppressive ideology. He warned against the authoritarian dominance of science. Scientific "facts" are now taught in much the same way that religious "facts" are taught, and science is obsessed with its own mythology, making claims far beyond its ability to justify them. He objected to the dogma of a single scientific method as limiting the activities of scientists. Similar to Kuhn, Feyerabend saw how many significant scientific advances came not from methodical processes but from serendipitous discoveries. The only "method" of science that made sense, he said, was "anything goes."

One scientist who has taken these critiques of science seriously is German physicist **Sabine Hossenfelder** (1976–). In her books, *Lost in Math: How Beauty Leads Physics Astray* (2018) and *Existential Physics: A Scientist's Guide to Life's Biggest Questions* (2022), she criticizes theoretical physicists as being beguiled by their own paradigms. Physicists' belief in mathematical beauty has become a dogmatic paradigm, so much so that this positivist belief in math now conflicts with the principle of scientific observation that goes back to Francis Bacon. Rather than derive ideas from observations, Hossenfelder says, theoretical physicists invent some mathematics that sound good to them and move forward with that paradigm. Current trendy paradigms such as supersymmetry, string theory, the multiverse, and grand unification theory are, she claims, ascientific—they do not come from scientific observation, and they are untestable. The supposed ability for science to self-correct is no longer happening. This is why physics has not made any breakthroughs in more than 40 years. Hossenfelder doesn't quite call for a Kuhnian revolution, but she does urge physicists to rethink their methods. Besides, she says, physics cannot answer life's biggest questions.

Many scientists today are resistant to any input from philosophy. Granted, some philosophers are highly critical of science, even accusing it of advancing racist, sexist, or imperialist ideologies, and we cannot blame scientists, who are people after all, for being resistant to harshly critical approaches. Nevertheless, a science that is ungrounded in self-critique about its methodology and implications is dangerous. A sound and productive philosophy of science will have the goals of increasing scientific accuracy and enhancing science's ability to help rather than harm society.

Globalization

We are becoming one world, the result of a long trend of increasing interconnectedness among the people of the world. Technology has enabled communication, trade, and travel to become quicker and easier. Anyone can converse with anyone anywhere in real time. The Internet has empowered people to access incredible amounts of information, learn almost everything about anything. People instead just watch videos of celebrities and post stupid memes. Too cynical? Well, like Nietzsche, some philosophers who have high hopes for humanity look at our global age of technology and are rather disappointed by the ways people behave.

Globalization has implications for political philosophy. Plato, Aristotle, and the modern political philosophers all held the view that states were relatively isolated and homogeneous within themselves. Not that states in prior centuries didn't have trade and immigration, but the idea of distinct societies with distinct cultural, if not geographic, borders was considered the norm. Globalization has forced people to give up the notion of cultural isolation. Some have welcomed it; some have resisted it. Powered by technology, the wave of globalization will continue, shrinking our world and our distance from each other.

We need to differentiate the globalization of the 2000s from the type of globalization that occurred during the age of European colonization of the rest of the world. Colonialism, which we will discuss later in this chapter, was an expression of economic exploitation and military power that inflicted European culture on other cultures. Today's globalization must be assessed in terms of the legacy of colonialism, but there is more openness from the West toward other cultures, and there is less, although still too much, denial and suppression of other cultures. Still, the ethics of cultural appropriation must be considered. What right do Western people and companies have to use and profit from the cultural creations of non-Western people?

Economic exploitation of workers in "third world" countries is still a significant problem. Marx's critique of 1800s European capitalism seems more true than ever when we consider the plight of workers in East Asian and Latin American countries who manufacture consumer goods for Western corporations. Some philosophers speak of today's global capitalism as a continuation of domination of the working class, now hidden from the sight of consumers because the exploitation now takes place in distant countries.

Some philosophers predicted problems associated with the pace of change and globalization. As early as 1927, **John Dewey** warned that it is difficult to organize the public sphere when it does not stay in place and that this would have negative effects on democracy. Canadian cultural critic **Marshall McLuhan** (1911–1980) wrote about the coming "global village" in which humanity is connected by technology. However, McLuhan predicted bad consequences, saying that the technological medium by which a message is transmitted would become more important that the content of the message—"the medium is the message." Anyone who didn't think of social media when they read that sentence is not paying attention.

Indeed, the moral issues of social media and social networking are the subjects of a new but very important field in philosophy. Phenomenologist and existentialist **Hubert Dreyfus** (1929–2017) in his essay, "Nihilism on the Information Highway: Anonymity versus Commitment in the Present Age" (written in 2004, before Facebook, Twitter, and Instagram), observed that the anonymity and distance allowed by electronic media meant that online interactions intrinsically lacked exposure to risk. Dreyfus said that we are not fully bodily present on electronic media, so we are shielded from the social risks of our behavior being disapproved of by others. Without risk, he said, there can be no true meaning or commitment in the social media realm. The Internet is, he says, like Kierkegaard's aesthetic sphere—promising us new and exciting experiences, and to be whoever we want to be, but without a chance of gaining a history and authentic self that is founded on firmness, balance, and steadiness.

Globalization is not all negative. **Kwame Appiah**, who has written primarily on moral philosophy, has addressed globalization with his theory of cosmopolitanism. In his book, *Cosmopolitanism: Ethics in a World of Strangers* (2006), Appiah defines cosmopolitanism as "universality plus difference," meaning that we don't ignore cultural diversity but that our universal humanity always takes precedence. Cultures matter, but people also matter. Cultural differences are to be respected, but only insofar as they do not harm our universal concern for people. We should first and foremost understand ourselves as citizens of the world. He goes on to say that our obligations to others go beyond sharing citizenship. We have a responsibility to learn about the practices and beliefs of others and their identities. Appiah is critical of all ethnocentrisms, both the Eurocentrism of white supremacy and the Afrocentrism of some radical black philosophers of race.

Technology

The effects of technology on society and individual people are also a concern for some philosophers. There is no doubt that technological advances have changed how people live. Technology is everywhere and has always been a part of life. Even something as primitive as a stone tool is technology—it is, after all, a tool made by a person with the intention of making life better. **Aristotle** had said that human *technè* (craft) sometimes imitates nature and sometimes completes what nature cannot finish. Aristotle's four causes have, as we saw, an application to considering technology. Bacon, in ushering in the new scientific revolution, also extolled the virtues of technology. He saw the link we still consider today between science and technology. For the most part, modernity has been typified by an enthusiastic embrace of technology and its perceived benefits.

The German idealists and the transcendentalists were predominantly negative about technology. They called for a simpler life returning more to nature, and although that did not preclude the use of technology, they saw the possibility that there was already too much technology. **Henry David Thoreau** eschewed technological inventions as "pretty toys which distract our attention from serious things. They are but improved means to an unimproved end." (*Walden*) This sentiment was in keeping with his deeply felt belief that we all need to return to a simple life unencumbered by a plenitude of possessions. We should possess nothing more than is needed for simple, direct tasks. With technology and industrialization, people have become tools of their tools.

Karl Marx noted the effects of technological developments on social developments. In his view, capitalism had developed because technological innovations had altered the means of production and enhanced the ability of the bourgeois class to exploit the labor of the proletariat. He further believed that technological innovations would help to liberate the working class from capitalism.

Not surprisingly, views as to whether technology is a great positive to humanity or at best an ambiguous one splits along the analytic–continental philosophical divide. From **Auguste Comte** to the present day, most analytic philosophers have seen technology as beneficial. This is understandable given how analytic philosophy bases knowledge on logic and mathematics, to which technology is strongly linked.

About the effects of technology, continental philosophers are more ambivalent and less positive, although to be honest that is their general disposition toward everything. **Martin Heidegger**, for example, who practiced a simpler rural life, in 1950 expressed concerns that technology was dehumanizing us, successfully predicting that television would soon come to dominate all communication. As mentioned in Chapter 15, the Frankfurt School observed that technological methods of culture dissemination had assimilated people into a mass consciousness dominated by the bourgeoisie. Some neo-Marxists have agreed with Marx on the connection between technology and capitalism and thus have condemned technology as a tool of capitalist oppression, although to be honest again, neo-Marxists tend to see everything as a tool of capitalist oppression. Arendt discussed how technology had leveled out much of human distinctiveness, with both positive and negative effects.

The postmodernists have perhaps offered the most powerful critique of technology. We covered some of their critique in Chapter 17, and we need not repeat it here. It is worth noting that postmodernists are skeptical of the optimism that science and technology will lead society into greater peace and happiness. Postmodernists tend to agree with the critique that technology, especially mass communication, has assimilated people into a mass consciousness that suppresses individuality and creativity. The proliferation of smartphones, beginning in 2007 with the Apple iPhone, has significantly altered the technological and communication landscapes. The long term effects of smartphones and social media apps have yet to be determined, but this is a growing area of interest for philosophers.

For the reasons given in the preface, this book has not covered ethical philosophy, but a brief note about the ethics of technology is necessary. A number of philosophers have remarked on the presence of technologies that can seriously harm, if not destroy, humanity. The specter of nuclear annihilation has haunted the world since the late 1940s. Some philosophers have warned that instead of a swift nuclear war apocalypse, we are engaged in a slow slide into apocalypse through our use of technologies that harm the environment. Technology produces many toxic chemicals and waste by-products, and our continued obsession with fossil fuels pollutes the environment and is causing climate change. The future of philosophy must include a healthy discussion of how we as a worldwide society should deal with the effects of our own technology.

Postcolonial Theory

The age of colonialism that had begun in the late 1400s supposedly ended sometime in the 1960s, by which time most former colonies had become independent nations. Postcolonial philosophers look at the ongoing legacy of colonialism, in particular the ideological justifications for colonial imperialism and oppression of non-European peoples. In short, colonialism justified itself as the enlightened Europeans bringing civilization to the rest of the world, whether the rest of the world wanted it or not.

The European powers exerted what Peruvian sociologist **Aníbal Quijano** (1930–2018) called the "coloniality of power." A political and economic world order emerged that divided the globe into those nations who held power and those nations that did not. Certainly, much of the activity of colonialism was the extraction of raw materials from foreign lands—such commodities as lumber, minerals, sugar, coffee, tea, tobacco, and slaves. However, raw materials could have been acquired by mutually beneficial trade. Colonialism was a practice of dominance and subjugation of indigenous people, often displacing them from their lands to make way for European peoples—what has come to be known as "settler colonialism." Centuries of subjugation and displacement means that the legacy of colonialism goes beyond economic issues. Postcolonial theory seeks to understand the effects that colonialism still has on the world, cultures, and individuals, with an eye toward ending colonial practices and restoring dignity and sovereignty to colonized people.

Frantz Fanon

Frantz Fanon inaugurated the philosophy of colonialism with his book, *The Wretched of the Earth* (1961). The book was certainly informed by Fanon's earlier thinking in *Black Skin, White Masks*, but it broadens those ideas about the experiences of Black people to the experiences of all oppressed people. Fanon had become deeply involved in the Algerian liberation movement, Algeria then being a colony of France, which kept control through harsh suppression of the Algerian people. Fanon was also interested in the Pan-African movement, the vision of uniting all of Africa in opposition to European colonialism. In a foreshadowing of intersectionality, Fanon looked at oppressions based on class, race, or national culture and considered them as having similar effects. All forms of prejudice rip away a person's ability to feel human, depriving him or her of the possibility of being a person.

Fanon said that the tensions caused by settler colonialism grow over time because the relationship of the settler and the native is one between binary opposites. Those tensions eventually become the catalyst for native violence against the settler, the colonizer who occupies native land. In this way, Fanon defended colonized people's use of violence to gain independence. He also stated that, because the colonizers did not consider the natives as human beings, the colonizers should not expect the natives to be bound by moral principles that apply to human beings. Also, because the colonizer maintains occupation of the land and control over the native population through violence, violent resistance by the natives is justified because it is the only language that the colonizer speaks.

Despite his condoning of violence, Fanon stressed the best solution to colonialism was to build up the humanity of the native. The native people needed to learn their own true history, reestablish their own culture, and develop their own consciousness of self. The Wretched of the Earth quickly became inspirational to anticolonial movements, including violent ones, across the world.

Edward Said, Gayatri Spivak, and Anti-Orientalism

Palestinian American cultural critic **Edward Said** (pronounced sa-YEED, 1935–2003) in his book, Orientalism (1978), he described how Western Europe had intellectually divided the world into a binary social relation, inventing the concepts of Occident and Orient. The "West" created the concept of the "East," despite the reality that those living in the "East" did not see themselves as such. So much discourse still today refers to "Western" and "Eastern" cultures as somehow qualitatively different. Said argued that the social construction of Orientalism falsely depicted the Middle East and Asia as a homogeneous cultural entity, unified in its inferiority to the European "West." Said thus reveals how white supremacy extends beyond the issue of Blackness. The reality of the enslavement of Black Africans created a distinct dynamic for anti-Black racism, but Orientalism is also a white supremacist dominance and dehumanization of the people of the Middle East and Asia.

Like the concept of Blackness, the concept of the Orient was created in the white world and continues to exist in negation to whiteness. The attitude of Orientalism has its roots in the Crusades of the 1000s, which saw the Islamic states of the Middle East as an evil scourge that needed to be eliminated. (Granted, the Islamic states had similar feelings about the Europeans, especially after the Crusades.)

Said focuses less on the political and economic exploitation of people in the "East" and instead focuses mainly on the academic field of Orientalism popular in Western Europe in the 1700s and 1800s. French and British scholars developed a structured set of assumptions and discursive practices that described and interpreted the people of the Orient. European paternalism exercised authority over the cultural products of Oriental societies, explaining their history, practices, and especially their literature. The Europeans pretended to know more about these people than the people did about themselves, often getting things very wrong. Said stated that this paternalistic characterization allowed Europeans to create a binary relation that could make them feel better about themselves. They were rational, ordered, and sensible people, whereas the people of the "East" were irrational, chaotic people who had strange and primitive beliefs.

In this way, Europeans were able to justify their expressions of power and superiority under the guise of their supposed knowledge about the "East." Said exposes the pretense of European scholarship being value free. It expressed the values of the "West."

Indian philosopher **Gayatri Spivak** (1942–) applied Said's concept of Orientalism to her native land. She says that Western scholars dismiss all non-Western forms of knowledge and discourse as mere myth and folklore. Using Gramsci's concept of the subaltern (see Chapter 15), Spivak explores the experiences of women who are socially and politically excluded from the hierarchy of power. She criticizes the ongoing cultural appropriations of Westerners who do not seek to listen to or understand subaltern peoples. In her essay, "Can the Subaltern Speak?" (1988), Spivak argues that subaltern people have been so dominated by colonialism that it is difficult for the authentic experiences and voices of marginalized people to emerge. The voices of colonized people were erased and the people alienated from their own culture and nature. Native people nevertheless remain powerful, despite being repeatedly denied.

Paulo Freire

Philosopher of education **Paulo Freire** (1921–1997) was concerned for those who suffered from colonial oppression in his native Brazil. As a schoolteacher, he tried to tackle the problem of widespread illiteracy in northeastern Brazil. He worked with government agencies on promoting literacy and grew to realize that the problems of illiteracy and poverty were related to authoritarian attitudes that were deeply ingrained in all aspects of society, even in how parents related to their children.

Influenced by John Dewey (see Chapter 12), Freire saw that education is more than learning skills—education is about people discovering themselves as creative agents and becoming more human. After teaching for years, he went back to school to get his doctorate and develop a philosophy of social justice.

Central to Paulo Freire's social philosophy is his insight that within oppressive dynamics, the humanity of both the oppressor and the oppressed is diminished. This idea is similar to Hegel's identification that the master–slave dialectic gives neither the master nor the slave sufficient recognition to realize him or herself.

Freire believed that political and legal reforms were on their own insufficient to change oppressive dynamics because people in all classes had internalized the historically pervasive authoritarian oppression. This includes the oppressed, who have internalized oppressive structures and are conditioned to keep their place in the social hierarchy. Worse, Freire realized, the oppressed, instead of striving for liberation, tend themselves to become oppressors. People embedded in oppressive dynamics become opportunistic oppressors—bosses of their workers, parents of their children, and other situations in which there is an imbalance of power.

In his 1968 book, *Pedagogy of the Oppressed*, Freire calls for an overhaul of pedagogy—the method and practice of teaching. While working as a teacher in the early 1960s, Freire came to realize that widespread illiteracy was related to authoritarian attitudes that bred an environment of oppressions. He saw that authoritarianism was deeply ingrained in all aspects of society, even in how parents related to their children. The value of education, for Freire, was not simply being better able to make a living in a profession but rather empowerment and transformation for an individual and community. Education is a process. Education, well done, leads to social justice.

Freire's philosophy of education was a response to the legacy of colonialism. Freire says that this traditional dichotomous and authoritarian model of education assumes that experts bestow their gift of knowledge to those who know nothing. This model not only perpetuates oppressive dynamics but also is an ineffective method of education. Freire called this the "banking concept of knowledge." The bank holds the knowledge, and people must come to the bank to receive it. The bank of knowledge is also separate from the people.

> Implicit in the banking concept is the assumption of a dichotomy between human beings and the world: a person is merely in the world, not with the world or with others; the individual is spectator, not re-creator. (*Pedagogy of the Oppressed* x)

Freire argued that this banking concept of knowledge perpetuates hierarchies of power, reaffirming the oppressive dynamics of powerful and powerless. Freire connects the banking model of education to colonialism. The oppressive dynamic of colonialism is that the colonizing culture sees itself as possessing value while the colonized culture does not. This binary paradigm extends to education. Even well-meaning teachers who wish to treat their students as valuable individuals are caught within a system of education that enforces the colonial dichotomy.

Education is never a neutral process, Freire says. Education presupposes about students either an inequality between teacher and student or the possibility of dialogue with students. The former presupposition perpetuates dichotomies of the banking model and traps students in hierarchies of power. The latter presupposition sees students as equal human beings deserving of trust and respect. It does not mean thinking all students know as much as the teacher. That would be counterproductive. It does mean empowering students to learn. It means seeing education as a process of facilitating practice and critical reflection. Education with the banking model does not appreciate the uniqueness of individuals. Individuals have an "infinite diversity of active tendencies," and education, and society as a whole, must account for this.

Nonheteronormative Philosophy

Definitely not least, but last in chronology, is the new and growing field of philosophy about people outside the traditional binary designations of norms about gender and sexuality. Heteronormativity is the traditional assumption that only male–female romantic and sexual relationships are normal. Any deviation from a straight male–female gender binary is considered psychologically or morally aberrant.

Nonheteronormative sexuality has long been dismissed or repressed by European and American societies. In one respect, the suppression and oppression of nonheteronormative people is similar to that suffered by women and people of color. However, heteronormative supremacy has a distinct character. The fear and loathing of nonheteronormative people cuts across gender, racial, and class distinctions. What should be obvious is that nonheteronormative people are people and, therefore, are entitled to recognition as people with basic moral consideration. We've seen some philosophers in this book whose nonheteronormative sexuality, and the oppression they suffered from society for it, formed part of their philosophy—for example, **Michel Foucault**, **James Baldwin**, and **Audre Lorde**. In the 1970s, serious academic study of homosexuality as a nonaberrant identity began. The gay rights movement also began, which has since expanded into rights for other nonheteronormative identities.

One philosopher who has written about nonheteronormative philosophy is American **Judith Butler** (1956–). She has written a series of books that have shown that gender is a social construction and that gender is therefore a set of concepts and stylized repetitive acts that reflect the dominant power structure. Gender, she argues, is performative—one acts male or female within the frameworks that determine for people what their possibilities are for gender, sex, and sexuality.

The supposed binary nature of biological sex has led to assumptions that gender and sexuality should also be binary. Butler calls instead for an open critique of sex and gender. For her, that includes how feminism has used the concept of "women" as an objective, discrete, ahistorical group. Butler sees this as a mistake that has reinforced the binary view of sex and gender. Instead of trying to define "women," Butler says that feminism should focus on providing an account of how power functions and shapes our understandings of womanhood.

Butler also takes aim at the concepts of homosexual and heterosexual, seeing them as limiting, binary identities. Her idea that sexuality is performative applies here also. One repetitively acts as a homosexual or heterosexual, matching one's behavior to imitate how the categorized identity is defined. This is the case even though acting as a homosexual may include exclusions and concealments.

Butler says that many of the performative acts of sex, gender, and sexuality are performed without conscious awareness. The social constructions of gender identities are social norms to which we conform because we are taught to do so. Such is the case for all social norms— that's why they are norms—these are the definitions of how we are to act to fit in with society (see Honneth in Chapter 15). Butler calls for breaking the socially defined linkage of sex with gender, allowing for people to develop their gender and desires freely and flexibly. One's gender and sexuality would still be performative, but an individual's acts would stem from who that person is, not from a social construction. Individuals would not have an identity limited to the expression of any binary structure.

Butler's work has been instrumental in the development of ideas of nonbinary gender identities and has helped establish the field of queer theory. Butler opened a door onto possibilities for dispensing with the traditional narratives that heterosexuality is the only acceptable norm, allowing for people not needing to take on compulsory identities as "man," "woman," "heterosexual," or "homosexual." We've seen in this book how when someone opens a door, people will go through it. This has indeed happened with this door to a society accepting of nonheteronormative identities.

When we've looked at previous times when these philosophical doors have opened, we've had the advantage of being able to analyze what happened from the perspective of many years later. Butler and others opened this philosophical door less than 30 years ago. It should not surprise us that the field of nonheteronormative philosophy is still very much in flux. Currently, there is much debate over approach, terminology, and goals.

One problem the field must resolve is that if "queer" is defined in opposition to "normal," than no matter how broad the concept of "queer" is, it remains a binary definition that can quickly become yet another binary opposition and excuse for division and oppression. The "transgender" label has become contentious with debate over whether a biological male has a right to demand to be treated as a woman or a biological woman as a man if they self-identify as such. If, as Butler contends, gender is a performative act, can one simply act like a woman and thus claim a legal right to be a woman? Although they agree that any person claiming to be "trans" should be free from hate directed at their nonheteronormativity, many feminists who have suffered the discrimination and oppression that comes with being a woman take issue with biological men claiming they are now also women. These feminists point out that sex is not gender, and some claim that the trans demand is trying to erase that distinction. It is a thorny dispute over a complicated set of issues.

That all nonheteronormative people should be recognized as having full human rights should be obvious. Actually, that all people should be so recognized is obvious. As we've heard a number of philosophers of feminism and race say, we need to respect differences and listen to individuals' lived experiences. We are all on a quest to build a better life. The best approach to our personal quest is to be open to understanding people for who they are and listening to what they have to tell us.

A Concluding Unscientific Postscript

Here we are at the end of this book, and how we are today has been shaped by the ideas and actions of the philosophers we have discussed. To give just two quick examples, in the last few years, the Black Lives Matter and #MeToo movements have been prominent in social consciousness. These movements for social justice are informed by the philosophers discussed in this book, and not just the most recent ones. As the world begins finally to deal with the climate crisis, philosophy will help frame the discussion. Philosophers we have discussed will also help us understand technological and political changes and help us find our way amid an increasingly diverse and complex world.

This book could be expanded another hundred pages and still not exhaust the subject of philosophy past and present. It is meant only as an introduction to this wonderful field of philosophy. Hopefully, this book will inspire you to explore philosophy further. You can find much more in-depth information on every philosopher and every topic discussed in this book. The references at the end will be helpful in your further exploration.

Also, I have regrettably not been able to discuss every idea of the philosophers covered, and I have left out other philosophers who are still interesting in their own right. I have told a story of the history of philosophy, but it is not the only story.

Today there are, of course, a great number of philosophers doing important work on important questions. Some of them I have had the honor of meeting and speaking with in person. I could list the names of dozens of philosophers active today who are doing important work, but I will not even try to do so because unavoidably I will leave someone out.

Most importantly, I hope this book has impressed on you the importance of philosophy's influence on our society and how we think and act today. No aspect of our lives has been unaffected by the thinking, research, and writing of philosophers. Philosophy still has much to offer us in helping us understand how we are, how we got here, and what we can be in the future.

Finally, I hope I have encouraged you to be a philosopher. Not necessarily to be a professional academic philosopher (although it is a great career) but to be a philosopher in the course of your own life. We have seen in this book how your experiences and choices affect your perceptions. We have also seen how your own freewill choices constitute who you are and what you can be. Being a philosopher is integral to being a person, to being any part of society. And, yes, being a philosopher can lead to greater personal fulfillment as you create your own future.

CHRONOLOGY

Ancient Era

BCE
509	Roman Republic established
449 to 431	"Golden Age" of Athens
431–404	Peloponnesian War ending in defeat of Athens
399	Death of Socrates
398–347	Plato active
347–322	Aristotle active
31	Octavian establishes Roman Empire

CE
ca. 30–50	Philo active
245–270	Plotinus active
313	"Edict of Milan" proclaims religions toleration
325	Council of Nicaea
384–430	Augustine active
410	Visigoths sack Rome
410–895	Age of "barbarian" invasions
455	Vandals sack Rome
476	Last Roman Emperor deposed

Medieval Era

ca. 930–950	Al-Farabi active
ca. 1010–1037	Ibn Sina active
1169–1198	Ibn Rushd active
1204	Sack of Constantinople
1209–1229	Albigensian Crusade against Gnostic Christians in Languedoc
1212	Battle of Las Navas de Tolsa; beginning of end of Muslim rule in Spain
1240	Translations of Aristotle and Islamic commentaries on Aristotle widely available in Catholic Europe

Renaissance Era

1317–1349	William of Ockham active
1347–1351	Black Death kills one-third of population throughout Europe
1447	Invention of the printing press

1453	Constantinople falls to Ottomans, Greek scholars and manuscripts flee to Latin west transmitting the rest of Plato to the west
1480–1519	Leonardo DaVinci active
1492	Christopher Columbus's first voyage to the new world
1494	Spain and Portugal agree to Treaty of Tordesillas which divides the world between them, ushering in the age of colonialism
1500	First Portuguese trading posts in India
1502	First slaves taken from Africa to the new world
1513	Niccolo Machiavelli writes *The Prince* though it is not published until 1532
1514	Mikołaj Kopernik begins development of heliocentric theory though he does not publish until on his deathbed in 1543
1517	Martin Luther produces his *95 Theses* intended to stimulate debate about church corruption and abuses
1521	Pope Leo X excommunicates Luther
1521	Spain conquers the Aztec Empire
1524	First rebellions and defections from Catholic rule commence over a century of wars in central Europe
1532–1533	Spain conquers the Incan Empire
1534	Henry VIII breaks with Rome and declares himself head of Church of England

Modern Era

1589–1613	William Shakespeare active
1597–1627	Francis Bacon publishes works on methods of philosophy and science
1600	Giordano Bruno burned at the stake for heresy
1604	"Kepler's Nova" lends further credence to notions of change in the heavens
1609	Johannes Kepler publishes his theory of planetary motion showing planetary orbits are not circular but elliptical
1610	Galileo publishes his discoveries in astronomy, the *Sidereus Nuncius*
1632	Galileo publishes *Dialogue Concerning the Two Chief World Systems* explaining the heliocentric theory; a year later the Inquisition forced him to recant
1618–1648	Thirty Years War
1624–1643	Political theory of Absolutism develops in France under reign of Louis XIII
1626–1649	Rene Descartes active; publishes *Discourse* in 1637, *Meditations* in 1641
1628	William Harvey publishes his theory of circulation of blood

1638	Galileo publishes *Two New Sciences* advancing theories on motion of objects
1637–1656	Thomas Hobbes active; publishes *Leviathan* in 1651
1642–1660	English Civil War, Oliver Cromwell's rule (1649–1658), Restoration of the monarchy in 1660
1643–1715	Reign of French King Louis XIV
1660	The Royal Society of London for Improving Natural Knowledge founded two months after the Restoration
1661	Robert Boyle in *The Sceptical Chymist* rejects the Aristotelian four elements and adopts a corpuscular view of matter
1665	Robert Hooke publishes *Micrographia* detailing his microscopic observations
1666–1714	Leibniz active, invents calculus in 1675
1678	Peace of Westphalia ends the Thirty Years' War
1685	Louis XIV revokes legal protections for protestants; brutal persecutions begin
1687	Isaac Newton publishes *Principia Mathematica*
1689	After the Glorious Revolution, William and Mary are named co-rulers of the United Kingdom
1689	British "Bill of Rights" lays out basic rights for all male citizens
1689–1695	John Locke's published writings on epistemology and political philosophy
1709–1713	George Berkeley's published writings
1726	Jonathan Swift publishes *Gulliver's Travels* satirizing scientists, especially the Royal Society
1739–1762	David Hume active
1754–1799	Immanuel Kant active
1762	Rousseau writes *The Social Contract*
1772–1775	Carl Scheele, Joseph Priestley, and Antoine Lavoisier independently discover oxygen
1774	Johann Wolfgang von Goethe publishes the novel, *The Sorrows of Young Werther*
1776	Adam Smith publishes *Wealth of Nations*
1776	James Watt sells the first copy of his vastly improved steam engine
1776	Declaration of Independence and Articles of Confederation written establishing the ideas of natural rights and the social contract in the new United States of America
1781	Kant's first edition of *Critique of Pure Reason*
1787	United States Constitution written
1789	Jeremy Bentham publishes his moral theory of utilitarianism
1789	Antoine Lavoisier publishes the first modern list of chemical elements
1789	French Revolution; "Reign of Terror" 1793–1794, chaos and war until 1799

| 1792 | Mary Wollstonecraft publishes *A Vindication of the Rights of Woman* |

Post-Kantian Era

1794–1814	Fichte active
1798–1802	The Jena Romantic circle meets
1799	Napoleon grabs power in France
1803–1815	Napoleonic Wars
1807	Hegel publishes *Phenomenology of Mind* and *Phenomenology of Spirit*
1808	Beethoven's *Fifth Symphony*
1813	Madame de Staël publishes *De l'Allemagne*, introducing German idealism to the rest of Europe
1830–1842	Auguste Comte develops positivism
1836	Transcendental Club founded in Cambridge, Massachusetts
1841–1855	Søren Kierkegaard active
1842–1883	Karl Marx active
1843–1869	John Stuart Mill active
1845	Margaret Fuller publishes *Woman in the Nineteenth Century*
1848	"The Year of Revolutions"—peasant and worker rebellions across Europe
1848	Marx and Engels' *Manifesto of the Communist Party*
1857	Herbert Spencer publishes the first theory of evolution
1859	Charles Darwin publishes *Origin of Species*
1864–1909	Charles Sanders Pierce active
1896	John Stuart Mill publishes *The Subjection of Women*
1872	Claude Monet's painting, *Impression, soleil levant*, sparks the Impressionist art movement
1872–1888	Nietzsche active, publishes *Beyond Good and Evil* in 1886
1874	Franz Brentano publishes Psychology from an Empirical Standpoint
1881–1949	John Dewey active
1889–1932	Henri Bergson active, publishing *Time and Free Will* in 1889 and *Creative Evolution* in 1907
1989–1935	Jane Addams active
1890–1910	William James active, beginning with *The Principles of Psychology*
1891–1936	Edmund Husserl active, publishes *Ideas* in 1913, the founding text of phenomenology
1895–1969	Bertrand Russell active, with Alfred North Whitehead publishes *Principia Mathematica* in 1910–1913
1897–1963	W.E.B. Du Bois active, publishes *The Souls of Black Folk* in 1903
1904–1969	György Lukács active, publishes *History and Class Consciousness* in 1923

1913–1928	Max Scheler active
1914–1918	World War I
1916–1933	Edith Stein active
1917–1918	Ludwig Wittgenstein writes the *Tractatus Logico-Philosophicus* while a soldier and then prisoner of war
1918–1939	The Frankfurt School is active
1920–1938	Alfred North Whitehead develops his natural theology, publishes *The Concept of Nature* in 1920 and *Process and Reality* in 1929
1926–1937	Antonio Gramsci writes his philosophical works while a political prisoner under the Italian fascists
1927	Martin Heidegger publishes *Being and Time*
1929–1941	Ludwig Wittgenstein develops his later philosophy which goes against the *Tractatus*
1929–1975	Hannah Arendt active
1932–1969	Karl Jaspers active, publishes *Reason and Existenz* in 1935
1933–1945	The Nazis suppress many philosophers' ideas
1939–1945	World War II

Post-World War II Era

1936–1976	Jean-Paul Sartre active
1946	Max Horkheimer and Theodor Adorno publish *Dialectic of Enlightenment*
1946–1997	Paulo Freire active
1946–1975	Michael Polanyi active
1947–1986	Simone de Beauvoir active, publishes *The Second Sex* in 1949
1949	Gilbert Ryle publishes *The Concept of Mind*
1951	Hannah Arendt publishes The Origins of Totalitarianism
1952	Franz Fanon publishes *Black Skin, White Masks*
1953	W.V.O. Quine writes "Two Dogmas of Empiricism"
1955–1968	Martin Luther King, Jr. active in Civil Rights Movement, wins Nobel Peace Prize in 1964
1955–1994	Claude Lévi-Strauss active
1959–2003	Jacques Derrida active
1960–1978	Louis Althusser active
1961	Franz Fanon publishes *The Wretched of the Earth*
1961–1984	Michel Foucault active
1962	Thomas Kuhn publishes *The Structure of Scientific Revolutions*
1962	John L. Austin publishes *How to Do Things With Words*
1962–	Jürgen Habermas active, publishes *Theory of Communicative Action* in 1981
1963	Betty Friedan publishes *The Feminine Mystique*
1963	Edmund Gettier publishes "Is Justified True Belief Knowledge?"
1963	Hannah Arendt publishes *Eichmann in Jerusalem: A Report on the Banality of Evil*

1963	James Baldwin publishes *The Fire Next Time*
1963	President John F. Kennedy is assassinated
1966	National Organization for Women (NOW) established
1968	Summer of student and worker protests in France, events influential on postmodernist and political theory
1968–2004	Jean Baudrillard active, publishes *The Consumer Society* in 1970
1968–2010	Mary Daly active, publishes *Gyn/Ecology: The Metaethics of Radical Feminism* in 1978
1969	The Stonewall uprising in New York City, sparking the gay liberation movement
1969–	John Searle active
1970	Shulamith Firestone publishes *The Dialectic of Sex: The Case for Feminist Revolution*
1970	Germain Greer publishes *The Female Eunuch*
1971	John Rawls publishes *A Theory of Justice*
1973	*Roe v. Wade* U.S. Supreme Court decision protects a woman's right to terminate her pregnancy
1973	Derrick Bell publishes *Race, Racism, and American Law*
1974	Robert Nozick publishes *Anarchy, State, and Utopia*
1978	Edward Said publishes *Orientalism*
1979–1998	Jean-François Lyotard active
1981	Angela Davis publishes *Women, Race and Class*
1981–2021	bell hooks active
1982	Carol Gilligan publishes *In a Different Voice*
1982–	Cornel West active, publishes *Race Matters* in 1993
1984	Audre Lorde publishes *Sister Outsider: Essays and Speeches*
1988–	Judith Butler active
1989	Kimberlé Williams Crenshaw introduces the concept of intersectionality in "Demarginalizing the Intersection of Race and Sex"
1991–	Axel Honneth active, publishes *The Struggle for Recognition: The Moral Grammar of Social Conflicts* in 2003
1994	The World Wide Web comes into general public use
1995–	Lewis Gordon active
1996	David Chalmers publishes *The Conscious Mind*
1997	Charles W. Mills publishes *The Racial Contract*
2001	September 11 terrorist attacks
2007	Apple releases the first iPhone
2008	George Yancy publishes *Black Bodies, White Gazes: The Continuing Significance of Race*
2013–	Black Lives Matter movement for social justice
2017–	#MeToo movement for social justice
2018	Sabine Hossenfelder publishes *Lost in Math: How Beauty Leads Physics Astray* and *Existential Physics: A Scientist's Guide to Life's Biggest Questions* in 2022

| 2020– | Global COVID-19 pandemic |
| 2022 | *Dobbs v. Jackson Women's Health Organization* U.S. Supreme Court decision removes a woman's right to terminate her pregnancy |

REFERENCES

A list of philosophical works mentioned in this book. When a free online version is available. I have added a Web address valid at the time of publication. Portraits of major philosophers were added if a royalty-free version was available.

Chapter 1

Plato. *Meno*. Project Gutenberg. http://www.gutenberg.org/ebooks/1643.
Plato. *Republic*. Project Gutenberg. http://www.gutenberg.org/ebooks/1497.
Plato. All books by Plato on Project Gutenberg. https://www.gutenberg.org/ebooks/author/93.
Plato portrait—Public domain. https://commons.wikimedia.org/wiki/File:Plato_Pio-Clemetino_Inv305.jpg.

Chapter 2

Aristotle. *The Categories*. Project Gutenberg. https://www.gutenberg.org/ebooks/2412.
Aristotle. *Metaphysics*. Translated by W. D. Ross and J. A. Smith. Wikisource. https://en.wikisource.org/wiki/Metaphysics_(Ross._1908).
Aristotle. *Politics: A Treatise on Government*. Translated by William Ellis. Project Gutenberg. https://www.gutenberg.org/ebooks/6762.
Aristotle portrait—Public domain. https://en.wikipedia.org/wiki/Aristotle#/media/File:Aristotle_Altemps_Inv8575.jpg.
Detail of *School of Athens*—Public domain. https://commons.wikimedia.org/wiki/File:Socrates_and_Plato_Socrates_y_Platon._Escuela_de_Atenas._Raffae.jpg.

Chapter 3

Augustine. *The City of God*. Edited by Marcus Dods. Project Gutenberg. http://www.gutenberg.org/ebooks/45304.
Augustine. *Confessions*. Translated by E. B. Pusey. Project Gutenberg. http://www.gutenberg.org/ebooks/3296.
Plotinus. *Enneads*. Translated by Kenneth Sylvan Guthrie. Project Gutenberg. https://www.gutenberg.org/ebooks/42930.
Augustine portrait—Public domain. https://en.wikipedia.org/wiki/File:Augustine_Lateran.jpg.
William portrait—Public domain. https://commons.wikimedia.org/wiki/File:William_of_Ockham.jpg.

Chapter 4

Bacon, Francis. *New Atlantis*. Project Gutenberg. https://www.gutenberg.org/ebooks/2434.
Bacon, Francis. *Novum Organum*. Project Gutenberg. https://www.gutenberg.org/ebooks/45988.
Descartes, René. *Discourse on the Method of Rightly Conducting One's Reason and of Seeking Truth*. Project Gutenberg. http://www.gutenberg.org/ebooks/59.

Descartes, René. *The Method, Meditations, and Selections from the Principles of Descartes*. Translated by John Veitch. Public Domain. https://archive.org/details/methodmeditatio00desc/page/n11/mode/2up. 1901.

Descartes, René. *Principles of Philosophy*. Translated by John Veitch. Project Gutenberg. http://www.gutenberg.org/ebooks/4391.

Montaigne, Michel de. *Essays of Michel de Montaigne — Complete*. Translated by Charles Cotton. Edited by William Carew Hazlitt. Project Gutenberg. https://www.gutenberg.org/ebooks/3600.

Bacon portrait—Public domain. https://commons.wikimedia.org/wiki/File:Francis_Bacon._Viscount_St_Alban_from_NPG_(2).jpg.

Descartes portrait—Public domain. https://commons.wikimedia.org/wiki/File:Frans_Hals_-_Portret_van_Ren%C3%A9_Descartes_(cropped).jpg.

Montaigne portrait—Public domain. https://commons.wikimedia.org/wiki/File:Portrait_of_Michel_de_Montaigne._circa_unknown.jpg.

Chapter 5

Hobbes, Thomas. *Leviathan*. Project Gutenberg. http://www.gutenberg.org/files/3207/3207-h/3207-h.htm.

Jefferson, Thomas. "Thomas Jefferson to John Trumbull." https://www.loc.gov/exhibits/jefferson/18.html. 1789.

Hooke, Robert. *Micrographia*. Project Gutenberg. https://www.gutenberg.org/ebooks/15491.

Locke, John. *Essay Concerning Human Understanding*. Project Gutenberg. http://www.gutenberg.org/files/10615/10615-h/10615-h.htm.

Camera obscura—Public domain. http://www.retrophotographic.com/pinhole.htm.

Hobbes portrait—Public domain. https://commons.wikimedia.org/wiki/File:Thomas_Hobbes_by_John_Michael_Wright.jpg.

Locke portrait—Public domain. https://commons.wikimedia.org/wiki/File:John_Locke_by_Herman_Verelst.png

Chapter 6

Burke, Edmund. *Reflections on the Revolution in France*. Wikisource. https://en.wikisource.org/wiki/Reflections_on_the_Revolution_in_France.

Duc de La Rochefoucauld, François. *Reflections; or Sentences and Moral Maxims*. Translated by J. W. Willis Bund and J. Hain Friswell. Project Gutenberg. https://www.gutenberg.org/ebooks/9105.

Hobbes, Thomas. *Leviathan*. Project Gutenberg. https://www.gutenberg.org/ebooks/3207.

Locke, John. *A Letter Concerning Toleration*. Wikisource. https://en.wikisource.org/wiki/A_Letter_Concerning_Toleration.

Locke, John. *Two Treatises of Government*. Wikisource. https://en.wikisource.org/w/index.php?title=Two_Treatises_of_Government&oldid=9693604.

Paine, Thomas. *Common Sense*. Project Gutenberg. https://www.gutenberg.org/ebooks/147.

Rousseau, Jean-Jacques. *Emile*. Translated by Barbara Foxley. Project Gutenberg. https://www.gutenberg.org/ebooks/5427.

Rousseau, Jean-Jacques. *The Social Contract*. Translated by G.D.H. Cole. Project

Gutenberg. http://www.gutenberg.org/files/46333/46333-h/46333-h.htm.

Schwitzgebel, Eric, Liam Kofi Bright, Carolyn Dicey Jennings, Morgan Thompson, Eric Winsberg. "The Diversity of Philosophy Students and Faculty in the United States." *The Philosophers Magazine*. 30 May 2021. https://www.philosophersmag.com/essays/244-the-diversity-of-philosophy-students-and-faculty-in-the-united-states.

Wollstonecraft, Mary. *A Vindication of the Rights of Men*. Wikisource. https://en.wikisource.org/w/index.php?title=A_Vindication_of_the_Rights_of_Men/Letter_to_the_Right_Honourable_Edmund_Burke&oldid=2235002.

Wollstonecraft, Mary. *A Vindication of the Rights of Woman*. Project Gutenberg. http://www.gutenberg.org/ebooks/3420.

Hobbes portrait—Public domain. https://commons.wikimedia.org/wiki/File:Thomas_Hobbes_by_John_Michael_Wright.jpg.

Leviathan title plate—Public domain. https://commons.wikimedia.org/wiki/File:Leviathan_by_Thomas_Hobbes.jpg.

Locke portrait—Public domain. https://commons.wikimedia.org/wiki/File:John_Locke_by_Herman_Verelst.png

Rousseau portrait—Public domain. https://commons.wikimedia.org/wiki/File:Jean-Jacques_Rousseau_(painted_portrait).jpg.

Wollstonecraft portrait—Public domain. https://commons.wikimedia.org/wiki/File:Mary_Wollstonecraft_Tate_portrait.jpg.

Chapter 7

Berkeley, George. *A Treatise Concerning the Principles of Human Knowledge*. Project Gutenberg. http://www.gutenberg.org/ebooks/4723.

Locke, John. *Essay Concerning Human Understanding*. Project Gutenberg. http://www.gutenberg.org/files/10615/10615-h/10615-h.htm.

Hume, David. *A Treatise of Human Nature*. Project Gutenberg. http://www.gutenberg.org/ebooks/4705.

Hume, David. *An Enquiry Concerning Human Understanding*. Project Gutenberg. http://www.gutenberg.org/ebooks/9662.

Berkeley portrait—Public domain. https://commons.wikimedia.org/wiki/File:George_Berkeley_by_Jonh_Smibert.jpg.

Hume portrait—Public domain. https://commons.wikimedia.org/wiki/File:David_Hume_Esqr.jpg.

Chapter 8

Hume, David. *An Enquiry Concerning Human Understanding*. Project Gutenberg. http://www.gutenberg.org/ebooks/9662.

Kant, Immanuel. *Critique of Pure Reason*. Translated by J. M. D. Meiklejohn. Project Gutenberg. http://www.gutenberg.org/ebooks/4280.

Kant, Immanuel. *Prolegomena to Any Future Metaphysics*. Edited by Paul Carus. Project Gutenberg. http://www.gutenberg.org/ebooks/52821.

Kant portrait—Public domain.
https://commons.wikimedia.org/wiki/File:Immanuel_Kant_3_(cropped).jpg.

Chapter 9

Fichte, Johann Gottlieb. *The Vocation of Man*. Translated by William Smith. Public
Domain. *Wikisource*. https://en.wikisource.org/wiki/The_Vocation_of_Man.

Hegel, Georg Wilhelm Friedrich. *The Phenomenology of Spirit*. Translated by James
Black Baillie. Internet Archive.
https://archive.org/details/phenomenologyofs0000hege_n6q1/mode/2up.

Staël, Germaine de. *De l'Allemagne* (French). Project Gutenberg. Part 1:
https://www.gutenberg.org/ebooks/66924. Part 2:
https://www.gutenberg.org/ebooks/67933.

Fichte portrait—Public domain.
https://commons.wikimedia.org/wiki/File:Johann_gottlieb_fichte.jpg.

Hegel portrait—Public domain.
https://commons.wikimedia.org/wiki/File:G.W.F._Hegel_(by_Sichling,_after_Sebbers).jpg.

Chapter 10

Congress.gov. "Constitution of the United States. Fourteenth Amendment."
https://constitution.congress.gov/constitution/amendment-14/.

Mill, James. "Essays on the Formation of Human Character." *Philanthropist* 3 (10): 93–
119. 1813.

Mill, James. "Government." in *Essays*. J. Innes. 1828.
https://archive.org/details/MILLJames1828EssaysonI.GovernmentII.Jurisprudenc
eIII.LibetyofthePress.

Mill, John Stuart. *A System of Logic, Ratiocinative and Inductive*. Project Gutenberg.
https://www.gutenberg.org/ebooks/27942.

Mill, John Stuart. *On Liberty*. Project Gutenberg.
https://www.gutenberg.org/ebooks/34901.

Mill, John Stuart. *Principles of Political Economy*. Project Gutenberg.
https://www.gutenberg.org/ebooks/30107.

Mill, John Stuart. *The Subjection of Women*. Project Gutenberg.
https://www.gutenberg.org/ebooks/27083.

Marx, Karl and Friedrich Engels. *Communist Manifesto*. Project Gutenberg.
http://www.gutenberg.org/ebooks/61/.

Marx, Karl. *Das Kapital*. Translated by Samuel Moore and Edward Aveling. Wikisource.
https://en.wikisource.org/wiki/Das_Kapital_(Moore,_1906).

Marx, Karl. "Economic and Philosophic Manuscripts of 1844." in *Classical Sociological
Theory and Foundations of American Sociology*. ed. Allison Hurst.
https://open.oregonstate.education/sociologicaltheory/chapter/economic-and-
philosophic-manuscripts-of-1844/. licensed under a Creative Commons
Attribution-ShareAlike 4.0 International License. No modifications made.

Marx portrait—Public domain. https://commons.wikimedia.org/wiki/File:Karl_Marx.png.

Mill portrait—Public domain.
https://commons.wikimedia.org/wiki/File:Stuart_Mill_G_F_Watts.jpg.

Chapter 11

Kierkegaard, Søren. *Either/Or, A Fragment of Life*. In *The Essential Kierkegaard*. Edited by Howard V. Hong and Edna H. Hong. Internet Archive. https://archive.org/details/essentialkierkeg0000kier. 2000.

Kierkegaard, Søren. *On the Concept of Irony with Continual Reference to Socrates*. In *The Essential Kierkegaard*. Edited by Howard V. Hong and Edna H,. Hong. Internet Archive. https://archive.org/details/essentialkierkeg0000kier. 2000.

Kierkegaard, Søren. *Journalen* JJ:167 (1843). *Søren Kierkegaards Skrifter*. Søren Kierkegaard Research Center. Public Domain. http://sks.dk/forside/indhold.asp.

Nietzsche, Friedrich. *The Joyful Wisdom*. Edited by Oscar Levy. Project Gutenberg. https://www.gutenberg.org/ebooks/52881.

Nietzsche, Friedrich. *The Will to Power: An Attempted Transvaluation of All Values. Books III and IV*. Translated by Anthony Ludovici. Project Gutenberg. https://www.gutenberg.org/ebooks/52915.

Nietzsche, Friedrich. *Beyond Good and Evil*. Translated by Helen Zimmern. Project Gutenberg. https://www.gutenberg.org/ebooks/4363.

Thoreau, Henry David. *Walden, and On The Duty Of Civil Disobedience*. Project Gutenberg. https://www.gutenberg.org/ebooks/205.

Kierkegaard portrait—Public domain. https://commons.wikimedia.org/wiki/File:Kierkegaard_portrait.png.

Nietzsche portrait—Public domain. https://commons.wikimedia.org/wiki/File:Nietzsche187a.jpg.

Chapter 12

Addams, Jane. A Belated Industry." American Journal of Sociology Volume 1. Number 5 Mar.:536-550. (1896). https://www.journals.uchicago.edu/doi/epdf/10.1086/210552.

Dewey, John. "Between Two Worlds" (1944). *Later Works Volume 17*. edited by Jo Ann Boydston. Southern Illinois University Press. 1981.

Dewey, John. *How We Think*. D.C. Heath & Co. Internet Archive. https://archive.org/details/howwethink02dewegoog/. 1910.

George, Henry. *Progress and Poverty*. Project Gutenberg. https://www.gutenberg.org/ebooks/55308.

James, William. "The Dilemma of Determinism" in *The Will to Believe. and Other Essays in Popular Philosophy*. Project Gutenberg. http://www.gutenberg.org/ebooks/26659.

James, William. *Pragmatism: A New Name for Some Old Ways of Thinking*. Project Gutenberg. http://www.gutenberg.org/ebooks/5116.

James, William. "The Dilemma of Determinism." in *The Will to Believe. and Other Essays in Popular Philosophy*. Project Gutenberg. http://www.gutenberg.org/ebooks/26659.

James, William. *The Principles of Psychology*. Project Gutenberg. Volume 1 - http://www.gutenberg.org/ebooks/57628. Volume 2 - https://www.gutenberg.org/ebooks/57634.

James, William. "The Will to Believe." in *The Will to Believe. and Other Essays in Popular Philosophy*. Project Gutenberg. http://www.gutenberg.org/ebooks/26659.

More, Thomas. *Utopia*. Project Gutenberg. https://www.gutenberg.org/ebooks/2130.

Peirce, Charles Sanders. "How to Make Our Ideas Clear." *Popular Science Monthly* 12 (Jan.):286-302 (1878). http://www.peirce.org/writings/p119.html.

Peirce, Charles Sanders. "The Fixation of Belief." *Popular Science Monthly* 12 (Nov.): 1-15 (1877). http://peirce.org/writings/p107.html.

Saint-Simon, Henri de. *L'Industrie*. 1817.

Tocqueville, Alexis de. Democracy in America. Project Gutenberg. Vol. 1 - https://www.gutenberg.org/ebooks/815. Vol. 2 - https://www.gutenberg.org/ebooks/816.

Addams portrait— No known restrictions on publication. United States Library of Congress's Prints and Photographs division. http://loc.gov/pictures/resource/cph.3a15774/

Dewey portrait— No known restrictions on publication. United States Library of Congress's Prints and Photographs division. http://hdl.loc.gov/loc.pnp/cph.3a51565.

James portrait—Public domain. https://commons.wikimedia.org/wiki/File:William_James._philosopher.jpg.

Peirce portrait—Public domain. https://commons.wikimedia.org/wiki/File:Charles_Sanders_Peirce.jpg.

Chapter 13

Bergson, Henri. *Creative Evolution*. Translated by Arthur Mitchell. Henry Holt and Company. Internet Archive. https://archive.org/details/creativeevoluti01mitcgoog. 1911 [1907].

Bergson, Henri. *An Introduction to Metaphysics*. Translated by T.E. Hulme. G. P. Putnam's Sons. Internet Archive. https://archive.org/details/anintroductiont02berggoog. 1912 [1903].

Flynn, Thomas. *Existentialism*. Oxford University Press. 2006.

Russell, Bertrand and Alfred North Whitehead. *Principia Mathematica*. Cambridge University Press. Wikisource. https://en.wikisource.org/wiki/Russell_%26_Whitehead%27s_Principia_Mathematica. 1910.

Stone, Allison. "The Politics of Clarity." *Hypatia*. 30(3): 613–619. 2015.

Whitehead, Alfred North. *The Concept of Nature*. Project Gutenberg. https://www.gutenberg.org/ebooks/18835.

Wittgenstein, Ludwig. *The Blue and Brown Books: Preliminary studies for the 'Philosophical investigations'*. Blackwell. 1972. Internet Archive. https://archive.org/details/preliminarystudi00witt.

Wittgenstein, Ludwig. *Philosophical Investigations*. Wiley-Blackwell. 1953.

Wittgenstein, Ludwig. *Tractatus Logico-Philosophicus*. https://www.gutenberg.org/ebooks/5740.

Bergson portrait—Public domain. https://commons.wikimedia.org/wiki/File:Henri_Bergson_(Nobel).jpg.

Proof 54-43 in Principia Mathematica. Volume I. 1st edition. p. 379 (Public domain source: http://quod.lib.umich.edu/cgi/t/text/pageviewer-idx?c=umhistmath&cc=umhistmath&idno=aat3201.0001.001&).

Russell portrait—Public domain. https://commons.wikimedia.org/wiki/File:Russell1907-2.jpg.

Whitehead portrait—Public domain. https://commons.wikimedia.org/wiki/File:ANWhitehead.jpg.

Wittgenstein—Public domain. https://commons.wikimedia.org/wiki/File:Ludwig_Wittgenstein.jpg.

Chapter 14

Heidegger, Martin. *Being and Time*. Translated by John Macquarrie and Edward Robinson. HarperPerennial/Modern Thought. Internet Archive. https://archive.org/details/beingtime0000heid_z1r4. 2008 [1927].

Jaspers, Karl. *Basic Philosophical Writings*. Edited by Leonard H. Ehrlich, Edith Ehrlich, and George B. Pepper. Ohio University Press. Internet Archive. https://archive.org/details/karljaspersbasic0000jasp. 1986.

Jaspers, Karl. *Philosophie*, Springer. Translated by E. B. Ashton, University of Chicago Press, 1969–1971 [1932].

Sartre, Jean-Paul. *Being and Nothingness: An Essay on Phenomenological Ontology*. Translated by Hazel E. Barnes. Philosophical Library. Internet Archive. https://archive.org/details/beingnothingness00sartrich. 1956 [1943].

Sartre, Jean-Paul. *Nausea*. Translated by Lloyd Alexander. New Directions. Internet Archive. https://archive.org/details/nauseasart00sart. 1964 [1938].

Sartre, Jean-Paul. "No Exit." Translated by Lionel Abel. Vintage Books. Internet Archive. https://archive.org/details/noexitthreeother00sart. 1955 [1944].

Scheler, Max. *Ressentiment*. Marquette University Press. Internet Archive. https://archive.org/details/ressentiment0000sche/mode/2up. 1994 [1915].

Heidegger portrait—Creative Commons Attribution-Share Alike 3.0 Unported license. Image cropped. https://commons.wikimedia.org/wiki/File:Heidegger_4_(1960).jpg.

Husserl portrait—Public domain. https://commons.wikimedia.org/wiki/File:Edmund_Husserl_1900.jpg.

Jaspers portrait—Public domain. https://commons.wikimedia.org/wiki/File:Karl_Jaspers_1910.jpg.

Merleau-Ponty portrait—Creative Commons Attribution-Share Alike 3.0 Unported license. https://commons.wikimedia.org/wiki/File:Maurice_Merleau-Ponty.jpg.

Sartre portrait—Public domain. https://commons.wikimedia.org/wiki/File:Sartre_closeup.jpg.

Scheler portrait—Public domain. https://commons.wikimedia.org/wiki/File:Scheler_max.jpg.

Stein portrait—Public domain. https://commons.wikimedia.org/wiki/File:Edith_Stein-Student_at_Breslau_(1913-1914).jpg.

Chapter 15

Adorno, Theodor W. *Minima Moralia: Reflections from a Damaged Life*. Translated by E. F.N. Jephcott. Verso. Internet Archive. https://archive.org/details/minimamoraliaref0000ador_p2l6. 2005 [1951].

Adorno, Theodor W. *Philosophy of New Music*. Translated by Robert Hullot-Kentor. University of Minnesota Press. 2006 [1949].

Adorno, Theodor W. and Max Horkheimer. *Dialectic of Enlightenment*. Edited by Gunzelin Schmid Noerr. Translated by Edmund Jephcott. Stanford University Press. Internet Archive. https://archive.org/details/pdfy-TJ7HxrAly-MtUP4B/mode/2up. 2014 [1944].

Arendt, Hannah. *Eichmann in Jerusalem: A Report on the Banality of Evil*. Viking. Internet Archive. https://archive.org/details/eichmanninjerusa00aren/mode/2up. 1963.

Arendt, Hannah. *The Human Condition*. University of Chicago Press. Internet Archive. https://archive.org/details/humancondition0000aren/mode/2up. 1958.

Arendt, Hannah. *The Origins of Totalitarianism*. Schocken Books. Internet Archive. https://archive.org/details/originsoftotalit0000aren. 2004 [1951].

Berlin, Isaiah. *Concepts and Categories*. Pimlico. Internet Archive.
https://archive.org/details/conceptscategori0000berl_t0u3. 1999 [1978].

Berlin, Isaiah. "Two Concepts of Liberty." In *Four Essays On Liberty*. 118-172. Oxford
University Press. 1969.

Dilthey, Wilhelm. *The Formation of the Historical World in the Human Sciences*. R.A.
Makkreel and F. Rodi (eds.). Princeton. NJ: Princeton University Press. 2002
(1910).

Du Bois, W.E.B. "Sociology Hesitant" in Nahum Dimitri Chandler (ed.). *The Problem of
the Color Line At the Turn of the Twentieth Century: The Essential Early Essays*.
New York: Fordham University Press. 2015.

Habermas, Jürgen. *The Structural Transformation of the Public Sphere: An Inquiry Into
a Category Of Bourgeois Society*. Translated by Thomas Burger. MIT Press.
Internet Archive. https://archive.org/details/structuraltransf0000unse. 1989
[1962].

Habermas, Jürgen. *The Theory of Communicative Action*. Translated by Thomas
McCarthy. Beacon Press. Internet Archive.
https://archive.org/details/theoryofcommunic01habe. 1984 [1981].

Honneth, Axel. *Disrespect: The Normative Foundations of Critical Theory*. Polity Press.
Internet Archive. https://archive.org/details/disrespectnormat0000honn/mode/2up.
2007 [2000].

Honneth, Axel. *Freedom's Right: The Social Foundations of Democratic Life*. Translated
by Joseph Ganahl. Polity Press. 2014 [2011].

Honneth, Axel. *The Idea of Socialism: Towards a Renewal*. Translated by Joseph Ganahl.
Polity Press. 2018 [2015].

Honneth, Axel. *Recognition: A Chapter in the History of European Ideas.* Translated by
Joseph Ganahl. Cambridge University Press. 2020.

Honneth, Axel. *The Struggle for Recognition: The Moral Grammar of Social Conflicts*.
Translated by Joel Anderson. Polity Press. Internet Archive.
https://archive.org/details/struggleforrecog0000honn/mode/2up. 1995.

Korsgaard, Christine. *Sources of Normativity*. Cambridge University Press. 1996. Kindle.

Ortega y Gasset, José. *Obras Completas*. Vols. 1–10.Jose Ortega y Gasset Foundation
Edition. Madrid: Taurus. 2004–2010.

Ortega y Gasset, José. *The Revolt of the Masses*. W.W. Norton & Co. Internet Archive.
https://archive.org/details/revoltofmasses0000unse/mode/2up. 1957.

Arendt portrait—Creative Commons Attribution-Share Alike 4.0 International license.
https://commons.wikimedia.org/wiki/File:Hannah_Arendt_auf_dem_1._Kulturkrit
ikerkongress._Barbara_Niggl_Radloff._FM-2019-1-5-9-16.jpg.

Dilthey portrait—Public domain.
https://commons.wikimedia.org/wiki/File:Wilhelm_Dilthey_zZ_seiner_Verlobung.jpg.

Du Bois portrait—Public domain.
https://commons.wikimedia.org/wiki/File:Du_Bois._W._E._B..jpg.

Gramsci portrait—Public domain. https://commons.wikimedia.org/wiki/File:Gramsci.png.

Habermas portrait—Creative Commons Attribution-Share Alike 3.0 Unported license.
https://commons.wikimedia.org/wiki/File:JuergenHabermas_retouched.jpg.

Honneth portrait—Creative Commons Attribution-Share Alike 2.0 Generic license.
https://commons.wikimedia.org/wiki/File:Axel_Honneth_2016-04-18_(cropped).jpg.

Horkheimer and Adorno portrait—Creative Commons Attribution-Share Alike 3.0
Unported license.
https://commons.wikimedia.org/wiki/File:AdornoHorkheimer.png.

Korsgaard portrait—Creative Commons Attribution-Share Alike 4.0 International license.
https://commons.wikimedia.org/wiki/File:Christine_Korsgaard_at_Amherst_Colle

ge_2.jpg.
Lukács portrait—Public domain.
https://commons.wikimedia.org/wiki/File:Luk%C3%A1cs-comisario-alimentos-hungr%C3%ADa--outlawsdiary02tormuoft.png.
Ortega y Gasset portrait—Public domain.
https://commons.wikimedia.org/wiki/File:JoseOrtegayGasset.jpg.

Chapter 16

Chalmers, David J. *Conscious Mind: In Search of a Fundamental Theory*. Oxford University Press. 1997.

Cohen, G.A. *Karl Marx's Theory of History: A Defence*. Princeton University Press. Internet Archive. https://archive.org/details/karlmarxstheoryo0000cohe_j5n3. 1978.

Gettier, Edmund L. "Is Justified True Belief Knowledge?" *Analysis*. 23 (6): 121–123. 1963.

Goldman, Alvin I. "Discrimination and Perceptual Knowledge." *The Journal of Philosophy*. 73 (20): 771–791. 1976.

La Mettrie, Julien Offray de. *L'homme Machine*. De l'imp. d'E. Luzac, fils. Internet Archive. https://archive.org/details/b33001443. 1747.

Nozick, Robert. *Anarchy, State, and Utopia*. Blackwell. Internet Archive. https://archive.org/details/anarchystateutop00nozi. 1974.

Rawls, John. *A Theory of Justice*. Belknap Press. Internet Archive. https://archive.org/details/theoryofjustice0000rawl. 1971.

Ryle, Gilbert. *The Concept of Mind*. Penguin. Internet Archive. https://archive.org/details/conceptofmind0000gilb/mode/2up. 1949.

Searle, John. *Intentionality: An Essay in the Philosophy of Mind*. Cambridge University Press. Internet Archive. https://archive.org/details/intentionalityes0000sear/mode/2up. 1983.

Searle, John. "Minds. Brains and Programs" *The Behavioral and Brain Sciences*. Volume 3. Issue 3. 417–424. 1980.

Searle, John. *The Rediscovery of the Mind*. MIT Press. Internet Archive. https://archive.org/details/rediscoveryofmin0000sear_e1u9. 1992.

Sen, Amartya. *The Idea of Justice*. Belknap Press. Internet Archive. https://archive.org/details/ideaofjustice0000sena/page/n7/mode/2up. 2009.

Wittgenstein, Ludwig. *Philosophical Investigations*. Translated by G.E.M. Anscombe. MacMillan Publishing. Internet Archive. https://archive.org/details/philosophicalinvestigations_201911/mode/2up. 1958.

Chalmers portrait—GNU Free Documentation License. https://commons.wikimedia.org/wiki/File:David_Chalmers_TASC2008.JPG.

Gettier portrait—Creative Commons Attribution-Share Alike 4.0 International license. https://commons.wikimedia.org/wiki/File:Edmund_L_Gettier_III_ca_1960s_umass.jpg.

Lévi-Strauss portrait—Creative Commons Attribution-Share Alike 3.0 Unported license. https://commons.wikimedia.org/wiki/File:Claude_L%C3%A9vi-Strauss_KNAW.jpg.

Rawls portrait—Public domain. https://commons.wikimedia.org/wiki/File:John_Rawls_(1971_photo_portrait).jpg.

Searle portrait—Creative Commons Attribution-Share Alike 4.0 International license. https://commons.wikimedia.org/wiki/File:John_Searle_speaking_at_Google_3.jpg.

Chapter 17

Barthes, Roland. "The Death of the Author." *Manteia*, no. 5. 1968.

Baudrillard, Jean. *America*. Translated by Chris Turner. Verso. Internet Archive. https://archive.org/details/america00baud_0. 1988.

Baudrillard, Jean. *The Consumer Society: Myths and Structures*. Translated by Sage Publications. Sage Publications. Internet Archive. https://archive.org/details/consumersocietym0000baud/mode/2up. 1998 [1970].

Baudrillard, Jean. *Simulacra and Simulation*. Translated by Sheila Faria Glaser. University of Michigan Press. Internet Archive. https://archive.org/details/simulacrasimula000baud. 1994 [1981].

Baudrillard, Jean. *Symbolic Exchange and Death*. Translated by Iain Hamilton Grant. Sage Publications. Internet Archive. https://archive.org/details/symbolicexchange0000baud/mode/2up. 1993 [1976].

Baudrillard, Jean. *The System of Objects*. Translated by James Benedict. Verso. Internet Archive. https://archive.org/details/systemofobjects0000baud/mode/2up. 1996 [1968].

Derrida, Jacques. *Of Grammatology*. Translated by Gayatri Chakravorty Spivak. The Johns Hopkins University Press. Internet Archive. https://archive.org/details/ofgrammatology1976derr. 1974 [1967].

Derrida, Jacques. *Voice and Phenomenon*. Translated by Leonard Lawlor. Northwestern University Press. 2011 [1967].

Derrida, Jacques. *Writing and Difference*. Translated by Alan Bass. Chicago: University of Chicago Press. Internet Archive. https://archive.org/details/writingdifferenc00derr_0. 1978 [1967].

Foucault, Michel. *The Archaeology of Knowledge and the Discourse on Language*. Translated by A.M. Sheridan Smith. Vintage Books. Internet Archive. https://archive.org/details/archaeologyofkno0000fouc/mode/2up. 2010 [1969].

Foucault, Michel. *The Birth of the Clinic: An Archaeology of Medical Perception*. Translated by A.M. Sheridan Smith. Vintage Books. Internet Archive. https://archive.org/details/birthofclinic00fouc/mode/2up. 1975 [1963].

Foucault, Michel. *Discipline and Punish: The Birth of the Prison*. Translated by Alan Sheridan. Vintage Books. Internet Archive. https://archive.org/details/disciplinepunish0000fouc/mode/2up. 1979 [1975].

Foucault, Michel. *The Order of Things: An Archaeology of the Human Sciences*. Pantheon Books. Internet Archive. https://archive.org/details/orderofthingsarc00fouc/mode/2up. 1970 [1966].

Foucault, Michel. *Madness and Civilization: A History of Insanity in the Age of Reason*. Translated by Richard Howard. Vintage Books. Internet Archive. https://archive.org/details/madnesscivilizat0000fouc_x6f3/mode/2up. 1973 [1961].

Foucault, Michel. "Truth and Power" in Faubion. James D. (ed.) *Essential Works of Foucault. Volume 3: Power*. The New Press. 1979.

Lyotard, Jean-François. *The Postmodern Condition: A Report on Knowledge*. Translated by Geoff Bennington and Brian Massumi. University of Minnesota Press. Internet Archive. https://archive.org/details/postmoderncondit00lyot. 1985 [1979].

Lyotard, Jean-François. *The Differend: Phrases in Dispute*. translated Georges Van Den Abbeele. University of Minnesota Press. Internet Archive. https://archive.org/details/JeanFrancoisLyotardTheDifferendPhrasesInDispute/mode/2up. 1988 [1983].

Lyotard, Jean-François. *The Inhuman: Reflections on Time*. Translated by Geoff Bennington and Rachel Bowlby. Stanford University Press. Internet Archive. https://archive.org/details/inhumanreflectio0000lyot/mode/2up. 1991 [1988].

Rampton, Roberta. "Fictional TV presidents more popular than Obama: Reuters-Ipsos poll." Reuters. https://news.yahoo.com/fictional-tv-presidents-more-popular-obama-reuters-ipsos-053009188.html.

Baudrillard portrait—Creative Commons Attribution-Share Alike 3.0 Unported license.
    https://commons.wikimedia.org/wiki/File:WikipediaBaudrillard20040612-
    cropped.png.
Derrida portrait—by Arturo Espinosa. Creative Commons Attribution 2.0 Generic license.
    https://commons.wikimedia.org/wiki/File:Derrida_Dibujo.jpg.
Foucault portrait—Public domain.
    https://commons.wikimedia.org/wiki/File:Michel_Foucault_1974_Brasil.jpg.
Lyotard portrait—Creative Commons Attribution-Share Alike 2.0 Generic license.
    https://commons.wikimedia.org/wiki/File:Jean-
    Francois_Lyotard_photographed_by_Bracha_Ettinger_1995.jpg.
Monet. Claude. "Impression. soleil levant"—Public domain.
    https://commons.wikimedia.org/wiki/File:Claude_Monet._Impression._soleil_levant.jpg.

Chapter 18

Astell, Mary. "A Serious Proposal to the Ladies for the Advancement of Their True and
    Greatest Interest." In *The First English Feminist: Reflections Upon Marriage and
    Other Writings*. Edited by Bridget Hill. St. Martin's Press. 1986 [1694].
Baumgardner, Jennifer and Amy Richards. *Manifesta: Young Women, Feminism, and the
    Future*. Farrar, Straus, and Giroux. Internet Archive.
    https://archive.org/details/manifestayoungwo0000baum_o1g7/mode/2up. 2000.
Beauvoir, Simone de. *The Second Sex*. Translated by H.M. Parshley. Knopf. Internet
    Archive. https://archive.org/details/secondsex00beaurich/mode/2up. 1953 [1949].
Burgess-Jackson, Keith. *Rape: A Philosophical Investigation*. Dartmouth Publishing. 1996.
Crenshaw, Kimberlé. "Demarginalizing the Intersection of Race and Sex: A Black
    Feminist Critique of Antidiscrimination Doctrine, Feminist Theory and Antiracist
    Politics," *University of Chicago Legal Forum*: Vol. 1989: Iss. 1, Article 8.
    http://chicagounbound.uchicago.edu/uclf/vol1989/iss1/8.
Daly, Mary. *Beyond God the Father: Toward a Philosophy of Women's Liberation*. Beacon
    Press. Internet Archive. https://archive.org/details/beyondgodfather00mary. 1973.
Daly, Mary. *The Church and the Second Sex*. Harper & Row. Internet Archive.
    https://archive.org/details/churchsecondsex0000daly/mode/2up. 1968.
Daly, Mary. *Gyn/Ecology: The Metaethics of Radical Feminism*. Becaon Press. Internet
    Archive. https://archive.org/details/gynecologymetaet00dalyrich. 1978.
Firestone, Shulamith. *The Dialectic of Sex: The Case for Feminist Revolution*. Bantam
    Books. Internet Archive.
    https://archive.org/details/dialecticofsexca00fire/mode/2up. 1970.
Fricdan, Betty. *The Feminine Mystique*. Dell Publishing. Internet Archive.
    https://archive.org/details/femininemystique0000bett_e9w2/mode/2up. 1964 [1963].
Gilligan, Carol. *In a Different Voice: Psychological Theory and Women's Development*.
    Harvard University Press. Internet Archive.
    https://archive.org/details/indifferentvoice00gill. 1982.
Gouges, Olympe de. *The Declaration of the Rights of Women*. Ilex Press. 1982 [1791].
Gournay, Marie de. "L'égalité des hommes et des femmes" ("On the Equality of Men and
    Women"). In La Fille d'Alliance de Montaigne. Edited by Mario Schiff. H.
    Champion. Internet Archive.
    https://archive.org/details/filledallianceyork00schiuoft/mode/2up. 1910 [1622].

Greer, Germaine. *The Female Eunuch*. MacGibbon & Kee. Internet Archive.
    https://archive.org/details/femaleeunuch0000germ/mode/2up. 1970.
hooks, bell. *Ain't I a Woman? Black Women and Feminism*. Routledge. Internet Archive.

https://archive.org/details/aint-i-a-woman-black-women-and-feminism_202102/mode/2up. 2015 [1981].

hooks, bell. *Feminist Theory: From Margin to Center*. South End Press. Internet Archive. https://archive.org/details/feministtheoryfr00hook. 1984.

Johnson, Allan G. *The Gender Knot: Unraveling Our Patriarchal Legacy*. Temple University Press. Internet Archive. https://archive.org/details/isbn_2901592133832/mode/2up. 1997.

Keller, Evelyn Fox. "Making a Difference: Feminist Movement and Feminist Critique of Science." In *Feminism in Twentieth-Century Science, Technology, and Medicine*, Edited by Angela N.H. Creager, Elizabeth Lunbeck, and Londa Schiebinger. University of Chicago Press, 98–109.

Lorde, Audre. "Age, Race, Class, and Sex: Women Redefining Difference." In *Sister Outsider: Essays and Speeches*. Crossing Press. Internet Archive. https://archive.org/details/sisteroutsideres00lord. 1984.

Millet, Kate. *Sexual Politics*. Doubleday. Internet Archive. https://archive.org/details/sexualpolitics00mill/page/n5/mode/2up. 1970.

National Organization for Women. "The National Organization for Women's 1966 Statement of Purpose." https://now.org/about/history/statement-of-purpose.

Signs: Journal of Women in Culture and Society. Volume 4, Number 1, Autumn, 1978. "Women, Science, and Society." Edited by Catharine R. Stimpson, and Joan N. Burstyn. https://www.journals.uchicago.edu/toc/signs/1978/4/1.

Sprague, Joey. *Feminist Methodologies for Critical Researchers*. Rowman & Littlefield. Internet Archive. https://archive.org/details/feministmethodol0000spra. 2005.

Stacey, Judith and Barrie Thorne. "The Missing Feminist Revolution in Sociology." *Social Problems*, Volume 32, Issue 4, 1 April 1985, 301–316. https://academic.oup.com/socpro/article/32/4/301/1734661.

Walker, Rebecca. "Becoming the Third Wave," *Ms.* Jan 1992, 2, 4. 39. https://aula.fundaciondeloscomunes.net/sites/default/files/walker_1992_-_becoming_the_third_wave.pdf.

Wollstonecraft, Mary. *A Vindication of the Rights of Woman.* Project Gutenberg. http://www.gutenberg.org/ebooks/3420.

Young, Iris Marion. "Throwing Like a Girl: A Phenomenology of Feminine Body Comportment Motility and Spatiality." *Human Studies* 3, 137-146. https://warwick.ac.uk/fac/arts/english/currentstudents/undergraduate/modules/fulllist/special/transnational/iris_marion_young.pdf. 1980.

Crenshaw portrait—by Mohamed Badarne. Creative Commons Attribution-Share Alike 4.0 International license. https://commons.wikimedia.org/wiki/File:Kimberl%C3%A9_Crenshaw_(32923595887).jpg.

Beauvoir portrait—Public domain. https://commons.wikimedia.org/wiki/File:Simone_De_Beauvoir2.jpg.

Friedan portrait—by Fred Palumbo. No copyright restriction known. Staff photographer reproduction rights transferred to Library of Congress through Instrument of Gift. Library of Congress. Prints and Photographs Division. NYWT&S Collection [Reproduction Number: LC-USZ62-115884]. http://loc.gov/pictures/resource/cph.3c15884/.

hooks portrait—by Alex Lozupone. Creative Commons Attribution-Share Alike 4.0 International license. https://commons.wikimedia.org/wiki/File:Bell_hooks,_October_2014.jpg.

Lorde portrait—by K. Kendall. Creative Commons Attribution 2.0 Generic license. Image

cropped.
https://commons.wikimedia.org/wiki/File:Audre_Lorde._Meridel_Lesueur._Adrienne_Rich_1980_(820298895).jpg.

Chapter 19

Anital, Tamar. "Artist Of The Week: Dr. Cornel West." https://www.mtv.com/news/6gh7v5/artist-of-the-week-dr-cornel-west. February 18, 2018.

Baldwin, James. *The Fire Next Time*. Watts. Internet Archive. https://archive.org/details/firenexttime00jame_2xq/mode/2up. 1963.

Bell, Derrick A. *Race, Racism, and American Law*. Little, Brown, and Company. Internet Archive. https://archive.org/details/raceracismameric00bell. 1973.

Belle, Kathryn Sophia (as Kathryn T. Gines). *Hannah Arendt and the Negro Question*. Indiana University Press. 2014.

Davis, Angela. *Women, Race and Class*. Random House. Internet Archive. https://archive.org/details/womenraceclass0000davi. 1981.

Du Bois, W.E.B. *The Souls of Black Folk: Essays and Sketches*. A. C. McClurg & Co. Internet Archive. https://archive.org/details/cu31924024920492/mode/2up. 1903.

Fanon, Frantz. *Black Skin, White Masks*. Translated by Charles Lam Markmann. Grove Press. Internet Archive. https://archive.org/details/blackskinwhitema00fran. 1967 [1952]

Gordon, Lewis R. *Bad Faith and Antiblack Racism*. Humanity Books. 1995.

Gordon, Lewis R. *Existence in Black: An Anthology of Black Existential Philosophy*. Routledge. 1996.

Gordon, Lewis R. *Existentia Africana: Understanding Africana Existential Thought*. Routledge. Internet Archive. https://archive.org/details/existentiaafrica0000gord. 2000.

Mills, Charles W. "Critical Philosophy of Race." *In The Oxford Handbook of Philosophical Methodology*. Edited by Harman Cappelen, Tamar Szabó Gendler, and John Hawthorne. Oxford University Press. 2016.

Mills, Charles W. *From Class to Race: Essays in White Marxism and Black Radicalism*. Rowman & Littlefield Publishers. 2003.

Mills, Charles W. *The Racial Contract*. Cornell University Press. Internet Archive. https://archive.org/details/racialcontract0000mill. 1997.

The New Negro: An Interpretation. Edited by Alain Locke. Albert and Charles Boni. Internet Archive. https://archive.org/details/the-new-negro/page/n9/mode/2up. 1925.

Sartre, Jean-Paul. *Anti-Semite and Jew*. Translated by George J. Becker. Schocken Books. Internet Archive. https://archive.org/details/antisemitejew0000sart/mode/2up. 1965 [1946].

Shelby, Tommie. "Is Racism in the 'Heart'?" *Journal of Social Philosophy*, 33: 411-420. https://onlinelibrary.wiley.com/doi/10.1111/0047-2786.00150. 2002.

West, Cornel. *Prophesy Deliverance! An Afro-American Revolutionary Christianity*. Westminster Press. Internet Archive. https://archive.org/details/prophesydelivera0000west. 1982.

West, Cornel. *Race Matters*. Beacon Press. Internet Archive. https://archive.org/details/racematters00west_0. 1993.

Yancy, George. *Black Bodies, White Gazes: The Continuing Significance of Race*. Rowman & Littlefield Publishers. 2008.

Yancy, George. "Walking While Black in the 'White Gaze'." The Stone. Opinionator. New York Times. Sept. 1. 2013.

https://opinionator.blogs.nytimes.com/2013/09/01/walking-while-black-in-the-white-gaze/.

Baldwin portrait—Creative Commons Attribution-Share Alike 3.0 Unported license.https://commons.wikimedia.org/wiki/File:James_Baldwin_37_Allan_Warren_(cropped).jpg.

Bell portrait—GNU Free Documentation License.
https://commons.wikimedia.org/wiki/File:Derrick_Bell_by_David_Shankbone.jpg.

Crummell portrait—Public domain.
https://commons.wikimedia.org/wiki/File:Alexander_Crummell.jpg.

Fanon portrait—Public domain.
https://commons.wikimedia.org/wiki/File:Fanon_et_M%27Hamed_Yazid_repr%C3%A9sentant_le_FLN_%C3%A0_la_conf%C3%A9rence_Pan_Africaine_en_Kinshasa_le_27_ao%C3%BBt_1960_(cropped).jpg.

Alain Locke portrait—Public domain.
https://commons.wikimedia.org/wiki/File:Portrait_of_Alain_LeRoy_Locke.jpg.

Shelby portrait—Creative Commons Attribution 2.0 Generic license.
https://commons.wikimedia.org/wiki/File:Tommie_Shelby_(6096472077).jpg.

West portrait—by Gage Skidmore. Creative Commons Attribution 2.0 Generic license. Image cropped. https://commons.wikimedia.org/wiki/File:Cornel_West_(39223875064).jpg.

Chapter 20

Appiah, Kwame. *Cosmopolitanism: Ethics in a World of Strangers*. W. W. Norton & Company. Internet Archive.
https://archive.org/details/cosmopolitanisme0000appi_v9i3. 2006.

Dreyfus, Hubert. "Nihilism on the Information Highway: Anonymity versus Commitment in the Present Age." *Background Practices: Essays on the Understanding of Being*. Edited by Hubert L. Dreyfus and Mark A. Wrathall. Oxford Academic. 2004.

Fanon, Frantz. *The Wretched of the Earth*. Translated by Constance Farrington. Grove Press. Internet Archive.
https://archive.org/details/wretchedofearth08fano/page/n3/mode/2up. 1963 [1961].

Freire, Paulo. *Pedagogy of the Oppressed*. Translated by Myra Bergman Ramos. Herder and Herder. Internet Archive.
https://archive.org/details/pedagogyofoppres00frei/mode/2up. 1970 [1968].

Kuhn, Thomas. *The Structure of Scientific Revolutions*. University of Chicago Press. Internet Archive. https://archive.org/details/structureofscie00kuhn. 1962.

Polanyi, Michael. *Personal Knowledge: Toward a Post-Critical Philosophy*. Routledge & Kegan Paul. Internet Archive.
https://archive.org/details/personalknowledg0000pola_p9p1. 1958.

Polanyi, Michael. *Science, Faith, and Society*. Oxford University Press. Internet Archive.
https://archive.org/details/sciencefaithands032129mbp/page/n3/mode/2up. 1946.

Hossenfelder. Sabine. *Lost in Math: How Beauty Leads Physics Astray*. Basic Books. 2018

Hossenfelder. Sabine. *Existential Physics: A Scientist's Guide to Life's Biggest Questions*. Viking. 2022.

Said, Edward W. *Orientalism*. Pantheon Books. Internet Archive.
https://archive.org/details/orientalism0000said_r4m0. 1978.

Spivak, Gayatri. "Can the Subaltern Speak?" In *Marxism and the Interpretation of Culture*. Edited by C. Nelson and L. Grossberg. Macmillan Education. 271-313. Internet Archive. https://archive.org/details/CanTheSubalternSpeak. 1988.

Thoreau, Henry David. *Walden, and On The Duty Of Civil Disobedience*. Project

Gutenberg. https://www.gutenberg.org/ebooks/205.

Butler portrait—by Miquel Taverna. Creative Commons Attribution-Share Alike 4.0 International license. Image cropped. https://commons.wikimedia.org/wiki/File:Judith_Butler_al_CCCB_2018.jpg.

Dreyfus portrait—by Jörg Noller. Creative Commons Attribution-Share Alike 3.0 Germany license. https://commons.wikimedia.org/wiki/File:Hubert_Dreyfus.jpg.

Freire portrait—by Leandro Melito. Creative Commons Attribution 3.0 Brazil license. https://commons.wikimedia.org/wiki/File:2016-07-04_-_Paulo_Freire_no_Portal_EBC.jpg.

Kuhn portrait— Creative Commons Attribution-Share Alike 4.0 International license. https://commons.wikimedia.org/wiki/File:Thomas-kuhn-portrait.png.

McLuhan portrait—by Bernard Gotfryd. Public domain. https://commons.wikimedia.org/wiki/File:Marshall_McLuhan_with_and_on_television_(cropped).jpg.

Polanyi portrait—Public domain. https://commons.wikimedia.org/wiki/File:Michael_Polanyi.png.

Said portrait—Creative Commons CC0 1.0 Universal Public Domain Dedication. https://commons.wikimedia.org/wiki/File:Edward_Said_and_Daniel_Barenboim_in_Sevilla,_2002_(Said).jpg.

Spivak portrait—by Robert Crc. Free art license. https://commons.wikimedia.org/wiki/File:Gayatri_Spivak_on_Subversive_Festival.jpg.

Made in the USA
Monee, IL
05 December 2023

48266805R00236